Tolley's Drafting Contracts of Employment

Second Edition

by

Gillian Howard LLB, Dip Comp Law(Cantab)

Industrial Relations Consultant and
Executive Consultant with
Curry, CH Hausmann, Popeck, Solicitors

Tolley Publishing Company Limited
A UNITED NEWSPAPERS PUBLICATION

Dedication

This book is dedicated to the three wonderful men
in my life – Barry, Daniel and Ben – without
whose patience, understanding and long
sufferance I could not have written it.

Published by
Tolley Publishing Company Limited
Tolley House
2 Addiscombe Road
Croydon Surrey CR9 5AF England
081-686 9141

Typeset in Great Britain by
Express Typesetting Ltd
Croydon, Surrey

Printed and Bound by
BPCC Wheatons Ltd, Exeter

Introduction to First Edition

This book is aimed largely at practitioners whether they be legal or personnel whose task it is to draft contracts of employment. Many of the clauses referred to in the book have been drafted by me in my practice and all I am aiming to do is pass on my experience on some of these matters. That is not to say that they are perfect and could not be improved.

I trust that for those new to this field you will find this book of help in what is a legal minefield.

I have given minimal legal analysis or case references but a certain amount has been included to guide the reader as to why a certain clause is phrased in such a way or why it is there at all!

We have included a complete Model Management Contract at the end of the book along with a set of Written Particulars, a Sick Pay Scheme and Holiday Policy.

I would like to thank in particular my Commissioning Editor, Sarah Blair, for first asking me to write this book and my Legal Editor, Stephen Barc, for the careful and thoughtful work he did on my manuscript and in pointing out my errors and omissions and for making some excellent changes to the text. Any remaining errors are my entire responsibility.

I am also indebted to my tutor and friend (formerly of Christ's College, Cambridge and now at King's College, London), Paul O'Higgins, for it was he who taught me and inspired me and gave me the love of labour law that I have today.

Lastly I would like to thank Barry, Daniel and Ben Howard, who have been so patient and caring over the months that I have been closeted in my office writing this book.

I seek to state the law of England and Wales as at 1 June 1990.

8 June 1990   *Gillian S. Howard*
                                                                      34 Lyndale Avenue
                                                                                London
                                                                              NW2 2QA

Introduction to Second Edition

I am delighted to have updated and rewritten the first edition of this book originally published in September 1990 and hope that this second edition provides some helpful ideas and precedents for practitioners and personnel specialists charged with the task of drafting contracts of employment.

Much has happened since 1990. Legislation in the form of the Trade Union Reform and Employment Rights Act 1993 has made changes to the requirement to provide Written Particulars of terms and conditions of employment, bringing into effect the EC Directive on Proof of the Employment Relationship. Other changes to contracts of employment as a result of the 1993 Act are described elsewhere in the book.

The tide of EC legislation has affected several of the personnel policies and the implications of the *Dekker* and *Webb* decisions in the area of pregnancy discrimination have led to a radical rewriting of my model maternity policy. I have also included some details on part-time contracts and terms and conditions for such contracts as there has been considerable development in this area from the EC.

Landmark cases have given guidance on the drafting and enforceability of post-termination restraint clauses such as restrictive covenants and non-solicitation clauses. In this respect the very helpful Court of Appeal decision in the delightfully-named *Office Angels v Rainer-Thomas and O'Connor* has clarified how far employers may restrict ex-employees from soliciting clients of the former employer and has clarified what constitutes legitimate business interests of employers.

The Wages Act 1986 has been clarified in the House of Lords in the case of *Delaney v Staples* – establishing that no claim for unpaid pay in lieu of notice lies under the Wages Act since payments in lieu of notice are categorised as damages for breach of contract and not 'wages'. As such any claims for payments in lieu of notice not paid had to be recovered in the common law courts.

However the House of Lords acknowledged that this state of affairs was most unsatisfactory and urged the Secretary of State to implement section 131 of the Employment Protection (Consolidation) Act 1978 in order to extend the jurisdiction of industrial tribunals to hear breach of contract claims. Implementation of section 131 now appears in the Trade Union Reform and Employment Rights Act 1993.

Since the last edition, ACAS has changed its practice in relation to effecting COT 3 settlements (pre-industrial tribunal). I have now included the COT 5 Practice Directive (July 1990) and some guidance of my own!

The revised COT 3 procedure has led to an increasing unwillingness for ACAS to become involved in COT 3 settlements much to the concern of lawyers and employers alike. At the Report Stage in the House of Lords of the 1993 Act, provisions were included for compromise agreements to be effected by legal representatives. The full details of this procedure are described in Chapter 11 on 'Settlements'.

The swiftness with which the Government is prepared to move on employment matters is no better illustrated than by the introduction of a further amendment on 24 May 1993 to the 1993 Act at the Third Reading in the House of Lords which in effect nullifies the Court of Appeal decisions in *Wilson v Associated Newspapers Ltd* and *Palmer v Associated British Ports* heard on 30 April 1993. These cases concerned employers who had offered pay rises to those who would accept personal contracts and forgo union bargaining for their terms and conditions. The Government introduced new subsections (3)-(5) to section 148 of the Trade Union and Labour Relations (Consolidation) Act 1992 whereby employers who choose to offer personal contracts in place of union bargaining arrangements may be protected from a claim of action short of dismissal against union members.

I have also included some tips on drafting termination agreements and settlements.

During the last two years I have been asked to draft some interesting contracts – for a hairdressing salon, a major firm of accountants and several Directors' Service Agreements – all of which I include as new Precedents. I have amended and updated my Model Sick Pay Scheme and have introduced a new Procedure for Dealing with the Malingerer (originally drawn up for an employer within a Health Authority!).

On a lighter note, I have included some more 'useful clauses' in the final chapter including a section on 'Workplace affairs and consensual relations'. Perhaps some lawyers or personnel practitioners may find this useful!

My special thanks go to my good friend and colleague, Janet Gaymer, Head of the Employment Department of Simmons and Simmons (Solicitors), with whom I have spent many enjoyable hours lecturing and discussing the subject of drafting contracts. I would particularly thank her for her helpful suggestions and kind permission to use some of her precedents in the chapter on Competition and Confidentiality.

As ever I would like to thank Tolley Publishing Co and in particular Robert McKay and Ashley Fillingham for their patience in permitting such a long gestation period for this second edition. All errors and omissions remain entirely my responsibility.

Finally I would like to thank all my many clients who have asked me to draft contracts and employment documents for them over the years. Through you, my book has been reborn!

I seek to state the law of England and Wales as at 1 July 1993.

Gillian Howard
34 Lyndale Avenue
Childs Hill, London NW2 2QA

1 July 1993

Contents

Contents

Contents

Abbreviations and References

General

COIT	=	Central Office of the Industrial Tribunals
CRE	=	Commission for Racial Equality
DES	=	Department of Education and Science
DSS	=	Department of Social Securety
EAT	=	Employment Appeal Tribunal
EC	=	European Community
EOC	=	Equal Opportunities Commission
EPCA	=	Employment Protection (Consolidation) Act 1978
ICTA	=	Income and Corporation Taxes Act 1988
NIC	=	national insurance contributions
PAYE	=	pay as you earn
RRA	=	Race Relations Act 1976
SAYE	=	save as you earn
SDA	=	Sex Discrimination Act 1975
SI	=	statutory instrument
SSP	=	statutory sick pay
TULRCA	=	Trade Union and Labour Relations (Consolidation) Act 1992
TURERA	=	Trade Union Reform and Employment Rights Act 1993

Law Reports and other references

AC	=	Law Reports, Appeal Cases
All ER	=	All England Law Reports
CA	=	Court of Appeal
Ch	=	Law Reports, Chancery Division
ChD	=	High Court, Chancery Division
HC	=	High Court
HCNI	=	High Court (Northern Ireland)
ICR	=	Industrial Cases Reports
IRLIB	=	Industrial Relations and Legal Information Bulletin
IRLR	=	Industrial Relations Law Reports
ITR	=	Industrial Tribunal Reports (1966-1978)
QBD	=	High Court, Queen's Bench Division
WLR	=	Weekly Law Reports

Table of Cases

Table of Cases

Table of Statutes

Table of EC Legislative Material

Table of Statutory Instruments

Chapter 1

The Prelude

1.1   There is probably great confusion on the part of anyone who is not a lawyer as to exactly what constitutes a contract of employment. Is it the offer letter? Is it the document headed 'Contract of Employment'? Is it the Staff Handbook or Personnel Manual? Is it the collective agreement? Or is it all of these documents? The answer is that, quite simply, it depends upon what the parties have agreed should form the contract and what terms are discretionary and outside the contract.

It is not uncommon for lawyers to hear a client, who may be an employee or ex-employee, stating categorically, 'No I do not have a contract'. What the employee may mean is that he does not have any written terms of employment. He certainly does have a contract although finding the terms may be problematic. In this connection note that sections 1–6 of the Employment Protection (Consolidation) Act 1978 as substituted by section 26 and Schedule 4 of the Trade Union Reform and Employment Rights Act 1993 (TURERA 1993), require employers to give each employee working eight hours a week or more, within two months of his commencing employment, a written statement of employment particulars – see Chapter 4 for more details. If the employer fails to provide such a statement, the employee may apply to an industrial tribunal under EPCA s 11, and the tribunal may specify the terms which ought to be included in the statement. Tribunals have no power to *enforce* the terms. A recent case illustrates that the jurisdiction of the industrial tribunal is to declare or imply the terms which, on the evidence, it concludes have been agreed between the parties. The tribunal has no power to invent particulars of terms of employment which the contract is not required to contain. Even with regard to mandatory or essential terms an industrial tribunal has no power to impose on the parties terms which have not been agreed – in other words, the tribunal will not draft the contract for the parties (*Eagland v British Telecommunications plc [1992] IRLR 323*).

This book is intended to show you – whether you are a lawyer or a personnel manager – that it is not difficult to draft the terms of a contract but it is important to draft them carefully. It is particularly important to give careful thought to what you (the employer or employee) want to cover, what is provided in the way of benefits and what duties and obligations will be expected.

Many disputes over contracts and unfair dismissal cases concern either the lack of any written terms or their lack of clarity. If, for example, a senior manager is given a directorship of one of the subsidiary companies, it is wise

1

to state what (if any) director's fees will become payable, at what date they will be paid, whether this is a discretionary or contractual payment and what happens to such fees in the case of a summary dismissal for gross misconduct. Similarly, if a company has special rules about holidays – there may be rules about the times of the year that holidays may or may not be taken – then careful thought should go into the drafting of such clauses so that all the points are covered and both parties, the employer and the employee, are clear about the terms of the contract.

Contract of employment/Contract for services

1.2   This book is not intended to cover contracts other than contracts of employment. It is important for employers to determine whether an employment contract is appropriate or whether an agency agreement or consultancy agreement would be more appropriate.

The tests for determining whether or not someone is an 'employee' for employment protection purposes is complex and best explained elsewhere. The position is outlined in Chapter 3, but for an excellent explanation readers should look no further than 'Tolley's Employment Handbook' by Elizabeth Slade and Nigel Giffin.

The tax position is also an important consideration for employers since they are liable to deduct PAYE and Class 1 National Insurance Contributions (NIC). If in any doubt about the definition of an employee for tax and NIC, readers should refer to the Inland Revenue booklets (P7)(1993) 'Employer's Further Guide to PAYE' and (P8)(1993) 'Employer's Basic Guide to PAYE' and to 'Tolley's Social Security and State Benefits'.

Some brief advice to employers would be to insist that there are only two situations where tax and national insurance should not be deducted – either where the person provides his Schedule D Number or tax certificate of self-employed status or where the person works under a limited company. In both those cases, he may render an invoice and be paid a gross fee. A copy of a contractor's agreement is contained in Chapter 3 **Precedent 4.**

The formation of the contract

1.3   The form that the contract may take varies greatly from a lengthy director's service agreement to a basic agreement to work and be paid! In *Ferguson v John Dawson & Partners (Contractors) Ltd [1976] IRLR 346*, the court heard that:

> 'The plaintiff came with four other Irishmen already working for the defendant and he asked, or perhaps one of his friends asked, if he could "come along". Mr Murray's evidence is: "I said he could start on Monday and that was it. But I did inform him that there were no cards; we were purely working as a lump labour force".'

There are essentially five key elements of a contract:

(*a*)   an offer;

(*b*)   an acceptance;

(*c*)   consideration (in employment contracts this essentially means that the employee carries out the work specified by the employer, in return for which the employer pays him);

(*d*)   terms that are certain; and

(*e*)   both parties intend to be legally bound by those terms.

The terms of a contract of employment must be agreed at the outset of the employment relationship. It is important to ensure that all the agreed terms (or at least the most important ones) are confirmed in writing. The terms of the contract agreed between the parties, whether confirmed in writing or not, are often referred to as *express terms*. In certain circumstances, a court or tribunal may, in addition to the express terms, imply terms into a contract which have not been specifically agreed between the parties. Such terms are referred to as *implied terms*, and may be implied using a variety of tests including 'business efficacy', 'the officious bystander', 'mutuality of obligations', and 'custom and practice' (see also 4.7 below).

The making and acceptance of an offer of employment is dealt with in Chapter 2. The remainder of this chapter is concerned with some important matters which commonly arise during the prelude to that stage – i.e. the advertisement, the application form, and the interview.

The advertisement

1.4   As a general rule the advertisement does not form part of the contract, so prospective or current employees may not normally sue upon any promise made in the advertisement. This is the rule unless the written terms are ambiguous or there are no written terms and conditions of employment. In both cases the courts and tribunals will look at the advertisement in order to interpret the contract.

Several cases should help to illustrate the point; in each of these, there was an alleged ambiguity in the contract itself. In *Deeley v British Rail Engineering Ltd* [*1980*] *IRLR 147*, a Mr Deeley answered an advertisement for 'Sales Engineer (Export)' and responded to it on an application form which was headed 'Sales Engineer (Export)'. The actual offer of employment was headed 'Sales Engineer' and this was the post which Mr Deeley accepted. His contract contained a wide flexibility clause giving his employers the right to require him to undertake any duties 'which the Railways Board may from time to time determine'. After several years, Mr Deeley suffered from a debilitating medical condition which rendered him unfit for any duties in a hot climate, so that he was unable to undertake any work in the Middle East which at that time was a very important part of the export area with which he was dealing. After

3

discussions and consultations with him, he was offered a comparable post dealing with domestic sales. He refused and was eventually dismissed.

The Court of Appeal agreed with the industrial tribunal and held that the Board had the contractual right to transfer Mr Deeley to a similar job relating to the UK market. They held that:

> 'It is the original words of the engagement which form the contract of employment. In the present case the words were clear and there was no reason for implying any words of restriction. Although the employers' advertisement and application form referred to the appointment of "Sales Engineer (Export)", the employers' offer of appointment and statement of terms and conditions referred to "Sales Engineer" and Mr Deeley's acceptance of that offer referred to that term. The contractual documents therefore omitted the word "export". . . . There was no necessity for there to be a limitation to that effect.'

Contrast that case with two other cases, *Pederson v London Borough of Camden* [*1981*] *IRLR 173* and *Financial Techniques (Planning Services) Ltd v Hughes* [*1981*] *IRLR 32*. In both cases the employees had been induced to apply for and accept the jobs in question on the basis of the wording of the advertisement. The courts in both cases were prepared to use the words of the advertisement to clarify and interpret the proper contract terms, which were otherwise unclear.

In *Pederson*, the advertisement referred to the post of 'Bar steward/catering assistant' but the advertisement described in detail the duties properly ascribed to a bar steward. On the basis of that advertisement Mr Pederson accepted the post. His offer letter did no more than refer to his job title of 'Bar steward and catering assistant'. In deciding that he had been dismissed by reason of redundancy when the Council no longer required a bar steward, the Court of Appeal concluded:

> 'The terms of the appellant's contract were set out in his letter of appointment but in construing that letter the court was entitled to look at the surrounding circumstances and in particular at the advertisement which led to him applying for the job which was on offer. The advertisement stressed very clearly that the primary function would be to perform the duties of a bar steward. Although the advertisement was not part of the contract there was a link between the written terms of contract and the advertisement.'

Perhaps the *Financial Techniques* case provides a more powerful example of the importance of advertisements in determining the terms of the contract. Here a Tax Consultant, Mr Hughes, had answered an advertisement which included these terms: 'The career prospects are exceptional and are linked to a sophisticated remuneration package which through a profit-sharing scheme offers a substantial earnings potential'.

The profit-sharing scheme was not mentioned at the interview nor in his offer letter but some time later he was notified that he was eligible to participate in the profit-sharing scheme. At no time was he told that the scheme was discretionary. A dispute arose over payment of the profit share following his letter of resignation. The company had unilaterally decided to offset the bonus earned in the previous quarter with the shortfall in the last quarter of his employment. The employee believed that this was breach of contract and sued for constructive dismissal.

The Court of Appeal had no difficulty in deciding that the

'. . . evidence pointing to the profit-sharing scheme being part of the contract was all one way. . . . The advertisement on the face of which he started negotiations had referred to "a sophisticated remuneration package, which, through a profit-sharing scheme, offers very substantial earnings potential". That kind of language was wholly inconsistent with the kind of situation which arises when employers offer discretionary bonuses to their employees. . . . The commonsense of the situation pointed to the fact that the respondent was negotiating with his employers on the basis that he was paid a salary plus the advantages of the scheme, if he qualified under it'.

There is an interesting twist to this case because the employers had attempted to argue that a subsequent document outlining some new terms of the bonus scheme had included the words: '. . . this document does not create a legal relationship' – thereby creating a non-contractual scheme. Furthermore, the employers argued that Mr Hughes had received this document and had failed to register any objection to it, thereby accepting that the new scheme offered was discretionary. The Court of Appeal rejected this view forcefully, holding: 'Silence seldom amounts to consenting to new terms'.

However, for other reasons, the Court of Appeal held that Mr Hughes had not been constructively dismissed.

In other cases, employers have been 'caught out' by misleading advertisements. In *Holliday Concrete (Testing) Ltd v Woods [1979] IRLR 301*, an advertisement which stated that the job would be 'for 15 months' was held to bind the employer to offering 15 months' employment or to pay damages for breach of contract when he terminated it earlier on grounds of redundancy. In another case, a job advertised as 'sales manager' was held to be misleading when the job turned out to be mainly clerical work (*Joseph Steinfeld & Co v Reypert, EAT 550/78*).

Discriminatory advertisements

1.5   One further point about the drafting of advertisements – care must be taken not to offend the anti-discrimination legislation. Here the employer, the agency who drafted the copy, the manager who drafted or approved the copy and the publisher may all be liable. [*Sex Discrimination Act 1975 (SDA), s 38; Race Relations Act 1976 (RRA), s 29*]. 'Advertisement' has a wide meaning covering every form of advertisement whether public or internal, whether published in a newspaper or journal or on the television, radio, notices, signs, displays, circulars, catalogues etc. [*SDA s 82(1); RRA s 78(1)*].

Advertisements will not be deemed to be discriminatory if the post falls under one of the 'genuine occupational qualification' exceptions. So, for example, a theatrical company advertising for a black male actor to play the part of Othello would neither offend the Sex Discrimination Act 1975 nor the Race Relations Act 1976. (As to what constitutes a 'genuine occupational qualification' for the purposes of each of those Acts, see SDA s 7 and RRA s 5 respectively.)

The use of words which have a sexual connotation such as 'waiter, salesgirl or stewardess' would be taken to indicate an intention to discriminate. Either different words such as 'waiting staff, sales staff or steward/stewardess' would have to be substituted or a disclaimer inserted such as 'applications are invited from both men and women'.

The Equal Opportunities Commission (EOC) or Commission for Racial Equality (CRE) are the only bodies empowered to bring proceedings in relation to alleged discriminatory advertisements. In one classic case, *EOC v Robertson [1980] IRLR 44*, the owner of a 'cash and carry' business advertised in the local newspaper for 'craftsmen, handymen' and had gone on to state '. . . a good job opportunity for a good bloke (or blokess to satisfy those damned fool legislators)'. Here the industrial tribunal found that he had intended to discriminate!

An advertisement was placed by an employment agency, headed 'Genuine career opportunities for Rugby Players', featuring a sketch of a male rugby player. The tribunal agreed with the EOC that this advertisement showed an intention to discriminate because it gave the impression that a woman applicant would be treated less favourably than a male. The picture gave the impression that the advertisement was directed at men rather than women (*EOC v Rodney Day Associates Ltd (COIT 7937/88)*).

Making promises at interviews

1.6   Care should always be taken at interviews not to make promises concerning terms and conditions of employment. If an employer does, he may be stuck with them! This may be particularly difficult where the promise contradicts the standard written terms or company policy. Whilst it is important to discuss some of the important terms and conditions with job applicants, it is very unwise to make any promises concerning changes to those terms at that time. A sensible course of action for any personnel officer or interviewing manager would be to reserve the company's position and write to the applicant at a later date.

The status of an oral promise which in fact contradicted the signed written terms came before the tribunals with an interesting result, in *Hawker Siddeley Power Engineering Ltd v Rump [1979] IRLR 425*. Here a Mr Rump had been promised at his interview that he would not have to agree to travel all over

England (mobility clauses are discussed further in Chapter 4). On the basis of that promise he accepted the job. Several years later he signed a contract of employment which included a mobility clause requiring him to work anywhere in the British Isles.

Some years later the company required him to transfer to Scotland (he had previously only worked in the South of England). Mr Rump refused to move relying on the oral promise that had been made to him at his interview. He was dismissed. Both the industrial tribunal and the Employment Appeal Tribunal concluded that the oral term to which he and his employer had agreed was the correct term of his contract. Even though there was a written term covering mobility that he had signed at a later date, that document neither provided conclusive evidence of what the correct terms were nor could it unilaterally change the previously agreed term that he would not be required to move outside the South of England. The EAT held that:

> 'In the present case the employee had no notice that the oral term he had secured was going to form no part of his new contract. The mere putting in front of him of a document and invitation to him to sign it could not be held to be a variation by agreement so as to exclude the important oral term which he had previously secured. Rather, if there was a variation at all to the contract, it was a unilateral variation which was not binding upon the employee. Alternatively . . . the employee in signing that agreement might have taken that the promise which had become a term of his contract and honoured as such, still applied.'

This case illustrates the dangers of not putting in writing what has been agreed between the employer and employee.

Holding out and making misrepresentations

1.7   In normal cases where a person applies for a job advertised in the media, he holds himself out to be competent for that job. In *Pinkerton v Hollis Brothers & ESA plc (21 July 1988, Court of Session, unreported)* for example, a Managing Director of a company was dismissed shortly after appointment for incompetence. He argued that since his contract of employment was silent as to the degree of skill required, there was no implied term that he had to demonstrate a particular level of skill. The Court of Session disagreed stating that the implied duty to serve 'loyally and faithfully' meant that he had impliedly promised to have the standard of skill that a reasonably competent Managing Director would possess. He could therefore be dismissed without notice for fundamental breach of such a term.

However, take the case of a job that is barely described in the advertisement and is one for which the applicant could not be expected to know whether he is or is not competent – at least, not until he gets to the interview! In cases where the applicant has no knowledge of the details of the job being advertised, interviewing managers must take care not to make misrepresentations about the job or about the ability of the job applicant to do the job. A manager (or his employer) who makes a misrepresentation which induces a person to enter into a contract may be sued for any losses sustained by that person as a result of that misrepresentation, under section 2(1) of the Misrepresentation Act 1967. Here the misrepresentation does not have to be fraudulent for the plaintiff to succeed, but there is a defence that at the time the person made such representation he had reasonable grounds to believe and did believe, up to the time that the contract was made, that the facts represented were true.

A case which went before the High Court, *McNally v Welltrade International Ltd [1978] IRLR 497*, illustrates this point. Here Mr McNally applied for a job advertised as 'operational staff required'. The advertisement stated that 'operators must have previous refinery experience and have held a similar position for a minimum of three years'. Mr McNally had worked as a chemical plant operator. Mr McNally was called for interview and at his interview he told the manager concerned, Mr James, that he had never worked in an oil refinery. Mr James said that the work would be very similar to the work he had been doing in his present job and that 'he would have no problem'. He was offered a job to work on an oil exploration rig in Libya and as part of his contract he had to agree to undergo several tests of competency.

Mr McNally resigned from his existing job, sold his house, uprooted his family and started work in Libya. After ten days his employment was terminated as a result of his failure to pass the required tests. He sued the parent company, the subsidiary company responsible for the Libyan operation and the interviewing manager, Mr James, for damages including general damages for the considerable worry and inconvenience suffered and won.

The High Court held that:

> 'In (a case) where the plaintiff had no idea what the job was, he could only rely on the defendant Mr James's advice to decide whether he was suitable for the job. Having in effect been told that the work involved was within the ambit of his experience, he relied on this advice and entered the contract. ... Since he relied on Mr James's misrepresentations that he was qualified for the job, there was a misrepresentation to which s 2 of the Misrepresentation Act applied.'

Please note that the Misrepresentation Act 1967 does not apply in Scotland. However equivalent provisions, contained in section 10 of the Law Reform (Miscellaneous Provisions) (Scotland) Act 1985, apply in Scotland.

Asking the right questions

1.8   There may be certain occupations which involve a high degree of trust. In such cases it is vital to ask the job applicant either on the application form or at the interview whether or not they have any criminal convictions other than 'spent' convictions by virtue of the Rehabilitation of Offenders Act 1974 (see below). The consequences of failing to make these most simple enquiries may lead a court to find that the employer has been negligent in his recruitment procedure should the employee commit a criminal act during the course of his employment.

In *Nahhas v Pier House Management (Cheyne Walk) Ltd, 1 February 1984 (QBD, unreported)*, the High Court found the employers vicariously liable for the criminal acts of one of their employees (a night porter in a select block of flats in Chelsea) and ordered the employers to pay damages including interest and legal costs to a resident whose jewellery had been stolen by the night porter. Here the employer had failed to make any reasonable enquiries about the background of their night porter and this, the High Court held, fell below the standard of care expected of an employer recruiting an employee in a position of trust. The porter had had 33 previous criminal convictions for theft and burglary!

A dishonest or evasive answer to a question about previous criminal convictions may give an employer a fair reason for dismissal should this be discovered at a later date (*Torr v British Railways Board [1977] IRLR 174*).

Rehabilitation of Offenders Act 1974

1.9   Under the Rehabilitation of Offenders Act 1974 it is unlawful to refuse to engage or to dismiss on the grounds of a spent conviction. Applicants with spent convictions are permitted to act towards a prospective employer as though they have not been convicted. This includes stating on a form and in an interview that they have not been convicted.

The Act applies only to terms of imprisonment of 30 months or less and certain fines and other sentences. There is an Order (SI 1975 No 1023, as amended by SI 1986 Nos 1249 and 2268) exempting certain professions and jobs from the scope of the Act. These include teachers, barristers, accountants, pharmacists, doctors, dentists, nurses, social workers and those involved with children. In addition, for the purposes of certain specified proceedings, offences involving fraud and dishonesty and offences in contravention of other legislation (for example, relating to companies, including insider dealing, and banking and financial services) are also excluded from the Act. This exemption principally affects sole traders, partners and those holding or who are to be appointed to senior positions (such as directors, managers, and controllers) in authorised businesses, or businesses applying for authorisation, under the Financial Services Act 1986 (see section 189 and Schedule 14).

The conviction becomes spent after a period of time (the 'rehabilitation period') which runs from the start of the sentence. Refusing to engage on grounds of a spent conviction is not a criminal offence and there is no action for compensation for refusing to employ someone on the basis of a spent conviction. [*Sec 4*].

The rehabilitation periods applicable to particular sentences are set out in two

Tables contained in section 5 of the Act. Table A, slightly simplified, is reproduced below.

Table A (reduced by half for persons under 17)

Sentence	*Rehabilitation period*
Imprisonment, youth custody, corrective training of 6–30 months	Ten years
Cashiering, discharge with ignominy or dismissal with disgrace from HM's service	Ten years
Imprisonment, youth custody, corrective training of less than 6 months	Seven years
Sentence of dismissal from HM's service	Seven years
Detention in service disciplinary proceedings	Five years
Fine or any other sentence subject to the Act	Five years

Table B, which is not reproduced here, applies to young offenders where the rehabilitation period runs from seven to three years.

It is automatically unfair dismissal to dismiss on the basis of a 'spent' conviction (*Taylor and Kershaw v Property Guards Ltd [1982] IRLR 175*). However, it may be fair to dismiss on discovery of a conviction which is not spent if this is material. In *William Craig v Innes (EAT 744/82)*, a betting clerk lied about a previous conviction which was not spent (on engagement). When his employers discovered he had a conviction, following a robbery at the shop which they suspected was an 'inside job', they dismissed him. This was held to be fair even though they did not know the exact nature of the conviction. They could not find out since this is a criminal offence.

Checking criminal records

1.10 As stated above, certain categories of employee are exempt from the provisions of the Rehabilitation of Offenders Act 1974 and it may be quite proper for an employer employing such staff to make thorough checks on their criminal records and other relevant employment matters. Official sources such as the police, the courts or government departments may be used in such cases and the Home Office regulates the procedures for making such checks.

However it is not lawful for employers other than in those excepted cases to make enquiries of any individual's criminal record although some employers use the services of private detective agencies or other sources who may provide such information. This practice is extremely dubious and could lead to a prosecution of either the agency/consultant or the employer or both for conspiracy to commit a criminal offence or aiding and abetting! It would be wise for any employers who know or suspect that job applicants are vetted in this manner to make sure that the practice is prohibited.

Under the Data Protection Act 1984 however, data subjects have a right to seek access to their criminal records stored on the police computers. It is therefore possible for a prospective employer to gain access to a job applicant's criminal record indirectly via the job applicant himself. Some employers require job applicants to provide a copy of a print-out of their criminal record as part of the recruitment process before any job offer is made. The Data Protection Registrar is aware of this practice and considers that this is an abuse of the Act. He has published a report (in March 1989) criticising this practice, and is considering whether a change in the legislation is necessary to outlaw it. An important point to note here is that the police computer records do not distinguish between 'spent' and 'unspent' convictions and therefore the information obtained may be out of date, inaccurate, irrelevant and in breach of the data protection principles in Schedule 1 to the Act.

(For a full and excellent article on this subject, see Marian Bell, 'Employing Ex-Offenders', IRLIB 390.)

Asking the wrong questions

1.11   Making enquiries about job candidates' family commitments or dependants or even plans to conceive is not itself unlawful but it may constitute unlawful sex discrimination under the Sex Discrimination Act 1975 if the answers are used to screen out female candidates – unless such questions can be objectively justified. In most cases they cannot be and the employer will be guilty of unlawful sexual or marital discrimination. Similarly asking about religious beliefs or using discouraging words to members of particular ethnic groups may also offend the Race Relations Act 1976. Several cases have illustrated this point.

In *Simon v Brimham Associates [1987] IRLR 307*, a firm of employment consultants interviewed a Mr S for a job and asked if he would be prepared to work for Arab employers. He was also asked his religion. The interviewer explained that 'if for instance you were of the Jewish faith, it might preclude your selection from the job'.

The Court of Appeal held that: 'Words or acts of discouragement can amount to treatment of the person discouraged less favourable than that given to other persons'. However, on the facts, it was held that Mr S was not discriminated against.

In *Adams v Strathclyde Regional Council (EAT 456/88)*, the EAT concluded that it is not inherently unlawful or discriminatory to ask about the number and age of a woman's children at the interview. Here a female job applicant was asked this question. She claimed she was so upset and angry at what she regarded as the discriminatory nature of the interview that she was unable to do her best for the remainder of the interview. She did not get the post; another woman was selected. The industrial tribunal and EAT both held that as a matter of fact the question was not discriminatory in the context in which it was raised.

The tribunal came to the conclusion that 'it was a question that could equally well have been asked of a male candidate'.

However, a word of warning – merely asking men the same question will not provide an automatic defence. The onus of proof will initially rest with the complainant to establish a *prima facie* case of discrimination. The evidential burden will then shift to employers to justify why a line manager needs to ask such questions!

In *Smith v North-Western Regional Health Authority (COIT 29270/86)*, the tribunal took a rather different view of such matters. Here, Mrs Smith applied for the job as 'leading ambulance person'. She was asked what arrangements she would make for her child if both she and her husband (also an ambulance driver) were on duty. She said she had satisfactory arrangements with relatives. She complained of sex discrimination when she was turned down for the job. The tribunal noted that a young man with a young child was not asked this question and that one of the interviewers said to Mrs Smith: 'Why did you bother to have a family if you always farm out your daughter?'.

The tribunal found that:

'Whilst it is proper for an interview panel such as this to enquire into the arrangements being made for the family it is indicative of a discriminatory frame of mind not to make similar enquiries of the male candidate with a young family.'

Mrs Smith won her case.

However where domestic or personal circumstances are relevant in that they might affect the performance of a job, merely asking questions about those circumstances will not in itself be discriminatory. So asking a candidate for police officer about her childcare arrangements was held not to be sex discrimination in *Woodhead v Chief Constable of West Yorkshire Police, EAT 285/89*. The tribunal however added that 'it would have been better if those conducting the interview had spent less time asking questions about the applicant's domestic circumstances and rather more about her previous background and experience in jobs she had been doing since these seem to be relevant to the work of a police officer . . .'.

Additionally, clause 23(c) of the Equal Opportunities Commission (EOC) Code of Practice recommends that

'questions should relate to the requirements of the job. Where it is necessary to assess whether personal circumstances will affect performance of the job (for example, where it involves unsocial hours or extensive travel) this should be discussed objectively without detailed questions based on assumptions about marital status, children and domestic obligations. Questions about marriage plans or family intentions should not be asked, as they could be construed as showing bias against women. Information necessary for personnel records can be collected after a job offer has been made.'

Industrial tribunals hearing cases of sex discrimination must take the provisions of the code into consideration.

Requests for photographs

1.12   Some employers ask for photographs of job applicants. This is particularly common for teaching posts and for certain public sector occupations. Whilst this is not in itself unlawful, employers should guard against this practice since in certain circumstances this could constitute an act of discrimination on racial or ethnic grounds. It could be the case, for example, where the job is in the service industry and the employer has no other reason for requiring a photograph other than to ensure that the candidates are white – on the basis that customers or clients would not deal with a person of any other ethnic group. It will be essential for an employer to be able to justify on solid, objective grounds, why a photograph of a job applicant is necessary. For example, any selection criteria which include the 'need to fit in with the rest of the department' may be strong evidence of racial or sexual discrimination.

In *Laudat v Hobbs Ltd (Case No 13950/89)*, an industrial tribunal has commented that:

> 'It could well be an act of discrimination if the job in question was for example for a barrister or a solicitor in a legal department of an organisation, or for a machine operator, to take two examples which were discussed during the case. We would say that as a general principle, a request for a photograph is generally at least capable of being discriminatory on racial or ethnic grounds.'

Applying selection criteria

1.13   It is essential to ensure that selection criteria are applied objectively. Where an industrial tribunal finds an inconsistent application of criteria and the moving of the goal posts for different candidates, they may draw an inference that there has been sex or race discrimination (*Camara v London Borough of Barking & Dagenham (No. 2) Case No 06681/87 reported in Equal Opportunities Review, Discrimination Case Law Digest, No. 3 Spring 1990, page 6*).

The Court of Appeal has recently applied a similar rule in two cases – *Dornan v Belfast City Council [1990] IRLR 179* and *Baker v Cornwall County Council [1990] IRLR 194*. Here the Court of Appeal (the Northern Ireland Court of Appeal in the former case) has ruled that if discrimination takes place in circumstances which are consistent with the treatment being based on sex or race, the industrial tribunal should be prepared to draw an inference that the discrimination was on such grounds unless the alleged discriminator can satisfy the tribunal that there was some other innocent explanation.

Key Points

- Do not have conflicting messages in advertisements.

- Make sure that all the copy for job advertisements is vetted carefully by an authorised officer of the company.

- Make sure that the application forms do not directly or indirectly discriminate against ethnic minorities or women (or men) – e.g. in interview assessment criteria avoid questions such as 'Does he/she fit in with the rest of the department?'.

- Take *detailed notes* of all interviews and keep them for a suitable period of time. Make sure the notes are legible! You may prefer to complete a pro forma interview sheet which notes standard information for all job applicants.

- At the interview explain all the important duties of the job and discuss the obligations of the employee and the employer. Refer to a copy of the relevant terms and conditions.

- At the interview ensure that a careful assessment is made in accordance with a job specification, a personnel specification and health profile which are all free of sex bias or racial bias.

- Do not ask questions which are irrelevant and which give the impression that there are discriminatory practices or sex-biased criteria, such as that women with young families are less reliable than others without dependants or men in general.

- Do not make promises at the interview about the job, job prospects or the competency of the applicant.

- Make sure that the agreed terms and conditions are clear and unambiguous and that they have actually been agreed.

- Put all the terms agreed between the parties *in writing* – either in the offer letter, the contract of employment, union agreement or Staff Handbook.

Chapter 2

Making the Offer

2.1   Once a decision has been made to make an offer of employment, great care must be taken to clarify whether the offer is conditional or unconditional. Many employers impose conditions that must be satisfied before the offer of employment can be accepted. Where this is the case, it is sensible to issue two 'offer' letters as set out at the end of this chapter. The 'first offer' letter, **Precedent 1**, sets out the employer's intentions to 'confirm' an offer of employment once the conditions have been satisfied. The first letter also advises the potential employee not to resign from his current employment until the offer has been confirmed in writing.

Conditions for offer of employment

References

2.2   It is almost standard practice to require satisfactory references before offering employment. A standard covering letter and reference request form, **Precedents 2** and **3**, are reproduced at the end of this chapter. Employers who fail to check references may well find themselves liable for any acts of negligence or criminal acts committed in the course of that employee's employment. An employer could be found to have failed to take reasonable care in his recruitment procedures if he has failed to obtain written references for any positions of trust, and could be held liable for negligence on the basis that he had failed to make checks (or adequate checks) prior to the start of the employment.

Any reference given may well include a disclaimer similar to the one in **Precedent 2**, which provides an employer with an exclusion from any legal liability in the giving of the reference. It may be worthwhile to include a disclaimer in relation to any reference given (whether oral or in writing). However, an exclusion must be reasonable having regard to all the circumstances obtaining when the liability arose or but for the notice would have arisen. [*Unfair Contract Terms Act 1977, ss 2(2), 11(3)*]. It would therefore be necessary to determine whether or not it is reasonable to exclude legal liability, knowing at the time of writing the reference that a prospective employer would rely on it to confirm or withdraw the offer of employment. Liability for a misstatement of facts may not be covered by a disclaimer if the reference purports to give facts which are ordinarily within the knowledge of the employer. However a disclaimer for a statement of opinion may be valid. Alternatively, a successful defence of estoppel may be raised by a defendant on the basis of the promise by the plaintiff not to sue for any negligent misstatement.

Questions of confidentiality and legal liability for negligence and defamation in relation to references cannot be dealt with in detail in this book but are well described in other publications (for example, *see* Gillian Howard and Christopher Southam, 'AIDS and Employment Law', Financial Training, 1987). However there are a number of points to be made here. Firstly, references given in confidence must be treated in confidence. The terms of any reference cannot be revealed to any prospective employees – this would be a breach of confidence on the part of the prospective employer.

Secondly, a reference must be honest and true to the best of the employer's ability. A prospective employer may be able to sue a former employer for negligence if a reference has been provided which falls below the standard of care that a reasonably careful employer would have adopted. An ex-employee may only have a claim in defamation if the reference is untrue and prompted by malice.

As a general rule, there is no legal obligation on employers to give references (other than under the LAUTRO rules where there is a very onerous duty to state a number of particulars). However, if the employer does give a reference, he owes a duty of care to the prospective employer to whom the reference is written, but no duty of care to the ex-employee about whom the reference is written – see *Spring v Guardian Assurance plc and ors* [*1993*] *IRLR 122*. In *Spring* the Court of Appeal held, (allowing an appeal from the High Court [*1992*] *IRLR 173*) that

> 'the giver of a reference owes no duty in the tort of negligence to the subject of the reference. His duty to the subject is governed by and lies in the tort of defamation. If it were otherwise the defence of qualified privilege in an action for defamation where a reference was given, or the necessity for the plaintiff to prove malice in an action for malicious falsehood would be by-passed. In effect a substantial section of the law regarding these two associated torts would be emasculated.'

The Court in so holding, approved the judgment of the New Zealand Court of Appeal in *Bell-Booth Group Ltd v AG* [*1989*] *3 NZLR 148* and overruled *Lawton v BOC Transhield* [*1987*] *IRLR 404*.

The decision in *Spring* was applied recently by the Court of Appeal in *Petch v Commissioners of Customs and Excise, The Times, 4 March 1993*, where an employer was required to answer queries from pension scheme trustees about a former employee's work record. However, leave to appeal to the House of Lords has been granted in the *Spring* case.

Where an offer of employment is made 'subject to receipt of satisfactory written references', it is the employer's final decision as to whether the references meet with his requirements. The test is subjective not objective. In *Wishart v National Association of Citizens Advice Bureaux* [*1990*] *IRLR 393*, a job offer was made 'subject to receipt of satisfactory references'. The references received were not satisfactory – they included details of a poor attendance record.

The Court of Appeal rejected the prospective employee's claim that it was breach of contract to withdraw the offer, since the conditional offer subject to satisfactory references was to be determined on an objective basis. The word 'satisfactory', held the court, 'should be given a subjective meaning in the present context'. (See also *Stapp v London Borough of Hillingdon, COIT 846/226*.)

Employers who fail to obtain written authority for references or checks from the application form may choose to use the 'Authorisation' form as set out in **Precedent 4**.

Documentary evidence

2.3   Other conditions for employment may include passing a medical examination or assessment, producing evidence of educational and professional qualifications and birth and/or marriage certificates. Evidence of age or marital status will be essential for occupational pension purposes whilst professional qualifications may be essential for certain categories of jobs. The first letter should include all these points. It may be desirable for candidates to bring along the originals of their certificates (birth/educational/driving licence/work permit etc.) at the time of the interview. In other cases it may be sufficient for the successful applicant to bring them along on the first day at work.

Medicals

2.4   Many offers of employment are subject to satisfactory medical assessments or examinations. Assessments may take the form of completion of a health questionnaire scrutinised by a company nurse or personnel officer. Medical examinations are normally conducted by medical practitioners – either a company doctor or doctor appointed by the company. Written consent to such examination must be obtained from the applicant. Any special tests, e.g. blood tests, AIDS tests etc., will be explained to the applicant at the medical examination and his informed consent obtained. Consent to disclosure of the results of any tests will also have to be obtained.

Whether or not the examination is to be carried out by the applicant's own doctor, the individual will have rights under the Access to Medical Reports Act 1988 and Access to Health Records Act 1990. The onus is on the employer to inform the job applicant of his rights and obtain his written consent. Copies of all the relevant forms and letters can be found in **Precedent 5**. A copy of a medical questionnaire is also reproduced in **Precedent 6**.

(For a fuller explanation of the 1988 Act, see 'Access to Medical Reports Act 1988 – Implications for Practitioners', Law Society's Gazette, Vol. 86, No. 13 and 'Occupational Health', October 1991, Vol. 43, No. 10.)

Qualifications

2.5   It may be regarded as a criminal offence for an employee including the self-employed to lie about a qualification in order to obtain or keep an employment. In *R v Callender [1992] 3 All ER 51 (CA)*, a self-employed 'accountant' passed himself off as being a member of the Chartered Institute of Management Accountants and the Institute of Marketing. On the strength of the false representations made on his CV to that effect, he was engaged by clients to keep their accounts and to submit their tax returns to the Inland Revenue. In fact he never did the work for which he was engaged but periodically submitted invoices to his clients claiming that accounts had been kept and tax returns submitted and he received payment from these clients.

He was convicted of obtaining a pecuniary advantage by deception under section 16 of the Theft Act 1968 in that he dishonestly obtained for himself the opportunity to earn remuneration in an office or employment as an accountant by falsely representing his qualifications. The Court of Appeal upheld his conviction on the basis that the word 'employment' in the definition of the offence of 'dishonestly obtaining a pecuniary advantage by deception' under section 16 should be given its ordinary literal meaning so as to include self-employed people such as accountants (solicitors and barristers could be added to this list!).

The Theft Act does not define 'employment' or 'office' and the court first took note of the view of academic writers most of whom suggested that the term 'employment' should be limited to the master-servant relationship (excluding the self-employed). The Court of Appeal however took another view and looked at the Oxford Dictionary which included the passive sense 'to be occupied'. The court said that if they took the more limited view:

'. . . . . there would be a yawning gap in the protection of the public afforded by section 16 of the 1968 Act through which a large number of dishonest persons can – by arranging matters so that they come within the definition of 'self-employed' – escape conviction and punishment for the kind of deceitful conduct of which the jury, by their verdicts in the instant case, found this appellant to be guilty.'

In the absence of any higher authority to the contrary, the court dismissed Mr Callender's appeal.

Trade union membership

2.6   The Employment Act 1990 made it unlawful for employers to discriminate against non-union members or union members at the point of recruitment. So any questions at the interview or on an application form or in a job advertisement which have the effect of screening out non-union members are unlawful. The relevant provisions are now contained in section 137 of the Trade Union and Labour Relations (Consolidation) Act 1992. In addition it is unlawful to exclude from recruitment those trade union activists on so-called 'blacklists'.

Confirming the offer

2.7   In an ideal world, it should be possible to check all these matters before allowing the individual to accept the job or start the employment. In such cases, the confirmation of the offer will be relevant. A copy of this letter can be found in **Precedent 7**. However, where an individual is permitted to commence employment before such matters have been checked, the wording of the offer letter will have to be amended. An amended clause is set out under the heading of **Precedent 8**.

Gaining qualifications as essential term of the contract

2.8   A number of employers recruit trainees in the expectation that they will gain further qualifications or professional status. Articled clerks in solicitors' practices or accountancy firms are obvious examples. However, the employer must make it clear in the offer of employment whether or not that offer, or indeed continued employment, is contingent upon passing examinations, gaining professional status or retaining the same.

Reneging on job offers

2.9   Once an unconditional offer has been made and accepted (which may be formally through a written acceptance or starting the job) any attempt unilaterally to withdraw the offer is breach of contract by the employer entitling the disappointed job applicant to sue for damages. Here damages are normally limited to the pay and contractual benefits which would have been enjoyed during the notice period. But in some cases the impact on future employment prospects may also be taken into account.

Two cases illustrate this point. In *Stubbes v Trower, Still and Keeling* [*1987*] *IRLR 321*, Mr S, a disappointed job applicant, successfully sued a firm of solicitors who had offered him employment as an articled clerk to start in September 1984, after he had sat the Law Society Finals. His offer letter read:

> 'I confirm that our salary scale in view of your age would start at £5,510 a year if you pass the whole of the final examination although it would be slightly lower than that if you start before the results of the final examination are known.'

Mr S accepted the offer. When the firm learnt that he had failed the examination and had no intention of resitting it, the firm wrote to him and told him that they would not accept him into service as an articled clerk. He sued for breach of contract and won. The Court of Appeal would not imply a term that Mr S would, at the start of his articles, either have passed the whole of the examination or be awaiting the results. The employers had at their disposal the means of securing this position by way of an express condition within the terms of their offer and this would have been consistent with Regulation 48 of the Law Society's Regulations. Mr S was awarded damages of £14,351. This included only £1,500 for the damage done to his prospects of future employment either as a solicitor or in some other capacity.

On this point the Court of Appeal held that:

> 'The approach in the present case should be the same as that for damages for personal injuries where a comparatively small conventional figure is awarded for loss of employment prospects unless there is solid evidence of what would have happened but for the accident. In the present case what might have happened if the appellant had entered service with the respondents was the matter of purest speculation as was the loss suffered from being deprived of the opportunity, apart from the direct loss of earnings, which was undeniably recoverable.'

In the second case, *Gill and others v Cape Contracts Ltd [1985] IRLR 499*, Mr Gill and his colleagues successfully sued Cape Contracts Ltd when they revoked an offer of employment to work at Sullum Voe in the Shetlands. They had originally worked as insulation engineers at Harland & Wolff in Northern Ireland. The jobs offered were for a minimum of six months and were accepted by the men. They resigned from their jobs in Northern Ireland. As a result of threatened industrial action from the Scottish workers if men from Northern Ireland were given the jobs, Cape Contracts revoked their offers of jobs.

In the Northern Ireland High Court, the men were awarded six months' wages but due regard was taken by the court that much of the wages offered (£358.00 per week) was paid for the inclement and inhospitable climate in Sullum Voe and since the men had stayed at home, they had not suffered that amount of damage. They were awarded £2,500 each.

Probationary periods

2.10   It is fairly common for employees to be offered employment subject to a satisfactory probationary period. This varies from three months to one or even two years. The wording of this clause must be carefully drafted; see the suggested wording in **Precedent 9**. Several issues are relevant here:

   (i)   the wording of the period of probation;

  (ii)   a provision to terminate at an earlier date (a 'break clause');

 (iii)   a power to extend the period;

  (iv)   details of what rules, procedures and benefits will apply during this period;

   (v)   reviews of performance during the period; and

  (vi)   confirmation of permanent employment in writing.

(i) The period of probation

An offer of employment subject to a 'six months' probationary period' is an offer of a fixed term contract for six months. A probationary period of 'up to' a certain length of time is preferable.

(ii) 'Break clause'

It is important to include a provision about notice during the probationary period. Such a provision, commonly referred to as a 'break clause', gives the employer (and the employee) the right to terminate the contract at any time during that period subject to either a specified period of notice or payment in lieu.

The position where no period of notice is specified was stated by Lord Denning MR to be as follows: 'In the absence of express stipulation, the rule is that every contract of service is determinable by reasonable notice.' (*Richardson v Koefod [1969] 1 WLR 1812*; see also *McClelland v Northern Ireland General Health Services Board [1957] 1 WLR 594*). 'Reasonable notice' has been deemed by the courts to last much longer than the statutory minimum notice set out in section 49 of the Employment Protection (Consolidation) Act 1978. In *Hill v CA Parsons & Co Ltd [1971] 3 All ER 1345 (CA)*, Lord Denning held that a senior engineer with long service should receive six months' common law notice. Where the contract of employment provides for the statutory minimum notice, it follows that during the first four weeks of employment, no notice or pay in lieu is due. (See Chapter 10 for further details.)

(iii) Extension

It will also be important to make provision for an extension of the probationary period should the employee not be up to the standard required. Some organisations have such a policy as a disciplinary measure since becoming a permanent member of staff attracts benefits not enjoyed in the probationary period.

(iv) Special rules

It may be important to outline what rules, procedures and benefits will apply during the probationary period. For example those companies with contractual disciplinary procedures will be in breach of contract if they dismiss the employee in breach of the procedure. In other words, for offences of minor misconduct or sub-standard work, most procedures provide for an oral warning and two written warnings before dismissal. Any attempt at dismissal during the first two years of employment (prior to enjoying employment protection) could lead to an action in the High Court for an injunction or damages. Quantum of damages would not be limited to the notice period but to the length of time that the employee would have been employed whilst the procedure was properly executed (subject to the general duty to mitigate). Injunctions in such cases have recently been granted in the public sector, albeit in rare cases, preventing the employer from executing the decision to dismiss until the correct procedure has been adopted.

For more details of some cases involving breach of contract, please see Chapter 12 'Other Clauses'. In order to avoid any problems, it would be wise to include wording such as that in **Precedent 10**.

(v) Reviewing the period

There may be reasons for extending the probationary period either because the standards of performance have not been achieved or for disciplinary reasons. It is important to spell out a right to extend the period in such cases.

(vi) Confirmation in writing

It is wise to confirm an employee's permanent employment particularly if terms and conditions will change following satisfactory completion of the period.

Temporary staff

2.11 Where temporary staff are obtained through agencies it may be wise to confirm who has checked references, qualifications, previous employment etc. It would be sensible to agree an indemnity clause and obtain a series of warranties from the agency. A comprehensive agreement can be found in **Precedent 11**.

Key Points

- Ensure that offer letters contain carefully worded offers of employment subject to certain conditions being satisfied.

- Check references carefully looking for dates of employment, positions held and other qualities needed for the job.

- Make sure that proper authorisation for references checks has been obtained from the employee.

- Insist that documentary evidence (the originals) are produced by the job candidate to verify information given.

- Check professional qualifications with the appropriate professional body.

- Take careful note that the requirements of the Access to Medical Reports Act 1988 and Access to Health Records Act 1990 have been considered in any pre-employment medicals.

- Make sure that criteria for employment such as trade union membership or non-union membership have now been eliminated.

- Draft clauses on probationary periods carefully.

- Include an exclusion clause from the warning stages of the disciplinary procedure in the first few months of commencement of employment, if appropriate.

- Insist on clear and fair terms of business with employment agencies.

PRECEDENT 1

First 'Offer' Letter

John Smith Esq
10, Noddy Street
Toytown
Nowhere NH1 1UP   Date

Dear John

Following your recent interview we are very pleased to tell you that we intend
to make you an offer of employment as .... (grade)
in the .... (Department) at the starting salary of £ .... per
annum, as soon as certain conditions are satisfied. These are set out below.
We would also point out that it is the Company's final decision as to whether
or not all these matters satisfy us.

We require:

1. satisfactory references (work and character);
2. a satisfactory medical report; and
3. documentary evidence of your stated qualifications/degree/diploma/
professional qualifications/licence under TSA/IMRO/LAUTRO etc./date
of birth/driving licence etc.
(*Delete where appropriate.*)

We would advise you not to resign from your present employment nor
authorise us to take up any references from your present employer until we
send you confirmation on the above matters. Once we have formally made you
an offer of employment in writing, please ring me so that we may agree a
starting date.

As we discussed normal office hours are ......am to ......pm Monday to Friday
inclusive but you will be expected to work such additional hours (which may
include weekends and Bank holidays) as the demands of the business require.

Full details of all your terms and conditions of employment are contained in
your Contract of Employment and the Staff Handbook and other Company
procedures and Policies, copies of which will be sent you when we make you
a formal offer of employment. We operate several generous employee benefit
schemes including a profit-sharing scheme, the details of which you will find
in your Contract of Employment and Staff Handbook.

If you wish to consider our offer of employment, would you please telephone
our resident nurse, Miss Mary Lamb, in the Personnel Department on
extension 2233, to arrange a medical examination as soon as possible.

Should you have any queries on any of the above, please do not hesitate to telephone me on the following number (insert telephone number).

Yours sincerely,

....
For and On Behalf Of

PRECEDENT 2

Request for a Reference

PRIVATE AND CONFIDENTIAL   Date

Dear Sir/Madam

RE: _____

The above-named person who has applied to us for employment has given your name as a referee. We understand he/she was previously employed by you as follows:

Position Applied For:
Employed By You From:
To:

It would be appreciated if you would kindly answer the questions on the attached form concerning the applicant. Any information you give us will be treated in the strictest confidence and without any liability on your part.

A stamped addressed envelope is enclosed for your convenience.

Thank you for your assistance in this matter.

Yours faithfully,

For and On Behalf Of
_____

PRECEDENT 3

To: Personnel Officer
XYZ Limited
1-15 Castle Street
Hammerbridge
London W16 2XQ

CONFIDENTIAL

RE: _____

1. Are the details given in our letter correct? If not please state the correct period of employment and/or position in your organisation:
_____

2. Did you find the applicant honest and capable? Please give details of any assessment or opinion you may have on these matters:
_____
_____

3. Was the applicant a) Punctual? _____
                              b) Capable? _____
                              c) Reliable? _____
                              d) Able to get on well with others? _____
4. Was the applicant able to work well under pressure?
_____

5. Was the applicant able to work without supervision?
_____

6. What was the applicant's absence record throughout his employment with you? Please give details of periods of absence:_____
_____

7. Did the applicant ever receive any disciplinary warnings during his employment, if so, what were they for? _____
_____

8. Why did the applicant leave your employment? _____

9. Would you re-employ the applicant? YES .... (tick) NO .... (tick)
10. Do you know of any reason why we should not employ this person?
_____

Additional information
_____
_____
_____

Name of Company _____
Signature _____ Position _____
Date _____19_____

PRECEDENT 4

Authorisation Form for Reference Checks

(Headed notepaper of company)

Name ....(Block Capitals)

I hereby authorise you to take up references from my previous employer(s), my present employer (once the offer of employment has been confirmed in writing) and the two people whom I submitted as personal referees. In addition, I hereby authorise you to take up other reference checks as deemed appropriate.

I authorise the Company to request that all corporations, companies, educational institutions, persons and former employers release information that they may have about me and release them from any liability and responsibility arising from so doing. I authorise credit agencies to release information that they may have about me to any authorised officer of this Company.

Signed................................ Date: ....

PRECEDENT 5

Access to Medical Report Form

(Headed notepaper of company)

Medical Consent Form (MCF 1)

The reasons for a medical assessment/examination have been explained to me. I have read an explanation of the Access to Medical Reports Act 1988 supplied to me by my Manager.

I consent/I do not consent to a medical examination and/or assessment by a doctor of the Company's choice.

I do/do not require access to the medical report upon me to be prepared following the medical examination/assessment prior to it being sent to .... (specify name and job title).

Signed .... Date ....

(Additional form printed below which will be sent with a copy of the Medical Report should access be requested before it is sent to the Company.)

Medical Report

I acknowledge receipt of a copy of the Report which was attached and consent to its supply to ....(name individual)

Signed............................... Date...........................

Authorisation Form (To GP or Consultant)

(AF 2)
To: .... (name of GP or Consultant)
.... (address)
....

I authorise Dr. .... (of the Medical Department of
.... Company Ltd) to seek from you a report on my medical history and current state of health.

I understand that the report is to be supplied by you within the terms of the Access to Medical Reports Act 1988. I have read an explanation of the Act supplied to me by .... (Name of Company).

I do not require access to your medical report upon me.*

I do require access to your medical report. I understand that I must communicate with you within 21 days of today to make arrangements for access.*
(Please delete whichever is inappropriate.)

Signed.................................... Date ....

Notice to Doctor
(To be sent only if access is required)

AMR (3)
To: .... (name of GP or Consultant)
.... (address)
....

NOTICE: Pursuant to Section 4(1)(a) Access to Medical Reports Act 1988

Mr/Ms.....................................requires access to your report before it is supplied and must within 21 days of the date above communicate with you in writing to amend any part of your report which he/she considers inaccurate or misleading and you should either amend your report or attach to your report a statement of Mr/Ms ....'s views. Before supplying the report, you must obtain his/her consent to your report being sent to us. If Mr/Ms.................................... fails to communicate with you within the said 21 days, after this period has elapsed, you should supply the report to the person named above in the consent form.

1 January 1990

Access to Medical Reports Act 1988 – Employee Explanation

The Access to Medical Reports Act 1988 gives you the right to have access to any report upon you made after 1 January 1989 which is to be, or has been, supplied by a Medical Practitioner, for example your own General Practitioner, a Consultant whom you have been seeing or a doctor from our own Medical Department/Company doctor.

You have the right to inspect or be supplied with a copy of the doctor's report before it is sent to the Company if you so indicate on the Consent Form which you will be asked to sign before you go for your appointment or examination or if you notify the doctor direct, before he/she has sent the report, that you wish to have access to it before it is sent to the Company.

Having been given access to the report, it cannot be sent to the Company without your consent. Before giving your consent, you have a right to request the doctor to amend or delete any part of his report which you consider inaccurate or misleading but if he/she refuses, you may require the doctor to attach to his/her report a statement of your views. You will continue to have the right to apply for access to the doctor for six months after he/she had made the report.

You will not have access to any part of the report if, in your doctor's opinion, disclosure would be likely to cause you or anybody else serious physical or mental harm or would indicate the doctor's intentions or would be likely to reveal information about or the identity of a third person unless that person has consented or is a health professional. You will be entitled to have access to the remainder of any such report. If the doctor is of the opinion that you should not have access to any of the report for the reasons above, he/she will notify you and will not supply the report unless you consent.

Prec 6 *Making the Offer (2)*

PRECEDENT 6

Medical Questionnaire

STAFF CONFIDENTIAL

PLEASE COMPLETE IN BLOCK CAPITALS

Surname	Date of birth
Forenames	Vacancy Ref. No.
Address	

Appointment applied for	National Insurance No.
Name and address of candidate's own doctor	National Health Service No.

Please answer all the following questions by circling the appropriate word: if the answer is yes, circle yes; if it is no, circle no.

	QUESTIONS	COLUMN	
		I	II
1	Are you a registered disabled person?	Yes	No
2	Have you ever received compensation or a disability pension?	Yes	No
3	Are there any medical reasons why you should not do shift work?	Yes	No
4	Are you able to carry out strenuous physical work including climbing ladders, working from scaffolding, bending, lifting and carrying?	Yes	No
5	Have you ever had to give up any previous job for medical reasons?	Yes	No
6	Have you been off work continuously for more than a month during the last five years?	Yes	No
7	Have you ever had any operations requiring hospital admission for five or more days?	Yes	No
8	Is your eyesight normal (with glasses if worn)?	Yes	No
9	Is your hearing normal?	Yes	No
10	(a) Do you regularly take tablets or medicine? (b) If so, what do you take?	Yes	No
11	Have you ever had any of the following:- (a) Diabetes?	Yes	No
	(b) Tuberculosis?	Yes	No
	(c) Angina?	Yes	No
	(d) Any other heart trouble?	Yes	No
	(e) Raised blood pressure?	Yes	No
	(f) Peptic, gastric or duodenal ulcer?	Yes	No
	(g) Indigestion for more than one week?	Yes	No
	(h) Back trouble, lumbago, sciatica, "slipped disc"?	Yes	No
	(i) Epilepsy, recurring blackouts or fits?	Yes	No

QUESTIONS	COLUMN	
	I	II
12 Have you ever had any of the following during the **past five years**:- (a) Bronchitis, asthma, pneumonia?	Yes	No
(b) Dermatitis, eczema or any other skin trouble?	Yes	No
13 Do you suffer from any of the following:- (a) Migraine or severe recurring headaches?	Yes	No
(b) Anxiety, depression or any other nervous complaint?	Yes	No
(c) Fainting attacks or giddiness?	Yes	No
(d) Ear trouble, discharging or infected ear?	Yes	No
(e) Kidney trouble or urinary infection?	Yes	No
14 If you have circled any answers in column 1 for questions 1 to 13, please give **very brief** details below:-		
15 Have you ever had any other serious illness? If Yes please give **very brief** details below:-	Yes	No
16 Have you consulted a doctor about your health during the past twelve months? If Yes please give **very brief** details below:-	Yes	No

I am willing to undergo a medical examination if required and I declare that the information I have given on this form is correct to the best of my knowledge.

I agree that the Board's Doctor may consult my own Doctor.

Signed: Date:

PRECEDENT 7

Confirmation of Offer

John Smith Esq
10, Noddy Street
Toytown
Nowhere NH1 1UP   Date

Dear John

Following my letter of ...., I am pleased to make you a formal offer of employment with the Company in the position of .... on the terms set out in my earlier letter and below. Once you have confirmed acceptance of this offer we intend to take up references from your present employer. Please note that in the unlikely event that we are not satisfied with this reference, the Company reserves the right to withdraw this offer of employment. Acceptance of this letter will give us authorisation to contact your present employer for a reference.

Your initial employment with us as .... will be on the basis of a probationary period of up to .... The company will assess and review your work performance during this time and reserves the right at any time during this period to terminate the employment with .... written notice. If you should feel that you are not suited to the job during this time you will be required to give .... written notice to terminate your employment with us. The Company also reserves the right to extend your probationary period should it be deemed necessary by the Company. Your appointment will be confirmed in writing should your probationary period prove satisfactory.

During your probationary period, the Company reserves the right in all cases (other than gross misconduct) to terminate your contract without any prior warnings or any disciplinary hearing by the giving of the written notice referred to above or payment in lieu/to reduce the number of official warnings for any acts of misconduct or poor work performance.* (*Delete whichever is inappropriate.*) You will nevertheless be obliged to follow all the procedures and rules laid down by this organisation.

Your terms and conditions are set out in the Contract of Employment attached and in the Staff Handbook enclosed with this letter. You will see that there are two copies of your Contract of Employment attached. For our records please will you sign both copies and the duplicate copy of this letter confirming your acceptance of this position.

Should you wish to raise any queries on any of your terms and conditions then please telephone me on the following number (insert telephone number).

As discussed with you, please will you bring all the original certificates of your educational, University/College and professional qualifications with you together with your birth certificate on your first day. Please do not send these in the post as they may go astray and please ensure that they are all original documents and not copies.

May I take this opportunity of welcoming you to .... and trust that your career with us will be both enjoyable and successful.

Yours sincerely,

....
For and On Behalf Of

I am pleased to accept this position under the above terms and I have read, understood and accept the above terms and the Terms and Conditions contained in my Contract of Employment and Staff Handbook attached, copies of which I have returned duly signed.

....
(Employee)

PRECEDENT 8

Amended Clause as to References in 'Confirmation of Offer' Letter

'Your employment is subject to satisfactory references and the Company's decision is final as to whether the references meet with our requirements. Your references will be taken up when you confirm your acceptance of the position unless you allow us to do so earlier. If any delay is incurred in our taking up the references and should you commence employment whilst we are waiting for a reply, it is understood that your employment is terminable forthwith (with no notice) in the event of such references falling short of our requirements. Every effort will be made to obtain references as quickly as possible.'

PRECEDENT 9

Probationary Periods

'1. Your initial employment with us as .... will be on the basis of a probationary period of up to ....

2. The Company will assess and review your work performance during this time and reserves the right at any time during this period to terminate the employment with .... notice. The Company reserves the right to make a payment in lieu of notice at any time other than in cases of gross misconduct where no notice or pay will be due.

3. If you should feel that you are not suited to the job during this time you will be required to give .... notice to terminate your employment with us.

4. The Company also reserves the right to extend your probationary period should it be deemed necessary at the entire discretion of the Company.

5. Your appointment will be confirmed in writing should your probationary period prove satisfactory.

6. Please note that the special rules relating to the disciplinary procedure will apply to you during your probationary period so please read these very carefully. In particular we would draw your attention to the fact that during this probationary period the Company reserves the right to waive all or some of the official warnings and may terminate your contract without any formal warnings at its discretion. Other than in cases of gross misconduct, the notice provision in paragraph 2 of this clause will apply.

7. You will also not be eligible for an interest-free season ticket loan until the completion of this period.'

PRECEDENT 10

Disciplinary Procedure

During your probationary period the Company reserves the right in all cases of poor performance or breach of the rules or unacceptable conduct to waive any or all of the official warnings and terminate your contract by giving you the required written notice or payment in lieu (other than in cases of gross misconduct). Please note that you are subject to all the Company's Rules and Policies from the start of your employment.

PRECEDENT 11

Terms of Agreement with Employment Agencies providing Temporary Staff

The .... Agency agrees to provide such staff as (Name of Company) may require upon the following terms which may be amended by (the Company) from time to time:

1. The Agency agrees to undertake a full and thorough check of any staff to be engaged on any work for (Name of Company) in whatsoever capacity, by obtaining and scrutinising written employment references covering the past X years (minimum of five years).

The following matters must be investigated and verified and copies of documents kept on file:

(a)   previous criminal convictions (other than 'spent' convictions) of individual or close family;

(b)   dates of previous employment, salary details and position held;

(c)   ability to keep all matters confidential;

(d)   reliability;

(e)   timekeeping record;

(f)   attendance record;

(g)   any previous disciplinary record;

(h)   documentary evidence regarding matters such as full name, address, age, work permit/driving licence (where necessary);

(i)   documentary evidence of educational and professional qualifications (where appropriate).

The Company reserves the right at any time to delete, add to or modify the above list of matters and the Agency will be notified when any such changes are made.

2. The Agency agrees upon request from an authorised Officer of the Company to send copies of any such written references or documentary evidence on any of the matters specified above or any other reasonable matters upon reasonable notice. Should any details of any matters covered in (a)–(i) above, reveal any negative matters or cause for concern, the Company reserves the right to refuse to engage any such individual or remove them from the Company premises without warning or notice.

3. The Agency agrees to indemnify the Company against any losses, costs, legal claims, damages or expenses arising directly or indirectly out of the acts

Prec 11 *Making the Offer (2)*

or omissions of the Agency or any of its staff. This includes but is not limited to any acts or omissions of any of the said Agency's staff whilst working on the Company's premises save where the Agency can prove to the satisfaction of the Company that it received satisfactory written references or documentary evidence on the matters covered in 1.(a)–(i) above or any other additional specified matters.

This indemnity will cover the immediate reimbursement of or cancellation of any engagement fees due to be paid or already paid by the Company to the Agency in relation to the engagement of any such individual(s) removed from employment with the Company or refused engagement upon the above terms.

Name of authorised officer .... Date ....
(Agency)

Chapter 3

Different Types of Contracts

3.1   There are a number of different types of contracts that an employer may choose to offer. Sometimes employment is permanent, sometimes it will be temporary. Lawyers and personnel managers responsible for recruitment need to be clear about the type of contract that they issue and questions such as whether staff are technically 'employees' for tax, national insurance or employment protection purposes will be relevant.

The temporary employment itself may be for one short period or for a series of short periods depending on the seasons, the workload of the business or the individual preferences of the person. 'Temps' employed by agencies will normally remain the legal responsibility of the agency. But in other cases the employer may employ such staff as 'direct' labour, in which case, there may be industrial relations implications – trade unions are sometimes reluctant for employers to employ 'temps' and have entered specific agreements about their use. Even where the 'temps' are direct labour, their interrupted employment with the same or associated employer raises the question of continuity of employment. In some cases, after two years of albeit interrupted employment, such workers may gain sufficient service to bring themselves within employment protection legislation.

As far as 'temps' from an agency are concerned, it is wise for employers to ensure that the agency has checked references, past employment etc. An agreement including warranties and indemnities for the terms of business for employers and employment agencies can be found in the previous chapter, **Precedent 11**. A model 'contractor's' agreement is included as **Precedent 4** at the end of this chapter.

An increasingly more common type of contract is a job share where two people share one job on a job-share or job-split basis.

Some work is termed 'casual' and even 'regular casual' and there has been a host of litigation as to whether or not 'casual regulars' are 'employees' or 'independent contractors'. In the latter case, they enjoy no employment protection rights.

Below we look at several different forms of contracts ranging from those for an indefinite period, those for a fixed term, those on a temporary or casual basis, those on a job share basis and those on a contract for services (i.e. freelance).

This book does not attempt to cover the complex subject of the law concerning the variation of terms and conditions of employment. However over the past few years there has been a growing practice amongst some employers to terminate collective agreements and offer incentives to staff to accept personal contracts and forego union bargaining arrangements. In recognition of this growing practice, there is a brief discussion of this subject at the end of the chapter.

'Employee' or independent contractor

3.2   It is essential to identify at the start whether or not the relationship is one of employer/employee or that of independent contractor. Whether or not a relationship constitutes a contract of employment is a matter of fact and degree to be determined by an industrial tribunal reviewing the facts of each case (*O'Kelly v Trusthouse Forte plc [1983] IRLR 369*). There may be more than one correct answer to the question whether a contract of employment exists. In the case referred to above, the Court of Appeal concluded that '. . . the precise quality to be attributed to the various individual facts is a matter of fact and degree'.

But if an industrial tribunal has erred in deciding whether on the true construction of the documents the complainant was an 'employee', the decision must be reversed.

The correct test(s)

3.3   The courts have applied a number of legal tests in order to determine whether an applicant is an 'employee'. Applying the correct test is a matter of law. The determination of the question whether the particular individual is an 'employee' is a matter of fact for the tribunal to decide. One of the most relevant tests used nowadays by the tribunals is that of 'mutuality of obligations'. In the *O'Kelly* case cited above, the industrial tribunal stated that '. . . whilst the relationship did have many of the characteristics of a contract of employment, there was one important ingredient missing – mutuality of obligation'.

At the heart of every contract of employment, there is an implied obligation on the company to offer work to its employees and on them to do the work when it was offered to them. This test was reiterated in the appeals of five trawlermen all based at the port of Hull. Here the fact that there was no mutuality of obligation led the Court of Appeal to hold that there was no global contract of employment covering the periods when the men were on leave at home between voyages. Evidence was brought that the men frequently worked for other employers during this period, thus negating their argument that they were still under a contract of employment during their leave and thus entitled to a redundancy payment when their services were not renewed (*McLeod v Hellyer Brothers Ltd, Wilson v Boston Deep Sea Fisheries Ltd [1987] IRLR 232;*

this was followed by the EAT in *Letheby and Christopher Ltd v Bangurah, EAT 639/86*).

The courts and tribunals will consider all the particular aspects of the relationship, no single factor being in itself decisive and each of which may vary in weight and direction. A tribunal must give such balance to the factors as seems appropriate, to determine whether the person was carrying on business on his own.

Here are the factors to be taken into account in determining this question:

(*a*)   Is the person taxed as self-employed? (i.e. does he pay Class 2 and 4 national insurance contributions and Schedule D income tax?)

(*b*)   How do they perform their work? With their own tools and equipment?

(*c*)   Can they sub-contract the work to others?

(*d*)   Who tells them what to do and how to do it?

(*e*)   Do they work for anyone else or are they working full-time for the same employer?

(*f*)   What are the terms of their contract? How are their hours controlled? Do they have holidays, sick pay, pension entitlement?

(*g*)   Are they employed as an integral part of the business?

(*h*)   Do they take any financial risk themselves?

(*j*)   Do they have any responsibility for management and investment?

(*k*)   Is the employer obliged to offer work and is the person obliged to accept it?

Casual workers

3.4   Casual workers are workers who are not provided with regular guaranteed work but who are called for employment when required. This may be on a regular or irregular basis. In some cases where casuals have worked regularly for the same employer without a break for several years, the tribunals have held that they are independent contractors and therefore not eligible for any employment protection rights. However, in other cases, on identical facts, the tribunals have held that they are employees and may therefore sue for unfair dismissal and/or a redundancy payment.

In the *O'Kelly* case referred to above, Mr O'Kelly and his colleagues had worked for many years virtually every week, often averaging 30 hours per week. The industrial tribunal found that since there was in theory no obligation on the employer to provide the work nor any obligation on the applicants to perform the work, they were not 'employees'. This decision followed the case of *Ahmet v Trusthouse Forte plc, EAT 124/82*, where the head barman at the Cafe Royal spent 17 years as a regular casual and retained the right to refuse to work although he had never exercised it. The EAT held he was not an 'employee'.

In contrast, in the case of *Four Seasons (Inn on the Park) Ltd v Hamarat, EAT 369/84*, the EAT found that a regular casual who had worked as a wine waiter for seven years was an employee. Here, he was only paid for the hours that he had worked and had received no sick pay or holiday pay. The industrial tribunal found that there was mutuality of obligation. Strangely, it would appear that the applicants in the first two cases had stronger cases than Mr Hamarat since they received holiday pay and were subject to the company's disciplinary rules and the grievance procedure. The company also deducted tax and national insurance from their wages.

The Inland Revenue's view regarding the taxation of casual workers' pay is set out in their Guidance Booklet on PAYE (Employers' Further Guide to PAYE (P7) (1993) at C1). (Also at C1, there are special notes for farmers who take on casual workers at harvest time.)

'Temporary' seasonal workers

3.5   Many workers work regularly each season but have breaks in service. They will not normally 'clock up' sufficient continuous service to enjoy the majority of the employment protection rights. However breaks in their service due to 'temporary cessation of work' may be regarded as continuous service and those breaks may count towards continuity of employment. [*EPCA 1978, Sch 13, para 9(1)(b)*]. In the latest of a long line of cases, *Sillars v Charringtons Fuels Ltd [1989] IRLR 152*, the Court of Appeal has confirmed that tribunals are entitled to adopt the mathematical test in determining whether or not breaks in service are 'temporary'. The tribunals may select the last two years prior to the last termination and compare the length of the appellant's last two periods of seasonal employment with the length of the last two periods of unemployment. In *Sillars*, the Court of Appeal upheld the EAT and industrial tribunal's decision that Mr Sillars did not serve continuously but had permanent breaks in his service during the 15 years that he had been employed as a seasonal driver delivering heating fuel. His last two years of employment were respectively 21½ weeks off and 30 weeks on; 27 weeks off and 27½ on. The Court of Appeal concluded that the breaks in service were by no means of a temporary or short duration. This was despite the facts that Mr Sillars was always given the same payroll number, had the same locker from season to season and was allowed to keep his personal belongings in that locker even when he was not working for the company, that both parties intended that he should work for the company each winter season, that seasonal workers received service-related pay increases and accrued seniority rights with regard to vacancies for permanent positions. These all pointed to the breaks not being permanent, but this did not mean they were only temporary.

Following the case, Charringtons has now changed its policy and provides new payroll numbers on every occasion that a seasonal worker is engaged!

Different types of contracts

Indefinite period/permanent

Private sector staff

3.6 The most common type of contract of employment provides for the contract to run until determined either by the employer for good cause or by the provision of notice or pay in lieu. This is known as a contract for an indefinite period. Quite often the employer will outline circumstances under which the contract may be determined. These may include:

(*a*)   gross misconduct;

(*b*)   inefficiency;

(*c*)   absence due to illness or injury for longer than six months or an aggregate of 26 weeks within a rolling period of twelve months;

(*d*)   wilful neglect of duties;

(*e*)   declared bankrupt or applying for or had made against him an Order in Receivership;

(*f*)   becomes of unsound mind or a patient within the meaning of the Mental Health Act 1983;

(*g*)   (if a director) prohibited by law from being a director of a company;

(*h*)   (if a director) resigns as a director of the company other than at the company's request.

Public servants

3.7 Different rules will apply to those working in public service which is not Crown employment (civil servants). Here, unless the contract provides for termination, the employment will continue until retirement unless the employer has dismissed for good cause or for a reason provided for in the contract. Such staff are commonly termed as having tenured employment, although there have been changes recently in the contracts of teachers and University staff who now no longer enjoy tenured employment (see below). Although civil servants are deemed not to have contracts of employment but to be employed at the pleasure of the Crown, they enjoy protection from unfair dismissal. [*EPCA 1978, s 138*].

The right to claim tenured employment has been borne out by a rather under-estimated decision in the House of Lords, *McClelland v Northern Ireland General Health Service Board* [*1957*] *AC 594*, concerning a senior clerical officer whose post was described as 'permanent and pensionable' but who was purportedly dismissed with six months' notice. Her contract only provided for termination for gross misconduct, inefficiency or unfitness for continued employment. Since she did not come within any of those categories, the House of Lords (by a narrow majority) held that her employers had no power to dismiss her.

3.7 *Different Types of Contracts*

Civil servants may also enjoy some form of security in employment until retirement unless dismissed for good cause. The wording of the Civil Service Code describes the employment as 'permanent' and makes provisions for the date of retirement. In *Secretary of State for Trade v Douglas [1983] IRLR 63* at *65*, the EAT held that the Civil Service Staff Codes provide for employment until retirement subject to earlier termination for good cause. (For a fuller explanation of the Civil Service Pay and Conditions of Service Code, see Davies and Freedland, 'Labour Law Text and Material' (Weidenfeld and Nicholson, 1984, pp 436-7).)

University lecturers

Some selected groups of employees who used to enjoy the security of tenured employment, no longer do so. Amongst this group were university lecturers, who until the Education Reform Act 1988 enjoyed protected employment and could only be dismissed for 'good cause'. This did not include dismissal for redundancy. The 1988 Act has now removed the security of tenure of academic staff of universities – this affects staff who have been appointed or promoted on or after 20 November 1987. Previously disputes arising out of the dismissal of academic staff were dealt with by the university visitor. Under the 1988 Act, the visitor's jurisdiction in this area had been abolished and university statutes are being amended so that academic staff can be dismissed by reason of redundancy as well as for good cause. (See the Education Reform Act 1988, ss 202–208.)

As mentioned above, the pre-Education Reform Act 1988 regime is still applicable to appointments made before 20 November 1987. This is illustrated in *Page v Hull University Visitor [1993] 1 All ER 97*. In *Page*, the appellant was appointed as a university lecturer in 1966. His appointment was subject to the university statute under which he was required to vacate his lecturing post on reaching retirement age. By the terms of his employment the contract could be terminated by either party on giving three months' written notice. He was dismissed by reason of redundancy and given three months' notice in June 1988. He petitioned the university visitor, arguing that under the provisions of the university statute, he could not be dismissed before retirement except for 'good cause'. The visitor dismissed his petition holding that he could either be dismissed for good cause or by the giving of three months' written notice.

The case reached the House of Lords, where it was held that the decision by the university visitor made within her jurisdiction was not amenable to challenge by judicial review on the ground of error of law or fact. Furthermore the university had not exceeded its powers in dismissing the appellant from his post as lecturer – his dismissal had been valid.

Automatic termination upon retirement age

It is also common, in addition to the inclusion of a notice period, for there to be a provision for determination of the contract automatically at the normal retirement date. An example of such a clause would be:

'Unless your employment has terminated at any earlier date, it will terminate without any further notice at the end of the month in which your (60th/62nd/65th) birthday falls.'

Note that, by virtue of section 3 of the Sex Discrimination Act 1986, the normal retiring age must be the same for both men and women.

Fixed term

3.8   Contracts may be drafted for a fixed term. They may express the termination date or provide a formula in order to ascertain the termination date. Care must be taken in the latter case to ensure that both parties understand what the termination date will be. In one case where an Oxford law student was given employment 'for the summer holidays', the personnel manager was horrified to learn, at the end of August, that the student had understood that the summer holidays continued until the start of the Michaelmas term in October! The personnel manager had meant the school holidays!

A common fixed term contract is that of a 'rolling' contract. Examples of all these types of clauses can be found in **Precedent 1**.

Probationary periods

3.9   Those drafting contracts should be aware of the legal implications of making an offer of employment 'subject to a probationary period of, e.g. six months'. Such an offer if accepted would be a contract for a fixed term, with the result that any termination prior to expiry date would lead to a claim for payment for the unexpired portion. A probationary clause should be most carefully worded so that it is not for a term certain and there should be a 'break clause' permitting termination before the expiry date. The recommended wording of a probationary clause appears in **Precedent 1**, Clause 4. (See Chapter 2 for more details.)

Contract for specific task

3.10   Contracts which last until the task has been performed or the project finished are yet another type of fixed term contract. Once the project has been completed, the contract automatically terminates without any need for notice. There is also no dismissal in law so the job holder will have no claim for damages or for compensation for unfair dismissal or redundancy pay.

In such cases, the duration must be uncertain. A local authority case, *Brown v Knowsley Borough Council [1986] IRLR 102*, illustrates the point. Mrs Brown was employed as a temporary teacher on a series of fixed term contracts. She was then issued with a contract which provided that her 'appointment will last only as long as sufficient funds are provided either by the Manpower Services Commission or by other firms/sponsors to fund it'. The EAT held that her contract came to an end 'upon the happening or non-happening of a future event and her contract had come to an end automatically when the happening or non-happening of the event specified in the letter took place'.

A standard clause which stipulates that the contract will automatically come to an end when the happening or non-happening of the event specified in the contract takes place can be found in **Precedent 1**, Clause 3.

Job share contract

3.11   A job share contract is most commonly offered to women returning from maternity leave. Such an arrangement must of course be open to both sexes otherwise a man may have a claim under the Sex Discrimination Act 1975. The contract may divide one job into morning and afternoon working, or specific days each week for each partner (say Monday to Wednesday for person A and Wednesday to Friday for person B), or one week on and one week off. In the last example, continuity of employment will be assured since the breaks in service will probably be viewed as an 'arrangement (whereby) he is regarded as continuing in the employment of his employer for all or any purposes'. [*EPCA 1978, Sch 13, para 9(1)(c)*].

An example of a job share contract can be found at the end of this chapter as **Precedent 2**. A career break, re-entry and retainer scheme can be found in **Precedent 3**.

Independent contractors/Freelancers

3.12   We have seen earlier in this chapter the tests adopted to determine whether or not a worker is an independent contractor or an employee.

It is vital for any employer to obtain satisfactory evidence of the tax status of an individual who purports to be self-employed. A letter from his accountant will not do! The evidence that should be obtained should include a certificate from the individual's tax inspector which is validated and agreed in writing by the employer's tax inspector. Provision of the person's Schedule D number may suffice. Failing such evidence, the individual should be regarded as a Schedule E taxpayer and PAYE and Class 1 NIC deducted from salary in the normal way.

Should consultants work for an employer, such as computer consultants, interpreters and translators or even employment law advisers, VAT registration may provide sufficient evidence of their tax status but this is not conclusive evidence and the tax office may require further proof.

It may be wise to include a warranty and indemnity clause in a contractor's agreement as to the tax position. A comprehensive contractor's agreement can be found in **Precedent 4**.

A standard executive's service agreement is also included in Appendix 1, as well as a typical contract for a hairdresser which contains restrictions after employment, including restrictions on advertising. A model contract for accountants can also be found in Appendix 1, containing special clauses regarding progress to partnership.

De-recognising unions and offering personal contracts

3.13 Recently, the Court of Appeal in two related cases, *Wilson v Associated Newspapers Ltd* and *Palmer v Associated British Ports*, *[1993] IRLR 336* held that the failure to offer pay increases to members of staff who would not accept personal contracts and thereby acquiesce in the de-recognition of the union of which they were members for collective bargaining purposes, amounted to action short of dismissal contrary to TULRCA 1992, s 146.

Section 146 provides, *inter alia*, that an employee has the right not to have action short of dismissal taken against him as an individual by an employer for the purpose of preventing or deterring him from being or seeking to become a member of an independent trade union or penalising him for so doing; or preventing or deterring him from taking part in the activities of an independent trade union or for penalising him for so doing.

On 24 May 1993, a late Government amendment to the Trade Union Reform and Employment Rights Bill was passed at the Third Reading in the House of Lords which effectively nullifies the Court of Appeal's decision in *Wilson* and *Palmer*. The amendment (contained in TURERA, s 13) inserts new subsections (3)-(5) into TULRCA 1992, s 148. Subsection (3) provides that:

'In determining what was the purpose for which action was taken by the employer against the complainant in a case where –

(a)   there is evidence that the employer's purpose was to further a change in his relationship with all or any class of his employees, and

(b)   there is also evidence that this purpose was one falling within section 146' –

the tribunal shall regard only the change in the employment relationship as the purpose for which the employer took the action, unless it considers that the action was such as no reasonable employer would take having regard to that purpose.

This subsection defines the way in which a tribunal should consider an employer's purpose when considering whether an employer has taken action short of dismissal against an employee for the purposes of preventing or deterring trade union membership. The provision is meant to clarify the protection in section 146 for an individual not to be prevented or deterred from being a union member or taking part in its activities and the right of employers to make and implement legitimate decisions about how they wish to negotiate with their employees.

Employers who wish to de-recognise unions and offer personal contracts will have to ensure that this is done without any overt or covert anti-union motive. Quite how significant a pay differential will have to be for those who accept personal contracts and accept no union recognition in the future in order to be viewed by a tribunal as a penalty and in breach of section 146, we shall have to wait and see.

Employers should be advised to tread carefully in making attractive offers to staff to opt out of union bargaining and accept personal contracts. Employers must be equally careful not to make overtly anti-union statements.

In *Wilson's* case, the Court of Appeal judged as important a statement of the newspaper's Editor that:

> 'He would prove in two years that the trade union was not necessary and the Chapel would wither away'.

This statement supported the contention that the employer's 'purpose' was anti-union rather than merely strategic or cost saving.

Key Points

- Make clear the status of the employment, whether it be temporary or permanent, for an indefinite period or for a fixed term.

- Make the fixed term certain and unambiguous.

- Identify clearly who is a freelancer or independent contractor and insist on clear evidence of tax status before permitting them to be paid gross without deduction of PAYE or NIC.

- Note that seasonal workers who continue to work for you on a seasonal basis may have continuous service despite their temporary breaks in service; this has implications for statutory employment protection such as unfair dismissal, maternity and redundancy payments.

- Draft service agreements carefully so that certain events such as insanity, bankruptcy or prolonged illness or injury may end the contract.

- Draft a clause in all contracts that they will automatically terminate upon the employee reaching his normal retirement date if the contract has not terminated earlier.

- Job share contracts may be drafted so that cover is ensured in the event of absence of one partner.

- Draft restrictive covenants carefully and include, if appropriate, 'touting for business' clause.

PRECEDENT 1

Clause 1

'The employee's employment will (unless lawfully terminated earlier under the provisions of this contract) be for a minimum term of *five (5)* years calculated from the commencement date and will continue thereafter unless and until terminated by either party giving to the other not less than *six (6)* months' written notice in advance to that effect (unless the party receiving the notice is willing to accept shorter notice) expiring at the end of the minimum term or of any subsequent month.'

Clause 2

'The employee's employment will (unless lawfully terminated earlier under the provisions of this contract) be for a minimum term of *one (1)* year calculated from the commencement date provided that on and with effect from each anniversary of the commencement date this contract shall be deemed to be renewed for a period of *one (1)* year unless either party shall have given written notice to the other to terminate this contract at the end of the then current term of *one (1)* year.'

Clause 3

'We are able to offer this appointment as a temporary .... in Grade X working in Department A. This appointment will last as long as sufficient funds are provided either by (sponsoring organisation)............... or by other firms/sponsors to fund it. Your salary and conditions of service are in the Company Handbook which is enclosed with this letter.'

Clause 4

'Your employment is subject to a probationary period of up to .... (week/ month(s)) during which time your performance and conduct will be carefully appraised and monitored. The Company reserves the right to terminate your employment at any time by giving you .... week(s) written notice or payment in lieu. You will be required to give us .... week(s) written notice should you wish to leave your employment. Please note that the Company reserves the right to reduce the number of official warnings as set out in the disciplinary procedure and may at its discretion merely give you notice or pay in lieu. The Company further reserves the right to extend your probationary period should this be considered necessary by management.'

PRECEDENT 2

Job Share Agreement – Some Special Conditions

BETWEEN

.... (the 'Company')

AND

.... (the employee, known as the 'Partner')

Date of Agreement ....

1. Job title ....

Name of Partner ....

2. Hours of Work

Your hours of work will be those agreed between the job share partners and management, and pay, annual leave and other benefits which are directly related to weekly hours will be on a pro-rata basis.

3. Public, Bank and Statutory Holidays

The two partners in the job will share the benefit of the Bank and Public Holidays on a pro-rata basis, i.e. according to the proportion of the job that each works. Since the timing of the holidays varies each year, the precise arrangements for sharing will be decided between the partners and management from year to year but where there is an imbalance so that a disproportionate number of days falls to one partner, the days to which that sharer is not entitled will either be unpaid or taken from annual leave entitlement or worked at a later date unpaid. The partner 'owed' leave will take it at a later mutually convenient date.

4. Sick leave

Entitlement to sick pay will accrue in accordance with the provisions of the Company sick pay scheme at the reduced rate of pay as set out in the partner's Offer Letter.

The qualifying days for SSP will be the days of the week that the partners actually work or are rostered to work. These may vary from time to time. In weeks when the partners are not due to work at all, then Wednesday of that week will be the qualifying day.

5. Cover for absences

In any case of annual leave, it is/is not* expected that the other partner will cover for the one on leave. However if one partner is absent from work for a significant period of time because of sickness or injury, or the half post becomes vacant for any reason, the remaining partner may be invited to work extended hours, possibly up to a standard full-time week, if personal circumstances allow for this.

Delete whichever is inappropriate.

6. Overtime

Overtime premia will be paid to a job share partner if the partners have *between them* worked more than 37* hours in any week or the other partner's hours have been credited through leave, sickness etc. Where one half of the post is vacant, however, overtime payments will only be paid if the remaining partner works more than 37 hours*.

*This may vary according to a Company's standard working week.

7. Pension

As you will be working less than 15 hours a week, you have an option whether or not to contribute to the Company's Pension Scheme. Would you please inform Personnel in writing whether you would like to contribute. You will be contracted out of the State scheme if you join the Company's scheme.

8. Attending meetings etc.

The partners agree that as long as they are given reasonable notice, either or both will agree to stay beyond their normal working hours for meetings etc. if requested to do so by their immediate manager or any other senior member of management.

PRECEDENT 3

Career Break Scheme

1. Who is eligible?

(a)   Any employee, male or female, who terminates their employment for *'domestic reasons'* (see definition below) is eligible for the Re-entry and Retainer Scheme.

(b)   *'Domestic reasons'* include:
  – leaving to have a baby;
  – leaving to care for children, dependants in need of care etc. (including elderly, disabled or sick dependants);
  – leaving to adopt a baby;
  – leaving to undertake successfully or unsuccessfully fertility treatment.

This list is not exhaustive and any decision on whether or nor a particular reason entitles an employee to enter the scheme will be made by the Personnel Director, whose decision will be final.

(c)   A *'dependant'* may include any person who is dependent upon the employee or ex-employee for care or for financial support and does not presuppose any family or blood relationship.

(d)   Except in exceptional circumstances, no individual will be permitted back on the Re-Entry Scheme until he/she has been on the Retainer Scheme for a minimum of two years.

2. Date of Entry to Scheme

Entrance to this Scheme will be effective from a date to be agreed between the Director of Personnel and the applicant.

3. Conditions: Retainer Scheme

(a)   The Scheme will be for a period of five years from the date the individual joined the Scheme.

(b)   The individual must work ten days in each calendar year following entrance to the Scheme. The individual will not be in any particular post but will be assigned duties to enable him/her to acquire and maintain skills, techniques and knowledge related to future employment.

(c)   The individual must attend an annual two and a half day course (called the 'refresher course').

(d)   The days during which the individual will work and attend the refresher course will be mutually agreed by the individual and the relevant Head of Department.

(e)   It is not permitted for any individual on this Scheme to take any paid employment except with the written consent of the Company.

(f)   The individual must inform the Company in writing of any change of address within two weeks of any change.

(g)   The individual may withdraw from this Scheme at any time by informing the Personnel Director in writing.

(h)   The Company agrees that, subject to the individual complying with the above conditions, it will:

>   (i)   provide ten days' work experience and a two and a half day refresher course each year;

>   (ii)   pay the individual for the days during which he/she attends the above, such payment to be calculated on the basis that the individual is employed on the same grade on which he/she was employed before leaving the Company;

>   (iii) provide facilities for career progression and support and counsellors to advise on training etc.

PLEASE NOTE: Except when undergoing work experience and refresher training, the individual is not employed by the Company.

4. Conditions: Re-Entry Scheme

(a)   The individual must notify the Director of Personnel in writing that he/she wishes to transfer onto the Re-Entry Scheme. A place will be allocated on the next available programme of re-induction training and employment will commence from the start of that programme which will be no later than six months from the date of the individual's letter.

(b)   Returners must attend the Company's programme of re-induction.

(c)   Following completion of the re-induction training, the returner will be provided with suitable employment wherever possible in the same department and on the same type of work that he/she was doing immediately before he/she resigned. If there is no suitable vacancy, the returner will be employed in a temporary position until a vacancy occurs.

He/she will be entitled to reject up to three alternative offers of permanent employment. If three offers are rejected, the Company will be under no obligation to offer further posts and the Company's obligations to the returner will cease.

(d)   The salary on taking up employment will be on the same grade or incremental point in the scale which had been reached on leaving.

(e)   The returner must complete a probationary period of up to six months after which the appointment will be confirmed.

(f)   The Company will provide facilities for support and counselling with regard to any appropriate training or other matters relevant to the employment or employee.

I..................................agree to abide by the terms of the Retainer and Re-Entry Schemes.

Date of joining the Schemes.....................................

Name...

Address...

PRECEDENT 4

Agreement for Professional Services

Dated ...., 19..

.............................Company of .... with registered offices at .... ('the Company') and .... with registered offices at .... ('the Contractor'), hereby agree as follows:

1.   Services to be performed

(A)   The Contractor shall perform for the Company the services (the 'Services') specified in Exhibit 'A' attached hereto [not included here] and incorporated herein for the period specified therein.

(B)   The Contractor shall if and for so long as the Company may require perform the Services on behalf of any Associated Company of the Company as if they were Services to be performed hereunder. In this Agreement the expression Associated Company means any company which is from time to time a subsidiary or a holding company (as those expressions are defined by section 736 of the Companies Act 1985) of the Company or any other company of which the Company's ultimate holding company, ... & Co ...., or any of its subsidiaries, holds at least 10% of the share capital having the right to attend and vote at general meetings.

2.   Payment for services

The Company agrees to pay the Contractor for the Services in accordance with the fee schedule contained in Exhibit 'A' hereto. Save as may be required by law the Company will make any payments due hereunder without deduction of any kind (including without limitation any deductions under the PAYE system or the Social Security legislation from time to time) and the Contractor hereby agrees to indemnify the Company against any costs, claims or expenses arising directly or indirectly out of the Company making such payments without deduction.

3.   Invoices

Invoices as to any amounts due under this Agreement shall be rendered to the Company by the Contractor on a .... basis. Invoices shall be payable by the Company within 30 days after receipt by the Company thereof.

The Contractor shall maintain accurate and complete records as to time spent and expenses incurred in its performance of the Services and shall allow the Company to examine such records from time to time upon request in order that the Company may ascertain the correctness of invoices submitted to the Company by the Contractor. In addition to these records, each of the Contractor's employees who participates in the performance of the Services shall complete daily Morgan Consultant timesheets which shall be approved and maintained by the Company.

4. Confidential information

(A) The contractor shall not and shall procure that its employees whose services may be provided to the Company hereunder shall not either during or after the termination of this Agreement:

— divulge or communicate to any person or persons except to those of the officials of the Company or an Associated Company whose province it is to know the same any of the secrets or any other information which they or any of them may receive or obtain in relation to the affairs of the Company or any Associated Company during the continuance of this Agreement;

or

— use for its or their own purposes or for any purposes other than those of the Company or any Associated Company any information or knowledge of a confidential nature which they or any of them may from time to time acquire in relation to the Company or any Associated Company but so that this restriction shall cease to apply to any information or knowledge which may come into the public domain (otherwise than through the default of the Contractor or any of its employees);

— for the avoidance of doubt, information or knowledge of a confidential nature includes, but is not limited to, any information which relates to internal controls, computer or data processing programs, electronic data processing applications routines, sub-routines, techniques or systems or business affairs and methods of operation or proposed methods of operation of either the Company, any affiliate of the Company, any Vendor of the Company, or any customer of the Company. Confidential information also includes information relating to the Company's employees. If in any doubt as to what constitutes confidential information the Contractor shall and shall procure that its employees seek guidance from an appropriate Company official.

(B) The Contractor agrees that it shall include and enforce such provisions in contracts of employment of individuals engaged in the performance of the Services as shall be necessary to ensure the non-disclosure of confidential information by such individuals.

5.   **Employees of Contractor**

(A)   For security purposes, the Contractor shall, prior to assigning any employee or subcontractor to participate in the performance of the Services, agree to require any such employee or subcontractor to furnish the Company with information required by the Statement of Information for Background Check attached hereto [not included here] and incorporated herein and signed by each such employee or subcontractor of the Contractor (the 'employee').

(B)   The Contractor will not permit any of its employees to perform the Services unless and until the Company has given the Contractor written authorisation.

(C)   The Contractor shall, upon written request of the Company, recall any employee of the Contractor engaged in the performance of the Services and shall, if requested by the Company, forthwith replace such employee with another individual acceptable to the Company.

(D)   Neither the Contractor nor any employee of the Contractor shall be or shall be deemed to be an employee of the Company for any purpose whatsoever.

(E)   Unless otherwise approved in writing by the Company, all individuals assigned by the Contractor to participate in the performance of the Services shall be employees of the Contractor. The Contractor shall not employ any subcontractor in connection with the performance of the Services without the prior written consent of the Company.

(F)   The Contractor shall have the continuing obligation to allow its employees to provide the Company with any additional information of the type required by Exhibit 'C' hereto [not included here].

(G)   Should the Contractor wish to replace one of its employees performing Services for the Company with another employee, prior approval, including security clearance (see paragraph 5 (A), above), must be obtained. When required, the Contractor will provide up to two (2) weeks of overlapping on-the-job training for the replacement employee at no charge to the Company.

6.   **Responsibility for injuries to persons and property**

The Contractor shall be solely responsible for all physical injuries, including death, to persons and all physical damage to property occurring on account of or in connection with the performance of the Services and shall indemnify and save harmless the Company from loss and liability including but not limited to liability for the payment of workers' compensation and disability benefits, upon any and all claims on account of such injuries to persons or physical damage to property and from all costs and expenses in actions which may be brought against the Company on account of any such injuries to persons or physical damage to property; provided, however, the Contractor shall not be obligated to indemnify and save harmless the Company from any loss and liability arising out of injuries or damage caused by or resulting from the negligence of the Company. The Contractor shall be solely responsible for any loss or expense incurred by the Company as a result of any act or lack of action on the part of employees of the Contractor, including but not limited to any direct or consequential liability or damage resulting from theft of material or services by any such employee.

7.   Term of Services and Agreement

The Services shall be performed within the term specified in the applicable Exhibit 'A' hereto; provided, however, that the Company may at any time terminate this Agreement and/or the Services upon four weeks' prior notice to the Contractor, and provided further, however, in the event that the Company in its sole and absolute discretion shall at any time determine that the Services are being performed in an unsatisfactory manner, it may immediately terminate this Agreement. Upon such termination, the only sum to which the Contractor will be entitled will be fees for such of the Services that have been rendered prior to the date of termination but not paid for.

8.   Rights to work product

(A)   The Contractor shall and shall procure that its employees shall promptly make a complete written disclosure to the Company of each invention, discovery or improvement, whether patentable or not ('Disclosed Subject'), conceived or first actually reduced to practice in connection with the performance of the Services. As to each Disclosed Subject, the Contractor shall and shall procure that its employees shall specifically point out the features or concepts which the Contractor believes to be new or different.

(B)   All written material, including reports, programs, manuals, tapes, card decks, listings and any other programming documentation prepared for the Company under this Agreement and each invention, discovery or improvement, including ideas, concepts, know-how or techniques, whether patentable or not, shall be deemed to be work made for hire and made in the course of the Services and shall belong exclusively to the Company. The Contractor agrees that it shall include and enforce such provisions in contracts of employment of individuals engaged in the performance of the Services as shall be necessary to ensure the exclusivity of ownership provided for in the preceding sentence. The Company shall have the right to obtain and to hold in its own name patents, copyrights, registrations, or such other protection as may be appropriate to the subject matter, and any extensions and renewals thereof. The Contractor agrees to give the Company and any persons designated by the Company any assistance reasonably required in order to perfect the rights defined

61

in this paragraph 8. The Contractor further agrees to periodically review the material prepared for the Company hereunder to ensure that no portion of such material is derived from any material which the Contractor does not have the right to use due to such material's being subject to a copyright, patent or other proprietary right.

9.   **Warranty**

The Contractor warrants that the work prepared for the Company hereunder shall not be improperly derived from any copyrighted or patented material or otherwise subject to or infringe upon any interest, proprietary or otherwise, of any individual or entity and agrees to indemnify and save the Company harmless from all loss or damage of any kind to which the Company may be subjected by virtue of a breach of this warranty.

10.   **General**

(A)   In performing the Services the Contractor shall at all times comply with all of the provisions set forth in Exhibit 'B' [not included here] (as amended from time to time), attached hereto and incorporated herein.

(B)   Any notice required to be given by either party hereunder shall be left at or sent by registered or recorded delivery post to the address shown on the signature page hereof. Any such notice shall be deemed to be served at the time when the same is handed to or left at the address of the party to be served and if served by post four days after the posting.

(C)   This Agreement, together with the exhibits hereto, constitute the entire agreement between the parties with respect to the subject matter hereof and supersedes in all respects all prior proposals, negotiations, conversations, discussions and agreements between the parties concerning the subject matter hereof and no subsequent alterations, amendments, changes or additions hereto shall be binding and valid unless reduced to writing and signed by each party.

(D)   This Agreement shall be binding upon and inure to the benefit of the parties hereto and their respective successors and assigns; provided, however, the Contractor shall not assign this Agreement or any other duty, obligation, interest or right hereunder without the prior written consent of the Company.

(E)   The Contractor shall not furnish the name of the Company or any of its Associated Companies' subsidiaries as a reference or utilise the name of the Company or any of its Associated Companies in any advertising or promotional material without the prior written consent of the Company or any of its Associated Companies.

IN WITNESS WHEREOF, this Agreement has been executed the day and year first above written.

Signed for and on behalf of   }

By:

Signed for and on behalf of
THE CONTRACTOR   }
By:

Chapter 4

Defining the Job

Written particulars of employment

4.1 There are several matters which by law must be spelt out in writing (often called 'the written particulars'). Sections 1–6 of the Employment Protection (Consolidation) Act 1978 as substituted by the Trade Union Reform and Employment Rights Act 1993 (see TURERA 1993, section 26 and Schedule 4) require employers to give all employees working at least **eight hours per week**, within **two months** of the beginning of their employment, a written statement of their main terms and conditions. The statement may be given in instalments provided that all the particulars are given to the employee within the two-month period and that those particulars required by section 1(2), 1(3)(a) to (c), (d)(i), (f) and (h), (see below) are included in a single document which is referred to as the 'Principal Statement'. The changes to sections 1–6 were introduced by virtue of the EC Directive on Proof of the Employment Relationship. These provisions are expected to come into force at the end of November 1993. (Note – changes effected by TURERA 1993 are printed in bold.)

The statement should contain the following details pursuant to section 1(2):

(*a*)   the names of the employer and employee;

(*b*)   the date on which the employment began;

(*c*)   the date on which the employee's continuous employment began (taking into account any employment with a previous employer which counts towards that period).

The statement, or the instalment, should also contain the following particulars pursuant to section 1(3):

(*a*)   the scale or rate of remuneration or the method of calculating remuneration;

(*b*)   the intervals at which remuneration is paid;

(*c*)   any terms and conditions relating to hours of work (including any terms and conditions relating to normal working hours);

(*d*)   any terms and conditions relating to any of the following:

   (i)   holiday entitlement including public holidays and holiday pay (with enough detail for the employee's entitlement including entitlement to accrued holiday pay on termination of employment, to be precisely calculated),

(ii) incapacity for work due to sickness or injury, including any sick pay provision,

(iii) pensions and pension schemes;

(*e*) the length of notice required from either party;

(*f*) the Job Title **or a brief description of the work for which the employee is employed;**

(*g*) **where the employment is temporary, the period for which it is expected to continue** or if it is for a fixed term, the date when it is to end;

(*h*) **the place of work or if the employee is required or permitted to work at various places, an indication of that fact and the employer's address;**

(*j*) **any collective agreements which directly affect the terms and conditions of the employment including, where the employer is not a party, the person by whom they were made; and**

(*k*) **where the employee is required to work outside the UK for more than one month:**

(i) **the period of work outside the UK,**

(ii) **the currency in which payment will be made,**

(iii) **any additional pay and benefits to be provided by reason of the work being outside the UK, and**

(iv) **any terms and conditions relating to the employee's return to the UK.**

Under section 2(5) where an employee is to begin work outside the UK for more than one month within two months of starting employment, the whole statement of terms and conditions will need to be provided before the employee leaves the UK.

'No particulars to give'

4.2 If there are no particulars to be entered under any of the headings relating to sickness, holidays or pensions or overseas working, that fact will have to be stated. This applies to any other terms and conditions required to be stated and so it appears to allow a statement to provide that no details exist where none exist under any particular heading (see section 2(1)).

However in *Eagland v British Telecommunications plc [1992] IRLR 323*, the Court of Appeal distinguished 'mandatory terms' (those required under section 1(2)(a) – (c) and 1(3)(a), (b), (e) and (f)) in that actual particulars must be given under those headings and 'non-mandatory' terms (those required under section 1(3)(c) and (d) in that no such particulars need be inserted if none have been agreed.

In *Eagland's* case the Court concluded that in the case of 'non-mandatory terms' an industrial tribunal could not invent a term where none could be shown to have been agreed between the parties, either expressly or by implication. In the case of 'mandatory terms', the Court felt that it was difficult to imagine a case where such terms fail to exist and if a 'mandatory term' was not included in the statement, a tribunal would probably have to imply one.

Note however that the particulars described as mandatory in *Eagland*, do not correspond exactly with those which are required by TURERA 1993 to be specified in the 'Principal Statement' (see 4.1 above) and which are therefore singled out as the principal particulars by the legislation.

Reference to other documents

4.3   A statement under section 1 allows reference to be made to 'some other reasonably accessible document' which 'an employee has reasonable opportunities of reading in the course of his employment' or is made reasonably accessible to him in some other way, for particulars listed in subsection (3)(d)(ii) and (iii) (sickness and pension provisions); and the law or a collective agreement for particulars listed in subsection (3)(e) (notice periods). Previously this type of reference was permissible for all of the terms.

Disciplinary note

4.4   The section 1 statement will have to include a note relating to disciplinary rules and procedures. Under new section 3(1) the note will have to include:

(*a*)   any disciplinary rules applicable to the employee or a reference to a reasonably accessible document which specifies those rules;

(*b*)   details of

   (i)   the person to whom the employee can apply if he or she is dissatisfied with any disciplinary decision, and

   (ii) a person to whom the employee can seek redress over grievances and the manner in which such applications should be made;

(*c*)   where there are further steps consequent upon any such application, details explaining those steps or a reference to a reasonably accessible document which explains them; and

(*d*)   a statement as to whether a contracting-out certificate is in force for the employment.

Subsection (1)(a)–(c) above will not apply to rules and procedures relating to health and safety. Only paragraph (b)(ii) needs to be complied with by employers with less than 20 employees.

Personal statement of changes

4.5   If there is any change to any of the terms about which particulars must be provided or referred to in the statement, the employer will generally have to give the employee a personal written statement detailing the changes. This must be given at the earliest opportunity and in any event no later than one month after the change or even earlier if the employee is to be required to work outside the UK for more than one month (section 4(i)).

Under the previous legislation, an employer could inform the employee of changes without actually providing the employee personally with a written statement.

This statement of change may refer to other reasonably accessible documents or a collective agreement as appropriate but only in respect of those matters where such a reference is permitted for the purposes of the section 1 statement (see 4.3 and 4.4(a) and (c) above).

If after an employee has been given a written statement and either, the name of the employer or the identity of the employer is changed in circumstances in which continuity of employment is not broken and no changes (other than the change of name) are made to the written particulars, the new employer will be required to provide employees with a written statement of this change in accordance with section 4(1).

If particulars of notice periods (section 1(3)(e)) have been given merely by reference to the law and the change results from changes to the law, then no notice of that change will be required.

The importance of ensuring that the terms as set out in the written statement are an accurate reflection of the terms and conditions is illustrated in the case of *Salvation Army v Dewsbury* [*1984*] *IRLR 222*. The commencement date is of critical importance where the two years' service qualification is in issue.

In the *Dewsbury* case, the 'Commencement date of employment' was expressed as 'May 1 1982'. This was a Saturday and Ms Dewsbury did not in fact commence work until the following Tuesday 4 May as Monday 3 May was a Bank Holiday. She was dismissed on 30 April 1983. The EAT held that she was to be taken as starting employment on 1 May for the purposes of calculating her continuous employment and she therefore had the requisite service (one year was all that was required in 1983) in order to present a complaint of unfair dismissal.

The EAT held that it was unlikely that Parliament should provide for Bank Holidays to delay the commencement of continuous employment. The EAT concluded that:

'... the phrase "starts work" in section 151(3) EPCA was not intended to refer to the undertaking of the full duties of the employment but to the beginning of the employee's employment under the relevant contract of employment ...'.

Other terms

4.6   There are other terms which it is sensible to spell out such as qualifications required, membership of professional bodies, dress and appearance, criminal convictions etc. Trade union membership was previously sometimes included as a term of the contract. However, section 1(1) of the Employment Act 1990 made it unlawful to refuse a person employment because he is or is not a member of a Trade Union. These provisions are now contained in section 137(1) of the Trade Union and Labour Relations (Consolidation) Act 1992. Employers must therefore not include such a term in any future contracts and ensure that any such requirement is removed from existing contracts.

Implied terms as to mobility and flexibility

4.7   Employers may wish to include, in contracts of employment, a carefully drafted express clause to cover job flexibility and mobility. Should such matters not be spelt out, the tribunals and courts have limited powers to imply terms as to flexibility and mobility. For example, a copy typist/clerk was held to be under an implied flexibility term to undertake photocopying duties (*Glitz v Watford Electric Co Ltd [1979] IRLR 89*). As far as more senior staff are concerned, they are expected to be as flexible as is reasonable to expect at that level of seniority.

The courts are prepared to imply mobility on the basis of what is reasonable. This depends on the nature of the employment, the custom and practice in the industry and the seniority of the employee. As far as blue collar workers are concerned, they are expected to be mobile 'within a reasonable daily commuting distance' (*Courtaulds Northern Spinning Ltd v Sibson and TGWU [1988] IRLR 305*). In contrast, senior managers are expected to be as mobile as the demands of the business dictate. Thus a general manager of a large insurance company was held to be under an implied obligation to serve the company 'wherever the company is located' (*Little v Charterhouse Magna Assurance Co Ltd [1980] IRLR 19*).

In some industries, the type of work requires workers to move from location to location. Such industries would include construction, banking and finance. In *Stevenson v Teesside Bridge and Engineering Ltd [1971] 1 All ER 296*, a steel erector was held to be under an implied duty to move from site to site in different parts of the country because of the custom and practice in the construction industry. In *Bouzourou v Ottoman Bank [1930] AC 271*, a bank was held not to have breached the contract (despite no express mobility clause) when they ordered an employee to move to another branch.

However, there is an overriding qualification on any implied requirement to be mobile. Where an employee's life would be at risk, the obligation to move to such a location ceases. For example, in *Ottoman Bank v Chakarian [1930] AC 277*, an Armenian, who had been sentenced to death in Turkey and had then escaped, was held not to be under any implied obligation to return to

Istanbul. There is, however, a difference between a general danger and a risk of personal danger. A professional espionage agent, a film stunt artist and a lion-tamer all have inherently dangerous jobs and it would be a breach of contract for them to refuse to work where required.

The courts are even prepared to imply terms where there is an express term as to mobility – these being that the employer will give reasonable notice of the move and provide reasonable financial assistance (in the case of a junior member of staff on a fairly modest salary). They are dealt with in the following paragraphs.

Implied duty to give reasonable notice and pay expenses

4.8   Even where there is an express clause on mobility, there is an implied duty on employers to give reasonable notice when exercising their right to move employees from one location to another and in some cases to pay certain expenses.

In one recent case, *United Bank Ltd v Akhtar [1989] IRLR 507*, the EAT held that even though the bank had an express mobility clause, it had been unreasonably exercised. Here Mr Akhtar was a junior employee on £560 gross monthly pay. He had been ordered to move from Leeds to Birmingham with six days' notice and no offer of financial assistance. His wife was ill and he needed time to sell his home so he requested a three-month delay with 24 days' leave so that he could sort things out. His employers' refusal to acknowledge his request and his subsequent resignation amounted to constructive dismissal.

Here the EAT held:

'The employers had committed a repudiatory breach of contract by the way in which they had sought to exercise their powers under the mobility clause in the contract of employment. . . .

There was an implied duty on the Bank to exercise their discretion under the mobility clause by implementing relocation or other allowances. . . . Their actions made the employee attempt the impossible.'

In a case involving a process operator (*McAndrew v Prestwick Circuits Ltd [1990] IRLR 191*), the Court of Session also held that the employer had been in breach of contract in requiring that employee to change his place of work at short notice. They held that:

'Where the right of an employer to transfer an employee is necessarily to be implied into the contract of employment, it is also necessary to imply some qualification of that term making the employer's right subject to qualifications both of reasonable distance and reasonable notice.'

Drafting express mobility clauses

4.9   Extreme care must be taken to draft express mobility clauses. They must be clear and unambiguous. The courts and tribunals will interpret ambiguous terms against the party attempting to enforce them. Since it is normally the employer attempting to rely on a mobility clause, it is even more important that the clause is drafted clearly. For example, the right to move an employee from 'site to site' is not the same as the right to move the employee from 'depot to depot'.

In *Litster v Fram Gerrard Ltd [1973] IRLR 302*, this distinction proved fatal to employers where the Civil Engineering Working Rule Agreement (incorporated into their employees' contracts of employment) provided only for transfer from 'one site to another'. The employers were in breach of contract in attempting to force their staff to move to another depot when their original depot closed down.

In contrast, where the mobility term is clear and unambiguous the courts will not interfere with the operation of such a clause. In *Rank Xerox Ltd v Churchill and others [1988] IRLR 280*, the company closed its office in the Euston Road in London and transferred to Marlow. The mobility clause in their employees' contracts read: 'The company may require you to transfer to another location'.

Here the EAT held:

'Where the words of the contractual term are clear and simple . . . there is no room for any implication . . . that it be construed on the basis of reasonableness as being restricted to a reasonable daily travelling distance.'

Two typical mobility clauses are set out as **Precedent 1** at the end of this chapter. The second clause commonly forms part of the contract of a member of a sales force.

Requirement to travel

4.10   It is arguable that certain occupations contain an implied obligation on the part of the job-holder to travel on business. Sales and marketing jobs would be typical examples. It is important to note that a standard mobility clause will not cover a requirement to travel on company business and it is therefore sensible to cover this point within the terms of any mobility clause. Such a clause is covered in **Precedent 1**.

Mobility clauses and sex discrimination

4.11   The inclusion of a blanket mobility clause into contracts of employment should be viewed with caution. It is arguable that such a clause may be unlawful as it may be regarded as indirect sexual or marital discrimination. [*SDA 1975, ss 1(1)(b), 3(1)(b)*]. This is because a far smaller proportion of women (particularly married women with children) than men, are able to comply with a mobility requirement. The Equal Opportunities Commission (EOC) issued a non-discrimination notice (pursuant to SDA 1975, s 67(2)) against the Leeds Permanent Building Society in respect of the mobility clauses in the contracts of employment of Head Office staff. This had led, in the opinion of the EOC, to a bar to women being promoted to management positions because of their inability to agree to be mobile. In practice, as it was admitted, Head Office staff did not have to be mobile! Since this requirement could not be justified, it was agreed that the mobility clause would be taken out of the contracts of Head Office staff and only inserted in certain management contracts where there was an actual requirement on the job-holder.

Expenses and clawback clauses

4.12   It is common for employers to offer relocation expenses either upon engagement or where employees are required to relocate (see also Chapter 8). It is sensible to include in the contract a provision requiring a written undertaking from the employee that he will repay the relocation expenses if he leaves within a minimum contracted period.

Relocation expenses can cover a wide range of items including legal charges, bridging loan assistance, interest free loan to cover advances of rent, deposits, excess housing allowances, removal expenses, disturbance allowances, travelling expenses and temporary accommodation costs etc. A typical clawback clause appears as **Precedent 2**.

Express flexibility clauses

4.13   There is a careful balance to be drawn between clearly defining the job title and the duties, and providing for flexibility within these definitions. The choice of job title is left to the discretion of the employer. A wide job title such as 'catering assistant', 'secretary', 'machine operator' provides the employer with the contractual right to move the person to any job within the definition of those job functions. There are other more important implications of a wide job title. Women returning from maternity leave have a right to return to their original job. [*EPCA 1978, s 45(1)*]. A specific job title gives a specific right to return to that job. A general job title provides the employer with the right to offer any job at that grade, in that capacity, at that location.

The definition of job title is also crucial in redundancy cases. EPCA 1978, s 81(2) defines 'redundancy' as such if wholly or mainly due to

'... (*b*) the fact that the requirements of that business for employees to carry out work of a particular kind, or for employees to carry out work of a particular kind in the place where (the employee made redundant) was so employed, have ceased or diminished or are expected to cease or diminish'.

Here, the courts have held that the statutory definition referred to above must be interpreted in the light of what the employee is employed to do under his contract and not what he has been doing in practice.

Thus, in *Runnalls v Richards and Osborne Ltd [1973] IRLR 124*, an HGV driver who had lost his licence and had been employed driving on the company's private road was dismissed when the company no longer required goods to be moved on the private road. The tribunal held that he had not been dismissed for redundancy since the company still required HGV drivers and that was what he was contractually employed to do. In contrast, a divisional contracts surveyor was held to have been dismissed for redundancy when the company decided to eliminate this position and employ only regional contracts surveyors (*Haden Ltd v Cowen [1982] IRLR 314*).

The balance between specifying the job duties and providing flexibility within that range of duties can be seen in the clause drawn up in **Precedent 3**. Where a job description is drawn up it is sensible to attach it as an Appendix to the contract so that those duties form part of the contract of employment.

Requirement to hold driving licence

4.14   Certain jobs such as HGV drivers, chauffeurs and members of a salesforce need to hold a valid, current UK driving licence. In some cases where HGV licences are held, these have to be renewed on an annual basis and a statutory medical examination has to be undertaken on such staff.

It is important to state whether a current, clean, full, valid, UK driving licence is essential and that the contract may be terminated should the job-holder lose that licence. It should be noted that where the employee has served two years' continuous service, the employer would have a designated fair reason for dismissal under the EPCA 1978 but he is expected to act reasonably in carrying out that dismissal. [*Sec 57(1)(b), (2)(c), (3)*]. For example, tribunals have held that drivers who have lost their licence for a short period only have been unfairly dismissed because someone else could have driven them for that period of time (*Appleyard v Smith (Hull) Ltd [1972] IRLR 19; Fearn v Tayford Motor Co Ltd [1982] IRLR 572*). In some cases the tribunals have been prepared to imply the requirement to hold a valid current driving licence (see, for example, *Tayside Regional Council v McIntosh [1982] IRLR 272*) but it is not safe to rely on this. A clause concerning a driving licence is set out in **Precedent 4**.

Requirement to have qualifications/experience

4.15   It is also important to stipulate whether certain educational or professional qualifications are required and the consequences of failing to have them or of being disbarred or disqualified from practising. For example, under the Financial Services Act 1986, there are certain occupations which require the acquisition of a licence from the appropriate regulatory body. Failure to acquire a licence or becoming disbarred would make it a criminal offence to continue to deal in that particular field. In some rare cases the courts appear to have accepted that where there is a statutory ban on the continued employment of the employee, it may be fair to terminate the contract. However, in *Sandhu v Department of Education and Science and London Borough of Hillingdon [1978] IRLR 208*, S was dismissed as a result of the DES ruling that he was unsuitable as a teacher, which would have made his continued employment unlawful by virtue of the Schools Regulations 1959 (SI 1959 No 364). The EAT held that it is not automatically fair to dismiss an employee where it is unlawful to continue to employ him, and remitted the case to be dealt with on its merits by a differently constituted industrial tribunal. It is important to cover these cases in the contract with an express clause. A typical clause can be found in **Precedent 4**.

It may also be prudent to include a requirement in the contract that the employee must notify the company of any change of personal circumstances such as change of address, status, loss of driving licence, loss or gain of qualification etc. Such a clause can be found in **Precedent 4**.

Work permits

4.16   Similarly, those workers who are not EC nationals are required to obtain UK work permits. It is a criminal offence for an employer to employ such a person without a valid work permit and it is therefore vital that a condition of the contract makes it clear that the contract may be terminated in the event of a permit not being obtained or being revoked. The term in the contract should include a requirement that the permit and passport be produced as evidence before the employment commences or at the start of the employment. (For more information on work permits, see 'Tolley's Employment Handbook'.)

Hours of work

4.17   It is a legal requirement to state any terms and conditions relating to hours of work. [*EPCA 1978, s 1(3)(c) as substituted by TURERA 1993*]. It is important to state the normal business hours, the actual hours of work required to be worked, whether additional hours such as in the evenings and weekends are required and whether there is any requirement to work on bank or statutory holidays.

Where there are flexitime arrangements these should be spelt out in the contract. Examples of such clauses can be found in **Precedent 5**.

Although this book is not intended to cover directors' service contracts, executive directors ought to be treated as employees and matters such as duties, outside interests etc. ought to be clearly spelt out. Directors are normally required to devote their whole time and attention to the business and their powers and duties need to be clearly drafted. A clause relating to powers and duties of directors can be found in **Precedent 6**. An executive's service agreement is contained in Appendix 1.

Dress, uniform requirements, conduct and appearance

4.18   In certain occupations there is a requirement to wear a uniform or protective clothing. Care must be taken to draft clear rules on such matters. In addition some companies require clear standards of dress and appearance to be maintained – for example, women are not permitted to wear trousers (e.g. *Schmidt v Austicks Bookshops Ltd [1977] IRLR 360; Kingston and Richmond Health Authority v Kaur [1981] IRLR 337*), men must wear sensible suits and ties and keep their hair above collar length. In contrast some organisations impose more unconventional requirements such as prohibiting the wearing of bright red lipstick and brightly varnished nails for female staff (*Murphy and Davidson v Stakis Leisure Ltd S/0534/89*).

However, a recent non-employment case in Northern Ireland has decided that it may be sex discrimination to insist upon discriminatory dress rules. In *McConomy v Croft Inns Ltd [1992] IRLR 561*, the Northern Ireland High Court held that a prohibition on men wearing earrings in the bar of a Belfast hotel was sex discrimination. Murray LJ said:

'It seems to me beyond question that the defendants' ground of refusal to serve the appellant in the bar while he was wearing an earring was that the appellant was a man. . . There is no doubt that the wearing of earrings by young men is very common today and since the refusal of the facilities specifically referred to in the 1976 Order [i.e. the equivalent of the Sex Discrimination Act 1975], viz. refreshment facilities, occurred in the present case, it would not be right in my view, to apply the doctrine [of *de minimis*] in this case.'

There may be aspects of sexual or racial discrimination here. For example, rules that women cannot wear trousers may indirectly discriminate against women (particularly against Sikh women, because they must keep their legs covered). (For a definition of indirect sex discrimination, see Sex Discrimination Act 1975, ss 1(1)(b), 3(1)(b), and for indirect racial discrimination, see Race Relations Act 1976, s 1(1)(b).) The courts have so far been reluctant to hold that dress requirements do unlawfully discriminate and employers have been able to justify these rules on the grounds of maintaining the company image or on grounds of health and safety.

A very limited exception in relation to Sikhs on construction sites has been provided by section 11 of the Employment Act 1989. By virtue of this section, a Sikh on a construction site is, at any time when he is wearing a turban, exempt from the requirement under the Construction (Head Protection) Regulations 1989 (SI 1989 No 2209) to wear a safety helmet. Neither a Sikh nor his employer will be liable in tort for any injury, loss or damage caused by his failure to comply with that requirement. [*Sec 11(4)*].

Precedent 7 sets out three typical clauses. Clause 1 relates to conduct, dress and appearance, and Clauses 2 and 3 set out alternative clauses relating to uniform and protective clothing.

Key Points

- Always include a detailed job description as part of the Contract of Employment.

- Draft a flexibility clause which allows for change in the scope and extent and range of the job duties.

- Draft a suitable mobility clause which is clear and covers the area of mobility required.

- Take care that any mobility clause could be justified in terms of the job needs – mobility clauses may be regarded as a form of indirect sexual or marital discrimination.

- Specify what qualifications are required for the job and the consequences (if any) of failing to achieve or retain them.

- Specify the requirement to travel on Company business if this is required.

- Include a clawback clause in the contract in relation to relocation expenses.

- Ensure that all qualifications, work permits etc. are checked before confirming job offers.

- Clarify the hours of work.

- Draft into the contract any special hours of work, flexitime arrangements etc.

PRECEDENT 1

Place of Employment

Clause A

Your place of employment is at our office at ...., London EC4.

During the course of your employment you may be required to work in the same or any similar capacity in any of the Company's Departments, Branch offices, subsidiary or associate Companies or locations within the UK. You will be eligible to receive relocation expenses as set out in the Company's Relocation Policy which is kept in the office of your Personnel Manager. Please note that you will be required to sign an Agreement as to repayment of these expenses or a proportion thereof should you leave within the minimum contracted period.

You may be required to travel in the UK or Overseas as Management may from time to time require should the need arise. This may involve travelling outside normal business hours and at weekends, Bank or Public Holidays should the need arise.

Reasonable expenses will be paid for such travel as laid down in the Staff Handbook or any other document concerning Expenses.

Clause B – Sales force

The territory which you are required to work is as stated at your interview and comprises 'sales bricks' which will be notified to you when you join. Management reserves the right to alter territorial boundaries and, if necessary, to require you to move house within the UK at the Company's expense, as laid down in the Relocation Policy.

Clause C – Alternative Clause

Your primary place of employment is:

....

but you will be required to work either on a temporary or permanent basis at any of the Company's other locations as you may be directed from time to time. You may also be required to travel on Company business for which you may either be provided with a company car or reimbursed for petrol or other reasonable travelling expenses.

PRECEDENT 2

'I .... agree to repay to the Company all moneys paid to me by way of relocation expenses, other than abortive purchase costs and temporary accommodation costs, should I leave voluntarily within .... months of the move.

I agree to the Company deducting these moneys from my final salary or any other moneys due to me upon my termination of employment. Should these sums not be sufficient, I agree to repay the said moneys upon any basis which is mutually acceptable.'

PRECEDENT 3

1. Job responsibilities

Your job title is .... Your duties will be fully explained to you when you commence employment with the Company. Your job description is attached as Appendix A to this Contract*. It is the Company's intention that any oral instructions or written descriptions of your job duties and responsibilities should serve as a guide to the major areas for which you will be accountable. Because of the changing nature of the business, the obligations upon you will inevitably vary and develop. The Company reserves the right at any time during your employment, upon reasonable notice, to require you to undertake any duties which fall within your capabilities and to move you from one department to another within the general office.

Delete if no written job description.

PRECEDENT 4

Requirement for driving licence

It is an essential condition of your employment that you hold and continue to hold a current, valid UK driving licence/HGV Class I, II, III Licence/ Advance Motorist licence. You may be requested to produce this at any time upon reasonable notice. If you have any endorsements or 'points' in your current driving licence, these must be reported to the Company.

Should you receive any criminal convictions for any motoring offences you must report the date and details immediately to your superior. You must also inform your supervisor/manager once you are charged with any such offence.

If you lose your driving licence through a conviction, this must be reported immediately to your supervisor/manager. Depending on the circumstances, this may result in the termination of your employment without any reference to the warning procedure set down in the disciplinary procedure.

Qualifications/Experience/Licence under appropriate Regulatory Body

Your employment (and continued employment) is conditional upon having and retaining all the educational, vocational, professional and any other appropriate qualifications that you stated you had when you completed your application form. It is also expected that the grades of all examinations taken conform with what you have stated on your application form. The Company also expects that you have had the work experience that you have stated on your application form or at your interview. The Company reserves the right to terminate your employment, with or without notice or payment in lieu, in any case where it is discovered you do not have the said qualification or experience, or where for whatever reason you fail to acquire any appropriate examination or licence or become disbarred from the appropriate Regulatory Body or Authority.

You will be required to bring the originals of all examination, under-graduate and post-graduate certificates and the certificates of any professional qualifications with you on your first day at work.

Work Permits

All non-EC nationals are required to hold a valid UK work permit before they obtain employment. It is a fundamental term of your employment that you have and continue to hold a valid UK work permit. You will be expected to produce your work permit together with your passport (your identity card will not suffice) on your first day at work. Please note that should you fail to produce these documents or should you for whatever reason have your work

permit revoked, the company reserves the right to terminate your contract
forthwith with no notice or pay in lieu and without reference to the warning
stages of the disciplinary procedure.

Change of personal circumstances

It is very important that you inform your Personnel Officer of any changes to
your personal circumstances such as change of address and/or telephone
number, next of kin, bank or building society details, dependants, marriage,
gain of qualifications, criminal convictions, loss of driving or other relevant
licences, loss of work permit etc.

It is expected that you have given all the correct details concerning age,
dependants, qualifications, grades of examinations passed etc. Should the
Company discover that you have provided any false information in this or any
other material respect, the Company reserves the right to terminate your
contract with or without notice or payment in lieu.

PRECEDENT 5

Hours of Work

Clause 1 – Normal working hours

Your working week is .... hours and you may be required to work .... hours per week. You are required to be punctual at all times.

Clause 2 – Flexible hours

The Company operates flexible working hours at all its offices. Core hours are 10.00 am to 12.00 noon and 2.00 pm to 4.00 pm when staff are required to be at work. Start and finish times may range from 8.00 am to 6.00 pm outside core time. These flexible working hours must, however, be agreed with your section head in advance and the flexible working arrangement will operate strictly on the proviso that the office must be manned at all times to a level agreed with your section head. Details of the flexible working hours arrangement are set out in the Staff Handbook. In any event you must work an average of .... hours a week at the end of each four-week statement period.

Clause 3 – No Normal Working Hours

Normal Business hours are .... per week, Monday to Friday inclusive from .... am to .... pm but due to the particular needs of our business, you are required to work such hours as the needs of the business dictates*/such additional hours from time to time*. This may include working in the evenings outside normal office hours, at weekends or on Bank, Public or Statutory Holidays. No additional pay or time off will be permitted. You will be issued with an appropriate security pass should you work outside normal office hours and you are expected to comply with the Company's security procedures at all times. This includes observing the notices concerning restricted areas where only authorised personnel are permitted to enter.

You are entitled to take one hour for lunch. The times at which lunch may be taken may vary from department to department depending on the needs of the business.

Clause 4 – Shift working

Your normal working hours are .... per week, Monday to Friday inclusive on a rotating/permanent shift basis as follows but which is subject to change at any time at the entire discretion of management:

Shift 1 ....to........Shift 2 ....to........Shift 3 ....to........Shift 4 ....to.......

You will qualify for a shift allowance. Meal break is one hour on shift(s).........
Where the needs of the business dictate you will be required to work
additional hours and on Saturdays and Sundays, Bank and Public Holidays. In
such cases you will qualify for overtime payments. A list of overtime rates and
shift allowances is available for reference in the Personnel Division. Any
changes of these rates will be notified to you from time to time.

Delete as appropriate.

PRECEDENT 6

Directors' Duties

1.1.   The Executive will exercise such powers and carry out such duties (if any) and observe such directions and restrictions in connection with the business of the Company as in each case the Board from time to time lawfully and reasonably directs him so to do.

1.2.   In addition the Executive shall carry out such duties and responsibilities as are included in Schedule 1 attached.

1.3.   The Executive shall use his best endeavours to maintain and improve and extend the business of the Company and will observe all proper and lawful directions of the Board.

1.4.   The Executive will devote his whole time and attention to the performance of his duties (except when on holiday as provided for in this Agreement) and EITHER [unless otherwise agreed between the Executive and the Company there shall be no specific terms and conditions relating to the Executive's hours of work] OR [the Executive's normal hours of work are ......am to ......pm Monday to Friday inclusive of one hour for lunch daily but the Executive will work such hours as may reasonably be required of him for the proper performance of his duties and shall not be entitled to receive any additional remuneration for work outside his normal hours].

1.5.   The Executive will, if required by the Company, serve the Company at any place of business of any Company in the Group or any associated company whether such place is used now or acquired later.

PRECEDENT 7

Conduct, Dress and Appearance

Clause 1

Because of the nature of our business, you are expected to conduct yourself at all times as would be expected of anyone working in the Finance Sector. The Company has published a booklet entitled 'Rules Book – General Standard of Conduct' and you are encouraged to read this carefully so that you are fully acquainted with all these rules. Briefly, although staff have freedom of choice of appearance in business dress, the rules require men to wear smart, business suits, tie and clean, smart business type shoes and tidy, above collar length hair. These rules are in common with most of the financial institutions in the City. It is forbidden for women to wear trousers or jeans but they are expected to wear smart, tailored, skirts, dresses etc.

Any failure to comply with these rules will render you liable to disciplinary action.

Clause 2

You are provided with a company uniform and it is a condition of your employment that you wear it as directed. You are responsible for keeping it clean and laundered and for this purpose you will be given a laundry allowance each month. You are provided with two sets of uniform annually. They must be returned in a clean and wearable state on your leaving the Company. Any failure to comply with these rules will render you liable to disciplinary action.

If it is a condition of your employment that you wear protective clothing and/or equipment, you will be told in your offer letter about any such rules. It is a strict requirement that you comply with these rules for reasons of health and safety. Breach of these rules will render you liable to serious disciplinary action which may result in summary dismissal.

OR

Clause 3

You are required to wear the uniform provided by the Company at all times during the working day. You are also required to keep the uniform in a clean and proper condition. The Company provides laundry facilities/a laundry allowance/OR expects you to keep your uniform clean and in a proper condition at your own expense. New uniform is provided from time to time depending on wear and tear.

You are also required to wear the safety clothing and protective clothing and equipment provided to you from time to time. It is your responsibility to keep this in a proper condition. New boots/filters for your face mask/rubber gloves etc. are available from your supervisor. It is up to you to ask for new clothing/ equipment when this is required.

You are strictly forbidden to take your uniform/clothing/equipment off site and must store them in the lockers provided.

Should you leave the Company, you are required to return all company property including uniforms etc. and these should be in a clean condition.

Chapter 5

Pay

5.1   By law, an employer must state in writing the scale or rate of pay or the method of calculating it and the intervals at which it is paid (e.g. weekly, four-weekly, monthly or by some other period). [*EPCA 1978, s 1(3)*]. There is also a legal obligation on the employer to provide the employee with an itemised pay statement at the time or before payment of wages is made detailing the gross pay, amounts of any variable and fixed deductions such as income tax (PAYE) and national insurance contributions (NIC), net pay and, where the net pay is paid in different ways, the amount and method of payment of each part payment. [*EPCA 1978, s 8*]. Fixed deductions such as PAYE and NIC need not be shown as specific items on each occasion but may be shown as one total deduction as long as the employer has given the employee a written statement of fixed deductions. [*EPCA 1978, s 9(1)*].

There is a strict definition of 'pay' for this purpose so tips given by customers to a waiter in a restaurant were held not to be 'pay' for the purposes of the itemised pay statement and the employer did not have to show them as items on the pay statement (*Cofone v Spaghetti House Ltd [1980] ICR 155*). The term 'pay' covers normal contractual pay, commission payments, bonus payments, overtime payments, and shift or other allowances. Whether the employee has a contractual right to such payments will depend upon the terms of the contract. It is vital to specify in the contract which payments are contractual and which are discretionary. A typical clause regarding pay can be seen in **Precedent 1**. It may be prudent to give details of the employer's tax office and reference so that any queries regarding an employee's tax can be dealt with by the employee and need not be processed through the Wages Department! Clause 1.5 of **Precedent 1** sets out a typical clause.

Variations in pay

5.2   In some organisations, pay rates vary depending upon size of location, geographical location, responsibilities etc. It will be important to ensure that the contract covers this aspect of pay so that when a member of staff is transferred, he has agreed to a variation in his pay (which may be a decrease) at the outset of his employment or at the time of moving. It is most sensible to explain the variations in pay at the commencement of employment and to cover this in the contract. A typical clause can be found in Clause 1.6 of **Precedent 1**.

Pay increases/reviews

5.3 Most employers provide for a review of pay on an annual basis. It is essential to make it clear in the contract whether any increases are contractual or discretionary. Some employers offer a contractual cost of living increase on an annual basis but merit or other increases are offered on a discretionary basis only. There is no obligation to offer a pay increase but this would be important to include from the employee's point of view. In particular, directors working under fixed term contracts will normally wish to see included some provision relating to the uprating of their salary over the period of the fixed term. A typical clause regarding salary increases can be found in Clause 1.4 of **Precedent 1**; see also Clause 1.2 of **Precedent 2**.

Where the contract is silent on the question of pay increases, the courts will not imply a right to an increase even where the employer has always paid one in the past. In *Murco Petroleum Ltd v Forge [1987] IRLR 50* the Employment Appeal Tribunal refused to find that the employer was in breach of contract when he failed to give one of his employees a pay increase despite the fact that she had received one for each of the previous ten years. Here the contract was silent as to increases in pay but the EAT held:

'An implied contractual obligation to an increase in pay is not part of the industrial structure and neither employers nor unions would wish it to be so. While for the last 25 years annual pay increases have been the pattern of life in the industrial field, that is not the same as saying that they are built into the contract.'

Overtime/shift allowances

5.4 Some employees who work overtime or outside normal daytime hours are entitled to be paid at the agreed overtime rates or shift rates. Others who work such hours are not entitled to any additional pay or time off in lieu. It is important to spell out whether such entitlement exists; see Clause 1.2 of **Precedent 1**.

Profit-share/Commission/Bonus

5.5 Where employees enjoy the benefit of a profit-sharing scheme or commission or bonus payments, the contract should make clear whether this is contractual or discretionary, the date on which these payments are made, the rate of such payments, when they become due and whether they are paid monthly, annually etc.

Where a profit-share or bonus on profits is paid, care must be taken to draft the clause in order to define what profits will be taken into account, how the profits will be determined and at what date, and whether the figures must be certified by the company's auditors. As far as directors are concerned, it is essential to clarify whether directors' fees are included in the salary or to be paid as an additional item. A typical clause concerning these and other points can be seen in **Precedent 2**.

5.6 *Pay*

Deductions from pay: pre-Wages Act 1986 position

5.6   Prior to the Wages Act 1986 (discussed below), the Victorian legislation known as the Truck Acts, together with the Payment of Wages Act 1960, governed the payment of wages for 'manual workers'. These were a series of statutes prohibiting any deductions (other than statutory deductions) from the wages of employees variously defined as 'servant in husbandry, journeyman, artificer, handicraftsman, miner or otherwise engaged in manual labour'. These Acts also provided that employers had to pay their wages in coin of the realm and any deductions from their wages by way of fines for damage to the employer's property or for negligent workmanship or for the use of tools and equipment had to be set out in the contract and agreed in advance by the workman. In addition, any such deduction had to be an amount which was 'fair and reasonable'.

Litigation over the Truck Acts ranged from:

— Who was a 'workman'? — A foreman was not (*Brooker v Charrington Fuel Oils Ltd [1981] IRLR 147*) but a so-called 'manageress' of a shoe shop was because in reality she was a sales assistant with some managerial responsibilities (*Riley v Joseph Frisby Ltd [1982] IRLR 479*); to

— What was 'current coin of the realm'? A giro-cheque *was* according to the county court judge in the *Brooker* case but this decision has been doubted by many!

The Wages Act 1986

5.7   The Wages Act 1986, which came into force on 1 January 1987, repealed the former restrictions on the payment of wages and replaced them with general legislation governing all employees.

Briefly, the Wages Act provides that subject to certain exceptions, contained in section 1(5)(a)–(f) (see 5.15 and 5.16 below) no deductions may be made from any worker's wages unless:

(*a*)   it is required or permitted by statute or provided for in the worker's contract; or

(*b*)   the worker has agreed in writing prior to the deduction being made.

[*Sec 1(1)*]. (For a fuller discussion see 5.14 below.)

Special rules for the deduction from wages of workers in retail employment are contained in section 2 (see 5.8 below).

Complaints under the Wages Act are heard by industrial tribunals. If successful, the tribunal may make an order for the employer to pay or repay any amount owed. The time limit for bringing a complaint is three months from the date of the deduction of wages, or the receipt of the payment, by the employer of which complaint is made (with the normal extension of time if the tribunal is satisfied that it was not reasonably practicable to bring the complaint within the relevant period).

Special rules for 'workers in retail employment'

5.8 In the case of 'workers in retail employment', section 2(1) provides that any deductions from their wages for cash shortages or stock deficiencies must be limited to 10% of their gross wages, save their final payment of wages when this limit will not apply. [*Sec 4*]. The employer must make such deductions within twelve months from the date on which he discovers any stock deficiencies or cash shortages (or within twelve months of the date when he ought reasonably to have discovered them). Similar provisions apply to payments made to his employer by a worker in retail employment on account of such shortages or deficiencies, pursuant to a demand for payment previously made by the employer. [*Sec 3*].

The definition of 'retail employment' in section 2(2) covers any worker whose job involves the sale or supply of goods or services, including financial services, directly with members of the public. So employees of the clearing banks and building societies are covered by this limitation.

Statutory definition

5.9 Section 7(1) of the Wages Act defines 'wages' as *inter alia*:

'. . . any sums payable to a worker by his employer in connection with his employment including:

(*a*) any fee, bonus, commission, holiday pay or other emolument referable to his employment, whether payable under his contract or otherwise;'.

Section 7(2)(*a*)–(*e*) excludes from the definition of 'wages' any payments made by way of advance of salary or loan, any expenses payments, pension or other payments made on retirement, any payment paid as compensation for loss of office, redundancy payments and any payments made otherwise than in the worker's capacity as a worker.

Non-payment of wages

5.10 According to the Court of Appeal in *Delaney v Staples (t/a De Montfort Recruitment)* [*1991*] *IRLR 112 (CA)* the non-payment of wages amounts to a deduction of wages within section 1(1) of the Wages Act. It was held that the scope of the expression 'deduction' had been extended by section 8(3) of the Act which provides that 'where the total amount of wages that are paid on any occasion are less than the total amount of wages that are properly payable the shortfall is to be treated as a deduction'. It followed from this that an industrial tribunal could entertain a claim by an employee that her employer failed to pay her commission and holiday pay which he ought to have paid.

5.11   *Pay*

The Court of Appeal in so holding approved the decision of the EAT in *Greg May (Carpet Fitters and Contractors) Ltd v Dring* [*1990*] *IRLR 19* and *Kournavous v JR Masterton & Sons (Demolition)* [*1990*] *IRLR 119* and disagreed with the contrary decision in *Barlow v Whittle* [*1990*] *IRLR 79* and *Alsop v Star Vehicle Contractors Ltd* [*1990*] *IRLR 83*.

Payment in lieu of notice

5.11   A second issue which arose in *Delaney* was whether payment in lieu of notice is to be regarded as damages and therefore recoverable in the county court or High Court, or 'wages' within the definition in the Wages Act (see 5.9 above) and thus subject to the jurisdiction of the industrial tribunal. The Court of Appeal concluded that such payments were not 'wages' within the statutory definition. On appeal to the House of Lords, [*1992*] *IRLR 191* (the issue of non-payment of wages referred to in 5.10 above was not the subject of appeal to the House of Lords) it was held conclusively, agreeing with the Court of Appeal, that a payment in lieu of notice did not constitute wages under the Act. Accordingly, an industrial tribunal did not have jurisdiction to entertain a claim for the failure by an employer to make a payment in lieu of notice following dismissal. A distinction was made between wages which are earned as a result of the provision of services under the employment and fall within the ambit of the Act, and payments in lieu of notice which become due after the contract has ended, and are not wages, since they are payments relating to the termination of the employment. This view accords with the decision of the EAT in *Foster Wheeler (London) Ltd v Jackson* [*1990*] *IRLR 412* and disagrees with the decision in *Kournavous v JR Masterton & Sons (Demolition) Ltd* (5.10 above) on this point.

Extension of powers of tribunals

5.12   In *Delaney*, Lord Browne-Wilkinson acknowledged *obiter* that the conclusion in that case 'produces an untidy and unsatisfactory result' in that an employee may be forced to bring two sets of proceedings – one in the industrial tribunal in relation to part of his claim (e.g. unpaid wages, holiday pay etc.) and another in the county court for damages for breach of contract. He felt that this would be 'wasteful of time and money' and would bring the 'law into disrepute'. He concluded that the Minister should consider whether to use his power under section 131 of the Employment Protection (Consolidation) Act 1978 to confer jurisdiction on industrial tribunals to deal with claims for breach of contract.

Section 38 of the Trade Union Reform and Employment Rights Act 1993 now amends section 131 and extends the power of the Minister to confer jurisdiction on industrial tribunals to hear certain claims for breach of contract.

Other payments within the meaning of 'Wages'

5.13   The statutory definition includes under-payment of wages under a Wages Council Order (*Mountford v Mazello Ltd, COIT 2009/212*) and holiday stamps which were unlawfully withheld from a bricklayer (*Travers v Townshend, COIT 2028/196*).

Clawback clause

5.14   Section 1(1) of the 1986 Act provides that a lawful deduction may be made from an employee's wages where:

(*a*)   it is required or authorised to be made by virtue of any statutory provision or any relevant provision of the worker's contract; or

(*b*)   the worker has previously signified in writing his agreement or consent to the making of it'.

To satisfy section 1(1)(a), it is obviously important for the employer to ensure that the terms of the contract are crystal clear when specifying when and in what circumstances the employee will be obliged to pay moneys from his wages. In any claim by an employee who alleges that an unlawful deduction has been made, the tribunals will be entitled to determine not just whether the contract authorised the type of deduction in question but also whether the deduction was justified on the facts.

In *Fairfield Ltd v Skinner* [*1993*] *IRLR 4*, the employee had agreed to pay for vehicle damage and private telephone calls from his van. The EAT held that even though as a matter of construction, the deduction falls within section 1(1)(a), the tribunal is entitled to look not only at the clause in the contract to see proper authorisation but must also examine the employer's reasons for making the deductions and consider whether there was any factual basis for making the deductions.

Section 1(1)(b) has been interpreted as meaning that not only must the employee in advance and in writing agree to repay any money due to the employer but the agreement must also contain the employee's agreement that any money owing may be deducted from the wages (or final wages where appropriate).

In *Potter v Hunt Contracts Ltd* [*1992*] *IRLR 108*, Mr Potter agreed to repay a course fee of £545 loaned to him by the respondents relating to an HGV driving course he had been sent on by his former employer. The terms of the agreement were set out in a letter which stated that if he left the respondents' employment within 24 months, he would be required to 'return the fee on a diminishing basis based on £22 per month'. Mr Potter's contract was terminated some five weeks after commencing employment still owing £523 under the agreement. Since his final wages only amounted to £278.50, he was paid nothing. The EAT upheld his claim that this was an unlawful deduction since to fulfil the condition laid down in section 1(1)(b), there must be a document which states with sufficient clarity the source from which the deduction was to be made – his wages – or that the deduction was authorised from that source. In this case, even though the loan agreement was in writing, any consent to deduction was oral.

5.15 *Pay*

A model agreement for the repayment of a loan from wages appears as **Precedent 4**.

Care will have to be taken in the future to provide for other deductions to be made in the contract – e.g. loss of pay for unauthorised absence, deduction of pay for stock or cash losses (all subject to the 10% rule for 'retail staff'). Unless these cases are specifically covered in the contracts, any such deductions or non-payments will be unlawful! Employers should ensure that if they wish to deduct (or withhold pay) in circumstances such as unauthorised absence (see Chapter 6 for more details), poor workmanship, carelessness or breach of the rules, they include a properly worded 'Indemnity Clause' in the contract. A model clause appears in **Precedent 3**. Such clauses will have to apply a limit of 10% for 'retail staff'.

Overpayments

5.15   A number of exceptions to the general rule as set out in section 1(1) of the 1986 Act are contained in subsection (5)(a)–(f). Section 1(5)(a) of the 1986 Act specifically excludes from the scope of the Act any deductions from wages made by an employer in respect of overpayments of wages. This section was interpreted narrowly in *Home Office v Ayres* [*1992*] *IRLR 59*, where the EAT held that an employer could make a deduction from wages in respect of an overpayment only where the deduction is a lawful deduction, and the reimbursement is of money to which the employer is lawfully entitled, i.e. that the employer could successfully recover the sum in a court of law. In other words the employer has to show that the money in question were paid by mistake of fact and not by mistake of law. 'Where there is a clear mistake which is obvious to both sides, the Act provides a quick and simple remedy to an employer but any issue as to the entitlement to the money deducted must be tried in the industrial tribunal.' (This was approved by the EAT in *Murray v Strathclyde Regional Council (S)*, *EAT 62/92* and in *Humber Workforce Contractors Ltd v Langley & others*, *EAT 369/91*.)

The EAT added that if an employer relies on section 1(5)(a) by way of defence to a claim under section 1(1), the employee would be able to raise a number of defences such as no overpayment, incorrect amount of deduction or the purpose of the deduction was not to reimburse or some other defence under the general law to the claim to deduct.

In *Ayres*, the employee successfully relied on the defence of estoppel on the basis that he had received the moneys in good faith and had spent it on normal living expenses.

In *The County Council of Avon v Howlett* [*1983*] *IRLR 171*, the Court of Appeal upheld the defence of estoppel in a claim by the Council to recover overpaid sick pay on the basis that:

'(*a*)   the plaintiff must generally have made a representation of fact which led the defendant to believe that he was entitled to treat the money as his own;

(*b*)   the defendant must have, bona fide and without notice of the plaintiff's claim, consequently changed his position; and

(*c*)   the payment must not have been primarily caused by the fault of the defendant.'

The EAT in *Ayres* referred to *Howlett*, but suggested that because of the complexities of the defence of estoppel it would be easier in such cases to rely on the simpler defence of 'change of position' as recognised by the House of Lords in *Lipkin Gorman v Karpnale Ltd [1991] 3 WLR 10*. This defence is 'available to a person whose position has so changed that it would be inequitable in all the circumstances to require him to make restitution or alternatively to make restitution in full' (*3 WLR 10* at *34, 35* per Lord Goff).

'Lawful' deductions from wages

5.16   Recently, in *Sunderland Polytechnic v Evans [1993] IRLR 196*, a case concerning a deduction from wages under section 1(5)(e) (deduction from wages where the worker has taken part in a strike or other industrial action), the EAT held that part of the reasoning in *Ayres* could no longer stand. As seen in 5.15 above, according to the EAT in *Ayres* the word 'lawful' was to be read into subsection (5)(a), enabling the industrial tribunal to determine any issue regarding entitlement to deduct. It followed that this reasoning should apply equally to each of the subsections of section 1(5).

However, it was clear from statements made during the statute's Parliamentary passage (which according to the House of Lords in *Pepper v Hart [1993] IRLR 33* could be used as an aid to construction, see 5.20 below), that there was no intention to give industrial tribunals the jurisdiction to determine the contractual validity of a deduction from wages by reason of industrial action. The employees' only remedy was to sue in the civil courts.

Is tax and national insurance a 'statutory' deduction from a payment in lieu of notice?

5.17   An issue that arises in many termination payments cases concerns the deduction of PAYE income tax from a payment in lieu of notice and whether or not this is a lawful deduction. The position as far as the Inland Revenue is concerned seems clear. If a payment in lieu of notice is provided for *in the contract* (this may be included in the provisions under 'Notice', see Chapter 10), then any such lump sum payment is to be regarded as a contractual payment and the normal PAYE deductions should be made. It is probable that national insurance contributions should also be deducted in the usual way.

However if the payment in lieu of notice is non-contractual, then this is not to be regarded as an 'emolument', but rather as damages for the employer's breach of contract which escapes liability for the general Schedule E charge. Termination payments exceeding £30,000 are taxable under section 188 of the Income and Corporation Taxes Act 1988 (as amended by section 74 of the

Finance Act 1988). However there is one important caveat here. If there has been an almost invariable custom or practice of paying employees in lieu of notice, then the Inspector of Taxes will regard such payments as taxable under the general principles of Schedule E as a lump sum payment which 'employees usually get'. In the writer's experience, no employer has appealed against such an assessment.

View of the Inland Revenue

5.18   In support of the above, it is useful to look at the recent guidance to employers regarding Pay As You Earn. In the 'Employer's Revised Guide to Pay As You Earn (1993) (P7)' Section L1, the Inland Revenue advises that lump sum payments liable to PAYE deductions are:

'1.   Lump sum payments that the employee has a contractual right to receive; or

2.   Lump sums which employees usually get.'

Just one word of warning. The word 'net' is frequently used and is intended to mean after deduction of tax. This is not the proper meaning of the word. The Oxford English dictionary defines 'net' as 'free from or not subject to any deduction'.

Employers should take care not to offer 'net' or 'nett' payments to staff unless it is intended to make these payments without any deductions otherwise the employee may sue under the Wages Act. Employers should take care to spell out in any written agreement concerning severance pay that the payment 'will have tax and national insurance contributions deducted'.

Payment of school fees

5.19   Some more fortunate employees receive the benefit of the payment of school fees as part of their contractual remuneration. Should this be the case then the payments constitute income from their emoluments and are assessable to income tax. In *Glynn v Commissioner for Inland Revenue [1990] 2 WLR 633*, a Hong Kong case, the school fees for a director's daughter were paid direct by the employer to the boarding school. There was a specific clause in his contract that apart from a specified monthly remuneration, *inter alia*, the company would pay the education costs of the children.

Although the arrangement provided for primary liability for the fees to rest with the company, the Inland Revenue contended that each sum paid by the company to the school was a perquisite of the taxpayer and liable to income tax. The director's argument, that a perquisite had to be a sum of money paid to the employee if it was to be taxed, was not accepted by the Privy Council. There was no difference between money paid to an employee pursuant to the contract of employment and money paid for the benefit of an employee by the employer pursuant to that contract.

This is well covered in Tolley's 'Taxation of Employments 1991-92'.

Taxation of reduced school fees

5.20 It has been a common practice amongst public schools to offer to the staff teaching at the school the benefit of reduced school fees for their children. The question that was recently considered by the House of Lords in *Pepper v Hart [1993] IRLR 33*, was whether the staff concerned should pay tax on the additional or 'marginal' cost incurred by the school to educate their children, or whether the tax should be based on a rateable proportion of all the school's running expenses – the 'average' cost.

The House of Lords ruled that the taxable benefit was to be quantified on the basis of the marginal cost to the school of educating the children. Where the marginal cost has been reimbursed (as in this case), there was no taxable benefit. In reaching this decision, the Law Lords (Lord Mackay dissenting) turned aside a rule of statutory interpretation that had been in place since the 19th century and held that Parliamentary materials including reported speeches in Hansard by the Minister or other promoters of the Bill may be referred to by the courts in order to interpret the Statute where:

(1) the legislation is ambiguous or obscure or would lead to an absurdity;

(2) the material relied on consisted of one or more statements by a Minister or other promoter of the Bill together with such other Parliamentary material as is necessary to understand such statements and their effects;

(3) the statements relied upon are clear.

This decision is relevant not only with regard to the payment of reduced school fees but also in any case where an employee receives free or discounted benefits from his employer. This will include, for example, British Rail employees and airline staff who travel free, employees buying goods at a discount from their employer, or the use of social and sport facilities provided by the employer. These employees will be taxed only on the marginal cost to the employer of providing the benefit and so long as they reimburse the employer for that cost no taxable benefit will arise.

Pay date

5.21 It is now more common for employers to pay their staff in the middle of the month. Should an employee resign without notice, or fail to attend work taking unauthorised leave after the pay date, he will have received pay in advance to which he is not entitled. It will be important to include a provision within the *Indemnity/Deductions/Overpayments* clause if the employer wishes to deduct any sums from final salary where certain moneys are owed to the employee and are outstanding and unpaid at the date of leaving.

Reductions in pay – quantum of damages

5.22 One final point. If an employer breaches the contract by unilaterally varying the terms and conditions and imposes a pay cut, the quantum of damages will not be limited to the notice period if the employees elect to remain in employment, having made clear their position that they do not accept the breach (*Burdett-Coutts v Hertfordshire County Council [1984] IRLR 91*).

In one important House of Lords' Appeal, *Rigby v Ferodo Ltd [1987] IRLR 516*, an employer purported to effect a pay cut during 1982 when the company was in a deep recession and in severe financial difficulties. The employees refused to accept the breach but continued working. One of the lathe operators brought an action for breach of contract. The employers argued that quantum should be limited to his pay during his notice period (twelve weeks). This argument was rejected by the House of Lords. Firstly, they held that, merely because the employer had committed a repudiatory breach of contract, this did not automatically bring the contract to an end. The innocent party had a choice whether or not to accept the breach – the principle that 'an unaccepted repudiation is a thing writ in water and of no value to anybody' was valid in cases of employment contracts. The employees had not accepted the breach by continuing to work since they had continued working under protest. Mr Rigby's claim was one for his agreed remuneration for services rendered or for damages for breach of an agreement to pay it. Damages were thus awarded on the basis of the shortfall for seven years (the course of the trial) between his agreed weekly wages of £192 and £162 (the reduced wages).

A clause permitting decreases in pay can be seen in Clause 1.6 in **Precedent 1**.

Key Points

- Define contractual pay and ensure that any other payments such as tips, commission payments, bonuses etc. are clearly expressed as contractual or discretionary.

- Define the pay date clearly.

- Express clearly whether there is to be any pay review and if so at what intervals.

- If necessary reserve the right to alter pay rates (up or down) depending on the grade or location.

- Clarify whether overtime is paid or unpaid.

- Ensure that there is an express term in the contract permitting deductions of pay for poor workmanship, losses, mistakes in payments, unauthorised absence.

- Ensure that there is provision concerning the right to make a payment in lieu of notice.

- Ensure that any payments in lieu of notice are paid with tax deducted if there is a contractual term.

- Ensure that the details and reference number of the Company Tax Office are provided. Employees can then sort out their own tax queries!

- Clarify the tax position regarding any other benefit provided to the employee even if they do not receive this directly. School fees paid direct to the school attract liability for tax as an emolument.

PRECEDENT 1

1. Salary

1.1. Basic salary

Your basic salary is £............ per annum payable monthly by direct credit transfer to your personal bank or building society account. This will normally be paid on .... day of each month. It will be your responsibility to ensure that your Personnel Officer has a note of your Bank or Building Society Account Name and Number and Sort Code Number.

1.2. Overtime/shift allowance

You are/are not entitled to the payment of any overtime for hours worked in excess of the normal business hours of this Company. You are/are not entitled to time off in lieu.

You are/are not entitled to receive the shift allowance applicable to you when you work shifts. Details of the current shift allowances can be found in the Personnel Manager's office/current union agreement etc.

1.3. Profit-Sharing Scheme

The Company operates a profit-sharing scheme in respect of your employment. The Board of the Holding Company meets each year to determine the percentage award to be made, based on the Company's profits for the preceding year. Any payments are distributed in the January of each year to employees on the payroll on the previous 31 December and the amount payable (if any) is announced in January of each year.

Please note that this profit-sharing scheme and any payments paid are discretionary. Any such scheme does not constitute a contractual term. The Company reserves the right at any time to vary or withdraw the scheme and will give you four weeks' notice of any such changes.

1.4. Salary increases

Your basic salary will be reviewed annually. There is no contractual entitlement to any increase in your basic salary but you will be notified in writing in any case where there is any change to your salary.

An itemised pay statement of your earnings and deductions will be sent to you on your normal pay date.

1.5. Tax Office

The Tax Office which deals with this Company is:
HM Inspector of Taxes

Ref:

Should you have queries on any matters relating to your personal tax, please will you contact the tax office direct.

1.6. Currently your rate of pay for this position at your present location is .... However should you transfer at your own request or at the request of the Company, you will be paid the current rate for that job at that location. Because there are variations in pay for your position depending on the location and size of the Branch/office/retail outlet/Region, your pay will automatically be adjusted at the appropriate time. This may involve an increase or a decrease in your pay. You will be required to agree to the relevant adjustments in your pay at the time of your moving by signing an acceptance form.

PRECEDENT 2

Remuneration

1.1. The Executive shall be entitled to receive by way of remuneration for his services as from the commencement date of this Agreement during the continuance of his employment a basic salary at the rate of £.................. per annum or at such higher rate as may from time to time be approved by the Company.

Such salary shall be inclusive/exclusive of any Director's fees payable to the Executive by any Company in the Group or any associated company [and accordingly either the Executive shall pay over to the Company all such fees received or to be received by him or his remuneration shall be reduced pro tanto].

1.2. The Board shall not less frequently than once a year review the basic salary referred to in para 1.1. above in the light of the increases in the cost of living, the profitability of the Company and the rates of remuneration then being paid to Executives holding similar positions in the industry.

1.3. The Executive's salary shall be deemed to accrue from day to day and unless otherwise agreed will be payable by equal monthly instalments on the last day of each month.

1.4. In addition to the said basic salary the Executive shall during his employment with the Company be paid in respect of each financial year of the Company an additional sum equal to .... per cent of the Company's net trading profits [as defined below in para 1.6.] in excess of £ .... The first payment shall be in respect of the Company's financial year ending ....

1.5. Any such said payments as described in para 1.4. above shall be confirmed by the Board.

1.6. The Company's net trading profits shall for the purposes of this Agreement be the net profits shown in the audited accounts of the Company for each financial year after deducting any portion thereof attributable to minority interests subject as follows:

1.6.1. they shall be excluding income from investments;
1.6.2. they shall be excluding any profits, gains, bonuses, surpluses, accretions, losses or deficiencies of a capital or non-trading nature whether realised or not, any taxation rebates or receipts;
1.6.3. they shall be before charging any taxation including income tax, profits tax, corporation tax and other taxation or profits or gains;
1.6.4. they shall be after charging the basic salary and any other additional remuneration payable under para 1.4. and any similar remuneration payable by way of percentage of profits under any service agreement between the Company and other officers or executives;

1.6.5. they shall be before charging dividend on the Company's issued share capital of all classes for the time being and general group management;

1.6.6. they shall be after making proper provision for doubtful debts and for accrued and/or ascertained liabilities and losses and after charging all trade, working, overhead and management expenses other than referred to above; depreciation as provided for in the audited accounts of the Company; appropriations to any staff or employee pensions or compensation payment and recurring grants in the nature of pensions.

1.7. The amount of the said net profits of the Company and of the said additional remuneration due to the Executive in respect of each financial year or part thereof of the Company payable to the Executive shall [unless previously agreed in writing between the Company and the Executive] be certified in writing by the auditors for the time being of the Company and such certificate if not disputed by either party [by notice in writing] within fourteen days of its delivery to them shall subject to para 1.8. be binding absolutely on the parties to this Agreement and the making of such certificate shall after the expiration of fourteen days be conclusive evidence of the amount of the said net profits.

1.8. The Company agrees that such certificate shall be issued by the Auditors within a reasonable time after the adoption of the Company's accounts in General Meeting provided that if the Auditors are unable or unwilling to issue such Certificate because they need to obtain further information on any matter relevant to the determination of the said net profits or if any question is raised by either party on any Matter raised in the Certificate within a reasonable time, then if there is no agreement between the parties, the matter will be decided by either a person (who will be an expert and not an arbitrator) whose decision shall be final and binding upon both parties or by the current President of the Institute of Chartered Accountants in England and Wales. The Company and the Executive shall pay one half of the cost of any chartered accountants appointed under this clause.

PRECEDENT 3

'Company Indemnity/Deductions from Salary/ Overpayments and Loss of Pay

Where any losses are sustained in relation to the property or moneys of the Company, client, customer, visitor or other employee, during the course of your employment caused through your carelessness, negligence, recklessness or through breach of the Company's rules or any dishonesty on your part, the Company reserves the right to require you to repay any of the said losses, either by deduction from salary or any other method acceptable to the Company (which will be no more than 10% of salary for retail staff). This may include paying the excess in any insurance claim made against the Company in respect of a motor accident for which you are responsible or are deemed to be responsible and this shall be recouped by way of deduction from your salary or any other method deemed acceptable to the Company.

This clause will also apply in cases of overpayment of any remuneration or any other payments (statutory, discretionary etc.) made by mistake or through any misrepresentation or otherwise.

The payment of sick pay is dependent upon you complying with all the rules of the sick scheme and this includes the rules concerning the notification of your supervisor by (time) on the first day of absence from work. Any day's leave which has not been notified to the Company in line with the rules will be treated as unauthorised absence.

The Company reserves the right to withhold payment or deduct from salary a day's pay for each day of unauthorised absence. Any decision concerning this matter will be made by your immediate superior who will notify Personnel and Payroll. Unauthorised absence is defined in the Company's sick pay scheme which forms part of your contract details of which are given in the Staff Handbook.

Should you fail to give proper notice to terminate or should you take unauthorised leave as defined above and should you have received your current month's salary by direct credit transfer or cheque or cash, the Company reserves the right to deduct the amount of pay which has been overpaid, taking the last day at work as the last day for which pay becomes due, from the following month's salary or from any moneys outstanding at the termination date.'

PRECEDENT 4

Agreement for Repayment of Loan

'I .... hereby agree to repay the loan of £ .... made to me by my employers .... by way of deduction each week from my wages in the sum of £ ....

In the event of my leaving the Company's employment, howsoever caused, within .... months from the date of this agreement, I agree that any outstanding moneys due to my employer in respect of this loan, may be deducted from my final salary/outstanding expenses/outstanding commission/bonus etc.

Signed   ....   Date   ....'

Chapter 6

Absence, Health and Sick Pay

Health requirements on recruitment

6.1   Many employers require a prospective employee to undergo a medical examination before he is permitted to accept the job offer. This condition may be provided for in the offer letter (see **Precedent 1** in Chapter 2). A medical examination may quite properly include intrusive or invasive tests such as blood tests and other tests such as the taking of urine samples, as long as the individual has given his informed consent. This has been clearly laid down at common law and by the Faculty of Occupational Medicine's 'Guidance on Ethics for Occupational Physicians' (4th edition, available from Royal College of Physicians, St Andrews Place, Regents Park, London NW1). A right of action for battery would arise where an individual was unlawfully touched in some way by a doctor where there has been no express or implied consent.

For consent to be informed entails a full explanation as to the exact nature of the tests. Recently some employers in the UK have included alcohol and drug addiction testing in their pre-recruitment medical screening.

The Faculty of Occupational Medicine, in the publication referred to above, has advised occupational health practitioners that they should not rely on implied consent on the basis that the individual has consented to attend the medical examination. In relation to urine testing for drugs and alcohol, doctors are advised by the Faculty that:

'... such tests may be acceptable at pre-recruitment examinations provided that the subjects are informed in advance of the nature of the test and later of the results. Great care should be taken to develop a testing protocol that includes the retesting of positive specimens in order to avoid the possibility of action being taken on a false negative.
... It should not be inferred from (the patient's attendance) that the individual necessarily agrees to the examination and to the disclosure of the result.'

Robust health, a requirement of the job

6.2   In certain industries robust health is of the essence. Whilst pre-employment medicals may be useful to screen for existing medical conditions, they are of little use as predictors of future health problems. It may be wise for employers who work to tight deadlines and who may be subject to expensive penalty clauses to include a clause in the contract that informs the job-holder of the need to maintain near perfect attendance at work and the consequences on the contract of spells of sickness absence. The oil exploration and construction industries are two typical examples.

Whilst a clause in the contract will protect an employer from a breach of contract and/or wrongful dismissal claim, in any claim for unfair dismissal an industrial tribunal will still have to be satisfied that the employer has a fair reason for dismissal and that he acted reasonably in treating that reason as a sufficient reason for dismissal. [*EPCA 1978, s 57(1)-(3)*].

In one rare case, *Leonard v Fergus & Hayes Civil Engineering Ltd [1979] IRLR 235*, an employer was held to have fairly dismissed an employee for ill health under a clause in his contract which stated:

'(1) Any man absent for two shifts in his 14-day working period will be classed as unsuitable for North Sea related work and his contract of employment will be terminated.

(2) An employee who is absent for one or more shifts on medical grounds must produce a document from the nurse or doctor to the effect that he is ill. The management reserve the right to investigate each document and to judge the case on its merits. If it is that the documentation is false or unjustified, the man will be marked absent for that day and will be penalised accordingly. If an employee is frequently absent on medical grounds he will be classed as unsuitable for the rugged conditions of North Sea related work and his contract of employment terminated.

If an employee is injured when carrying out work for which he was employed, he will be offered alternative employment for what he is capable of doing if the injury is not serious.

Any employee who falls ill on the Rig during his shift must report to the foreman or ganger and the medical officer on the Rig before he leaves the Rig. Any employee who fails to follow this procedure will be penalised as per (the disciplinary procedure).'

Despite the fact that Mr Leonard had been absent on previous occasions due to ill health, he was dismissed following a spell of absence due to an injury sustained on the rig.

The Court of Session held that despite the fact that the employer had not obtained a medical report nor had they consulted him with a view to discovering whether or not he was likely to be fit for work in the future (as laid down in *East Lindsey District Council v Daubney [1977] IRLR 181*, an earlier authority on ill health dismissals), here there were special circumstances and conditions which did not make the dismissal unfair despite the lack of any fair procedure being followed.

'In the present case, the relationship between the appellant and the respondents was of an exceptional and special nature and the EAT's observations in *East Lindsey* had no relevance to the particular circumstances of this case. This was not a case where the respondents were considering the dismissal merely on general grounds of ill health. This was a case in which they decided to dismiss him, in terms of a special contract of employment because he had failed to meet an essential requirement of his employment, namely, that he must not be frequently absent on medical grounds. In light of the special requirements of the contract of employment, it could not be said that there was no material on which the tribunal were entitled to conclude that the respondents had satisfied the (statutory test in EPCA 1978, section 57(3)).'

This case must now be read in the light of the most important House of Lords' decision in *Polkey v A E Dayton Services Ltd [1987] IRLR 503* (see judgment of Lord Bridge), where a failure to follow a fair procedure will normally (but not inevitably) render a dismissal unfair.

A proposed clause for a contract of employment appears in **Precedent 1**.

Legal position on sick pay

6.3   There is a statutory requirement for employers to state any terms relating to incapacity for work due to sickness or injury, including any payments which may be made. [*EPCA 1978, s 1(3)(d)(ii) as substituted by TURERA 1993*]. If there are no agreed terms concerning sick pay, an employer will be entitled to rely on the common law. In a line of early decisions the courts held that where there were no express provisions relating to sick pay and no implied term to the contrary, there was a presumption that there is a contractual right to sick pay (see, for example, *Orman v Saville Sportswear Ltd [1960] 1 WLR 1055*). If this is correct, it is clear that an employer would be liable to pay sick pay at the normal rate of pay subject to deductions of any state sickness benefit, or inclusive of any Statutory Sick Pay for a reasonable period (*Howman and Son v Blyth [1983] IRLR 139*). In that case, the EAT judged what was a reasonable period of time for sick pay to be paid by looking at what the general practice was in the industry concerned; here, the EAT took note of the relevant union agreement, which was the National Working Rule Agreement for the Building Industry.

Statutory Sick Pay (SSP)

6.4   Some employers do not provide any occupational sick pay and may therefore wish to exclude any liability. This should be made clear in the contract, so as to avoid the problems referred to above. In such a case the employer's liability would be limited to Statutory Sick Pay (SSP). SSP was first introduced under the Social Security and Housing Benefits Act 1982 (SSHBA), which was amended by subsequent Social Security Acts. The relevant legislation has now been consolidated in the Social Security Contributions and Benefits Act 1992 (SSCBA 1992), sections 151-163 and

Schedules 11 and 12. The Social Security Administration Act 1992, a separate consolidating statute, contains the provisions on the administration of SSP. A typical clause can be found in **Precedent 2**. In some cases employers may wish to provide an explanation about SSP. In some cases this appears in the Staff Handbook, in other cases in the 'Written Terms and Conditions of Employment'. An explanation of SSP appears in **Precedent 3**.

Is occupational sick pay a contractual entitlement or discretionary?

6.5   Whilst the rules concerning SSP are laid down by statute governing when and whether SSP is to be paid, the rules concerning occupational sick pay lie entirely at the discretion of the employer (or to be determined by agreement with the trades unions).

The payment of sick pay by the employer whether on a full or part pay basis may be a contractual entitlement or may be discretionary. In either case it is important to ensure that payment of occupational sick pay is only made where the rules have been followed. Where an employee has not followed the company's rules, he will not be entitled to occupational sick pay. **Precedent 4** sets this out clearly.

Furthermore, even if occupational sick pay is a contractual entitlement, there is no rule of law which entitles an employee to be protected from dismissal prior to the exhaustion of sick pay (*Coulson v Felixstowe Dock and Railway Co [1975] IRLR 11*) nor would he have a right to sue for the outstanding sums if he is dismissed prior to the end of his sick pay benefit (*Smiths Industries Aerospace and Defence Systems Ltd v Brookes [1986] IRLR 434*). The rule for SSP is similar; entitlement to SSP normally ends on the same day that the contract ends. [*SSCBA 1992, s 153*]. However, Regulation 4 of the SSP (General) Regulations 1982 (SI 1982 No 894) provides that liability to pay SSP will continue where it is proved that the employer dismissed the employee solely or mainly to avoid paying SSP.

It may be wise to clarify the position in relation to the continued payment of sick pay in the contract or in any agreement. Some employers go further and include a term reserving their right to terminate the contract at the end of any sick pay entitlement. This clause in itself would not satisfy an industrial tribunal that the employer had acted reasonably but it may be important where there is either a fixed term contract with a considerable proportion still to run or where the notice provisions generally are more generous than the statutory terms.

As far as the statutory position is concerned, section 49 of the Employment Protection (Consolidation) Act 1978 sets out the minimum periods of notice, while Schedule 3 to that Act sets out the rights of an employee during the notice period. These include the right of an employee, who is absent from work during that period because of sickness or injury, or by virtue of holiday entitlement, to be paid at the rate at which he would have been paid if he had been at work. Any payment made by the employer by way of sick pay (which for this purpose includes SSP) or holiday pay will go towards meeting the employer's obligations under Schedule 3.

Senior executives with service agreements typically have clauses concerning their absence from work due to sickness or injury reserving the right on the part of the company to terminate the agreement without any further notice.

Two typical clauses concerning sick pay and termination can be found in **Precedent 5**.

Scope of sick pay scheme

6.6   It is important to define the scope of the sick pay scheme in the contract, so as to cover the following matters:

(1)   purpose of the sick pay scheme;

(2)   definition of unauthorised absence;

(3)   rules on eligibility;

(4)   benefits provided;

(5)   the 'sick year';

(6)   rules on notification;

(7)   rules on evidence;

(8)   exclusions;

(9)   rules relating to non-payment;

(10)   conduct during sickness absence;

(11)   accrual of holidays during sick leave;

(12)   claims for sick leave during holidays (including public or statutory holidays);

(13)   loans during periods of sickness absence.

Purpose of sick pay

6.7   Most occupational sick pay schemes provide for sick pay to be paid where an illness or injury prevents the employee from doing the work that he is employed to do. SSP can only be paid in such circumstances. According to the statutory provision (SSCBA 1992, s 151(4); see also SSP General Regulations (SI 1982 No 894), Reg 2(1)), SSP can only be paid where:

'. . . the employee concerned is or is deemed (by) Regulations to be incapable by reason of some specific disease or bodily or mental disablement of doing work which he can reasonably be expected to do under that contract.'

It is commonly believed to be the case that once an employee notifies his employer that he is ill, all his duties and obligations under that contract are suspended. This is not so. Where an employee is off sick, he is relieved of the obligation to perform such services as the sickness from which he is suffering prevents him from carrying out, but not all the employee's obligations are suspended (*Marshall v Alexander Sloan & Co Ltd [1981] IRLR 264*).

It is therefore important to clarify, within the terms of any sick pay scheme, the circumstances when sick pay will be paid. The purpose clause is set out in **Precedent 6**.

Defining unauthorised absence

6.8   It is important to define when absence will be authorised and unauthorised and the consequences regarding pay and disciplinary action. A simple definition of unauthorised absence can be found in **Precedent 7**.

Some organisations define trigger points for disciplinary action for lateness and unauthorised absence. In some cases lateness is defined as 'any time after the start of a shift'. A number of occasions of lateness within a defined period leads to the first stage of the disciplinary procedure. Similarly one or several instances of unauthorised absences may lead to disciplinary action. It is now wise to be cautious about treating cases of absence whether genuine or otherwise as immediate cases for discipline.

In a leading case concerning persistent, intermittent absence, *Lynock v Cereal Packaging Ltd [1988] IRLR 510*, Mr Justice Wood cautioned employers to treat such cases 'with sympathy, understanding and compassion'. He added that these are not normally cases where the ordinary industrial relations jargon of 'warnings' are appropriate. He suggested that employers should 'caution' employees – rather than warn. Perhaps all he meant was that any warning letters should be written in an understanding and sympathetic manner.

Rules on eligibility

6.9   If sick pay is only to be paid to employees with a minimum length of service, this must be stated in their terms and conditions. For example, in some firms sick pay is not paid during a probationary period or for the first few months of service.

Benefits

6.10   Occupational sick pay may be paid at full, basic pay, average pay, half pay or at a flat rate. This should be clearly spelt out. Any SSP paid on a day that any remuneration is due offsets any liability to pay that remuneration (if it is less than the SSP payment) and any remuneration (occupational sick pay, occupational maternity pay etc.) paid on any day offsets any liability to pay SSP. [*SSCBA 1992, Sch 12, para 2*].

'Sick year'

6.11   A company's sick year may be the calendar year, its financial year, the fiscal year, a rolling twelve months starting with the first day of sickness or a rolling twelve months from the anniversary date of starting the job. There is no sick year for SSP. There is a liability to pay 28 weeks' SSP in any period of incapacity for work or linked spells subject to a three-year 'cut-off'. It is important to spell out the 'sick pay year' for occupational sick pay purposes. Furthermore, it is important to clarify when sick pay entitlement recommences after the employee returns to work should the company not define any 'sick year'.

A typical clause setting out the benefits and eligibility rules are set out in **Precedent 8**.

Notification rules

6.12   There should be clear rules on notification which should cover:

(*a*)   the time that notification must be made;

(*b*)   the person to whom notification must be made;

(*c*)   the information required to be given;

(*d*)   the intervals at which regular contact must be made;

(*e*)   special rules for staff with no telephone;

(*f*)   penalties for failure to notify according to the rules.

Some model notification rules appear in **Precedent 9**.

Evidence of sickness

6.13   It will be important to spell out what documentary evidence will be required. For SSP purposes, employers can only ask for medical evidence after seven calendar days of sickness [*SSP (Medical Evidence) Regulations 1985 (SI 1985 No 1604), Reg 2*] but other evidence of illness or injury is also acceptable (apart from medical statements). The DSS has suggested that certificates from chiropractors, herbalists and Christian Scientists may be accepted by employers if they so wish ('Employer's Guide to Statutory Sick Pay' (NI 227), paras 80-81). It is more common for employers to require self-certificates for the first seven calendar days of sickness and medical statements thereafter. For occupational sick pay purposes, if the rules provide, employers may require medical certificates (private certificates) for any day's sickness absence.

It is important to make clear that a medical statement in itself may not provide conclusive evidence for sick pay purposes. The tribunals have accepted that employers are entitled to look behind medical certificates. In *Hutchinson v Enfield Rolling Mills Ltd [1981] IRLR 318*, an employee, whose doctor had medically certified 'sciatica', was seen marching on a TUC rally. The employer refused to pay sick pay arguing that he had contradictory evidence as to the employee's alleged unfitness for work. The employee's claim for constructive dismissal failed. Anyone drafting a sick pay scheme should cover this point. One doctor carefully wrote 'ergophobia' on a medical statement. It was only when the personnel manager looked up the meaning in the dictionary that he learnt it meant 'morbid fear of work'!

It is also important to stress that only *acceptable* reasons for absence on self-certificates will trigger sick pay. The rules must make it clear that payment and authorisation for absence will only be given where the supervisor is satisfied with the reason given on the self-certificate. One employee completed a self-certificate after a day's absence which was counter-signed by his supervisor. Upon closer inspection the employee had completed the 'Reason for Absence' box with the immortal word 'Knackered'!

An example clause relating to evidence of sickness or injury appears in **Precedent 10**.

Conduct during absence

6.14　What action an employer proposes to take if an employee is suspected or seen participating in certain activities during a period of sick leave must depend upon the rules of the scheme. Whilst undertaking any form of alternative employment during any such time would almost certainly be regarded as misconduct and in certain cases gross misconduct, there may be other activities which might cause the employer to become concerned. It is therefore sensible to include some guidance on these points.

For example, should an employee provide a medical certificate with details of any form of back complaint or injury, it would not be expected that they undertake the leading part, every evening of their week's absence, in a production of the local amateur dramatic society! Similarly an employee who self-certifies (or produces a medical statement) alleging 'Gastroenteritis' would not be expected to be found eating a meal in a restaurant.

An example of wording of such clauses appears in **Precedent 11**.

Medical examinations

6.15　There may be occasions during the course of employment when a medical examination may be required. Determining fitness for work where there is an underlying medical problem, or where there is work-related illness or injury, is an obvious instance. In other cases an employer may wish to ascertain whether an employee has an alcohol or drug addiction problem. It is important to include a term in the contract (or contractual sick pay scheme) which requires an employee to submit to a medical examination. No individual can be forced to submit to a medical examination and his informed consent must be obtained on each occasion should any tests or assessment be carried out. However it may be argued that an unreasonable refusal to undergo a medical examination, particularly where the employee has agreed to do so in the contract, may give the employer grounds for suspension of sick pay and discipline or even eventually dismissal in serious cases. The rules on sick pay must make it clear that pay may be suspended where an employee unreasonably refuses to undergo a medical examination. However there is still a duty on the employer to explain the nature, purpose and extent of the examination even where there is an express clause in the contract. Two cases illustrate this point.

In *Meade v Smiths Industries Aerospace and Defence Systems Ltd (COIT 1979/ 129)*, Mrs Meade had been off work for several weeks with vertigo. The personnel officer asked her to attend for an examination with the company doctor but refused to tell her the reason for it. She had refused to attend until she was given a reason which the company refused to do. They then asked the company doctor to visit her home 'on spec'! The company then stopped her sick pay even though she was still unfit for work. She then agreed to attend for an examination if her sick pay was restored. This the company declined to do and they then dismissed her. The tribunal found the dismissal was unfair on the grounds that they had failed to explain the reasons for their request for a medical examination, they had failed to try to meet Mrs Meade's objections to their request and they had failed to warn her that her continued refusal could result in her dismissal.

In *Whitbread and Co plc v Mills [1988] IRLR 501*, Ms Mills thought she had been asked to attend for an examination in connection with her claim for personal injuries as a result of an accident at work. It was in fact, but unknown to her, to assess her fitness to return to work. Neither was she told that it was normal practice to submit to a full medical examination. Her sick pay then ceased and she was told that she could appeal against this decision. During her appeal she then made complaints of improper conduct against the company doctor. She was asked to return to another meeting but was not told that this was a disciplinary hearing which could result in her dismissal. Her subsequent dismissal was found unfair on the grounds that the company had not acted reasonably in not telling her about the nature of the medical examination and in not informing her that she was the subject of a disciplinary hearing for making allegations against the company doctor.

A standard clause regarding medical examinations can be found in **Precedent 12**.

Return to work

6.16   In some industries, there is a statutory requirement to be medically examined before returning to work after suffering certain medical conditions (for example, see the Merchant Shipping (Medical Examination) Regulations 1983 (SI 1983 No 808) and the Food Hygiene (General) Regulations 1970 (SI 1970 No 1172)). In other cases, employers require staff absent for more than a prescribed time to be checked by the company doctor prior to returning to work. A standard clause on this point can be found in **Precedent 12**.

In other organisations, employees must see their supervisor in a 'Return to work' interview and complete a self-certification form in the presence of their supervisor. In certain companies, the computer provides a personalised self-certification form with a resumé of the previous twelve months' absence record at the bottom of the form.

Exclusions

6.17 The excluded classes for SSP can be found in **Precedent 3**. Occupational sick pay schemes may operate different exclusions such as injury in any other outside employment (whether paid or unpaid) or self-inflicted injuries and excessive sickness absence. The rules of the scheme must make clear when sick pay will not be paid even in genuine cases. A standard list of exclusions from occupational sick pay is set out in **Precedent 13**. It includes exclusions for smoking-related illness or disease and may be appropriate in companies which operate 'No Smoking' policies.

Employers must also take care not to provide for exclusions which discriminate against women or ethnic minority groups. For example, it has been held to be a breach of the principle of equal pay under Article 119 of the Treaty of Rome to exclude part-timers from sick pay arrangements (*Rinner-Kühn v FWW Spezial-Gebaüdereinigung GmbH & Co KG [1989] IRLR 493*). Such an exclusion indirectly discriminates against women because a considerably larger proportion of women as compared to men work part-time. Unless this could be justified, it is an act of unlawful discrimination. Although in this case the woman was barred from the State Sick Pay Scheme (anyone working 10 hours a week or less or 45 hours a month or less), the same principle could be applied to employers' sick pay schemes if such an exclusion existed.

Similarly, if sick pay claims are excluded during maternity leave or restricted to claims for sickness other than those connected with pregnancy or confinement, then this too could be a breach of the Equal Pay Act 1970 or Sex Discrimination Act 1975 (depending on whether the scheme was a contractual entitlement or a discretionary benefit). In *Coyne v Export Credits Guarantee Department [1981] IRLR 51*, claims for sick pay following maternity leave were only allowable upon medical certification that the absence arose from some illness unconnected with confinement. Since men were not covered by any 'similar' restriction – all they had to do was produce a medical certificate and they were entitled to six months' paid sick leave – the industrial tribunal found that this term was a breach of the Equal Pay Act.

When the provisions of section 23 of, and Schedule 5 to, the Social Security Act 1989 come into force (for the purpose of implementing the EC Directive 86/378 relating to equal treatment for men and women in occupational social security schemes), employers will be required to continue all employment-related benefits during the whole of any period of paid maternity leave.

113

6.18   *Absence, Health and Sick Pay*

Similarly an absolute exclusion of claims for sick pay during any extended leave may be unlawful under the Race Relations Act 1976 since the vast proportion of staff who take extended leave are from amongst the ethnic minorities whose native country is not the UK.

Loans during absence

6.18   Where an employee has been injured through a work accident or an accident outside work, any earnings received during any time off work will be discounted from any award of damages. Any damages awarded may be reduced by the amount of State benefits already paid and likely to be paid during a period of up to five years from the date of the accident or injury. [*Social Security Administration Act 1992, ss 81, 82, formerly Social Security Act 1989, s 22, Sch 4*]. In addition, any remuneration or earnings from employment will also be deducted in full. Any payments received from an employer's permanent health insurance scheme will also be deducted from any damages (*Hussain v New Taplow Paper Mills Ltd [1988] IRLR 167*).

Thus it may be prudent for employers to make provision in the contract for no earnings to become due during such time off but to offer a loan which must be repaid when damages are awarded or settlement received. Examples of two loan arrangements and a Loan Agreement Form can be found in **Precedent 14.**

Sickness during holidays

6.19   It is essential to spell out whether claims for sickness during holidays will be permitted and whether there are any special rules relating to sickness immediately prior to or following a bank or public holiday. The rules may range from the normal rules for sick pay applying in any case of sickness, whether it be on annual leave or not, to an exclusion from any claim for sick pay once annual leave has started. It is common for claims of sickness during holidays to have to be supported by strong medical evidence such as a hospital report or medical certification. Self-certification will not normally be acceptable in such a case. The terms of the sick pay policy should make this clear.

Accrual of holiday during sick leave

6.20   It is also important to cover the position of the accrual of holiday during sick leave particularly during long-term sick leave since it will accrue and become due to be paid upon termination of employment as well as normal pay during the notice period [*EPCA 1978, Sch 3*] unless there is a provision to the contrary.

A typical policy on both the matters above can be seen in **Precedent 15**.

Private medical insurance

6.21   Some organisations offer private medical insurance to employees and their families under a Group Scheme. Such items are deemed to be emoluments and thus a taxable benefit in kind. If the company offers insurance cover abroad it is prudent to state what cover, if any, is provided. In *Reid v Rush and Tompkins Group plc [1989] IRLR 265*, the Court of Appeal held that an employer is under no duty of care to insure an employee who works abroad on company business against special risks, nor is there any duty on the employer to inform the employee about those special risks and advise him to obtain insurance cover. However, although the Court of Appeal held that at common law, the employer is under no duty to provide insurance cover in such a situation, it is good practice to do so and to advise the employee accordingly. (It is arguable that there may be some liability on the employer under section 2(2)(a) of the Health and Safety at Work etc. Act 1974.)

In some organisations staff who are sent to work abroad are given special medical kits with syringes, needles etc. and special arrangements are made to send out blood or other blood products in any emergency. This practice has become more common since the advent of AIDS and is a particularly important consideration where staff are working in countries where AIDS is endemic.

A typical clause appears in **Precedent 16**.

Permanent Health Insurance (PHI)

6.22   Some employers provide generous terms covering Permanent Health Insurance Schemes. Most schemes are insurance-based and guarantee salary continuation (often on a percentage basis) after a certain minimum period of absence from work (typically after six months) if the employee is unable to resume work at that time.

Implied duty upon employer to pay

6.23   As a general rule, it is always important to identify those benefits which form part of the contract which the employer is obliged to pay for, and those which are paid only at the employer's discretion. Employees are sometimes referred to the Staff Handbook for the details of some of the benefits mentioned in the written statement. As such the terms of the Staff Handbook are incorporated into the written statement and are given contractual status.

Problems have arisen in relation to insured benefits such as PHI when for one reason or another the insurance company has refused to pay the benefit. The courts have been left to decide who should pay the benefit and upon what basis.

In *Rutherford v Radio Rentals Ltd (21 November 1991, unreported)*, the Inner House of the Court of Session held that an employer may be obliged to pay an amount prescribed under an accident insurance policy incorporated into the employee's contract of employment, providing that employee qualifies under the terms of the insurance policy. This is the case even in circumstances where the insurance company refuses to honour the policy.

Here the employee concerned suffered a back injury carrying televisions in the course of his employment and was dismissed from his job on medical grounds. He sued the company on the basis that the Staff Handbook, incorporated into his contract, provided for personal accident cover in the form of earnings-related insurance. The handbook specified that subject to the terms and conditions contained in the insurance policy, an employee who was permanently and totally disabled from carrying out his usual occupation should be paid a benefit equivalent to five times his average annual earnings. The insurance company rejected Mr Rutherford's claim on the grounds that it did not fall within the stated terms. Mr Rutherford claimed that as he was permanently and totally disabled, the employee company itself was contractually obliged to pay him the sum, as prescribed in the Staff Handbook.

The claim by Mr Rutherford was formulated as an action in debt for the recovery of a sum due rather than as an action for damages for breach of contract.

The Inner House held that if there was any dispute between the company and the insurer about the contract between them, then that would be a matter for them to resolve, without involving Mr Rutherford.

In relation to the obligation on the part of the employer to pay the sum due, the Inner House concluded that even though Mr Rutherford's contract of employment did not contain any express term requiring the company to make any payment, certain terms had to be implied to give the contract business efficacy. This included an implied term that the '. . . policy entered into should satisfy the terms of the contract between Mr Rutherford and the company by providing cover in circumstances envisaged in that contract. . . .'.

Suggested wording

6.24   In order that an employer offering insured benefits protects himself from having to pay even where the insurance policy will not pay, it is suggested that such benefits are carefully described as discretionary and not forming part of any contractual entitlement. The following wording may be inserted:

'. . . only in so far as the terms of the Policy provide for cover and in any such cases as the Insurance Policy provides for and pays for such cover'.

A model procedure for Dealing with the Malingerer appears in **Precedent 17,** and a Supervisor's Briefing Paper on absence control appears as **Precedent 18.**

Key Points

- Include a term in the contract about robust health or any other special health requirements or pre-conditions for employment.

- Obtain the written, informed consent of any person who is required to undergo any medical examination or tests e.g. blood or urine tests for alcohol or drug dependency.

- Ensure it is clear whether occupational sick pay is contractual or discretionary.

- Ensure that there are clear rules concerning the non-payment of occupational sick pay upon certain events or conditions (in order not to fall foul of the Wages Act 1986).

- Ensure that there are clear notification and evidence rules.

- Ensure that if certain categories of illness or injuries are to be excluded from the occupational sick pay scheme these are carefully drafted.

- Ensure that there is a contractual term relating to a requirement to submit to medical examinations.

- Consider including a term relating to a loan during any period of absence caused by an accident whether work or third party and provide a loan agreement.

- Ensure that no discriminatory terms are included in any sick pay scheme such as exclusions of part-timers, pregnancy or maternity cases etc.

- If staff are to be sent to work abroad, ensure that either they are covered for sickness and accidents or are advised that they are not covered so that they may take out their own insurance cover.

PRECEDENT 1

'Special Health Requirements

Because of the rigorous and sometimes difficult working conditions on North Sea Oil platforms, it is essential that the Company employs only staff with robust health. It has been fully explained to you at your interview what conditions you are likely to expect on the platforms and the nature of the shift patterns that you are expected to work. It is for this reason that we insist that every job applicant pass a thorough medical examination. We also require that at any time during your employment with the Company, should you suffer any illness or injury which is likely to affect your ability to perform any duties expected of you or your ability to attend work on a regular and efficient basis, you are expected to inform the Medic on duty immediately. The Company may have to take steps, after consultation with the Company doctor, the member of staff concerned and his doctor, to terminate the employment. The trigger for any such action will be absence lasting more than 14 consecutive days (i.e. one whole shift) or two spells of absence in a rolling twelve months. The Company however will endeavour wherever possible to offer paid sick leave in accordance with the Company's Sick Pay Rules until you are fit to return to your duties. It may be impossible however due to the nature of our business to extend leave of absence with pay for the full duration of the sick pay benefit scheme or for any substantial amount of time after sick pay has run out.

It is for the reasons set out above that any false information regarding previous work experience or medical history will be viewed very seriously. In most cases the Company will treat such conduct as gross misconduct for which the normal penalty is summary dismissal.'

PRECEDENT 2

Clause concerning SSP and other Entitlements

1. Statutory Sick Pay (SSP)

The Company pays Statutory Sick Pay (SSP) as long as you have complied with all the statutory rules. These are clearly laid out in the Staff Handbook.

2. Additional sick pay

The Company may pay sick pay in addition to SSP at its entire discretion. In any case, the rules set down in the Company's Sick Pay Policy must be followed.

It is essential that you follow the absence reporting procedure otherwise your absence may be deemed to be unauthorised for which you may not be paid and for which disciplinary action may be taken.

PRECEDENT 3

Statutory Sick Pay – an Explanation for Employees

1. Introduction

The SSP rules can now be found in sections 151-163 and Schedules 11 and 12 of the Social Security Contributions and Benefits Act 1992.

(The SMP rules can be found in sections 164-171 and Schedule 13 of the Social Security Contributions and Benefits Act 1992.)

Under the prior Social Security and Housing Benefits Act 1982 as amended, Statutory Sick Pay (SSP), is paid by the employer through the normal payroll. This replaces the State Sickness Benefit which was paid by the old Department of Health and Social Security (DHSS – now called DSS).

SSP is payable for up to 28 weeks in any period of incapacity for work or linked periods.

2. Amount of SSP

There are two rates of SSP depending on your average earnings in the eight weeks preceding the first day of sickness absence. The rates for the tax year 1993/1994 are:

Average weekly earnings	*SSP per week*
Less than £55.99	NIL
£56.00 to £194.99	£46.95
£195.00 or more	£52.50

SSP counts as normal pay and as such is subject to deduction of income tax and Class 1 National Insurance Contributions (NIC), pension contributions and any other lawful deductions.

3. Eligibility for SSP

All employees (including married women paying the reduced NIC) are eligible for SSP provided:

(a) Your average weekly earnings are at least at the lower earnings limit (LEL) for Class 1 NIC – 1993/1994 this stands at £56.00.

(b) You are incapable of work for four or more consecutive days (a period of incapacity for work – PIW), including Saturdays and Sundays and Public and Bank Holidays.

Sickness on these days must be reported by employees whether or not you would normally work as this may affect entitlement to SSP. Periods of incapacity for work (PIWs) separated by less than eight weeks (i.e. 56 days or less) count as one single period of incapacity.

Please note that spells of sickness lasting less than four days do not count for SSP purposes and therefore cannot link with any earlier spells.

(c) You are sick on 'qualifying days'. These are the days which have been agreed with your Company as the days on which SSP will become due. This Company has agreed Mondays to Fridays (five qualifying days in each week).

The first three qualifying days in any PIW or linked PIWs count as waiting days and no SSP is payable. On the fourth and subsequent qualifying days, SSP will fall due.

Please note that if you are already being paid sick pay by your employer, you cannot receive SSP in addition. Your employer's liability to pay any SSP will be discharged if he is paying you more than the SSP due. Your employer (unless he is a small employer, see below) will now only be able to reclaim 80% of the SSP paid from the NIC paid at the end of each month. No further recoupment is now permitted by way of deduction of a percentage figure of all SSP payments made each month. In 1990/1991 (the last year for which this recoupment applied) the additional percentage recoupment was 7% on all SSP payments. This and the reduction of the 100% reimbursement to 80% was introduced in the Statutory Sick Pay Act 1991 and came into effect on 6 April 1991.

A special dispensation is given to 'small employers' through Small Employers' Relief (SER) which enables them to recover 100% of their SSP payments, but only after a six-week period of payment. A small employer is defined by regulations as an employer whose NI contribution payments do not exceed a set threshold within a qualifying tax year. In the tax year 1992/93, the relevant figure was £16,000 and remains unchanged for 1993/94.

(d) You do not fall into any of the following categories on the first day of a PIW:

(i)   over 65 years of age (men), over 60 years of age (women);

(ii)   employed on contracts for a specified period of three months or less;

(iii)   average weekly earnings over the last eight weeks was less than the LEL;

(iv)   where sickness benefit, invalidity benefit, State Maternity Allowance or Unemployment Benefit following entitlement to Invalidity Benefit has been paid or become due within the last 57 days.

Here you will be given a 'linking letter' from the Department of Social Security (DSS) which you must hand over to your employer. It will notify your employer of the date from which SSP will become due;

(v)   you are a new starter and have done no work at all when you fall sick;

(vi)   you fall sick during a strike i.e. you are 'participating in a strike or have a direct interest in a strike';

(vii)   you are pregnant and fall sick within the 'disqualifying period' – this can start at any time from the 11th week before the expected week of confinement (EWC) up to the 6th week;

(viii) you have already received 28 weeks' SSP in a single PIW or linked PIWs – there is a 'cut off' after three years even if you have not exhausted your 28-week entitlement;

(ix) you are outside the EC;

(x) you are in legal custody.

These exclusions only apply at the start of any period of incapacity and will continue throughout the PIW or linked PIWs. You will be sent a form SSP 1 'Changeover Form' by your employer.

4. Purpose of SSP

SSP can only be paid when *you* are genuinely ill and are incapacitated from doing any work that you are employed to do or could reasonably be expected to do. Your employer may be entitled to investigate your reasons for absence before making any payments of SSP to you.

5. State Sickness Benefit

You may be eligible to receive State Sickness Benefit or State Invalidity Benefit. The rates differ from SSP in that they are not paid at a flat rate and are not subject to tax.

If you are being paid sick pay by your Company you will need to inform them of any State benefits you may be receiving as this will normally be deducted from your pay.

6. Authorisation of SSP

SSP may be withheld if there is any reason to believe that you are not ill or that your illness or injury does not prevent you from working. Furthermore if you fail to comply with any of the rules such as those concerning notification and evidence you may not receive SSP or may experience some delay. The Regulations provide a right of appeal to an Adjudication Officer at the DSS if you believe that SSP has been withheld incorrectly. Your employer will provide you with a written statement of the reason for any non-payment.

7. Leavers

If you are still sick when you leave the Company's employment, you will be sent a Leaver's Statement (SSP 1(L)). You should give it to any new employer if you obtain new employment within eight weeks of receipt of the form.

8. Recovery of SSP and NIC

Your employer (unless he is a 'small employer – see 3 above) is now only entitled to recover 80% of the SSP paid from their NICs.

9. Records

Employers are obliged to keep records for three years from the end of the tax year to which they relate, showing:

(a)   the dates of each reported PIW;

(b)   details of the agreed qualifying days;

(c)   details of the SSP paid to each employee;

(d)   dates when SSP was withheld, with reasons;

(e)   any leaver's statements received from new employees;

(f)   copies of any leaver's statements issued.

10. DSS inspections

DSS Inspectors are empowered to make spot checks to ensure that employers are correctly applying SSP rules and to investigate the circumstances of individual cases.

PRECEDENT 4

Absence from Work due to Sickness or Injury – Rules, Procedures and Benefits

1. Preamble

The following sections set out information about the Company's Scheme for sick pay and absence from work due to injury or sickness. It is a condition of your employment that you abide by the terms of this Scheme.

Any benefits, whether sick pay or permission to be absent, will only apply where you have complied fully with the letter and spirit of the following points. Please make sure that you read very carefully the rules of the Scheme and that you understand exactly what you must do in the event of any sickness or injury which prevents you from working.

Any sick pay paid by the Company is paid at its entire discretion and none of the benefits described below form part of any contractual entitlement.

The Company reserves the right to withdraw or modify any or all of the terms of this Policy at its discretion. Any change will be notified to all employees and will affect both existing or any new staff.

Payments made under this Policy are made as full or part payment for any wages during any period of absence due to sickness or injury, subject to all the rules and conditions laid down in this Policy. Any such payments shall include any Statutory Sick Pay (SSP) payments where they fall due.

During the first six months of employment, members of staff are normally only eligible for SSP when this becomes due.

2. Purpose of the Sick Pay Scheme

The Company will provide generous sick pay at its discretion where the circumstances and/or the member of staff merits it. Sick pay is designed to alleviate hardship and anxiety in cases where an employee is unable to carry out his/her duties because of an illness or injury.

The Sick Pay Scheme operates on trust and the Company leaves it to the integrity and honesty of individual employees to comply with the spirit of the Scheme as well as the detailed rules set out below.

It should be understood that anyone who is suspected or caught abusing the Scheme will be dealt with under the disciplinary procedure which may result in a formal warning or, in serious cases, dismissal with or without notice or pay in lieu depending on the seriousness of the case.

Prec 4 *Absence, Health and Sick Pay (6)*

This section describes:

- what you must do when you cannot work due to sickness or injury (page   );
- what you must do as a new employee (page   );
- what sick pay you may be entitled to (page   );
- exclusions from sick pay (page   );
- absence due to negligence of third parties (page   );
- medical examinations (page   );
- the procedure for the supervisor when an employee reports sick (page   );
- examples of forms (pages   ).

PRECEDENT 5

Clause 1

'Please note that management reserves the right to terminate the contract of any employee absent through sickness or injury at any time. The mere payment of sick pay will not affect any decision to dismiss. There is no rule that sick pay must have been exhausted before management may take a decision to dismiss. In normal cases, management will obtain a full medical report and discuss the position with the employee (and union representative) concerned. Redeployment to suitable employment will normally be considered prior to any decision to terminate the contract.

Subject to the provisions of the EPCA 1978 as amended, if for an aggregate period of not less than......working days in the period of 12 months ending with the date of notice, you have been incapacitated by reason of ill health or injury from performing your duties under the contract, the company may terminate the contract by written notice of the minimum period to which you are entitled in accordance with the provisions of section 49, EPCA 1978 as amended.'

Clause 2

Termination

'If the Executive is prevented by illness, accident or other incapacity from fully carrying out his duties under this Agreement for a period exceeding { } consecutive months or at different times exceeding in aggregate { } days (whether working days or otherwise) in any one period of 12 consecutive months, it will be lawful for the Company (without prejudice to any other rights it may have at law in respect of any of the matters mentioned above) by written notice to the Executive to terminate his employment forthwith.'

PRECEDENT 6

Purpose of the Sick Pay Scheme

The Company will provide generous sick pay at its discretion where the circumstances and/or the member of staff merits it. Sick pay is designed to alleviate hardship and anxiety in cases where an employee is unable to carry out his/her duties because of an illness or injury.

The Sick Pay Scheme operates on trust and the Company leaves it to the integrity and honesty of individual employees to comply with the spirit of the Scheme as well as the detailed rules set out below.

It should be understood that anyone who is suspected or caught abusing the Scheme will be dealt with under the disciplinary procedure which may result in a formal warning or, in serious cases, dismissal with or without notice or pay in lieu depending on the seriousness of the case.

Please note that in any case an employee may be requested to attend the Company's premises if he is fit enough to do so either at the start or during any sickness absence. In the alternative, management reserves the right to ask any member of management to visit a sick employee at home or in hospital – such visits will not normally be unannounced. Appointments that are mutually convenient will be made. Only in the event of any failure to contact the employee or where serious abuse of the Scheme or company rules is suspected will management reserve the right to make a visit to the employee's home without an appointment.

The Company reserves the right, upon proper medical advice, to determine whether an employee is fit or unfit for any duties which it would be reasonable to expect that employee to perform. Employees will be given every opportunity to put forward their own medical evidence before any final decision is taken.

PRECEDENT 7

Defining 'unauthorised absence'

Unauthorised absence is defined as follows:

An employee who fails to turn up for work at the appropriate time will be deemed to be unauthorised absent, for which no payment will be made and for which disciplinary action may be taken UNLESS the absence is due to:

(a) genuine sickness and this has been notified to the company according to the rules;

(b) leave for which prior permission had been granted (in writing where appropriate) by the immediate manager;

(c) genuine reasons outside the employee's control which are acceptable to the company.

Please note that should the Company have any reason to doubt the validity of the illness or injury or the reason given for the absence, the Company reserves the right to withhold pay for all or part of the absence and may issue a formal warning (which could eventually lead to dismissal) or even dismiss if such conduct was deemed to be gross misconduct under the Disciplinary procedure, should the circumstances warrant it.

Any employees whose past absence record causes concern or whose absence record is higher than the average of those working in the same location may receive an extended written warning which may last longer than normal written warnings. If this should happen, the warning letter will make clear how long the warning will last and the reasons for the extended warning.

PRECEDENT 8

Your Sick Pay

If you are absent from work and your illness or injury prevents you from working, you (may be) (are) entitled to the following sick pay benefits, provided that you have complied with all the rules of the Scheme set out in this booklet and provided that the Company is satisfied with the reasons given for the absence.

Depending on your length of service, the following benefits may apply:

Length of Service	Full Pay period (Weeks)	Half Pay period (Weeks)
0 months – X months	X	Y
X months but less than Y years	XX	YY
Y years but less than Z years	XXX	YYY
Z years and over	XXXX	YYYY

The benefits as set out above run for a rolling twelve months starting with the first day of your sickness absence.

OR

Periods of absence occurring at intervals will be treated as cumulative within the rolling twelve months. Once you have returned to work for a period of......complete weeks of work, i.e. excluding any rest weeks on which you may have suffered any illness or injury, your maximum entitlement to sick pay is resumed.

Please note that any employee who has a record of persistent or excessive sickness absence may be refused Company sick pay for any future period of absence.

Absences due to accidents arising outside work are treated separately and may be subject to the rules contained under the heading 'Loans during periods of absence' on page   .

PRECEDENT 9

Notification of Absence

If you are absent from work due to any illness or injury which incapacitates you from doing any work that you are employed to do, the following rules must be observed in order to qualify for payment and for authorised leave:

Notify your supervisor

It is your responsibility to notify your supervisor by telephone as soon as you fall sick and you know that you will be unable to attend work.

You must give sufficient details on the telephone about the nature of your illness or injury and you must give some indication as to when you will be able to return to work. Should your absence be caused by any illness or injury of a highly personal nature, then as long as the Company doctor/nurse/Personnel is satisfied with your explanation, he/she will merely relay details about your absence but will keep confidential all personal details.

You must continue to regularly update your supervisor throughout your absence either by telephone or by post.

The supervisor will then inform Personnel that you are absent from work and will relay to Personnel details as to when you have said you will be likely to return to work.

Staff who do not have a telephone will be required to inform Personnel upon joining. Special arrangements will apply in any such case. Staff will be required to send a letter by first class mail to reach their Supervisor on their second day of absence. Please make sure that the letter is clearly dated. The Company will date stamp the letter upon receipt.

PRECEDENT 10

Evidence of Illness or Injury

Self-certification (for seven calendar days or less)

Should your absence last less than seven calendar days (counting Saturday and Sunday) you will be required to report to your Supervisor immediately you return to duty and complete a Company self-certification form. *The reasons given by you for your absence must satisfy your Supervisor before he will authorise your absence and counter-sign the self-certificate.* Should your supervisor have any doubts about the reasons given by you or for any other reason, he may not counter-sign the self-certificate. This may result in either non-payment of sick pay or a delay in payment until more senior management has reviewed your case. Until your self-certificate is counter-signed by a member of management no sick pay can be authorised.

In such a case, the position will be discussed with you, first in the context of an informal counselling interview. Depending on the outcome of that meeting, you may be formally warned should the circumstances warrant it.

When your self-certificate has been counter-signed by your supervisor, it will then be forwarded to Personnel/Payroll.

Medical statements

If you are absent for more than seven calendar days (including Saturdays and Sundays) or as soon as you know that you will be away from work for more than seven calendar days, you must get a medical statement from your own doctor. This must be sent immediately to Personnel who will forward a copy to your Supervisor. You will be required to let your supervisor know when you will be fit to return to work. Your supervisor will send a copy of any self-certificates to the Company doctor and Personnel.

In certain cases and at the entire discretion of the Company you may be required to produce medical statements for any day or days of sickness absence either at your own expense or at the Company's expense. This rule does not apply to the payment of SSP during the first seven calendar days of any sickness absence.

All medical statements obtained from your doctor covering the total absence save for the first seven days must be sent straight to Personnel.

It is your duty to ensure that your absence is covered by a current medical statement at all times.

Please note that all medical statements submitted must satisfy your supervisor and whilst medical statements normally provide adequate evidence of unfitness for work, they may not be conclusive evidence depending upon other factors and the circumstances surrounding your particular case.

Should there be any query or problem regarding any medical statements submitted, this will be discussed with you and the matter may be referred to a higher level of management for investigation and further action may be taken if necessary.

PRECEDENT 11

Conduct during Sickness Absence

To help you understand what might raise doubts or queries in the mind of your supervisor concerning any medical statements (or self-certificates), the Company has drawn up some guidelines for employees concerning their conduct and activities during any periods of absence due to sickness or injury.

In all cases of sickness or injury which necessitates taking time off work, it is expected that the employee will do his utmost to facilitate a speedy return to fitness and to work. In this regard, employees are trusted to act sensibly and honestly.

The Company would not in the normal case expect any employee who is absent from work due to sickness or injury to:

(a)   participate in any sports, hobbies or social activities which are in any way inconsistent with their alleged illness or injuries or which could aggravate the illness or injury or which could delay recovery;

(b)   undertake any other employment whether paid or unpaid. If you declare yourself incapacitated from work in relation to your employment with us, it will not be deemed proper conduct to undertake any other duties whilst off sick. Clearly the Company would expect you to do everything to aid a speedy recovery;

(c)   engage in any work around the home in terms of home improvements or the like;

(d)   engage in any activity which is inconsistent with the nature of the alleged illness or injuries (e.g. be seen walking round town with bags of shopping whilst suffering from an alleged injury).

Any case involving a breach of this part of the policy will be looked at on a case by case basis but disciplinary action may be taken which could include summary dismissal.

PRECEDENT 12

Medical Examinations

You may be required to submit to a medical examination during or after any absence from work due to sickness or injury or at any time deemed necessary by the Company during your employment. You will be required to give your consent to a report being sent to management concerning your fitness or otherwise to work or on any other relevant matter.

Medical reports

Should the doctor appointed by the Company require details of your medical history, you will be required to give your written consent giving him permission to contact your doctor (your GP or your Consultant) for your medical records or for a medical report – subject to your rights under the Access to Medical Reports Act 1988 and Access to Health Records Act 1990.

You may also or in the alternative be required to submit to a medical examination by an independent consultant (whether medical or otherwise) at the Company's expense. You will be required to give your written consent to a report being sent in confidence to the Company doctor who in turn will disclose to management any relevant details regarding your fitness to work. No confidential medical details will be disclosed to management neither will any diagnosis be given except in cases where any doctor regards this as paramount for your or other people's health and/or safety. In any event your consent will be sought first before any such disclosure is made.

The doctor appointed by the Company will be responsible for liaising with your own GP who will be kept fully informed about your case. It is expected that you will co-operate in this procedure and you will be required to give such consent as necessary in order to progress your claims for sick pay.

Confidentiality

All medical information will be kept confidential but you may be required to give your consent to any medical reports or records kept by your GP being sent to the doctor appointed by the Company for him/her to base a report on your fitness or otherwise, that report may then be sent to a senior Manager.

Until the Company is satisfied with the outcome of those enquiries, the Company reserves the right to withhold all or part of Company sick pay and if the circumstances warrant it, Statutory Sick Pay (SSP).

Reporting infectious disease(s)

You should also report any contact with anyone suffering from an infectious or contagious disease and it will be up to the Manager in charge of your office to determine whether you should come to work or stay home on full pay. Such leave would not count against any sick pay.

Second opinions/Light work

The Company reserves the right to ask for a second opinion (normally from a qualified medical practitioner or nurse) on whether any particular illness or injury would necessarily incapacitate an employee from doing such work for the Company.

In addition, the Company reserves the right to require an employee to undertake any reasonable duties having due regard to the nature of the illness or injury and this may mean that the employee will be able (after being signed off as fit for work by his doctor) to attend for work and undertake alternative or light duties or work shorter hours for a period of time. In such a case the Company may, at its discretion, 'red circle' (maintain) the employee's normal earnings or may offer the rate of pay applicable to those alternative duties/ shorter hours. This will in any event be fully discussed with you first.

Return to work

Upon your return to work you may in certain circumstances be required to present a certificate from your doctor confirming that you are fit for work. In any such case you will be contacted and asked to obtain such a certificate. You may also be required to submit to a medical examination by a doctor appointed by the Company before being allowed back to work. The decision of management will be final, following consultation with the doctor, as to whether you are fit to return to work. Management, at its entire discretion, reserves the right to refuse to permit any member of staff to return to work should the circumstances warrant it.

PRECEDENT 13

Exclusions

There is no entitlement to any Company sick pay (this may include the withdrawal or non-payment of SSP in some cases) where in the opinion of the Company:

(1)   you have knowingly entered false information on any form (including a self-certification or application form); this is regarded as serious misconduct which could result in serious disciplinary action being taken;

(2)   you have failed to follow the Policy and Rules explained in this part of the Handbook;

(3)   there are any serious doubts about the circumstances surrounding your claim for sick pay;

(4)   your absence record in previous years is in the opinion of management excessive;

(5)   your absence is caused by negligence, recklessness or carelessness by you in not observing standard safety practices or by wilful misconduct at work – in addition to withholding sick pay management reserves the right to take any appropriate action it deems fit including disciplinary action where necessary;

(6)   your absence is caused by any self-inflicted illness or injury as defined by management from time to time; this may include any illness or injury which was in the opinion of management primarily caused by your failure to heed medical advice;

(7)   your absence is caused through injury in any dangerous sport as defined by the Company – in this respect you are advised to take out your own personal accident insurance cover;

(8)   your absence is caused through illness or injury occasioned at any outside employment (whether paid or unpaid) or activities such as a charity parachute jump or run;

(9)   your absence is caused through any smoking-related illness or disability, in the written opinion of a medical practitioner;

(10)   your absence is caused by elective surgery or medical treatment unless undertaken upon the advice of a registered medical practitioner and confirmed as necessary by any doctor appointed by the Company – this may cover cosmetic surgery or dental treatment; treatment for infertility; sterilisation operations etc.

PRECEDENT 14

Clause 1

Loans during periods of absence

If you are absent through injuries caused by the actionable negligence of a third party in respect of which damages are recoverable, you must inform your supervisor/Personnel immediately. Any payment that may be made for all or part of any such absence (other than SSP) shall be by way of a loan which must be repaid in full. If damages are settled on a proportionate basis, the Company will require full details. The amount of any repayment required in those circumstances will be determined by the Company but will not exceed the actual damages recovered or the part thereof identified as loss of earnings.

In circumstances where no claim is made or where no claim can be made, you may, at the Company's discretion, be paid up to your maximum sick pay entitlement regardless of any other period of absence which may have occurred over the previous eight weeks.

You will be required to sign a Company Loan Form in respect of this loan.

Clause 2

A person employed by this Company who is absent from duty as a result of an accident in the United Kingdom shall not be allowed paid sickness absence if there is a claim for damages against a third party in respect of the accident, but sums amounting to not more than the sums which would have been paid had the absence been due to ordinary sickness shall be advanced to such a person after abatement to take account of any entitlement to Statutory Sick Pay. He or she will be required to undertake to refund, from any damages received, the full amount of the sums advanced, less such part of that amount as is proportionate to any contributory negligence or fault on the part of that person, or, if the claim is settled by a lump sum in which no specific amount is identifiable as loss of earnings, to refund the advance to the same extent as the total claim is successful, or such other amount as is, in the opinion of the Head of Department, fair and reasonable.

Any period of absence in such a case shall, if a refund of the sums advanced is made in full, be ignored for the purposes of reckoning sickness absence or, if a refund is made in part only and covering therefore part only of the period of absence, there shall be reckoned as sickness absence only that part of the total period of absence for which no refund is made.

'Accident' includes any event which causes personal injury.

ACCIDENT LOAN FORM (Optional to include for 'industrial injury' as well as third party)

TO: ABC plc

I, (full name in block capitals) ....
hereby acknowledge that any payments, other than Statutory Sick Pay, which ABC plc may make to me during my absence from work as a result of an accident which took place on .... are made as a loan (without any admission of liability on the part of the Company).

I undertake to repay this loan in full from such damages or settlement as I may receive in respect of the said accident immediately on receipt of the same.

*I agree that the said moneys loaned to me by the Company may be deducted from my salary (each month at the rate of £ ....) (Optional)

Signed .... Date.........................

PRECEDENT 15

Clause 1

Sickness before or during a holiday

Subject to the Rules as set out in the section on 'Conduct during sickness absence' if you should fall ill before you are due to start your annual holiday and you inform your Supervisor or Manager immediately, the Company may at its entire discretion treat that absence as sick leave and further annual leave may be granted at a time to be agreed with senior management.

However should you fall sick once your holiday has commenced, then the Company reserves the right to treat that as holiday and not as sick leave. In such cases, holiday pay will be paid and the absence will not be regarded as counting towards your sickness entitlement.

In genuine cases however, where you are actually prevented from taking your holiday through sickness or injury, if you notify your Manager immediately and submit medical evidence which satisfies the Company, the Company at its entire discretion may grant you further leave either paid or unpaid.

You will have to return to work for an uninterrupted period of .... weeks before you may take any further holiday entitlement and the normal rules on holidays will prevail.

Accrual of holiday during sick leave

OPTION 1

Holiday entitlement will accrue during any period of sick leave where the employee is in receipt of full pay or SSP only. If the employment is terminated as a result of sickness or injury then all holidays which have accrued during that holiday year will be paid with the final salary.

OPTION 2

Holidays will only accrue during any period of sick leave at the discretion of a senior Manager. The Company reserves the right to withhold all or part of any holiday pay which may have accrued during any period of sick leave.

If the employment is terminated as a result of sickness or injury the Company reserves the right to withhold all or part of any holiday pay which may have accrued during this period.

PRECEDENT 16

Private Medical Insurance

The Company has an arrangement with a private insurance company to provide you with free medical cover. You will become eligible and may elect to join the Scheme which covers you and your immediate family (spouse and children up to the age of 18) from your date of entry into the Company. At that time you will receive full details of this Scheme. Currently the cost of this insurance is a personal taxable benefit.

Medical insurance on Company business abroad

The Company insures all employees travelling abroad on Company business for medical expenses of up to £50,000 on each trip. Normally you are not required to inform the Insurance Department prior to travelling abroad but where you are suffering from a serious medical condition, full details must be disclosed to the Insurance Department before travel commences. Medical expenses may be settled by the employee out of currency and reclaimed on his return or may be charged on credit to the Company. In either case details must be submitted to the Insurance Department on return to this country. For other trips employees are advised to obtain additional medical cover.

Baggage

The Company Insurance Policy also covers accidental loss or damage to baggage up to a limit of £1,250 per person. The limit for any one item is £250. The Insurance Department must be notified if this limit is to be exceeded.

Personal accident

Employees travelling abroad are not covered against accidents abroad because the Company's death in service and accident and disablement policy is deemed to be sufficient. Should employees wish to provide additional cover at their own expense arrangements can be made with the Insurance Department.

Health Screening

Through......(name of company) we provide all employees over the age of 40 with an annual medical examination at the company's expense. This is completely voluntary and the medical report remains entirely confidential to the employee.

There is a special medical screening programme for women (Well Woman Screening) regardless of age. Wives of male employees can also benefit from this arrangement at a discounted cost. These services are arranged annually through..........(name of company) at our expense. Again these services are entirely voluntary and the medical report remains entirely confidential to the employee.

Staff over 35 are advised to visit their doctor for a blood pressure check once every two years. If you have to pay for this service the Company will reimburse you.

A booklet in the Personnel Department sets out these services in more detail or you could contact ....(name of company)'s medical centres direct quoting our reference number 000000000 (full medical screening) or XXXXXXXXX (Well Woman Screening).

PRECEDENT 17

Dealing with the Malingerer

1.   Asking for leave and it is declined

Employees who ask for leave and it is declined may still feel that they are entitled to take it or may have already booked the holiday and therefore decide to take it anyway. The following procedure is suggested:

(a)   Manager to call the employee into the office the afternoon before the first day of the leave requested.

(b)   To make opening remarks such as:

'You are looking very well today, etc.'

(c)   Remind employee of the refused leave application and produce the form with the refusal marked, dated and signed.

(d)   Ask the employee to confirm that he has understood that the leave has been refused, why it has been refused and to confirm that he will be at work on ....day.

(e)   Explain how the Company views going absent in breach of an express instruction not to take the leave i.e. that it is regarded as gross misconduct. Explain why it is gross misconduct.

(f)   Confirm that if in the unlikely event he is unfit for work, the Manager will require medical evidence which is acceptable to him and self-certificates may not suffice.

(g)   Confirm the conversation in writing, date and sign it and give employee a copy.

2.   Employee fails to attend work

1.   If the employee fails to attend work on a day that he should be at work, ring the telephone number and note down the number of times the telephone rings, the times of the day the number is tried and confirm with the operator that there is no fault on the line.

2.   Keep careful dated notes of this procedure.

3.   If the employee telephones the Manager, return the call immediately!

4.   If the answerphone is on, leave an urgent message that the Manager requires a conversation with the employee as soon as he feels fit enough to speak!

5.   State on the answerphone (if there is one) that the Manager is so concerned at the non-appearance at work, that he/she intends to visit the employee at home and can he confirm when it would be convenient.

6.   Visit and search for the individual. Make a note if the house is locked up. Visit a neighbour and explain that the individual has not been seen at work and enquire if he knows where the employee is.

7.   Leave a note that you called (you will have written one in advance and taken a copy). This note will state that you called, that there was no-one in and that you require an immediate telephone call to explain where the employee is and why he is not at work.

8.   You may also require an immediate medical examination (during or after the absence) by the Occupational Health Physician (OHP).

9.   You are entitled to treat going on holiday whilst claiming sickness as gross misconduct as this is regarded as fraud (making a fraudulent claim on sick pay); breach of mutual trust and confidence (lying on the self-certificate); flagrant breach of an express instruction not to take holiday.

10.   You are entitled to look behind a medical certificate if you have evidence of conduct inconsistent with the illness or injuries.

11.   A full disciplinary hearing should follow with all the evidence presented and the employee asked for an explanation.

12.   The decision whether or not to take disciplinary action and if so what should be taken.

13.   An opportunity to appeal should be given.

PRECEDENT 18

Absence Control for Supervisors – Briefing Paper

The absence levels for your department are now running at ....% losing .... working days as a result. The figures for 1992 are considerably worse than the figures for 1991 and are the worst amongst all the other companies in our industry.

The Company is now firmly committed to getting those figures down to more manageable levels and to this end we are asking each Departmental Manager to become more responsible for his team and to monitor closely individual records.

We are setting a new procedure in motion which if diligently carried out by all Managers should lead to a reduction in casual absence and a more careful monitoring of genuine sickness cases.

In order to have some consistency the following are the procedures to follow in controlling absence. Managers will be more responsible for responding to absence for own teams and for recording their actions.

Short-term absences

1. Trigger points to interview individuals

(1)   4 separate spells of absence in a rolling 12 months or 2 spells in a 3-month period; or

(2)   10 consecutive days of absence or more in a rolling 12 months or 5 days in a 3-month period; whichever happens first.

2. First interview of concern

The first meeting should be with the Manager once this trigger level has been reached. This is an informal counselling session and is not in any sense a disciplinary interview. You are expected to handle this meeting with sympathy, understanding and compassion!

You must have the individual's absence record with you at the meeting. A simple calendar with the SICK days marked in red will also be useful to identify patterns, frequency or curious coincidences in days taken off as sickness, e.g. school holidays, Bank and Public Holidays, annual leave, spouse's or partner's annual leave, sporting fixtures, refusal of leave etc.

Documents to be produced in the first counselling session

(a)   The absence record should be set out in three columns:

(1) the number of work days of absence in the left hand column;

(2) the number of spells in the middle column; and

(3) the reasons for the absence in the right hand column.

(b)   You should have attached all the self-certificates and any medical certificates to the record.

(c)   You should total the first two columns. You should investigate any pattern(s).

(d)   You should go through the reasons for the absences with the individual and try to find out which of the following six reasons is relevant (do not lead the individual but invite him to volunteer what lies behind all these absences).

(e)   If you have picked out the worst record in your department, then you must tell the individual that fact – the worst thing that can happen is for him to tell you of someone with a worse record within your working group!

Reasons for non-attendance

Several possible reasons lie behind persistent, intermittent absence and they include:

(1)   an underlying medical condition which is undiagnosed;

(2)   a problem with work or colleagues or supervisor;

(3)   a family, personal or domestic problem;

(4)   an attitude or motivational problem i.e. mere laziness;

(5)   a problem with a business or other interest outside work;

(6)   a response to a refusal for time off or in response to a particular shift or evening duty.

PLEASE BE AWARE THAT IF YOU GIVE CARERS' LEAVE OR DOMESTIC LEAVE, OFFER THIS IN APPROPRIATE CASES.

You will be expected to explore with the individual what lies behind the absence. Careful, persuasive and attentive questions and answers ought to be able to give you a clue as to the reason for the non-attendance at work.

It is essential that you take notes of this meeting and record what you say and what the employee has said. You will then attach these notes to any subsequent record of a warning. You must give the individual a copy of these notes after they have been typed up. If possible, although it is not essential, get the individual to sign at the bottom of the notes that they are a true and accurate record of the interview which took place on ....(date).

1. Medical problem

In order to ensure that the individual does not actually have an undiagnosed medical condition, you should ask for the answers to the following questions:

(1)   Have you been to see a doctor?

(2)   If the answer is 'No', then you can request that he/she is examined by your Occupational Health Physician (OHP) or GP. You must ask him/her to sign a consent form giving his/her consent to the examination and to a report (or answers to the relevant questions) being sent to you. Your OHP or the GP should be sent a copy of the absence record with copies of any self-certificates or medical certificates and ask him/her the following question:

'Is there any serious underlying medical condition which explains all these absences from work?'

SEE LETTER 1 BELOW.

If the answer is 'Yes', then further discussions must take place with the OHP or GP (with the written consent of the individual) to find out whether the condition can be treated and whether or not the individual is fit to attend work during treatment.

2. Other explanation for absences

If the answer from the medical report is 'No, there is no underlying medical condition', then you must explore the other reasons with the individual at a further meeting.

3. Second interview of concern

In this second interview, the employee must be counselled about his/her absence record and advised that if there is not 100% attendance at work, further action including disciplinary action will have to be taken. His/her record should be further reviewed within a reasonable interval (say after one complete shift or one or two weeks) and if the absences continue and there is no underlying medical condition, then he/she must be issued with a warning letter (detailed below). A review of the attendance record should continue at the end of each complete shift (or weekly or fortnightly) until you are satisfied. With delicate handling the absence record should improve.

4. 'Sympathetic Warning' letters – 'NOTIFICATIONS OF CONCERN' (see below)

If a warning letter becomes necessary, then it should be given to the individual after a formal interview with a fellow colleague present if he/she so wishes. Please be sure to tell him/her that he/she has a right to have a colleague present. These should be 'sympathetic warning letters' rather than disciplinary warning letters as per the normal disciplinary procedure for breach of company rules.

5. Further 'warnings'

If the absences continue and you are unable to discover whether there are particular problems in this case, you will have to issue further sympathetic written warnings – a first written warning and then a final written warning.

6. Dismissal

Should the record continue, consideration will have to be given to dismissal. BEFORE dismissal is effected, it is essential to seek and consider suitable alternative employment.

It should be made clear to the individual at each stage and in the warning letters, the problems that are being caused in terms of lost production, health and safety, morale amongst the rest of the staff etc. by his/her continued absences.

Employees with poor or excessive records

For employees with a history of high absence levels, who have a persistent record of poor attendance, it may be appropriate to issue slightly different warnings (a) or (b):

(a)   To state in their warning letters that because of their bad attendance record in the past, should they fail to improve or sustain any improvement, they will go back into the same Stage or next Warning Stage of the procedure i.e. if they have been issued with a first written warning and this then lapses, they will not go back to the oral warning stage but will either go back on a first written warning or straight to a final written warning despite the original first written warning having lapsed;

OR

(b)   To state in the 'sympathetic' warning letter that because of their poor attendance record over .... months/years, their warning will last for an extended period, e.g. two years and not twelve months.

*It is essential that the warning letter spells out why this slightly unusual procedure is being applied and how long the warning will last.

(c)   Issuing 'Well Done' letters after the warning has lapsed is a positive measure.

(d)   Computerised records may allow for each self-certificate generated by the computer to be individualised and by this means the computer may be able to generate the previous twelve months' absence record by spell and duration and cause at the end of the self-certificate.

Note to management

One way to ensure that line managers will monitor absence in this way is to write into their annual targets the responsibility to reduce absence levels in their departments/area and properly control absenteeism and sickness absence. Once a year Managers can be appraised on this!

Long-term or chronic sickness cases

Monitoring short spells of absence is fairly easy since you can see the employee on his return to work. Long-term absence is less easy to assess what is happening. You can ask the OHP or Company-nominated doctor to examine the employee away on sick leave after fourteen/twenty-eight days of absence.

If you are concerned about an employee, you should arrange for someone to visit him. You should telephone (or ask Personnel to telephone) the employee concerned to make an appointment.

NEVER MAKE UNANNOUNCED VISITS UNLESS YOU HAVE BEEN UNABLE TO CONTACT THE INDIVIDUAL AND ARE CONCERNED ABOUT HIS WELFARE OR WHEREABOUTS.

These calls and visits are firstly to enquire how the employee is and about his progress. You should try to ensure that the employee is receiving satisfactory medical treatment. PLEASE ENSURE THAT ALL THESE CALLS AND VISITS ARE RECORDED IN WRITING!

The OHP or nurse can offer an excellent second source of information and guidance working with the GP or hospital. Employees cannot refuse a reasonable request to be seen by the OHP. If they do, then that can be used as part of the case against the employee when/if the decision to dismiss is taken. However with careful counselling and spelling out the consequences of not co-operating with a medical examination, the employee may be persuaded!

If an employee is off work for a long spell and is very ill, perhaps that person's Manager ought to arrange to visit that person personally so that the Manager can show his concern as well as assess the situation first hand. Take a box of chocolates or flowers and a card round!

Summary for long-term or chronic ill-health cases

1.   Request a medical report along the lines of letter 2 below.

2.   Use guidelines on when to start this procedure from Appendix 3, DSS 'Guidance to Employers on Statutory Sick Pay' NI 227 (see attached).

3.   Consult the employee personally and arrange to visit. Discuss the medical report and ask the individual whether he agrees as to the likely date

of return. Discuss sick pay entitlements, ending of sick pay, SSP and Invalidity Benefits, employment of temporary cover, employment of permanent replacement etc.

Also discuss suitable alternative employment upon return or modified job duties.

4.   Consider the medical report and prognosis.

5.   Before taking the decision to dismiss consider alternative duties, modified job duties, less hours etc. with the consequent effect on pay (with the employee's written agreement to any changes) or agree to 'red circle' earnings if this is possible. Be aware that red circling should not last forever.

6.   If the decision to dismiss is to be taken, ensure that the person with that authority takes the decision. Communicate that decision to the individual personally and sensitively. Allow him to appeal against the decision if he so wishes and notify him of this option.

7.   Be prepared to consider new medical reports if they are available.

8.   The employee is only entitled to request another medical report other than from the OHP or the GP if he is consulting a specialist and the management has not received any specialist's report, the OHP report is woolly or indeterminate, the OHP has not actually examined the patient but merely reviewed the files or where the continued employment of the individual would pose a risk of health and safety to that individual or others.

Letter 1: Model Letter of Enquiry for Persistent Intermittent Absence

Doctor's name ....

Address ....

Please acknowledge receipt of this letter if there is likely to be any delay in replying.

Dear Dr ....

Re: Name ....

Address ....

In order for us to plan the work in the department, administer Statutory Sick Pay and our own occupational sick pay and assess the likelihood of any recurrence of this absence, it would be helpful to have a report on the above-named employee who is a patient of yours.

We have included his/her signed consent form and we undertake to you that all his/her rights under the Access to Medical Reports Act 1988 have been explained in a leaflet which we sent to him/her with the consent form. You will see that he/she has indicated that he/she wishes to have a copy of your report before/after* (delete as applicable) you have sent a copy to us.

His/her work as an .... has the following major features:

Management responsibility for ....

Seated/standing/mobile

Light/medium/heavy effort required

Day/shift/night work

Clerical/secretarial duties

HGV/medium/private driver

Other ....

The absence record for the past year is summarised as:

Last year, total days' absence ....

This month ....

Previous months ....

We include copies of all the relevant self-certificates and medical statements.

Please will you report whether upon examination of the above-named employee you have been able to find any serious underlying medical condition which explains this pattern of absence?

I would be grateful for an early reply and enclose a stamped addressed envelope. Please attach your account (at the BMA recommended scale) to your report and we will be pleased to settle this with you.

Yours sincerely,

Signed ....

Name (Block capitals) ....

Role in Company ....

Letter 2: Model Letter for Long-term or Chronic Sickness Absence Case – Addressed to Employee's General Practitioner or Consultant

Doctor's name ....

Address ....

Dear Dr ....

Re: Name of Patient ....

Address ....

In order for us to plan the work in the department, administer Statutory Sick Pay and our own occupational sick pay and assess the likelihood of a return to work in the near future and the recovery of our employee, it would be helpful to have a report on the above-named employee who is a patient of yours.

We have included his/her signed consent form and we undertake to you that all his/her rights under the Access to Medical Reports Act 1988 have been explained in a leaflet which we sent to him/her with the consent form.

You will see that he/she has indicated that he/she wishes to have a copy of your report before/after* (delete as applicable) you have sent a copy to us.

His/her work as an .... has the following major features:

Management responsibility for ....
Seated/standing/mobile
Light/medium/heavy effort required
Day/shift/night work
Clerical/secretarial duties
HGV/medium/private driver
Other ....

The attendance record for the past year is summarised as:
Last year, total days' absence ....
This month ....
Previous months ....

I have your patient's permission to enquire:

1.   What is the likely date of return to work?

2.   Will there be any disability at that date?

3.   How long is it likely to last? Will it be temporary or permanent?

4.   Is he/she likely to be able to render regular and efficient service in the future?

5.   Is (are) there any specific recommendation(s) you wish to make which would help us to find him/her alternative employment if that is necessary and if there is an opportunity for redeployment (e.g. no climbing up ladders, no driving etc.)?

6.   Do you recommend that your patient continues with any medication or treatment when he/she returns to work? If so could you indicate whether this would affect his/her ability to undertake his/her duties or necessitate any time off work (and if so how much)?

I would be grateful for an early reply and enclose a stamped addressed envelope.

Please would you contact me if your reply will be delayed for any reason.

Please attach your account for your report and we will be pleased to settle this with you according to the BMA recommended scale of fees.

Yours sincerely,

Signed ....
Name (Block capitals) ....
Role in Company ....

'Well Done' Letter

(Headed Company Notepaper)

Dear .... Date ....

I am writing to thank you for the effort you have made throughout 1993 to attend work following the official warning on .... (date).

The Company is naturally extremely concerned about the level and cost of casual absenteeism and intends to take some positive measures to deal with the problem.

It is particularly heartening to note that since your warning your own record shows that you lost no time at all from work this year.

On behalf of management I should like to extend my sincere appreciation to you for your excellent attendance and our hope and expectation that it will continue during this year despite the warning lapsing from your record.

Signed .... (Manager)

Sympathetic Oral Warning (to be recorded) –
NOTIFICATION OF CONCERN

Employee's Name ....
Location/Department ....
Date of oral warning ....
Offence ....

An oral warning was given to the above-named employee in respect of his/her unacceptable absence record as set out in our absence control procedure. Details of the absence record are attached.

I saw him/her on an informal basis on .... (date) when I asked for any explanation of his/her absence record. We had a long session together when we discussed at length his/her absence record and the reasons for it. I told him/her that if he/she had any personal problems or difficulties he/she could tell me in confidence or go to see our Company nurse/doctor. I also referred him/her to Dr .... on .... (date) and received a report (attached) which did not indicate any medical problem.

I have now advised him/her that unless his/her attendance record makes an immediate, significant and substantial improvement during *the next two shifts* and is sustained for the next twelve months, he/she will be given a first written warning.

I will review ....'s (name) absence record on .... (date) and after each shift, for a period of twelve months. If the attendance record improves and is sustained over the next twelve months, this oral warning will lapse.

I have advised him/her that he/she should come to see me if he/she has any problems with which the Company can help.

Signed ....
Status ....

(A record of those present at the interview and summary notes of the main points should be attached)

First Sympathetic Written Warning – SECOND NOTIFICATION OF CONCERN

Employee's Name ....   Date ....
Location/Department ....

Further to the disciplinary hearing which took place on .... (date)
I confirm that you have been given a first written warning for failing to
achieve/maintain a satisfactory attendance record. Over the past ....
(weeks/months) your absence record has been .... (state number of
days/spells).

I have discussed your record with you on two previous occasions and have
tried to find out why your record is unacceptable. You have not been able to
produce any explanation which satisfies me so regretfully, I have had to issue
you with a first written warning.

In accordance with the disciplinary procedure/absence control procedure, if
there is the required improvement in your attendance which is maintained
over the following twelve months, this warning will lapse. However should
your attendance not improve or be sustained over the next twelve months or
should you commit any further disciplinary offence, then you will be given a
final written warning.

I trust that you will be able to attend work on a regular basis and achieve a
100% attendance record. If you have any problems which make it impossible
for you to attend work, I would urge you to tell me immediately so that we can
try to find a satisfactory solution. I have explained to you the difficulties we
face when you fail to attend work and the effect that this has on the running
of the Company. I trust that this warning will lead to the improvement
required and that no further action will be necessary. I have also reminded you
of the facility for confidential counselling should you need this.

Signed ....
Status ....

(A record of those present at the interview and summary notes of the main
points should be attached to the Company's copy of this letter)

Final Sympathetic Written Warning – FINAL NOTIFICATION OF CONCERN

Employee's Name ....   Date ....
Location/Department ....

Further to the disciplinary hearing which took place on .... (date) I confirm that you have been given a final written warning for failing to achieve/maintain a satisfactory attendance record. Over the past .... (weeks/months) your absence record has been .... (state number of days/spells). I have discussed your record with you on three previous occasions and have tried to find out why your record is unacceptable. You have consistently been unable to provide a satisfactory explanation.

In accordance with the disciplinary procedure/absence control procedure, if there is the required improvement in your attendance which is maintained over the following twelve months, this warning will lapse. However should your attendance fail to improve or be sustained over the next twelve months or should you commit any disciplinary offence, we will have no option but to terminate your contract.

I trust that this warning will lead to the desired improvement and that no further action will be necessary. You have a right of appeal within .... working days to .... should you consider this warning unfair.

I have also reminded you of the facility for confidential counselling should you need this.

Signed ....
Status ....

(A record of those present at the interview and summary notes of the main points should be attached to the Company's copy of this letter)

Dismissal Letter

Employee's Name ....   Date ....
Location/Department ....

Further to the disciplinary hearing which took place on .... (date) in view of your previous unacceptable attendance despite counselling and formal warnings, I hereby give you notice to terminate your employment with the Company on ....*

*Your employment therefore ceases forthwith as at the date of this letter. You will receive a payment in lieu of any notice together with any outstanding payments due to you.

OR

You will/will not be required to work out your notice and you will/will not be given a payment in lieu of notice.

(*Delete whichever is appropriate.)

If you consider that this decision is unfair, you may appeal against it to .... within ....working days. Please briefly state your grounds for appeal.

Signed ....
Status ....

(A record of those present at the disciplinary interview and summary notes of the main points should be attached to the management's copy of this letter)

Chapter 7

Holidays

The law

Annual holidays

7.1 There are no general legislative rules which require employers to give employees annual holidays. This is normally covered by an express term in the contract by virtue of EPCA 1978, s 1(3)(d)(i) (as substituted by TURERA 1993), which requires the employer to state in writing what the holiday entitlement is. In rare cases an employee may be able to rely on an implied term through custom and practice; thus, in *Tucker v British Leyland Motor Corporation Ltd [1978] IRLR 493*, the employees were entitled to rely on custom and practice to the effect that they were allowed to take Christmas Day and New Year's Day as holidays, and it was a breach of that term for the management to insist that they worked on those two days and took two days' holiday at some other time. In some cases workers are covered by Wages Council Orders which lay down minimum holiday entitlements (there are also statutory provisions in the Agricultural Wages Act 1948). There are proposals in Article 5 of the Draft EC Directive on Working Time for a minimum of four weeks' paid holiday. In many cases trades unions have negotiated holiday entitlement and arrangements for other leave; for example, the Amalgamated Engineering Union (AEU) negotiated an agreement in 1979 giving four weeks' paid annual leave to all its members covered by the national agreement with the Engineering Employers' Federation (EEF).

Bank and public holidays

7.2 There are designated bank holidays laid down by the Banking and Financial Dealings Act 1971. Although this lays down the list of designated bank holidays, the Act only applies to employees working in banks and other financial institutions. However 'bank holidays' are recognised by most employers, although some employers may make special arrangements concerning these days (see below).

In addition there are certain days which are customary holidays (known as public holidays) and other days which may be public holidays by Royal Proclamation (such as on a day of a royal wedding).

The current list of bank and public holidays runs as follows:

7.3 Holidays

England and Wales	Scotland	Northern Ireland
1 January	1 January	1 January
Good Friday (public holiday)	2 January	17 March
Easter Monday	Good Friday	19 March
First Monday in May	First Monday in May	Good Friday (public holiday)
Last Monday in May	Last Monday in May	Easter Monday
Last Monday in August	First Monday in August	Last Monday in May
Christmas Day	Christmas Day	12 July
Boxing Day	Boxing Day	Last Monday in August
		Christmas Day (public holiday)
		Boxing Day

If any of the above days falls on a Saturday or Sunday, the following Monday is a holiday unless that Monday is already a holiday in which case the Tuesday becomes the holiday.

The contract

7.3 In many cases, the written terms and conditions or the offer letter will specify holiday entitlement and may then refer to the holiday policy contained in the staff handbook, collective agreement, or personnel manual. Detailed rules concerning annual leave and bank and public holidays will be important. Most disputes concerning holiday pay will be referred to the county court or High Court as a claim for breach of contract, but where the employer disputes the amount due and holds back an amount, this will come under the Wages Act 1986 and will be referred to an industrial tribunal. Any claims for unfair dismissal in any case concerning annual leave or holiday pay may be referred to an industrial tribunal.

The details of a holiday policy are set out below. These may be specified in the contract itself or in any document referred to therein.

Common terms and rules of a holiday policy include:

(a)   the holiday year;

(b)   authorisation of leave;

(c)   length of leave;

(d)   rules concerning leave;

(e)   basis of holiday pay;

(f)   bank and public holidays;

(g)   holiday entitlement;

(h)   holidays in year of commencement;

(j)   special leave including 'educationals', religious holidays and sabbaticals;

(k)   holidays and the notice period;

160

(*l*)   holiday pay upon termination including cases of gross misconduct;

(*m*)   maternity leave and holidays;

(*n*)   holidays and shift workers;

(*o*)   compassionate leave;

(*p*)   extended leave;

(*q*)   disciplinary rules and holidays.

1. The holiday year

7.4   It is essential to spell out the holiday year during which time all annual leave must be taken. Most policies specify whether any annual leave untaken at the end of the holiday year can be carried over to the next year. A typical clause appears in **Precedent 1**.

There may be special rules concerning the carry over of untaken leave. In some organisations a maximum number of specified days may be carried forward and taken within the first few months (specified) of the next holiday year. In other organisations untaken holidays will be forfeited. In yet other organisations, employees who are unable to take their full annual leave entitlement for operational reasons may be given pay in lieu.

2. Authorisation

7.5   Annual leave may normally only be taken with the prior agreement of the manager or head of department. There may be rules concerning the normal notice that must be given and in many cases, holiday leave forms must be signed.

Anyone refused leave may be reminded in writing of the reason and this should be recorded on their file. This will be important if the leave is taken as alleged sick leave (see below under 'Gross misconduct'). Should an employee be dissatisfied with any decision he may pursue this through the grievance procedure. A clause on this point can be seen in **Precedent 1**.

3. Length of leave

7.6   In some organisations there may be rules regarding the maximum amount of leave that may be taken at any one time. In others employees are exhorted to take a minimum period of leave so that they can benefit fully from their holidays. In the financial sector it is common for staff to be required to take a minimum of three weeks' leave, so that if the Bank of England or other body wishes to check on any irregular dealing, they will have three clear weeks to do so!

4. Rules concerning leave

7.7   In some organisations, there is a prohibition on the taking of leave during certain times of the year when the company is busy. In other organisations part of the annual leave entitlement must be taken during a certain period. In some organisations there is a factory shutdown for two weeks in the summer and staff are obliged to take two weeks' annual leave during this time.

In other organisations the business closes during the whole of the Christmas period, reopening on the day after the New Year's Day holiday. In such cases staff may be required to take a certain number of days' leave during this time, the days of which are notified to them each year.

In the case of *Silentnight Ltd v Pitfield and Pitfield, EAT 106/82*, it was held to be gross misconduct to return late after the factory fortnight shutdown as it was clearly spelt out in the rules that taking time off immediately before or after the shutdown was a dismissible offence.

A clause on this point can be seen in **Precedent 1**.

5. Holiday pay

7.8   In cases where pay does not vary, employees will receive their normal pay. In cases where employees work on a shift rota or earn overtime pay, it will be essential to spell out how holiday pay is calculated. It may be basic pay, contractual pay, average pay (averaged over the twelve weeks prior to the employee's leave or over the previous tax year based on the earnings stated on the last P60).

It is also essential to spell out whether the company will pay any holiday pay in lieu of any holiday untaken at the end of the holiday year.

A typical clause on holiday pay is set out in **Precedent 2**.

The need to spell out clearly what holiday pay will be paid was illustrated in a case under the Wages Act 1986 (*Humber Workforce Contractors Ltd v Langley & Ors, EAT 369/91*).

6. Bank and public holidays

7.9   It is important to specify whether employees are required to work on a designated bank or public holiday and whether this attracts additional pay and/or time off in lieu.

Some organisations specify the arrangements that will be made where an employee is absent through sickness on any day immediately before or after a bank or public holiday. In some cases no days are paid and no time off in lieu is given. This is a fairly typical clause in relation to blue collar workers. A clause is set out in **Precedent 3**.

7. Holiday entitlement

7.10   The amount of holiday entitlement often varies according to service. Some organisations offer extra days' annual leave depending on length of service. It may also vary according to the grade of the employee. In one organisation senior staff may take any amount of annual leave at their discretion but five weeks' annual leave is taken for the purposes of determining accrued holiday pay upon termination. **Precedent 4** sets out a common arrangement.

8. Holidays in year of commencement

7.11   It is common to provide that only the pro rata entitlement will be permitted to be taken in the first year of service and that a certain specified period of employment must be served before any holidays will accrue. Any holidays already booked by a new starter should be discussed at the interview and it should be agreed whether this will be honoured and whether it will be paid or unpaid. **Precedent 5** contains such a clause.

9. Special leave

Educationals

7.12   In certain industries staff may be on leave for part business reasons and whether this counts as annual leave must be clearly spelt out. For example, in the travel business 'educationals' are offered to staff by tour operators and hotels (at no cost to the staff). The staff are sent to holiday locations and hotels so that they are better able to understand the nature of the holiday or the standard and services of the hotel. In some travel firms, 'educationals' may form part of the annual leave entitlement.

Sabbaticals

7.13   In some companies, long serving members of staff are offered paid or unpaid sabbaticals. In some cases this is to have time to write or research books or projects. In other cases it is for a complete break from work for mental and physical refreshment. This is normally offered only once during a period of employment and in some cases a written report has to be produced. It is essential to spell out all the rules for such leave and to clarify what contractual benefits will cease to apply during such leave.

Religious holidays

7.14   Other organisations recognise the religious holidays of members of staff such as those of the Jewish faith, Muslims etc. The rules may specify the amount of notice and the cover required should the members of staff wish to take time off on such days as part of annual leave.

7.15 *Holidays*

Additional leave

7.15   In certain organisations, it is recognised that some time off which is alleged to be sickness absence may in fact be time off work to wait in for delivery men, look after a sick child, attend a sports day at school or go to a hospital, dental or doctor's appointment. Since this may only require a few hours off work (whereas at least one whole day will be taken for alleged sick leave), some employers have granted additional days' leave for such purposes which may be taken in hourly units.

A typical series of clauses appears in **Precedent 6**, relating to all the categories of special leave referred to above.

Holidays and notice periods

7.16   It is wise to reserve the right to require staff to take their untaken holiday entitlement during their notice period particularly where the employee will not be required to work out his notice. Otherwise accrued holiday pay will have to be given as well as the notice pay.

In other cases where it would be inconvenient for the employee to be away from work during his notice period, the holiday policy should specify that there may be cases where the employee may not take any untaken holiday but may be required to work for operational reasons. In such cases any accrued holiday pay will be paid in lieu.

Precedent 7 sets this out.

Holiday pay upon termination

7.17   Where there is holiday pay due to be paid at the termination date, the policy should express how a day's pay will be calculated. In many cases a fraction of the annual salary is found by dividing the annual salary by the number of actual working days in any year.

Where holiday in excess of entitlement is taken, it is essential to specify that any days in excess will be deducted from final salary or any payments due upon termination. This is set out in **Precedent 8**.

No notice or short notice

7.18   Where an employee gives no notice or leaves during his notice period, an employer may, if there is an express clause in the contract, deduct from any final salary payments the amount of pay equivalent to the number of days' short notice. This is one financial penalty open to an employer in such a situation.

A clause in **Precedent 8** sets this out.

Maternity leave

7.19 It is essential to spell out how holiday entitlement is to be treated before and during maternity leave. Care must be taken to treat maternity leave in the same way as any other leave otherwise denial of such benefits may be held to be sex discrimination. It would be wise to treat holidays accruing during the maximum 40 weeks' maternity leave period (to which women are entitled provided that they have been continuously employed for two years or more at the beginning of the eleventh week before the expected week of childbirth) in the same way as holidays accrue during sick leave (see 6.20 'Absence, Health and Sick Pay') in order to avoid a claim of sex discrimination.

The new EPCA 1978, s 35 (inserted by TURERA 1993, s 23) gives a right to pregnant women, irrespective of their length of service, to fourteen weeks' maternity leave. Under the new section 33, 'an employee who is absent from work at any time during her maternity leave period shall, subject to sections 36 and 37 [see below], be entitled to the benefit of the terms and conditions of employment [save for remuneration] which would have been applicable to her if she had not been absent (and not been pregnant or given birth to a child)'.

Under sections 36 and 37, an employee will not be entitled to the rights conferred under section 33, unless she notifies her employer of the fact of her pregnancy and of the intended or actual start date of her maternity leave period.

Therefore, provided that the notification requirements are complied with, holidays will accrue during the fourteen weeks' maternity leave period. Employers should therefore ensure that during any remaining maternity leave, holiday accrual is treated in the same way as during any other leave arrangements, otherwise they may be faced with a claim for equal pay or sex discrimination.

The maternity provisions contained in TURERA 1993 are expected to be implemented by October 1994 as required by the EC Pregnant Workers' Directive.

Before a woman takes maternity leave it is important to clarify whether she should take all accrued leave before her maternity absence begins, whether this will be paid as holiday pay at the start of her absence or whether she may save it for when she returns. If she plans to return in a new holiday year she should be advised accordingly and payment should be made or the holiday taken prior to her leaving.

A clause on this point appears in **Precedent 9**.

Shift workers

7.20 There should be special rules concerning holiday entitlement for any workers who work abnormal weeks or shift patterns. A typical clause can be found in **Precedent 10**.

Extended leave

7.21   Extended leave is commonly granted in companies where there are many workers whose native country of origin is not the UK. The policy normally grants a period of unpaid leave but clear guidelines need to be set. Documentary evidence of the return date may be required and in many cases the policy lies at the discretion of management.

Any letter that an employee may be required to sign should set out the agreement to return on the due date in clear terms. Any letter purporting to state that the employee agrees that his contract will terminate should he not return on that date will be void (*Igbo v Johnson Matthey Chemicals Ltd [1986] IRLR 215*, where the Court of Appeal held that such a letter was contrary to EPCA 1978, s 140(1)). The employer cannot argue that by not allowing the employee to return because of his delayed return to work, there has been no dismissal but a mutual agreement to terminate.

If an employee walks out of his job, or commits any other breach of contract, repudiatory or otherwise, and then subsequently claims that he is entitled to resume or continue his work, his contract is only terminated if the employer expressly or impliedly accepts repudiation on the part of the employee. This will constitute a dismissal in law by the employer. In any complaint by the employee of unfair dismissal, the employer will have to show that he acted reasonably in the circumstances of the case, in accordance with EPCA 1978, s 57(3).

In *London Transport Executive v Clarke [1981] IRLR 166*, where the non-return of an employee from Jamaica resulted in the employers accepting his conduct as a repudiation of the contract, it was held that applying the principles outlined above, the employers had acted reasonably in the circumstances in treating that conduct as a sufficient reason for dismissing him. The circumstances were that Mr Clarke had a very poor attendance record and on several occasions his request for leave of absence to visit Jamaica was turned down. He threatened to take the time off anyway and complain to the Commission for Racial Equality. He then went absent without permission and without notifying the company. He had in fact gone to Jamaica leaving his family in Britain. He failed to respond to any of the letters his employer sent seeking an explanation for his absence but a few weeks later his wife wrote asking for leniency for her husband and stating that he would be back the following month. The company wrote to Mr Clarke and told him that his name was permanently removed from their books. On his return the following month he produced a medical certificate from a doctor in Jamaica covering him for exactly the 49 days of his absence. He alleged that he had sent it but it had never been received.

Gross misconduct

7.22   In some cases taking unauthorised leave of absence may constitute gross misconduct which warrants summary dismissal. A shop steward, who had been refused a week's leave but took it anyway, was seen in Majorca but returned and self-certified as having had 'Gastric stomach', was held to have committed gross misconduct (*Bailey v BP Kent Oil Refinery Ltd [1980] IRLR 287*). See also 7.7 above.

It is important to reserve the right to withhold any accrued holiday pay in such a case (*Greg May (CF & C) Ltd v Dring [1990] IRLR 19*), but it will be up to a tribunal to determine whether the conduct was such as to constitute gross misconduct. If it is not, not even an express clause such as the one in **Precedent 13** will provide any defence to a claim of an unlawful deduction under the Wages Act 1986.

Key Points

- Spell out the annual leave entitlement.

- Define the 'holiday year'.

- Spell out the rules relating to Bank and public holidays.

- Spell out whether there is extra pay or time off in lieu of any Bank or public holidays worked.

- Spell out the rules for the amount of leave permissible to be taken at any one time, whether leave must be taken at a particular time or is not permitted to be taken at a particular time.

- Spell out any extended leave arrangements.

- Spell out entitlement in year of commencement of employment.

- Spell out how holiday pay is calculated and in what circumstances accrued holiday pay may be paid upon termination (including the rules in cases of gross misconduct).

- Spell out the rules for sickness during holidays, accrual of holidays during maternity leave and accrual of holidays/holiday pay during sick leave.

- Spell out any special arrangements for leave such as unpaid, sabbaticals, religious holidays etc.

PRECEDENT 1

General Rules

1. The Holiday Year

The Holiday Entitlement Year runs from 1 April to 31 March. You are required to take your holiday between those dates (i.e. between 1 April to 31 March the following year).

2. Carry-over rules

You may not carry forward any holiday untaken by 31 March in any year nor will any pay in lieu be made.

OR

In certain cases you may be permitted to carry over no more than ten days' untaken leave. This must be taken by 30 June in the next holiday year and only with the express permission of your Manager.

3. Agreement required

All holidays must be taken at times approved by your Manager or a Director. In agreeing holiday leave the Manager will consider the requirement to maintain a satisfactory level of operation within the division or department concerned. Holiday leave forms are available from the Personnel Department and these must be completed and signed by your immediate Manager before leave is properly authorised.

Should you be refused leave for any reason this will be fully explained to you and a written note will be given to you and recorded in your personnel file.

Should you disagree with any decision you have a right to pursue this under the Company's Grievance Procedure.

4. Amount of leave to be taken

Two weeks is the maximum that can be taken at any one time.

OR

All staff will be required to take at least two weeks at one time in order for them to have a thorough break and rest.

Prec 1 *Holidays (7)*

5. Ban on holidays during certain periods

No holidays can be taken during....................(state months). This is the Company's busy period and no member of staff will be permitted to take annual leave at this time.

6. Required holiday periods

(IN CASES WHERE THERE IS A HOLIDAY SHUTDOWN PERIOD)

All staff are required to take their annual summer holidays in the two weeks designated in July as the Company Annual Holiday Fortnight Shutdown. You will be notified of the exact dates at the beginning of each calendar year.

Because of the nature of our business and the need to keep production going up until the last day before the holiday shutdown and to start up production as soon as the holiday is over, it is a strict condition of your employment that you remain at work up to and including the day before the shutdown and return to work punctually at the normal starting time on the day that the company starts work after the holiday has finished.

It is regarded as gross misconduct, for which summary dismissal is a penalty, for any member of staff to go absent immediately before or after the holiday fortnight. In cases of genuine sickness, the Company will require satisfactory medical evidence to cover any absences immediately prior to or after the holiday shutdown and may require a second opinion. In any case, no payment will be made to any member of staff who is absent immediately prior to or after the holiday fortnight shutdown.

All staff are advised that they must ensure that any holidays or flights are booked with the requisite holiday dates in mind. No extension of time or alteration of these dates is permissible.

OR

All staff will be required to take certain days of annual leave during......(state period, e.g. Christmas through to New Year). These days vary each year and they will be notified to all members of staff in writing as soon as they are known.

PRECEDENT 2

Holiday Pay

Holiday pay is calculated on the basis of your current basic rate of pay (i.e. basic excluding any overtime, bonuses etc.).

OR

For staff whose earnings vary, your holiday pay is based on your average earnings based on the average of the twelve weeks prior to the start of your annual leave *or* based on the average pay as stated on your last P60.

There will be no payment in lieu of any holidays not taken.

PRECEDENT 3

Public and Bank Holidays

A. All Public and Bank Holidays are permitted as paid holidays in addition to your normal Holiday Entitlement. Any additional holidays will be notified to staff. If a Public or Bank Holiday falls on a Saturday or Sunday, an alternative date will be notified to all staff.

OR

B. Due to our 24-hour operation we do not close on Bank or Public Holidays. Some staff will be required to work on those days from time to time and they will be notified to employees in the usual way on their shift rotas. Any such staff will be paid at time and a half.

Any employee who works on a Bank or Public Holiday will be entitled to a day off in lieu at some later date at a mutually convenient time.

C. You will not be paid for any Bank or Public Holiday however should you be absent (other than on Company business or unless expressly authorised) immediately before or after a holiday occurs. If the absence was caused by genuine sickness, you may be paid at the entire discretion of the Company should your Manager so agree. In any event a medical certificate must be produced for any such days of sickness absence.

OR

If you should fall sick on a Bank or Public Holiday (on which you are not required to work) you will be paid your normal holiday pay and no alternative day will be given in lieu.

OR

To qualify for payment for a Bank or Public Holiday you must be and remain at work until normal finishing time on the last working day before the holiday and return to work at the normal starting time on the first working day after. Any employees who are sick on days on or surrounding a Bank or Public Holiday will have to satisfy their Manager that their sickness absence is genuine. A medical certificate by itself may not be conclusive evidence and the Company reserves the right to withhold pay in any case where there are genuine doubts and initiate disciplinary action if appropriate.

PRECEDENT 4

Holiday Entitlement

Clause 1

Your holiday entitlement is four weeks in any holiday year calculated at one and one third days per completed calendar month. For the purpose of calculating the amount of accrued holiday entitlement only complete calendar months will count. Holiday entitlement will be rounded up or down to the nearest half day.

In addition you will be entitled to one extra day's annual leave for every complete year of service up to a maximum of five extra days' leave after five complete years' service.

Clause 2 – For Senior Management

You may take holidays at your discretion by agreement with your appropriate departmental head or director. For the purposes of calculating contractual entitlement in the event of termination of employment, any payments in lieu of holiday will be based on entitlement of five weeks per annum. Details of all the rules relating to holidays can be found in the Leave Section of the Staff Handbook.

PRECEDENT 5

Holidays in Year of Commencement

(A) During your first year of service, unless otherwise agreed by your immediate superior, you will not normally be allowed to:

(i)   take any holiday before you have completed three months' service without any sickness or unauthorised leave subject to (B) below. However any new employees starting within three months of the end of the holiday year should take any holiday accrued by the end of the holiday year;

(ii)   take more holiday than you have actually accrued.

(B) If a new employee has already booked a holiday and has discussed this at his interview, then, if agreed in writing, the Company will honour this prior commitment and he will be permitted to take this without pay.

PRECEDENT 6

Special Leave

Clause 1 – Educationals

The Company reserves the right to treat 'Educationals' as part of the holiday entitlement and employees should ascertain the position in this respect with their immediate Manager before accepting an 'Educational'.

Clause 2 – Sabbaticals

1. The Company provides long serving staff with the opportunity to take a sabbatical. This applies after ten years' continuous service and can only be applied for once during employment. It is provided at the entire discretion of the Company and must be taken at a time convenient to the Company so that adequate cover can be arranged.

2. Any member of staff wishing to apply must submit their request in writing stating what are the perceived benefits for the Company and the employee, the reasons for wanting to apply and what they intend to do during this leave.

3. The Company provides......weeks/months' paid leave of absence during which time the employee is encouraged/will be expected to undertake research in a particular field/complete a paper/book/travel within or outside the UK for a complete break away from work. It is expected that the employee will be mentally and physically refreshed after this break.

4. A written report must be submitted on completion of such absence.

5. During the absence the following contractual benefits will continue to accrue and apply:
......

The following benefits will not accrue or apply:
......

6. At least......weeks' notice must be given of the intended date of return where this has not been set prior to taking the leave.

7. No other paid employment can be undertaken during this leave except with the prior written permission of your Head of Department.

Clause 3 – Religious holidays

Subject to the needs of the business and to reasonable notice being given, employees will be allowed to use their holiday entitlement to observe special religious holidays.

Clause 4 – Additional leave

Staff with at least......years' continuous service will be permitted five extra days' leave which may be taken in hourly or half daily units. This time is expected to be used for hospital, dental and doctors' appointments, domestic reasons such as waiting for delivery men, looking after a sick child, attending sports days at schools etc. Staff will be trusted to account for this time and to mark it on the holiday chart accordingly.

PRECEDENT 7

Holidays and Notice Periods

The Company reserves the right to require that any outstanding holiday entitlement is taken during any period of notice whether given by the employee or the Company. No holiday pay will be paid for any outstanding holidays untaken at the leaving date.

OR

The Company reserves the right to require the employee to serve out his notice in order to assist the smooth running of the department and effect a smooth handover. In such a case the employee will be advised that the Company cannot agree to him/her taking any outstanding leave during the notice period but will be paid accrued holiday pay in lieu.

PRECEDENT 8

Holiday Pay on Termination of Employment

If you leave the Company's employment you will receive pay for any accrued holiday outstanding. This pay will be calculated by deducting holidays already taken from the amount of holiday accrued in that holiday year to the date of leaving. A day's pay for these purposes will be calculated on the basis of the number of actual working days in a year after deducting weekends – by dividing this figure (*1/260/261ths*) into annual gross salary.

Should holiday already taken exceed entitlement, the Company shall require you to repay an amount equivalent to the number of days by which you have exceeded your entitlement. The Company reserves the right to deduct this sum from any moneys, whether final salary, bonus or commission outstanding, expenses etc., from your final salary payment.

The Company reserves the right to withhold any accrued holiday pay to which you may have been entitled should you be summarily dismissed for gross misconduct.

Holiday pay may also be withheld in whole or in part should you fail to give proper notice of termination of your contract or should you leave before the said notice has expired. In such a case your holiday pay will be reduced by the number of days' notice not worked.

In any case where the Company agrees to waive the need for you to work out your notice, the above paragraph will not apply.

PRECEDENT 9

Maternity Leave

1. 14 weeks' maternity leave

For those women taking 14 weeks' maternity leave your holiday will accrue during your leave.

2. Holiday entitlement for leavers

Should you have any holiday entitlement outstanding immediately before you stop work and you do not intend to return (or do not have the right to return to work) then we will pay any outstanding accrued holiday pay on your leaving date.

3. Status of holidays for those entitled to maximum 40 weeks

You will be advised before you start your maternity leave whether you have any outstanding holiday entitlement. You may either take this before taking your maternity leave, have it paid up as if you were a leaver or agree with your manager to carry it over and take it after you come back from your leave. The times when you take this leave must be approved and agreed with your manager.

Your holiday entitlement will continue to accrue during your maternity leave.

4. Taking holiday upon return

You may take your accrued holiday entitlement after you return, in single days if you choose, but you should arrange to do this well in advance and only with the prior agreement of your immediate manager. In any event you must return to work for a minimum uninterrupted period of four weeks before you may take any holiday entitlement.

Some staff have found the facility of single days of leave useful as it allows mothers to take a day off to be with their baby if their baby is ill, to go for a check up or just to enjoy a day off with their baby!

PRECEDENT 10

Shift Workers

Holiday entitlement is normally expressed in terms which equate 5 days' holiday with one calendar week. Where employees have a system of work involving other than 5 days in each week, the holiday entitlement will reflect the particular work pattern.

For example, in a normal case of normal holiday entitlement of 25 days, a holiday entitlement of 20 days per annum will apply to employees with a 4-day week working pattern.

PRECEDENT 11

Compassionate Leave

Limited leave with or without pay may be granted for bereavement of a close relative or for other similar reasons.

Entitlement will be at the discretion of each Head of Department and the following are guidelines only:

(1) Time off with pay will normally be granted to attend a funeral of a member of the immediate family e.g. spouse, child, parent, brother or sister.

(2) Where an employee is responsible for making the funeral arrangements up to three days' leave may be authorised.

(3) Time off for serious illness of a member of the immediate family may be granted. Whenever possible holiday entitlement should be used to cover at least part of the allocation of compassionate leave.

PRECEDENT 12

Extended Leave

1. The Company may grant up to six weeks' unpaid leave in addition to normal holiday entitlement in order to enable an employee to visit a relative in the employee's country of origin.

2. The policy is operated at the entire discretion of the Company and may be modified or withdrawn at any time.

3. The policy only applies to staff with at least......years' continuous service. The Company reserves the right to refuse an application for extended leave to anyone with a poor attendance or time-keeping record.

4. The employee will be required to provide documentary evidence of their date of return. The Company will normally require sight of the air tickets and employees are advised that they should book their return journeys at least 48 hours before the due date of return to work. This will take account of any delayed air journeys.

All employees taking extended leave will be given a letter and asked to sign it confirming their agreement to return upon the due date. The same or similar job will be provided upon their return.

Management reserves the right to discipline anyone who fails to return without an acceptable reason. In most cases illness or injury will not be accepted unless supported by a hospital report confirming treatment as an in-patient.

The employee in any such case will be required to submit to a full medical examination on their return by a doctor of the Company's choice.

Anyone caught abusing this scheme may cause the scheme to be suspended from the rest of the workforce for a period of time determined by the Company.

PRECEDENT 13

Gross Misconduct and Holiday Pay

Any person taking unauthorised leave e.g. when permission has been refused or where permission has not been sought or where the reason or the evidence is unacceptable, or immediately before or after the Company's annual fortnight shutdown, will be dealt with under the disciplinary procedure. Such conduct may be deemed in serious cases to be gross misconduct for which summary dismissal is the normal penalty. In all other cases other disciplinary action may be taken and no pay made, or pay deducted if payment has already been made.

In any case of gross misconduct, management reserves the right to withhold any accrued holiday pay.

Chapter 8

Fringe Benefits

8.1   There are a range of other benefits provided by employers which may be contractual or discretionary. They include company cars, expenses, pensions and life assurance, private medical insurance, tools, clothing and equipment, personal loans and house purchase schemes, season ticket loans, wedding gifts, long service awards, employee share option schemes, payment of telephone rental, relocation expenses, subsidised meals etc.

A recent House of Lords' decision now makes it clear that, in certain circumstances, an employer is under a contractual obligation to take reasonable steps to bring to the employee's attention, the existence of a 'valuable right' or benefit, to which he may be entitled (*Scally and others v Southern Health and Social Services Board and ors (Northern Ireland)* [*1991*] *IRLR 522* – see 8.16 below).

Company cars

8.2   It is perceived by many employees that one of the most valuable fringe benefits is a company car. If a company car is to be provided as part of the remuneration package then this should be spelt out in the contract. In some cases the car is provided on a leasing agreement. In other cases the car is purchased outright by the company. The rules relating to cars should include:

(*a*)   whether the car is a contractual item or merely provided for business needs;

(*b*)   documentary evidence from the driver required by the company;

(*c*)   the expenses paid for by the company;

(*d*)   the value and renewal policy;

(*e*)   insurance requirements;

(*f*)   return of car upon termination;

(*g*)   consequences of drinking alcohol whilst in possession of or driving a company car;

(*h*)   requirement to pay the excess in any claim.

The tax rules concerning company cars are complex. Briefly company cars are a taxable item if provided by an employer for private use, and the taxation of the car is based on both the benefit derived by the recipient and the cylinder capacity, cost and age of the car. However, from 6 April 1994 the system of taxing company cars will change from one based on engine size to one linked to the manufacturer's list price. Generally, the scale charge will be set at 35% of the list price of the car (see 'British Personnel Management', CCH Editions). There are additional tax rules for directors and higher-paid employees (as to which, see E. Slade and N. Giffin, 'Tolley's Employment Handbook').

Some companies set out clear rules about drinking alcohol whilst driving a company car. In some cases, company car drivers are prohibited from drinking alcohol and this rule may also apply where the employee uses his own car for company business. If the rules permit, an employer may reserve the right to withdraw the company car where there has been an incident of drink driving or a conviction for such an offence. It is clearly important that if employers wish to reserve this right, it must be carefully drafted in the contract or company car policy which forms part of the contract.

Some companies require an employee who is involved in, or causes, more than a specified number of car accidents to pay the excess as stated in the company car insurance policy. Similarly there may be a requirement to pay for any unreasonable damage to the car upon its return or upon termination of employment. Both cases must be clearly stated, otherwise any such deductions from wages would be unlawful under the Wages Act 1986.

Precedent 1 sets out a typical policy. **Precedent 2** sets out the terms to be specified in the contract.

Expenses

8.3   Should employees be authorised to use the expenses of the company for business purposes this should be made clear in the contract. The details of expenses policies vary from organisation to organisation and they are normally found in a separate document. A typical clause is set out in **Precedent 3**.

Pensions, death in service benefits and private medical insurance

8.4   Employers must state in writing any terms and conditions relating to pensions and pension schemes. Now both employers and employees can opt out of the State Scheme (SERPS); from 1 July 1988, the Social Security Act 1986 gave individual employees the right to contract out of SERPS by taking out their own personal pension schemes. Employers must obtain a contracting-out certificate from the Occupational Pensions Board (for more details, see 'British Personnel Management', CCH Editions). Most large employers provide an occupational pension scheme either on a contributory or non-contributory basis.

Employers in the UK must take care not to exclude part-time workers from their pension schemes particularly taking care not to specify minimum hours' requirements as eligibility for joining the pension scheme. This has been judged a breach of the equal pay principles and unlawful in *Bilka-Kaufhaus GmbH v Weber Von Hartz [1986] IRLR 317*, in which the European Court of Justice ruled that the exclusion of part-timers from the company pension scheme was unlawful discrimination and a breach of Article 119 of the Treaty of Rome which provides for equal pay for equal work.

In *Kowalska v Freie und Hansestadt Hamburg [1990] IRLR 447*, the ECJ ruled that it would be indirect sex discrimination to exclude part-timers from benefits unless this could be objectively justified. The ECJ went on to say that the disadvantaged group of workers 'must be treated in the same way and have the same system applied to them as the other workers in proportion to their hours of work'.

Employers in the future will have to look to the pension ages set in their pension scheme, access to pensions and the pension benefit, following the landmark decision of the European Court of Justice in *Barber v Guardian Royal Exchange Assurance Group [1990] IRLR 240*. Here, the ECJ has ruled that inequality in the pension ages, inequality in relation to access to the pension, and inequality in relation to pension benefits as between men and women is a breach of Article 119 of the Treaty of Rome. The implication for UK occupational pension schemes is staggering, since most occupational pension schemes set their pension ages at 65 for men and 60 for women, and other benefits are derived by reference to those ages.

In a similar case on a slightly different point with regard to equality in an occupational pension scheme, Mr Clarke is now pursuing his case before the European Court of Justice (*Clarke v Cray Precision Engineers Ltd*).

A typical clause on pensions can be seen in **Precedent 4**.

Tools and equipment

8.5   Where tools and equipment have to be provided by law (e.g. eye goggles must be provided under the Abrasive Wheels Regulations), these must be provided free of charge. [*Health and Safety at Work etc. Act 1974, s 9*]. However any other tools and equipment, uniforms etc. may be provided either free of charge, at cost price, or under any other similar arrangement.

As far as the tax position is concerned, any uniform, clothes, tools and equipment or allowances for such items may be provided and reimbursed with no tax liability for the employee, by virtue of Extra-Statutory Concession A1. The Inland Revenue do not require evidence of actual expenditure.

Other types of clothing (e.g. chauffeurs' uniforms) are not regarded as taxable benefits as long as such clothing cannot be used except when the job is being performed.

Loans

8.6 Some organisations offer personal loans, house purchase loans/ mortgage subsidy/low interest loans and season ticket loans. Clear rules must be laid down as to method of payment and eligibility. In some cases a minimum period of service must be served whilst in other cases the loan is open only to higher grades of management. Other conditions such as repayment of loan upon release from the mortgage may also need to be included.

Typical clauses appear in **Precedent 5**. The author is grateful to the publishers of 'British Personnel Management', CCH Editions, in permitting the reproduction of one of the clauses on personal loans, house purchase loans and season ticket loans.

The tax position on loans both interest free and interest bearing is set out briefly in **Precedent 5**. A model loan agreement is also set out in **Precedent 5**. For more details see Tolley's 'Taxation of Employments' and for loans to directors, see Tolley's 'Director's Handbook', Chapter 7.

Relocation expenses

8.7 It is becoming increasingly common for employers to offer relocation expenses both to new staff and existing staff whom they request or require to move. Indeed, in a difficult labour market and in an area such as the South of England where property prices are high, there may be little incentive for staff to move either away from the South or to the South unless a sufficiently attractive relocation package is provided. This may involve agreeing to purchase the house being sold or agreeing to pay for the costs of bridging the cost of the mortgage payments for the old and new house until the former house is sold.

In certain cases, the courts have been prepared to imply a term that the employer will provide reasonable relocation expenses (e.g. *United Bank Ltd v Akhtar [1989] IRLR 507*). (See Chapter 4 for more details.)

Employers who provide such expenses may commonly require the employee to sign a 'clawback' clause requiring the employee to repay some or all of the expenses should he leave the company within a certain prescribed time. Two typical clauses on relocation expenses and a 'clawback' clause are set out in **Precedent 6**.

Training expenses

8.8 Many organisations provide extensive training courses for staff. In some cases this involves considerable expenditure on the part of the company and time away from work on the part of the employee. In some cases the employee is given paid leave of absence of one or two years in order to obtain a professional qualification. In such cases some employers require a commitment of a certain period of employment following the courses. An agreement on the part of the employee to repay part of the moneys is sometimes required. Whether this is enforceable is now open to doubt. In *Electronic Data Systems v Hubble (unreported)*, Mr Hubble challenged the validity of a promissory note that he signed agreeing to repay £4,500 before undertaking an expensive training course costing the company many thousands of pounds in excess of £4,500. The case was settled out of court, so no decision has been recorded yet in relation to a private sector employer. In a previous case, *Strathclyde Regional Council v Neil [1984] IRLR 14*, Strathclyde Regional Council was successful in recovering a proportion of the costs borne by the employer for her social worker's course. The Sheriff Principal held that her written agreement to remain in their employment for a further two years, or to repay the proportion of costs corresponding to the unexpired portion of the minimum contracted period of further employment was valid and enforceable against her.

A typical clawback clause appears in **Precedent 7**.

Payment of telephone rental and installation charges

8.9   In some organisations certain staff may be provided with a telephone, with the cost of installation and rental charges paid for by the company. In most cases this applies to employees who need to be on call, staff who frequently use the telephone to transact company business at home or where the employee is a member of a sales team. Details concerning cessation of payment of the rental and other charges also need to be included.

A typical clause appears in **Precedent 8**.

Share option schemes

8.10   An increasing number of employers are offering Employee Share Option Schemes (ESOPs). There are certain tax concessions available on such schemes. There are three main type of schemes – profit sharing, savings-related share option and approved share option schemes. In respect of the latter, there is no simple standard procedure for approval by the Inland Revenue. There are complex rules relating to the granting of approval for share option schemes. Some share option schemes give a right to employees to acquire shares dependent on an employee reaching a performance target. In an interesting decision (*Inland Revenue Commissioners v Burton Group plc [1990] STC 242*), the High Court ruled that the approved share option scheme operated by the Burton Group could provide for certain adjustments to be made to the employees' rights to acquire shares in the company after the options had been granted. Prior to this decision, it was thought that for entitlement to acquire shares under options to depend on reaching subsequent performance targets was permissible, so long as the relevant conditions were clearly defined on the grant of the option. Now it has been decided that certain conditions can be imposed after the option-grant with the result that, on grant, an employee may not be in a position to ascertain how many (if any) shares he ultimately stands to acquire, nor the conditions which may apply to determine the level of entitlement.

In relation to savings-related share option schemes, there are considerable tax concessions introduced under the Finance Act 1980. Here employees and directors have an option to buy shares at a later date, fixed at a price when the option is granted from funds saved for that purpose. The shares must be bought from the proceeds of an approved SAYE savings contract with either a building society or the Department of National Savings. Employees can opt to receive money and interest gained on the proceeds of their savings contracts and need not buy shares. No income tax is payable on the options when they are granted or on any share value increase when they are used to buy the shares. The SAYE contract agrees the payment of between £10 and £100 per month for five or seven years. Tax relief is only granted on Inland Revenue approved schemes. The rules are complex and written application for approval for such schemes must be made to the Inland Revenue Technical Division, Public Enquiry Room, West Wing, Somerset House, London WC2R 1LB.

Tax relief for approved share option schemes is not dependent upon SAYE savings contracts and was introduced in the Finance Act 1984. Under these schemes, the company offers employees the option to use its own savings arrangements to buy shares. No income tax is payable on the value of the shares either at the time the option is granted or when it is exercised provided that certain conditions are satisfied including the conditions that the option is not exercised less than three or more than ten years after it was obtained and employees do not use their options to buy shares within three years of doing so under this or any other share scheme.

Effective exclusion clauses

8.11   It may be attractive for employers offering generous terms and conditions for share option schemes (or indeed any other benefits), to seek to limit their liability by contract to pay such benefits after the termination of employment. It is essential that employers draft any such clause in the contract very carefully. For example, if the clause is drafted so that the option cannot be exercised if the employee ceases to be employed 'for any reason', then if the employee is dismissed or resigns, the employee will not be able to exercise his option. This will be the case even if the employee is dismissed in breach of the contract (*Micklefield v SAC Technology Ltd [1990] IRLR 218*).

Even though an employer may try to draft a water-tight agreement, the courts will look to see whether any exclusions or waiver of liability on the part of the employer is lawful under the terms of the Unfair Contract Terms Act 1977 (UCTA).

In *Chapman v Aberdeen Construction Group plc [1991] 1 IRLR 505*, the Court of Session considered the effects of an exemption clause purporting to exclude liability under a share option scheme under which rights lapsed upon termination. The clause in the scheme provided that:

'It shall be a condition of the scheme that in the event of dismissal of a participant from employment he shall not become entitled to damages or

189

compensation or any additional damages or compensation by reason of any alteration of his rights or expectations under the scheme.'

The Court held by a majority, that the exclusion clause in the share option scheme was void since it was contrary to section 23 of UCTA. Section 23, which applies only to Scotland, renders void a term in a secondary contract which purports to exclude a right or remedy under the Act in respect of a primary contract. It was held that 'the purpose of section 23 is to prevent rights in a primary contract being cut down or extinguished by a provision in a secondary contract which could not have been achieved had the provision been incorporated in the primary contract'.

As the exclusion clause was in the secondary contract, i.e. the share option scheme, any term in that contract which purported to exclude or restrict a right or remedy arising out of the primary contract – the contract of employment – was unlawful under section 23.

In the *Micklefield* decision referred to above (which was not cited in *Chapman*), the facts were similar but the High Court treated the share option scheme as the primary rather than the secondary contract, because it was common ground between the parties that the rules of the share option scheme were incorporated into the employee's contract of employment. Thus the Court focused on section 3 of UCTA, which prevents contracting parties from excluding or restricting liability for breach of contract in England and Wales, rather than section 10, which deals with evasion by means of a secondary contract (the equivalent of section 23, mentioned above).

The Court in *Micklefield* held that section 3 of UCTA did not apply because paragraph 1(e) of Schedule 1 (which also applies only to England and Wales) excludes the application of sections 2 to 4 of the Act from any contract 'so far as it relates to the creation or transfer of securities or of any right in securities'. It is interesting to note that the exclusions in Schedule 1 do not apply to section 10 (evasion by means of a secondary contract – see above), and thus the result in *Micklefield* might have been different had the share option scheme been a secondary contract instead of being incorporated in the primary contract, i.e. the contract of employment.

Until the position is clarified by a higher authority, the possible effects of UCTA should be carefully considered by all those who draft and administer contracts of employment and fringe benefit schemes.

Wedding gifts

8.12   Several organisations (mainly those in the food manufacturing and baking industry) offer staff with a minimum period of service who are getting married, a wedding cake up to a certain fixed cost or a contribution towards the cost of their wedding cake. Where both partners are employed by the company the value may be increased.

Long service awards

8.13   It is fairly common practice for employers to make presentations for long service and to offer a gift upon retirement. Long service awards may include cash payments and/or extra holidays, a gift of the person's choice (up to a fixed limit) or a presentation of a gift chosen by the company (e.g. this may be a watch or clock).

Any cash payment is taxable but as a gift of equivalent value it is tax free (except premium bonds). A deferred award may sometimes be made after retirement or termination of employment in which case the tax will not be deducted by the company.

Other fringe benefits

8.14   There are a range of other fringe benefits which include subsidised or free meals, school fees, discount on company or other goods, use of credit cards etc. Any meals provided free are normally subject to tax as they are regarded as a taxable benefit, but there may be a relaxation of this rule in catering or food manufacturing companies. Some employers either pay the school fees for their staff or offer a substantial reduction in the fees where the employee is a teacher at the school which the child attends. See the House of Lords' decision in *Pepper v Hart [1993] IRLR 33* reviewed at 5.20 'Pay' for the tax implications of the payment of reduced school fees and other free or discounted benefits provided by an employer.

Some companies provide management staff with a company discount card which entitles the employee to a discount on those goods or services for private use. Hotel companies may commonly provide this benefit and a typical discount may be in the range of 10% on the total bill. A typical policy is contained in **Precedent 9**.

Contractual versus discretionary benefits

8.15   Where contractual benefits are provided, failure to provide them or compensate for their loss during a notice period will be breach of contract for which the employee may sue either in the county court or High Court. In breach of contract claims, loss of discretionary fringe benefits will not be recovered. In contrast, in unfair dismissal claims before tribunals, compensation for loss of fringe benefits may be awarded (*Norton Tool Co Ltd v Tewson [1972] IRLR 86*). It may be a sensible form of protection from any action for breach of contract to provide that certain benefits are discretionary only, particularly if the employer wishes to reserve the power to modify or withdraw the benefit.

Implied obligation on employers to inform staff about benefits

8.16   The House of Lords held in *Scally and ors v Southern Health and Social Services Board and ors (Northern Ireland) [1991] IRLR 522* that the employer had breached his implied duty at common law arising out of the contract of employment in that he had failed adequately to notify employees of their rights and benefits. The Law Lords held that there was a contractual obligation owed by an employer to an employee to take reasonable steps to inform him of a 'valuable right'. The obligation arises when three conditions are satisfied:

(1)   where the individual has not negotiated his terms and conditions of employment on an individual basis but they have been agreed in the course of negotiations between the employer and a trade union;

(2)   where there is a valuable right which is however contingent upon the employee taking certain action; and

(3)   where it is not realistic to expect the individual employee to know the details of these terms and conditions unless they are drawn to his attention.

In *Scally*, the employer had published a document in 1975 called 'Easy to Read Guide to Improved Health and Personal Social Services Superannuation for Northern Ireland' and a further leaflet 'SDT' which gave additional information about purchasing added years of pension entitlement. Strangely, but perhaps not unusually, these documents remained firmly with Unit General Managers and Personnel Departments and were not actually passed to staff who were affected by these changes to their pensions!

The Lords ruled that the law provided no means of ensuring that the intended beneficiaries of the opportunity to buy added years became aware of it, so that it would be a matter of chance whether or not any member of staff was able to take advantage of the new benefit. It was unrealistic to expect that young doctors embarking upon a career in the health service should appreciate the necessity to enquire into the details of the superannuation scheme to which they were contributors in order to be in a position to enjoy its benefits. It followed that there must be an implied obligation on either the employing authority or the Department of Health to take reasonable steps to bring the relevant provisions to the notice of employees in time to avail themselves of the opportunity to buy added years if they decided to do so.

The court held, *obiter*, that there was probably a distinction between those terms which the employer offered in the contract of employment and those terms which arise within a personal pension plan taken out by an individual employee. In such a case the employer would not be under any obligation to ensure that the employee was aware of and fully understood the terms of the Pension Policy.

Implications for employers

8.17   The judgment in *Scally* will apply not only to employers who negotiate with trade unions and other representative bodies, but also to those who do not negotiate on an individual basis and instead incorporate terms and conditions from lengthy staff handbooks and personnel manuals into the contract of employment.

Although this case was concerned specifically with pension rights, the principles will apply equally to sick pay schemes, Permanent Health Insurance Schemes, and all other benefits, where the employee must take some sort of action in order to avail himself of the benefits. The corollary may also be true – that there is an obligation on the employer to point out sanctions and penalties such as changes in the disciplinary rules or new rules.

Key Points

- Ensure that the contract defines whether a benefit is a contractual entitlement or a discretionary benefit.

- Ensure that company car policies form part of the employee's contract and that clear guidance is laid down concerning type of car and additional items provided, insurance, expenses, renewal and conditions for its return.

- If relocation expenses are to be paid, define what expenses are to be paid and whether there is to be a clawback agreement requiring repayment if the employee leaves the Company within a defined period.

- If expensive training courses are to be provided, thought should be given to similar clawback clauses.

- If telephone installation or expenses are to be paid, it is essential to spell out in what circumstances such expenses are paid and when they may be withdrawn.

- Any share option schemes need to be carefully drawn up by a tax lawyer!

PRECEDENT 1

Company Cars

1. Provision of company cars

You will have been notified in your offer letter whether you are entitled to a company car. The following policy applies:

(a) Business needs

A company car may be provided to you in accordance with the Company's business needs on the basis of the employee's business mileage which must be not less than 5,000 miles a year.

(b) Irrespective of business mileage

A company car may be provided, irrespective of business mileage for Executives on Grades......and above.

2. Schedule of cars

The range of cars available is related to the individual's grades as follows:

(Specify grades)

3. Factory fitted options and dealer fitted extras

(Specify who can order what, e.g. radio, sunshine roof, metallic paint, automatic transmission etc.)

4. Retention period

(Specify what the retention periods are in accordance with the Grade of the car and mileage and job change.)

5. Provision of fuel

Scheme A

The employee will be responsible for purchasing petrol and oil and the cost is reclaimed through petty cash according to the laid down rate. Daily travelling between home and normal place of work is defined as private mileage.

Prec 1 *Fringe Benefits (8)*

Scheme B

The employee is taxed on the benefit of the car and car fuel and the Company issues the employee with a credit card for all charges of petrol and fuel used in the company car in the UK and overseas for business or private use. No mileage allowance is payable for business journeys.

6. Company car expenses

(Specify whether:

(a) washing, garaging, overnight parking are chargeable expenses;

(b) it is necessary to obtain authority for use abroad;

(c) fines for parking are paid by the Company.)

7. Insurance

(Specify whether the insurance covers:

(a) claims by third parties for property damage and personal injury;

(b) costs of defending any claims;

(c) other drivers apart from the employee;

(d) accident damage to the car;

(e) trailers;

(f) loss or damage to property;

(g) legal costs of defending a charge of manslaughter or reckless driving.)

8. Accident procedure

(Specify)

9. Use of car abroad

(Specify)

10. Authorisation of other drivers

(Specify)

11. Hire of cars

(Specify whether there are any special rates when hiring a car for personal use.)

12. Withdrawal of company cars

Where an individual ceases to be eligible for a car allocated on the basis of business need, as a result of a change of job or changes in the nature of the job, the car may be retained until the next normal change-out when it will not be replaced. The individual may be given the option to purchase the car at the change-out at the discretion of the Executive in charge.

PRECEDENT 2

Company Car – Terms in the Contract

If you are entitled to receive a car you will be notified of this in your offer letter. The car is provided in accordance with the Company Car Policy which may be amended from time to time. The car is provided to you on condition that you have and retain a valid full UK driving licence.

You are required to produce to the Company's insurance department a copy of your driving licence and those of any members of your family eligible to drive the car. The Company Group Insurance Policy will cover you, your spouse and any children provided that you and they all have a valid, clean, UK driving licence. Any convictions for driving offences or endorsements must be disclosed to the Insurance Departments (other than 'spent' convictions) together with details of any claims already made in connection with any motor accident in the last ten years.

The Company will meet the costs of repair, tax and the insurance premium of the car together with any petrol.

The Company reserves the right to institute any rules which are reasonable relating to cars and may change the rules at any time. The Company may also withdraw the car at any time or amend the value of the car permitted at any time. Due written notice will be given to you of any such changes.

Should your employment terminate for whatever reason, the Company reserves the right to make a cash allowance in lieu of the use of the car during the notice period. The car will have to be returned upon leaving the Company or on any date determined by the Company in a clean and proper condition. The Company reserves the right to alter or withdraw any cash allowance to reflect the condition of the car or the need for any repairs.

You are expected to act at all times with the utmost care when driving your company car. You are not expected to drink alcohol at any time during your working day or whilst on Company business if you are driving either a company car or your own car. Soft drinks are always available either at lunchtime or at a social function arranged by the Company or for a work colleague (birthday, leaving party etc.).

If you are charged or convicted of any drink driving offence whilst driving a company car, the Company may at its discretion withdraw the car for any period of time it thinks fit. This provision may also apply to any case where you are unfit to drive through the consumption of alcohol whether or not you have been charged by the police.

Should you be responsible for more than......motor accidents in any twelve-month period, the Company may require you to pay the excess as stated in the Company's Car Insurance Policy in respect of any claim made against the

Company. This may be by deduction from your wages (or final salary) or any other method deemed acceptable to the Company.

In any case where the Company deems fit, should you be responsible for any unnecessary damage to the car (other than normal wear and tear), whether to the outside or to the inside or the fabric or additional extras fitted to the car, you will be required to repay to the Company any or all expenses required to repair the said damage. This may be by deduction from your wages (or final salary) or any other method deemed acceptable to the Company.

PRECEDENT 3

Expenses

You will be reimbursed all reasonable expenses relating to travel, accommodation, entertainment and other out-of-pocket expenses incurred on authorised Company business upon production of all reasonable receipts in accordance with the Company's Travel and Entertainments Policy.

PRECEDENT 4

Pension, Life Insurance, Long Term Disability and Medical Insurance Plans

The Company operates a voluntary, non-contributory Pension and Life Insurance Scheme for all employees over the age of 25. There is a Contracting-Out Certificate in force in respect of all employees covered in this Scheme. An explanatory booklet entitled 'Pensions and Long Term Disability Plans' is given to you on engagement. It is assumed that all employees over the age of 25 wish to participate in the Scheme unless Personnel are notified to the contrary. You will also be covered by a Long Term Disability Plan.

The rules on eligibility and benefit etc. for the Pension, Life Insurance and Long Term Disability Plans are governed exclusively by formal documents which are available for inspection in the Personnel Division.

The Company reserves the right to withdraw or amend any of the rules or benefits of the Schemes at any time and reserves the right to terminate any employee's participation in the Schemes at any time.

The Company also has a Medical Insurance Scheme which is paid for by the Company. The Scheme operates on the terms and conditions which are in force from time to time. The Company reserves the right at any time to amend or withdraw the Schemes or vary the scale or level of benefit currently in force and may at its entire discretion terminate any employee's participation in the Scheme.

PRECEDENT 5

Policy of Company A

House Purchase Loans/Low Interest Loans/Mortgage Subsidy

The Company provides house purchase loans to its employees provided that at the time they seek the loan they have at least one year's service with the Company, have reached 25 years of age and an appropriate management grade.

The loan which will not be for more than 95% of the purchase price or valuation, whichever is the less, will be up to four times current salary to a maximum of £......

Interest will be repayable at 5% per annum and repayment will be made monthly. The full loan must be covered by an endowment assurance assigned to the Company with a maturity date no later than normal retirement.

Termination of subsidy

In the event of the employee ceasing to be a registered mortgagee (either sole or joint) of the property for which this subsidy applies, the employee agrees to inform the appropriate Personnel Officer in the Company immediately. The payment of this mortgage subsidy will cease upon removal of the employee's name from the mortgage documents.

The subsidy is made on the understanding that should the employee cease to be a registered mortgagee and fail to inform the Company upon the terms above, the employee will be liable to repay the difference between the mortgage subsidy and the full commercial rate from the relevant date and may render himself liable to serious disciplinary action.

Should the employee remain responsible for paying the relevant mortgage and should he be able to produce documentary evidence of such payments to the satisfaction of the Company, the Company may at its entire discretion continue to make the employee the subsidy on the said mortgage.

OR

Should any employee in receipt of the subsidy be able to show to the satisfaction of the Bank that they are making an actual contribution to the mortgage despite not being the formal mortgagee, the Bank at its entire discretion may continue to pay the subsidy in cases where severe hardship may ensue.

Termination of employment

If the employee resigns, immediate repayment must be made of any outstanding loan. However, whilst alternative finance is sought, loan repayments may continue at the existing market rates.

Personal loans

Loans will be granted to employees with at least six months' service to enable them to purchase a car or other vehicle. Employees may borrow up to 50% of the cost of the vehicle up to a maximum of £...... Interest will be chargeable at 2% and the loan repayable by 24 equal deductions from pay.

Season ticket loans

Staff with at least six months' service may have an interest-free loan from the Company for the cost of an annual, six-monthly or monthly season ticket provided that the cost is not less than £......in annual terms and up to a maximum of 20% of annual salary or £2,000 whichever is the less. Repayment will be in ten monthly instalments for annual tickets (five months for half-yearly tickets).

Policy of Company B

All loan arrangements must be authorised by the Executive in charge and a loan agreement (see below) must be signed in advance of any loan being made.

1. Domestic loans

(a) Loans for domestic purposes may be made up to a maximum of £1,000 on the authority of the Executive in Charge. Authority may be delegated to immediate subordinates for domestic loans not exceeding £250.

(b) Repayment may be spread evenly in weekly/monthly instalments over a period not exceeding five years.

(c) The rate of interest on new loans will be...... However this rate may change from time to time and the Company reserves the right to change the rate of interest as it deems fit.

The first £250 of any loan may be interest free.

2. Starters loans

Loans to avoid hardship may be made to new employees and to those who change from weekly to monthly pay.

(a) Executives in charge or their authorised nominee may grant such loans.

(b) Interest at......rate will normally be charged.

(c) For new employees on weekly pay, a loan of up to one week's net pay may be granted. Such loans are to be repaid within twelve weeks. For new employees on monthly pay, a loan of up to two weeks' net pay may be granted after the employee has worked two weeks. Such loans are to be repaid within six months.

For employees changing from weekly to monthly pay, a loan of up to the net amount that would otherwise have been received between the last weekly payment and the first monthly payment may be granted. Such loans are to be repaid within twelve weeks.

Tax position of interest free loans

The tax position of interest free loans is as follows:

1. Interest free loans normally confer a taxable benefit upon the recipient calculated by reference to an official deemed rate of interest.

2. No such benefit arises in the following circumstances:

(a)   loans made to employees other than 'higher paid' employees or directors;

(b)   cases where deemed interest amounts in the year to less than £300 or if tax relief would have been given had the interest been paid by the employee (1993/94);

(c)   where a company housing loan is provided to an employee whose income does not exceed the basic rate band and that loan taken together with other loans from all other sources does not exceed £30,000 (it should be noted that as mortgage interest is only relieved at the basic rate, a higher rate taxpayer will pay tax at 15% on the interest on the first £30,000 to the extent that income exceeds the basic rate band) (1993/94);

(d)   where upon a change of residence resulting from the commencement of new employment, or an alteration of duties in the existing employment or from an alteration of the place where such duties are normally to be performed, a bridging loan is provided to help finance the gap between the purchase of a new home and the sale of the old home, but only to the extent that any unused part of the £8,000 exemption is available (as computed by a statutory formula) after deduction of all other items in the relocation package (1993/94); and

(e)   where bridging loan expenses are not provided under a relocation package consequent upon a company initiated change of residence and the loan is raised at least partly because of a gap between the purchase of the new residence and the sale of the old residence and to the extent that the loan does not exceed the market value of the interest in the former residence and is not used in redeeming a loan on the former residence or acquiring the new residence. Such expenses are, like (d) above, only exempt up the £8,000 ceiling taking into account all other eligible expenses (1993/94).

Interest bearing loans

Where a company charges interest it should be paid gross and not under deduction of tax. The borrower should be able to claim income tax relief in respect of housing and bridging loans subject to the limit set by the Inland Revenue.

Model Loan Agreement

EMPLOYEE LOAN FORM (To be used for domestic and starters loans only)

TO: .... (name of employing company)
FROM: .... (name, address and payroll number
.... of employee)
....

I hereby acknowledge that a .... (enter type of loan) has been advanced to me by the Company on the following conditions:

(1)   The loan is interest free and I undertake to repay the loan at £......per week/per month* by deductions from my wages/salary* until the full amount is repaid to the Company.

(2)   The loan is subject to the official rate of interest on beneficial loans which is currently......%. However this rate may change from time to time and the Company reserves the right to change the rate of interest as it may deem appropriate. I undertake to repay the loan at £......plus interest due on the reducing balance by weekly/monthly* deductions from my wages/salary* until the full amount is repaid to the Company.

Any outstanding amount of loan is repayable in full on termination of my employment and may be deducted from my final wages/salary*.

I agree to the above terms and conditions and authorise deductions as detailed above to be made from my wages/salary* payments made to me by the Company.

Signature .... Date.........

Delete as appropriate.

PRECEDENT 6

Relocation Expenses

Relocation expenses are only payable where an existing employee is required by the Company to move home or a new employee is granted such expenses by the Executive in charge.

These may include:

(a) *Professional fees* – legal, Building Society and estate agent fees and disbursements including private survey fees where appropriate.

(b) *Removal and storage and insurance* costs should this be necessary.

(c) *Visits* to new location – for employee and immediate family in order to find suitable housing – the number of visits to be agreed with Executive in Charge.

(d) *Travelling or temporary accommodation* if necessary.

(e) *Telephone installation* (except where employee does not previously have a telephone).

(f) *Disturbance allowance* – against receipts for costs of alterations of curtains, carpets, household equipment etc. Total allowances not to exceed 15% of basic annual gross salary at the time of taking up the new appointment. Receipts must be kept for at least six years in case they are required for Inland Revenue purposes.

(g) *Additional housing cost allowance (AHCA) for move to higher cost housing area* – paid only to staff required by the Company to move to an area where housing costs are higher than in the present location. To assist with added mortgage costs the difference between the former and current mortgage will be paid in full in the first year and reduced by one fifth in each of the next four years. Within Inland Revenue limits, which vary from time to time, some or all of this allowance is tax free. The AHCA is not pensionable.

Agreement To Repay Relocation Expenses

(Headed notepaper)
Date

I, ...(name of employee), being employed by ABC plc, having received relocation expenses of £XXXX (give details of all items and amounts provided), do hereby agree and undertake to remain in the service of the Company for a minimum period of ......(months/years) following the date of my relocation* or payment of such moneys*. In the event of my voluntarily leaving the Company's service before the expiry of the said minimum period, I undertake to refund to the Company an amount proportionate to the unexpired portion of the contracted minimum period of service whether this be by way of deduction from my final salary or any other moneys payable or paid upon termination of my employment or by any method acceptable to the Company.

Signed

....
(Employee)

Insert whichever is appropriate.

PRECEDENT 7

Agreement for Repayment of Expenses, Grant etc. for Training Course

(Headed notepaper)
Date

I, ...(name of employee), being employed by ABC plc, in consideration for being granted grants, expenses etc. in accordance with the Company's training and career development policy, to undertake an appropriate course of studies, do hereby agree and undertake to remain in the service of the Company for a minimum period of......(months/years) following the completion of my course. In the event of my voluntarily leaving the Company's service before the expiry of the said minimum period (or terminating my studies before completing the course), I undertake to refund to the Company an amount proportionate to the unexpired portion of the contracted minimum period of service calculated on the basis of:

(a) the salary, superannuation and National Insurance Contributions in respect of authorised leave of absence for attendance at the classes/course;

(b) the course fees for the full course of studies;

(c) all examination fees;

(d) grants towards the cost of books and materials paid to me or on my behalf by the Company while undertaking the course of studies;

(e) all other expenses paid in connection thereto, including travel expenses.

I agree to my employer deducting the said sums from my final salary or any outstanding moneys due to me.

Signed

....
(Employee)

PRECEDENT 8

Telephone Installation and Rental Charges

The Company will pay the rental charges for one telephone at an employee's home under certain circumstances.

This policy will apply to:

(1) where there may be an urgent requirement, specified in a written procedure, that under certain circumstances an employee must be contacted at home in order to avert possible danger to Company personnel, products or equipment,

(2) to staff who as part of their job specification are frequently required to use the telephone to transact Company business at home, or

(3) where the employee is a member of a sales team.

The Company will not be responsible for any tax liability on the employee by reason of the Company agreeing to reimburse telephone expenses.

The cost of all calls made on Company business will be reimbursed by the Company. Claims for reimbursement must be authorised by the employee's superior.

Those costs borne by the Company will only apply to those not already on the telephone prior to the identification of the Company requirement or those relocating and eligible for Company expenses.

Costs will only include expenses for standard British Telecom equipment.

Those currently receiving payment for their telephone rental who do not meet the criteria will be given twelve months' notice of termination of the arrangement and on termination will receive a taxable sum equivalent to the gross of twelve months' rental. Should the rental by then have been declared taxable income, a sum equivalent to the actual estimated cost of the rental only will be paid.

In the event of the employee moving to a post not qualifying for this payment, it will cease after presentation of the British Telecom bill nearest to the date of transfer.

PRECEDENT 9

Personal Discount Card

Eligibility

All management grades over X are eligible to a Company Personal Discount Card which currently entitles them to a discount of 25% on meals, refreshments and hotel accommodation in any of the Company's hotels and restaurants.

Terms

A list of scheduled establishments is available from........These terms apply only to services provided by the establishment in the normal course of business and in public rooms. They are normally limited in the case of a restaurant to parties of no more than ten including the card holder and in the case of hotel accommodation to the card holder and immediate family who live in the home. Other arrangements may be possible and can be arranged with the manager of the establishment.

Use of credit card

The card is available for business and personal use but in all cases the sum net discount is charged to the personal account of the individual concerned. Should the expense be incurred for business purposes the individual should recover the net amount as personal expenses through petty cash.

Control of credit cards

Only Executives in Charge may authorise the provision of credit cards and details of the rules for use will be issued by......Department.

Chapter 9

Competition, Confidentiality and Restrictive Covenants

During the employment

Working in competition

9.1   Employees are under a duty to work honestly, faithfully and loyally for their employer and there is an implied term in their contract that they will not work in competition or otherwise for anyone else or for themselves during their working hours (*Beloff v Pressdram Ltd [1973] 1 All ER 241; Nova Plastics Ltd v Froggatt [1982] IRLR 246*). However it is not possible to prevent an employee from undertaking any employment outside working hours other than any in competition with the primary employer. In *Hivac Ltd v Park Royal Scientific Instruments Ltd [1946] Ch 169* employees of a leading hearing aid manufacturer worked for a rival firm on their day off. Here, their primary employer was entitled to an injunction to stop them doing so, since their knowledge of the manufacturing process would inevitably aid the rival firm and damage the primary employer's business.

Just because an employee has a full-time job, he cannot be prevented from undertaking other paid employment but where this other employment prevents him from adequately performing his duties with the primary employer, an employer may wish to restrict outside working. Some employers require advance knowledge of any outside business interests and consider it to be a breach of contract and good faith should disclosures not be made.

Conflict of interest/Declaration of interests

9.2   In certain jobs in central and local government and in other organisations such as housing associations, there may be a requirement to declare any outside interests and a prohibition on any outside interests which cause a conflict of interest. In other cases, there may be a prohibition on the use by any employee of a contractor or supplier used by the employer because of any possible influence etc.

Some organisations also prohibit the acceptance of any (or any other than token) gifts or hospitality from any supplier, contractor etc.

To sum up, in the absence of contractual terms concerning activities outside working hours, an employee must not:

(1)   engage in any spare time activity which places him *in competition* with his employer – e.g. he should not attempt to compete with his employer for the same contracts, or design or supply products which he has designed or supplied for his employer;

(2)   use or disclose any of his employer's trade secrets or confidential information or put himself in a position where he is likely to do so.

Precedents 1 and **2** cover all these issues.

Duty of confidence – confidential information

9.3   The duty to keep the information of an employer confidential whilst the employee is in employment comes within the implied duty of good faith. When an employee leaves the employment, he is free to use the skills and knowledge gained in his former employment save his former employer's trade secrets. Information, even confidential information, which the employee has learnt and remembered will not be protected *after* employment unless it can properly be termed a trade secret. Ex-employees will be free to use or disclose to others any confidential information other than trade secrets which they take away in their head. But is is strictly forbidden to make or copy lists of information such as the employer's customers for use after the employment ends. Neither is it permissible deliberately to memorise such lists even though there is no implied restriction on an ex-employee from canvassing or doing business with customers of the former employer. 'This', said one judge, 'is no more than fair and honourable dealing'. (*Robb v Green [1895] 2 QB 315*).

There are three categories of information, only the third of which can be properly protected from disclosure or misuse *after* the employment has ended (*Faccenda Chicken Ltd v Fowler [1984] IRLR 61 at 65-66* – High Court; this decision was upheld by the Court of Appeal, as to which see 9.5 below).

(*a*)   Information of a trivial character or information which is easily accessible from public sources of information e.g. a published patent specification. This cannot be reasonably regarded as confidential at all.

(*b*)   Confidential information which must be kept confidential by an employee during his employment. This is information which he has been told is confidential or which is obviously so from its nature. Once learned it necessarily remains in his head and becomes part of his own skill and knowledge. So long as his employment continues he cannot use or disclose it other than for his employer's business. But when he is no longer in the same service, the law allows him to use his full skill and knowledge for his own benefit in competition with his former employer.

(*c*)   Specific trade secrets so confidential that even though they may necessarily have been learned by heart and even though the employee may have left the employer's service, they cannot lawfully be used for anyone's benefit other than the employer's.

The High Court suggested that employers could protect information which was not a trade secret or its equivalent, after the employee had left the employment, by means of a restrictive covenant. The Court of Appeal rejected this view but held that even where the employer had included a restrictive covenant, in the context of employment, the courts will not enforce it 'unless the protection sought is reasonably necessary to protect a trade secret or to prevent some personal influence over customers being abused in order to entice them away'. (*Faccenda Chicken Ltd v Fowler [1986] IRLR 69* at 76).

Drafting the clauses – finding the 'Golden Nuggets'

9.4   Great care must be taken when drafting confidentiality clauses, non-competition clauses and restrictive covenants in order that they are not struck out for uncertainty or on the grounds that they are too wide or too imprecise. Should all restrictions of this nature be covered in a series of sub-clauses, there is a real danger that if one sub-clause fails, the court would strike out the whole of the clause and all the other sub-clauses would fall.

Anyone drafting these clauses may wish to draft entirely separate clauses covering confidentiality, non-competition, non-solicitation, non-enticement and restraint of trade. Lord Dervaird in *Hinton & Higgs (UK) Ltd v Murphy and Valentine [1989] IRLR 519* gave some useful guidance to drafters (see 9.19 below 'Severing the clauses').

Lord Dervaird went on to explain why a preamble allowing the deletion of a clause found by the court to be unreasonable was such a vital protection in such cases:

'Although the courts will not make contracts for the parties, in the present case the parties themselves had agreed in advance that they would accept as continuing to bind them such part of the arrangements which they had made as the court finds by deletion only to be alterations which permit the restriction to be regarded as reasonable. Since that involved not rewriting the contract but selecting that version of it which the parties *inter alia* had made with each other and enabling the bargain so modified to stand, there was no reason why the court should refuse to perform that role.'

It is extremely important for confidentiality clauses to be confined to restricting the use and disclosure after employment of the company's trade secrets. These have been called the '*golden nuggets*' and as such should be clearly illustrated in the body of any such clauses. Clear, precise and detailed instructions will have to be taken from clients with regard to particular employees as the 'golden nuggets' of which they have knowledge, will differ depending upon the person involved. It is not sensible to leave it to any court to identify which information can properly be classified as 'trade secrets'.

Confidentiality clauses

Trade secrets

9.5   The courts will only prevent an ex-employee from using or disclosing information if the information can properly be classed as a 'trade secret' or is of such a highly confidential nature as to require the same protection as a trade secret. Examples of information which has been held to be confidential and properly belonging to the employer include sources of supply, lists of customers, price lists, costings, tables of stress factors of various components manufactured by the company, and the make-up of next season's mail order catalogue.

There is some useful judicial guidance as to what are trade secrets and what can be properly protected after the employment has ended. In *Thomas Marshall (Exports) Ltd v Guinle [1978] IRLR 174*, the court put forward a series of tests which if satisfied could convince a court that the information being sought to be protected was confidential:

—   Does the owner believe disclosures would be injurious to himself or advantageous to rivals or others?

—   Does the owner believe that it is still confidential (that it has not already become public knowledge)?

—   Are these beliefs reasonable?

—   The information must be judged in the light of the practices of the particular trade or industry.

In *Printers and Finishers Ltd v Holloway (No 2) [1964] 3 All ER 731*, the test of confidentiality was put like this:

'The test is whether a man of average intelligence and honesty would think that there is anything improper in putting his memory of the matters in question at the disposal of his new employers.'

In *Faccenda Chicken Ltd v Fowler [1986] IRLR 69*, the Court of Appeal stated that although there was no general definition of a trade secret, certain matters such as secret manufacturing processes, chemical formulae, designs or special methods of construction clearly fell within the definition.

The Court of Appeal stated that certain factors would influence any court in deciding whether or not the defendant had knowledge of any trade secrets, which the court would restrain him from using or disclosing. These are as follows:

(*a*)   The nature of the employment – whether the employee was sufficiently senior to handle confidential material in the normal course of his employment. Here the employee can be expected to realise its sensitive nature to a greater extent than if he were employed in a more junior role and only seldom had access to confidential material.

(*b*)   The nature of the information itself – one factor will be whether or not the information is restricted to only a few employees.

(*c*)   Whether the employer has impressed upon the employee the sensitivity and confidential nature of the information.

(*d*)   Whether the information can be easily isolated from other information which the employee is free to use or disclose. The fact that the alleged confidential information is part of a package and that the remainder of the package is not confidential is likely to throw light on whether the information in question is really a trade secret.

The courts now appear to take a less rigid approach and have concluded that trade secrets, in today's world of multinational business with worldwide interests, may also include highly confidential information of a non-technical or non-scientific nature. Employers are entitled to have such information protected – albeit for a limited period of time after the employee has left the employment.

In *Lansing Linde v Kerr [1991] IRLR 80*, Staughton LJ stated, as summarised in the headnote, that:

'A trade secret is information used in a trade or business which, if disclosed to a competitor, would be liable to cause real or significant damage to the owner of the secret. In addition, the owner must limit the dissemination of it or at least not encourage or permit widespread publication. Trade secrets can thus include not only secret formulae for the manufacture of products but also the names of customers and the goods they buy.'

Butler-Sloss LJ stated that:

'In the age of multinational businesses and worldwide business interests, information may be held by very senior executives which, in the hands of competitors, might cause considerable harm to the companies employing them. "Trade secrets" has to be interpreted in the wider context of highly confidential information of a non-technical or non-scientific nature, which may come within the ambit of information the employer is entitled to have protected, albeit for a limited period.'

Confidential information and motive of employer

9.6   Some employers may believe that items of information such as business plans cannot be used by staff after they have left the employment, such information being in the nature of a 'trade secret'. However the courts may well hold that such information does not of itself constitute a 'trade secret' and as such cannot be restrained from use after the employee has left the employment. In deciding whether or not to grant an injunction, the courts will also examine the motive of the employer in seeking the injunction. Employers are not entitled to protect themselves from competition, even from former employees.

In one case, the High Court ruled that a corporation was not entitled to prevent former employees from using confidential information in a business plan, because the information for which protection was sought was not sufficiently confidential to require the same protection as a 'trade secret' (*Berkeley Administration Inc and Ors v Mc Clelland and Ors [1990] Fleet Street Reports 505*). In this case dicta in the *Faccenda Chicken* case (9.5 above) was approved and followed.

In the *Berkeley Administration* case, a group of companies known as Cheque Point Group were the market leaders in the field of independent bureaux de change. In 1988, two employees, M and C, who had been employed by the Group in senior positions (M was a lawyer) were dismissed. After their dismissals they drafted a business plan to set up a rival company. On the basis of the projections in this business plan, they hoped to raise venture capital. Shortly afterwards they invited A, who was employed by the Group to join them and later recruited two more former colleagues. The Group then brought legal action against the ex-employees alleging they had wrongfully misused the confidential contents of a business plan and financial projections known as the 'Blue Book'.

The Group contended that their business plan was confidential; that the items relied on were sufficiently confidential to be protected when the employees ceased to work for the Group; that it could be inferred from alleged similarities appearing in the respective business plans that the employees had used those items of information. The information in question was allegedly derived from an Appendix in the Blue Book, namely:

(*a*)   the average operating profit per bureau de change;

(*b*)   the average profit in the first year of operation as a percentage of a subsequent year's profit;

(*c*)   the average capital cost per bureau;

(*d*)   the average number of annual transactions per bureau; and

(*e*)   the average value of each transaction.

The court held that the alleged similarities were not real and that only through a tortuous series of mathematical calculations could the employer achieve any degree of similarity between the two business projections. There was no evidence that the employees had used the information in the Blue Book for their own financial projection.

None of the information was sufficiently confidential to come within the criteria laid down in the *Faccenda Chicken* case (above). For an implied obligation of confidentiality, all the circumstances of the case needed to be taken into account, i.e.:

(1)   Nature of the employment – whether the employee habitually handles confidential material; if he does then he owes a higher duty of confidentiality.

216

(2)   The nature of the information itself.

(3)   Whether the employer has impressed on the employee the confidential nature of the information.

(4)   The extent to which the information can be easily isolated from other information the employee is free to use.

The Blue Book had limited access and each copy was numbered and a record made of every person who had a copy. Nevertheless the court held that the information was not sufficiently confidential to merit protection.

The employees had on their own admission relied on information from the Group but not from the Blue Book in order to assess the average number of transactions per bureau de change. C who had drawn up the business plan had divided the number of customers by the number of the Group's bureaux which were in operation at the end of 1987. The Group had announced the number of customers they had in a Press advertisement and the number of bureaux could hardly be held to be confidential. Nor could the capital cost per bureau be held to be confidential. Anyone with experience could assess what kind of location was necessary and then make enquiries of suitable estate agents. This was not confidential information even if it had come from within the Group. Assessing the average value per customer transaction came as a result of their general knowledge of the bureau de change business and was acquired by persons working in the business.

Precedent 2 covers confidentiality clauses, and also sets out a confidentiality agreement for third parties with whom an agreement has been made, and to whom confidential information is to be disclosed. Two confidentiality agreements for existing staff can be found in **Precedent 6**.

Duty to disclose wrongdoings of others

9.7   As a converse to this issue, whether or not there is any duty upon employees to disclose, in this case, the wrongdoings of others including their colleagues, superiors or even the company itself, will depend either upon the status of the employee – only directors are under a fiduciary duty to disclose the wrongdoings of others even if this implicates themselves (*Sybron Corporation v Rochem Ltd [1983] IRLR 253*) – or upon the existence of an express clause on this point. This is covered in Chapter 12 and **Precedent 1** of that chapter.

Defining the confidential information in the agreement

9.8   There is far more chance of a confidentiality agreement being enforceable if the agreement expressly defines the types of confidential information which are covered by the agreement. In some cases, express restrictions on disclosure of confidential information may prevent an employee from working for a rival employer where there is real possibility of disclosure of confidential information which could seriously harm the employer's business (although the courts have concluded that a more appropriate form of restriction would be a restrictive covenant – see below).

One example of such a case, *Norbrook Laboratories Ltd v Smyth (30 September 1986, High Court (NI))*, involved a research chemist, Mr Smyth, working for Norbrook Laboratories who had been testing the company's products. He sat on a committee in which the results of new products were discussed. In particular he had been dealing with a new drug called 'Amalycin'. Their main rivals, Pfizers, had complained about its safety to the US Federal Drugs Administration. Pfizers then offered Mr Smyth a job with them. Norbrook sought an injunction to enforce a confidentiality agreement whereby he agreed not to work, for a year after his employment ended, in any employment in which he could be 'required or expected to use or disclose confidential information' that he had acquired in the course of his employment. The agreement then contained a detailed clause defining the types of confidential information which were covered. The judge, in granting the injunction, held that he 'could not see anything in the definition of confidential information to justify the conclusion that the agreement attempted to restrain Mr Smyth from using his general know-how'.

The exact extent of the restriction must be carefully spelt out. Words such as 'work for' will be given a sensible meaning (*Hinton & Higgs* (9.4 above)). 'It must' stated Lord Dervaird, 'be related to the type of work which the employer performed'. This will include both working for another rival employer and working as a sole trader or independent consultant.

The scope of all such clauses will be strictly interpreted. Thus in *WAC Ltd v Whitlock [1990] IRLR 23*, where a clause prevented any shareholder from carrying on any competing business for two years after they ceased holding shares, the court held it did not cover a shareholder who had become a *director* of a rival firm. This was not 'carrying on' a competing business.

Here the Court of Session held:

> 'The clause in question prohibited a shareholder from personally carrying on business in competition with the company but it did not impose any restriction on his right to be a director or an employee of another company which carried on business in competition. . . There is a clear distinction between an individual carrying on a business and a company carrying on a business. The clause did not therefore cover the situation of the defender since he had not set up in competition on his own account but had merely become a director of a competing company.'

However the courts will enforce covenants if they are reasonable. In *Systems Reliability Holdings plc v Smith (Ch D) [1990] IRLR 377*, a covenant in an agreement providing that a company agreed to buy an employee's 1.06% shareholding in the company and that the employee should not carry on after dismissal a business competing with that of the company was not in restraint of trade merely because of the smallness of the shareholding.

It is important for any lawyer drafting such clauses to identify with the client the categories of information which can properly be classified as confidential information and trade secrets. It is advisable that employers list in a schedule attached to the contract, examples of trade secrets that would be applicable to the particular individual. The courts have recently issued a broadside to lawyers and employers not to rely on wide and ill-defined clauses – the courts will not draft the clauses for the parties! It will not be sufficient to require the employee not to misuse or disclose 'confidential information'. This generic term will not be acceptable as sufficiently precise and some clear examples will be required.

In *Malden Timber Ltd v Leitch, 6 September 1991, Court of Session (Outer House)* (see 9.14 below) it was held that:

'One cannot stipulate for the protection of "confidential information" and leave it to the court to find content for that expression in the event of a dispute. To do so is to depend upon the Court to define rather than construe the limits of the obligation. The adoption of wide and unqualified terminology in the drafting of the contract in this case in my opinion is such as to lead necessarily to the view that the restraint sought is considerably wider than necessary to provide reasonable and adequate protection of what might have been the legitimate interests of the pursuers. Overall I considered that the provisions were aimed at the protection of the pursuers against competition rather than at the protection of legitimate interests.'

Enforcing confidentiality clauses

Use of injunctions

9.9   The onus rests with the employer to enforce such clauses against the former employee(s) by way of injunction and/or damages. Clearly an injunction is the most powerful weapon in the hands of the employer since his primary concern is to prevent any further misuse of disclosure of his information. An injunction may be sought but will be granted only for a limited period since the information usually has a limited life. The courts take the view that:

'An injunction to prevent defendants from taking an unfair advantage of the springboard that they gained by the misuse of confidential information should not normally extend beyond the period for which the unfair advantage may reasonably be expected to continue.' (*Roger Bullivant Ltd v Ellis [1987] IRLR 491*).

In this particular case, the High Court granted an injunction for one year restraining an ex-employee from contracting with certain people whose names appeared on an index card of trade contacts which was removed from the employer's premises by their former employee.

It is essential for employers attempting to restrain ex-employees to spell out 'with particularity the trade secret or similar confidential information to which he lays claim'. (*Lock International plc v Beswick [1989] IRLR 481*). In other words, it is essential in any application for an injunction 'that the injunction can be framed with sufficient precision so as to enable the person injuncted to know what it is he is prevented from doing'. (*Lawrence David Ltd v Ashton [1989] IRLR 22*).

In the first ruling of its kind, the Court of Appeal approved an injunction against an ex-employee to restrain him from fulfilling a commercial contract already made with a third party, as opposed to entering into a future contract (*PSM International plc and anor v Whitehouse and Willenhall Automation Ltd [1992] IRLR 279*).

The injunction also restrained the ex-employee (managing director) from using confidential information obtained from his former employers.

PSM designed and manufactured equipment for use on the production lines of a customer, CR Ltd. The managing director acquired control of another business (WA Ltd) while still employed by PSM and subsequently gave six months' notice to terminate his contract on 12 June. On 17 June WA Ltd submitted five quotations signed by W and his sister-in-law, which were similar or identical to those submitted by PSM – including the same spelling mistakes! All WA Ltd's quotations were similar or identical to those previously signed on behalf of PSM by W except for one of the quotes which was subject to a seven per cent uplift in price. CR Ltd subsequently placed their orders with WA Ltd.

During a meeting in August the Chief Executive became suspicious that W might be in breach of contract as he wished to leave in September. Subsequently, unaware of W's involvement in WA Ltd or that eleven employees were to leave and join WA Ltd, PSM issued a Writ against W and sought an Anton Piller Order to search and seize documents relating to the case which W held in his possession. It was then that W's activities came to light.

W was served with an interlocutory injunction preventing him from:

(*a*)   working either on his own behalf or for WA Ltd in competition with PSM up to 31 December 1991 without prior consent;

(*b*)   enticing away PSM's suppliers and employees;

(*c*)   making use of or divulging any trade secrets belonging to PSM including drawings, quotations, pricing and costings or any other financial documents and business strategies.

W appealed against the restrictions on the use of trade secrets.

PSM also sought an injunction against WA Ltd prohibiting them from directly or indirectly fulfilling the orders placed with them by CR Ltd and making use of or divulging any trade secrets including drawings, quotations, pricing and costings or any other financial documents and business strategies. WA Ltd appealed.

The Court of Appeal modified the wording of the injunction to define clearly the trade secrets which W was prohibited from using. The court also upheld the injunction against WA Ltd even though it had the effect of restraining them from fulfilling a contract with a third party. It was held that although the courts should be wary of doing so, they clearly had the power in appropriate circumstances to grant an equitable remedy such as an injunction even though it interfered with the contractual rights of innocent third parties.

Use of Anton Piller Orders

9.10   In the *Lock International* case, Mr Justice Hoffman admitted that the courts had too readily in the past granted *ex parte Anton Piller* orders (which allow for search and seizure) and *ex parte* injunctions in cases of alleged breach of confidential information. He stated that:

'Applications for *ex parte Anton Piller* orders against employees who have joined competitors or started competing businesses of their own should be approached with scepticism. . . . The practice of the court has allowed the balance to swing too far in favour of the plaintiffs and *Anton Piller* orders have been granted with insufficient safeguards for respondents.

The three essential pre-conditions for making an *ex parte Anton Piller* order are first, there must be an extremely strong *prima facie* case; secondly, the damage, actual or potential, must be very serious for the applicant; and thirdly, there must be clear evidence that the defendants have in their possession incriminating documents or things and that there is a real possibility that they may destroy such material before any application *inter partes* can be made.'

Even where there is strong evidence that an employee has taken undoubtedly specific confidential information such as a list of customers, the court will only grant an order where there is a paramount need to prevent a denial of justice to the employer. Since such orders allow for a violation of the privacy of the ex-employee who has had no chance to put his side of the case the courts will now not readily grant them *ex parte*.

Factors such as the need on the part of the employer to show an 'extremely strong *prima facie* case' and 'clear evidence that the defendants had in their possession incriminating documents' or that there was 'a grave danger or real possibility that they might destroy the evidence' will now be critical in such cases.

Further judicial guidance on the measure of damages and the application of Anton Piller Orders in cases of alleged breach of confidential information has now been given in *Universal Thermosensors Ltd v Hibben and ors [1992] 3 All ER 257*. In particular some useful guidance as to the safeguards that should apply when executing such an Order and proper professional practice of solicitors serving the Order has been given. This guidance is in line with the cautious approach favoured by Hoffmann J in the *Lock International* case (see above) with regard to the use of Anton Piller Orders in such cases.

9.10 Competition, Confidentiality, Restrictive Covenants

In the *Universal Thermosensors* case, the employer (the plaintiff), who manufactured temperature measuring equipment, alleged that the employees (the defendants), who had left the plaintiff company and set up a competing business (TPL), had taken information about their customers with them. There were no restrictive covenants in the contracts of employment regarding setting up a competing business.

The plaintiff alleged breach of confidential information and obtained an Anton Piller Order which was executed early one morning at the homes of three of the defendants and at their business premises. None of the defendants were present at the place of business when the order was executed. Documents and components were seized and taken away. The plaintiff also obtained an interlocutory injunction restraining the defendants from soliciting, entering into or fulfilling contracts with any of the plaintiff's customers referred to in the seized documents. The company, TPL, had to cease trading as a result of this order.

The two main issues which remained at the full hearing before the High Court were:

(*a*) the plaintiff's claim for damages for the misuse of confidential information; and

(*b*) the defendants' claim for damages on the plaintiff's undertaking given when the interlocutory injunction was granted.

In relation to (*a*) above, the High Court ruled that:

'When assessing damages for the wrong done to a plaintiff by a former employee's misuse of confidential information each case had to be considered on its own facts and there was no irrebuttable presumption that once it was shown that the defendant had stolen documents containing confidential information and that he had used those documents in soliciting orders, any business resulting from the orders derived from the wrongful use of the confidential information so that the defendant was accordingly liable in damages.

Whether particular business obtained by the defendant was obtained as a result of misuse by him of the plaintiff's confidential information or whether the defendant already knew the name of the particular customer or contact was a question of fact.

On the facts, with one small exception the plaintiff had failed to establish that TPL's business was acquired as a result of the misuse of confidential information or that, but for TPL acquiring those orders, the plaintiff would have done so in whole or in part. Accordingly, with that exception, the plaintiff's claim for loss of profits failed.'

In relation to (*b*) above, it was held that:

'If by misuse of confidential information TPL had already made contact

222

with a customer and had received an order, the misuse occurred when the plaintiff's customer was approached and an injunction to restrain TPL from fulfilling that order would go too far as it would not be aimed at preventing further misuse of confidential information. The effect of the injunction restraining TPL was to put TPL out of business and the plaintiff in a better position for the future than if there had been no misuse of information and in those circumstances the protection given to the plaintiff by the injunction went beyond that required for the proper protection of its legitimate rights.'

The defendants were therefore entitled to damages under the plaintiff's undertaking, however only modest damages of £20,000 would be awarded in view of the fact that the defendants had to pay the plaintiff's compensation for the benefits derived from the wrongful use of the plaintiff's confidential information.

On the question of the appropriateness of making an Anton Piller Order, the court held that:

(1)   Execution of Anton Piller Orders should be subject to the following safeguards:

(*a*)   an Order should be executed only on working days in office hours when a solicitor can be expected to be available so that the defendant may obtain legal advice;

(*b*)   if the Order is to be executed at a private house, and it is at all likely that a woman may be alone in the house, the solicitor serving the Order must be, or must be accompanied by, a woman;

(*c*)   in general Anton Piller Orders should expressly provide that unless it is seriously impracticable a detailed list of the items removed should be prepared at the premises before they are removed and that the defendant should be given an opportunity to check that list at that time;

(*d*)   an injunction restraining those on whom it is served from informing others of the existence of the Order should be for a limited period not as long as a week;

(*e*)   the Order should provide that unless there is good reason, it should not be executed at business premises, save in the presence of a responsible officer or representative of the company or trader in question;

(*f*)   consideration should be given to devising some means appropriate to the facts of the case, by which the plaintiff is prevented when the Order is executed at a competitor's premises from carrying out a thorough search of all the competitor's documents.

(2)   When making the Order judges should give serious consideration to the desirability of providing that the Order should be served by an experienced solicitor familiar with the workings of an Anton Piller

Order other than a member of the firm of solicitors acting for the plaintiff, that the solicitor should prepare a written report on the execution with a copy served on the defendant and that report should be put before the court within a few days at an *inter partes* hearing, preferably before the judge who made the Order.

Restrictive covenants: Non-competition, Non-dealing and Non-solicitation

9.11   Covenants which restrain employees from working for a rival employer or working for the former employer's clients or customers or setting up a rival business in competition after they have left the employer's employment are *prima facie* void as being in restraint of trade. For them to be upheld, they must not be contrary to public policy, and no wider than is reasonably necessary to protect a proprietary right or interest of the employer. They also have to be reasonable in terms of geography, scope and time.

A recent case illustrates how closely the courts will examine the subject of the restraint (i.e. what the employer is attempting to protect) and will decide whether this is really a subject upon which the employer has a real proprietary interest or whether the covenant is being used as a means to prevent an ex-employee from using his personal qualities, skills and attributes.

In *Cantor Fitzgerald (UK) Ltd v Wallace and ors [1992] IRLR 215*, the High Court refused to uphold a restrictive covenant preventing ex-Eurobond brokers from working for a rival because the employers had no legitimate business interest to protect.

Five Eurobond brokers resigned en masse announcing they intended to work for a rival company. They had agreed in their contracts that they would not compete with their employer for six months after their employment terminated. The employer sought to claim a proprietary right by virtue of the customer connection built up during the course of their employment.

The employer argued that the work of a Eurobond broker was unique. The employees had built up a special relationship with the traders dealing in Eurobonds. In order to establish such relationships, brokers need the qualities of speed, accuracy and trustworthiness. This last quality was particularly important for the creation of business because traders would only deal with brokers with reputations for integrity. Financial or technical knowledge was not necessary and it only took a short time to pick up the jargon and market habits. The employer argued that if the covenants were not upheld, they would lose all their Eurobond business as clients would tend to continue to deal with brokers whom they trusted and in whom they had confidence even after they had moved to another company.

The Judge reiterated the basic legal principles that (*a*) the employer must show a proprietary interest attaching to his business, (*b*) that the employer is not entitled to protect himself from mere competition from employees and (*c*) that employees cannot be prevented from using their own skills, knowledge and experience even if acquired in the service of the employer.

He concluded that, where the true skill and art of a job relate solely to the personal qualities of the employee such as his temperament attributes and his ability to get on with people, an employer cannot claim a proprietary right by way of customer connection built up during the course of employment because the customer connection is nothing more than those personal qualities.

A typical non-competition or restrictive covenant clause appears in Clause 3 of **Precedent 3**. This type of clause restricts an ex-employee from setting up a rival business and prevents him from working for a competitor.

Restrictions on area

9.12   Ex-employees may only be restrained from competing in an area where the employer has legitimate business interests and only to the area where they have actually worked for the employer. In addition they cannot be prevented from working for *any* customer or client of any other companies in the group unless there are special circumstances which justify such a restriction. Area covenants may in many cases be unnecessary if it is the activity of dealing with clients that the employer wishes to prohibit – see *Office Angels Ltd v Rainer-Thomas and O'Connor [1991] IRLR 214* discussed at 9.16 below.

If, for example, an employee is restrained from working in a competing business or setting up a competing business within a 25-mile radius of the employer's business, this may be too wide and may be unenforceable if a smaller area would have been adequate to protect the employer's legitimate business interests. In *Spencer v Marchington [1988] IRLR 392*, an employment agency failed to obtain an injunction restraining one of their ex-employees from setting up a rival agency because their existing customers all fell within a 20-mile radius of the agency whilst the non-competition clause prohibited competition within a 25-mile radius.

Here the court held that: 'A restriction is too wide to be enforced if its area was more than was adequate to protect the employer's legitimate business interests'.

In *Greer v Sketchley Ltd [1979] IRLR 445*, the employer failed to enforce a restrictive covenant because the restrictive covenant purported to cover the whole of the UK whereas the employer's business interests only lay in the Midlands and the London area. The ex-sales and marketing manager could not be prevented from working in Scotland for a rival firm. Here the Court of Appeal held that the covenant was 'unreasonably wide in its geographic application'.

In the *Hinton & Higgs* case (9.4 above), the clause lacked any geographical reference – it merely attempted to prohibit any competition by declaring:

'It is a condition of your employment that upon leaving, you will not work for any previous or present client of the Hinton & Higgs Group of Companies without the permission of the Board of Directors for a period of at least 18 months.'

The Court of Session refused to grant an injunction on the grounds that:

'. . . the clause was unreasonably wide insofar that it placed no geographical limitations on the restrictions. Where the activities of the employer are limited to the UK, there is no justification against competition worldwide'.

The court went on to define this further:

'Even if the restriction (were) in practice . . . confined to the UK, in the absence of some special circumstance there is no ground for considering it necessary for the protection of the interests of an employer that ex-employees be restricted from working for any client of any other company in the group.'

In other words, ex-employees cannot be prevented from working with or for or dealing with clients or customers with whom they never had any business dealings prior to their leaving. In *Marley Tile Co Ltd v Johnson* [*1982*] *IRLR 75*, a restriction covering the whole of Devon and Cornwall – an area of 200 miles in length and between 50 and 100 miles wide – was held to be too wide to be reasonable. In this case it would have led to a prohibition on about 2,500 customers in the area concerned. Lord Denning held that: 'The defendant could not possibly have known or come into contact with more than a small percentage of them'.

It is therefore essential to draft the covenant with a limitation on any restriction to clients or customers with whom the employee has had any business dealings during the period of, say, twelve months prior to the termination of his employment (Clause 1 of **Precedent 3**).

Scope

9.13 Restrictive covenants can only prevent unreasonable competition with the former employer. This means that only legitimate business interests will be protected and the scope of the restriction must be carefully defined. In the *Marley Tile* case (above) a restrictive covenant attempting to prevent any activity involving 'the supply, sale or fixing of products similar to those of the plaintiffs' was held to be too wide because the company's business related to roofing materials and the clause as drafted was '. . . far removed from roofing. Thus if a greengrocer's shop had been re-roofed by the plaintiffs, the defendant, in the management of a small "do it yourself" shop, could not sell timber to be used for the vegetable and fruit racks in the greengrocer's shop'.

In an earlier case, *Littlewoods Corporation Ltd v Harris* [*1977*] *1 WLR 1472*, the Littlewoods Organisation obtained an injunction restraining its former senior director, Mr Paul Harris, from working for the GUS Corporation, one of its main rivals, because the clause specified the competitors for whom it was prohibited to work and it was to last for twelve months only and 'it was the one way of the employers protecting their position'.

More recently, in *JA Mont (UK) Ltd v Mills* [*1993*] *IRLR 172* the Court of Appeal rejected as unreasonable a clause purporting to prevent the joint managing director of a paper tissue company from working for 'another company in the tissue industry within one year of leaving (our) employment'.

Since this restrained him from working 'in any capacity whatsoever and indeed in any sector of the tissue industry', the clause fell and was unenforceable.

The court held that:

> 'As a matter of policy the Court should not too urgently strive to find within restrictive covenants *ex facie* too wide, implicit limitations such as alone could justify their imposition . . . . .'

The Court of Appeal refused to grant an injunction with regard to a narrower and more reasonable restriction, more accurately targeted at those of the employer's interests that could be legitimately protected. In other words they refused to ignore the unenforceable covenant and by way of an ancillary order restrict the ex-employee from breaching his duty of confidentiality.

This case reinforces the view that it is critical to consider drafting separate and severable clauses with regard to confidentiality, trade secrets, area covenants (where appropriate), non-solicitation and non-dealing clauses, prohibition or touting for business.

Draughtsmen must take care not to draft such wide covenants in terms of its scope otherwise the courts will hold that the clause is too wide and excessive and therefore contrary to public policy. The courts will either decline to redraft the clause, find implied clauses or substitute altogether a more reasonable restraint. Care must be taken to specify the exact nature of the occupation(s) within the *particular or relevant sector* of the industry in which the employee is restrained from working. For example the clause should state that the employee is restrained from working in the same or similar capacity and in the particular sector of the industry as the one in which he has been working for the last twelve months prior to the termination of his employment.

Lawyers should strive to take careful instructions in order to understand the precise and exact nature of the sector of industry and products with which the client is involved and then draft appropriately, a narrow clause seeking only to restrict the individual from taking up the same or similar employment in the particular sector of the industry in which the employer is involved and in which the employee works or has worked.

Time

9.14   Restrictive covenants must be reasonable in relation to the length of time they purport to restrict competition. Clauses between one to two years appear to be common and in the main are enforced for this limited period.

In *Malden Timber Ltd v Leitch, 6 September 1991, Court of Session (Outer House)*, a restrictive covenant purporting to prevent the employee from working for a competitor for *five years* after the termination of employment was held to be excessive in view of the nature of the employer's business. Here the business involved the wholesale and retail sale of timber, timber products and building materials. The Court of Session reiterated the well-established principle that the employer's right to restrict the ex-employee's freedom of action after the employment has ended is limited to:

'. . . a period no greater than is reasonably necessary to protect the employer's legitimate trading interests. An employer is not entitled to protect himself from mere competition . . . . The Courts will take into account various factors such as the relative strength of the parties' positions, less harm will be caused by granting the injunction if it subsequently turns out to be unjustified, than by refusing it if it turns out at the full hearing that an injunction should have been granted.'

In looking at the length of the purported restriction (five years), the court commented that in the business of retail and wholesale timber suppliers, there is constant review of pricing and credit policies. Information of that kind must have a limited life where supplies have to be purchased on annual contracts or short-term arrangements and where rapid turnover is necessary to generate the cashflow central to business efficiency.

In these circumstances a five-year limitation was excessive and 'nothing indicated a need for protection for longer than, at most, about half of the five-year period sought'.

Non-solicitation/Non-dealing clauses

9.15   Non-solicitation and non-dealing clauses are subject to the same restrictions as those discussed above. Here the employee is not specifically restricted from working for a rival or on his own behalf. He may be prohibited from soliciting or canvassing or accepting any work from the employer's existing customers or clients for a period of time. The restrictions must relate solely to those clients or customers with whom the employee had business dealings and not all the employer's clients – see *Office Angels Ltd v Rainer-Thomas* discussed at 9.16 below.

Whether 'solicitation' means *actively* seeking work from a customer or client of the former employer or whether the restriction can apply when a customer approaches the ex-employee was discussed in *John Michael Design plc v Cooke [1987] 2 All ER 332*. In this case the plaintiffs, a firm of shop fitters, obtained an injunction against a former employee who had obtained the business of Horne Brothers, the male outfitters. The ex-employee argued that the injunction should exclude from its scope any customer who wanted to do business with him and would not place their business with the plaintiff company no matter what the outcome of the legal proceedings. The High Court said that this was irrelevant, and accepted that a non-solicitation clause could cover a customer of a former employer who had made the approaches to the ex-employee. In contrast, in another case concerning the enforcement of a non-solicitation clause, *Merrill Lynch Pierce Fenner v Besman, 5 December 1985*, the Court of Appeal ruled that it would take account of the impact that an injunction would have on the right of an innocent third party to place their custom with the plaintiff company's former employee if they so wished.

Distinguishing area covenants from non-solicitation/non-dealing clauses

9.16   In *Office Angels Ltd v Rainer-Thomas and O'Connor [1991] IRLR 214*, the Court of Appeal restated the distinction between an area covenant which precludes the employee from operating a business within that geographical location and a non-solicitation/non-dealing clause which prohibits the employee from doing business with the company's clients. Area covenants may in many cases be superfluous if it is the activity of dealing with clients that the employer wishes to prohibit. In such a case a carefully worded non-solicitation and non-dealing clause will suffice.

In *Office Angels*, the defendants left the employee company on 23 October and opened their own agency on 1 November called Pertemps City Network (London) Ltd. The agency took over premises in Fenchurch Street and dealt with permanent and temporary staff. The defendants were shareholders and directors in the new company, and were also responsible for managing the temporary employment work. Their new office was within one kilometre of their former office.

The contracts of the employees included Clause 4.5 which provided

'. . . that in the course of his or her employment . . . the employee has dealings with clients of the company and in order to safeguard this goodwill the employee agrees:

(a)   He or she will not at any time during the six months immediately following the termination of his or her employment, whether on his own account or on behalf of any other person, firm or corporation, solicit custom from, deal with or supply (in connection with the trade or business of an employment agency) any person, firm or corporation who or which was a client of the company at any time during the period the employee was employed by the company.

(b)   He or she will not at any time during the six months immediately following the termination of his or her employment, whether on his own account or on behalf of any other person, firm or corporation, engage in or undertake the trade or business of an employment agency within a radius of three thousand metres of the branch or branches of the company at which the employee was employed for a period of not less than four weeks during the period of six months prior to the date of such termination or in the case of a branch or branches in the Greater London area then within a radius of 1,000 metres.'

An interim injunction was granted against the employees, who thereafter took offices just outside the one kilometre radius and spent most of their time canvassing for business – both from former clients and temps who were on the Office Angels 'books'.

The High Court held that:

1. Clause 4.5(a) (the non-solicitation clause) was too wide and therefore unenforceable as it covered all 6,000-7,000 clients of the plaintiff in all its branches, whilst only some 100 were known to the defendants in their particular branch.

2. Clause 4.5(b) (the area restriction) was broadly necessary to protect the goodwill which consisted of the client base and a secretarial base of temporary workers.

On appeal, the Court of Appeal held, allowing the appeal, that although the employer's connection with its pool of temporary workers constituted a legitimate business interest and could therefore be protected by contract, the introductory wording in Clause 4.5 (see above) clearly indicated that the clause as a whole was intended to protect its clients. The plaintiff could not now go behind that stated purpose by arguing that the restriction also applied equally to its pool of temporary workers.

Furthermore, a geographical restriction covering most of the City of London was inappropriate and unreasonably wide and would by itself do little to protect the plaintiff's client connection as client orders were placed over the telephone and it was of no concern to them where the office was located. A properly worded non-solicitation clause would probably have been more appropriate to protect the plaintiff's pool of temporary workers.

In any event, the restriction in Clause 4.5(b), placed a disproportionately severe restriction on the defendants' right to compete with the plaintiff after leaving its employment and went further than was reasonable in the interests of the parties.

Lessons in drafting

9.17   It is vital to give careful instructions to lawyers drafting these clauses. If a non-solicitation clause (properly worded) will suffice, then an area covenant may be deemed to be unreasonable and unnecessary.

For lawyers drafting these clauses, it is important to think carefully about the interest sought to be protected. Are clients physically located within a reasonably defined location and could this interest be protected by a non-dealing or non-solicitation clause? Or is the business a retail or service business where your clients visit your premises to receive the service (e.g. hairdresser, estate agent etc.), where an area covenant may be reasonable?

Non-solicitation and non-dealing clauses must be limited to those clients with whom the employee dealt. A blanket prohibition will be deemed to be too wide.

Non-dealing clauses and new clients

9.18   As a general rule, the courts will not enforce non-dealing clauses which attempt to stop an ex-employee from obtaining new business. But in the case of a sale of a business, the purchaser may wish to protect his newly acquired business, particularly where he has paid handsomely for the goodwill, from any activities of a competitive nature by the vendor. This would include the activities of the vendor attempting to secure new business away from the company that has just been sold. In such cases, the courts have enforced such clauses, particularly where there is some form of consideration for the goodwill.

In *Allied Dunbar (Frank Weisinger Ltd) v Weisinger* [1988] *IRLR 60*, a sales consultant had been paid £386,000 for the goodwill of his practice by a major insurance company, Allied Dunbar. In consideration of that agreement, he had agreed not to solicit any existing customer for a period of two years and he had agreed to act as a consultant for Allied Dunbar for a period of two years. Unfortunately his activities with Allied Dunbar did not prove to be satisfactory and the consultancy was terminated by mutual agreement. He then sought to obtain employment with a rival firm.

Here the covenant had been taken by the vendor for the protection of the goodwill of a business sold by the covenantor as opposed to the case where an employer takes a covenant from an employee.

Here the High Court held that:

> 'It is well established, that in order to protect the goodwill of a business, it may be legitimate to require the vendor to retire completely for a period of time from any form of competing business . . . . To protect the goodwill of a business which they had bought . . . . (the plaintiffs could show that) the prospects of obtaining new clients or professional firms was obviously part of the goodwill of the defendant's practice and therefore an interest which it was legitimate for them to protect . . . . They were entitled to require the defendant to abstain from undermining their chances of success by accepting those clients himself . . . .

A non-dealing covenant, particularly one extending to new clients, is difficult to police and enforce and depends to an unacceptable degree on the honesty and co-operation of the covenantor. Where as in the present case the purchaser has paid £386,000 for the goodwill of a business, he is entitled to protect his investment by a suitably worded covenant which does not depend upon the vendor's honesty and co-operation . . . .

In order to show that a covenant is reasonable as between the parties, it is sufficient to show that it is no greater than is reasonably required to protect the legitimate business interests of the covenantee.'

A model clause for such a case appears in Clause 2 of **Precedent 3**.

Enforcing restrictive covenants

9.19 It is common practice to draft restrictive covenants and other post-termination clauses so that they will become operative 'upon the termination of the employment howsoever caused'. However clever the drafting of the contract, it cannot alter the true legal position or the status of the contract. It is still good law that the guilty party to a contract will not be permitted to enforce any terms of that contract in their favour (*General Billposting Co Ltd v Atkinson [1909] AC 118*). Thus if the employer has wrongfully terminated the contract and the repudiation has been accepted by the employee, this brings the contract to an end and all outstanding contractual obligations of the injured party are in law discharged. Thus the employer will not be permitted to enforce any of the post-termination clauses.

In *Briggs v Oates [1990] IRLR 472*, for example, a firm of solicitors drafted a partnership agreement which *inter alia* provided for a restrictive covenant preventing the partner for a period of five years after the partnership terminated 'for whatever reason [from practising] as a solicitor from an office within a radius of five miles from Market Place, Huddersfield . . .'

The partnership agreement was terminated without proper notice. Mr Oates accepted the breach, left and set up a practice some 120 yards away from the original office. Mr Briggs sought to enforce the restrictive covenant.

The High Court held that since the partnership had been terminated in breach of the terms of the agreement, the restrictive covenant was unenforceable.

'In the circumstances under which the defendant's employment came to an end, the restrictive covenant in his contract of employment was not binding upon him and could not be enforced. It could not be accepted that the restriction applied irrespective of the manner in which the employment had come to an end because it referred to determination "for whatever reason".

The breach of contract for which the employers were responsible was accepted by the defendant as putting an end to the contract. In such a case, outstanding contractual obligations of the injured party are in law discharged together with the contract. The result does not depend upon the construction of the contract . . . .'

Severing the clauses

9.20   If upon a true construction of a single covenant there are two or more distinct areas of restraint, e.g. restrictive covenant, confidentiality clause and non-solicitation clause, the court may test the validity of each distinct clause separately. Any clause which is deemed to be unreasonable may be severed and the remaining clause(s) may be enforced. The clauses must all be independent of each other and if deleted must not alter the meaning of the remainder of the clauses. This is what is sometimes called the 'blue pencil test'. The key point here is not whether the words are grammatically severable but whether the parties intended to cover more than one type of restraint. It is therefore preferable to keep all these issues in separate and distinct clauses and then preface them all with the preamble suggested in the *Hinton and Higgs* case (see 9.4 above). Lord Dervaird in this case suggested that these words be added:

'In the event that any such restriction shall be void would be valid if some part thereof were deleted . . . such restrictions shall apply with such modifications as may be necessary to make them valid or effective.'

This case serves as a useful lesson to those drafting contracts to make sure that each clause is separate and severable! However, this preamble may render the clause void for uncertainty, – so use it with caution!

In a recent case, *Rex Stewart Jeffries Parker Ginsberg Ltd v Parker [1988] IRLR 483*, the court severed certain clauses prohibiting solicitation of customers of associated companies but left standing the central clause relating to the 'central prohibition preventing the soliciting of those who were customers up to the time of the termination of the defendant's employment. So limited, the covenant was not unreasonable and was therefore valid'.

'Touting' for business – intentions versus actions

9.21   In any case where the employee is 'touting for business' before he leaves, whether this be canvassing opinions or contacting the employer's suppliers and customers in order to prepare to leave and set up a rival business, the courts have held that it is not a breach of the implied duty of good faith and will not give an employer good grounds for summary dismissal. In order for an employer to protect himself from such activity, an express clause on this point must be included in the contract. A model clause appears in Clause 2 of **Precedent 3**.

In *Laughton and Hawley v Bapp Industrial Supplies Ltd [1986] IRLR 245*, the EAT held that:

'An employee does not breach the duty of loyalty merely by indicating an intention to set up in competition with his employer in the future. Whilst it is entirely understandable that an employer should be suspicious of an employee in such circumstances, unless the employer has reasonable grounds for believing that the employee has done or is just about to do a wrongful act, he is not justified in dismissing him . . . unless it can be shown that there were reasonably solid grounds for supposing that he was doing so in order to abuse his confidential position or information with his present employers . . . .

An employee with experience in a particular industry who is intending to leave, whether to join a competitor as an employee or to set up in competition on his own account, commits no breach of contract in doing so *unless there is either a specific term in his contract to that effect* which does not fall foul of the doctrine against restraint of trade, or he is intending to use the confidential information of his employer other than for the benefit of his employer.'

In two more recent cases, the issue of 'touting for business' was examined further and in one of the cases, *Laughton* (above) was distinguished. However it is clear that employees must be careful about their actions and activities if they wish to leave their employment to set up a rival business even where there is not express restriction in the contract.

The EAT in *Tithebarn Ltd v Hubbard, EAT 532/89* held that a mere intention to set up in competition with one's previous employer is not a breach of the implied terms of loyalty and fidelity and trust and confidence and so does not constitute misconduct. Although the EAT did hold that there was evidence upon which a different industrial tribunal might have come to the opposite conclusion.

Mr Hubbard was employed as a national sales trainer who approached one of the sales team and asked him if he would be interested in joining him to set up a competing venture. When Mr Hubbard was dismissed on the grounds that he had breached the implied term of loyalty and fidelity, the tribunal and the EAT held that Mr Hubbard's actions had merely amounted to 'a mere discussion for the future, an intention by Mr Hubbard to set up a business and an invitation that in due course Mr Perrett might care to join him'.

This said the EAT was

'. . . not a breach of the express terms of Mr Hubbard's contract nor a breach of the implied terms of fidelity and trust and confidence. Even though there existed other evidence which might clearly have pointed to a contrary view, there was no error of law in the Tribunal's decision.'

Whilst in *Marshall v Industrial Systems & Control Ltd, EAT 439/91* the EAT held that where the employee's acts go beyond the intention to set up in competition and includes firm plans to secure the employer's best client for his or her new venture, a dismissal for gross misconduct will be justified.

In *Marshall's* case, the managing director of a firm marketing engineering products approached two other members of staff with an idea to market a particular piece of software manufactured by Boeing which was the company's only profitable product and to which the company had exclusive European distribution rights. A draft business plan fell into the hands of the Board and Mr Marshall was dismissed for gross misconduct.

The EAT distinguished *Laughton's* case and said the facts were very different here.

'The managing director of a company together with another important manager proposed to try to persuade another senior manager to leave the company to join them in their plan for which concrete arrangements had been made, to deprive the company of its best client. Under these circumstances the tribunal could not be faulted for holding that the employer had acted reasonably in dismissing the employee.'

Warranties and indemnities

9.22   Should an employer or a recruitment agency attempt to induce any employee to break any of these restrictive clauses, they might be sued (by way of an application for an injunction and/or an action for damages) by the original employer for committing a number of torts, namely unlawfully interfering with contractual relations, inciting a breach of contract or aiding and abetting one!

The courts will only refuse to grant an injunction where it would have the effect of an order for specific performance of the contract of employment by in effect requiring the employee to remain in the employ of the original employer. In the main, such cases have been concerned with 'personal services' such as exclusive contracts to manage the business affairs of individuals such as sportsmen and women, personalities etc.

In *Warren v Mendy [1989] IRLR 210*, a boxer became disillusioned with his manager and decided to break an exclusive management contract with his former manager, Mr Warren. He sought and obtained the services of a commercial agent, Mr Mendy. Mr Warren's application for an injunction to prevent Mr Mendy from committing the tort of unlawful interference with contractual relations failed on the basis that:

'It is well settled that an injunction to restrain a breach of contract for personal services ought not to be granted where its effect will be to decree performance of the contract. *There is no comparable objection to the grant of an injunction restraining the performance of particular services for a third party because, by not prohibiting the performance of other services, it does not bind the servant to his contract.*'

It may therefore be wise to include a warranty and indemnity clause particularly in senior staff contracts where it is known or believed that such restrictions exist. A model clause appears in **Precedent 4**.

On a point of practice it is prudent for any new employer to require sight of the former employment contract in order to satisfy himself that no such restrictions exist.

Confidentiality clauses versus restrictive covenants?

9.23   In *Lawrence David Ltd v Ashton [1989] IRLR 22* (see also 9.9 above), the court gave employers a little hint – if they cannot identify with sufficient precision the trade secrets or confidential information to enable a 'proper injunction to be granted', then they should 'exact covenants from their employees restricting their field of activity after they have left their employment and not by asking the courts to extend the general equitable doctrine to prevent breaking of confidences beyond all reasonable bounds'.

'Garden leave' clauses – Are they enforceable?

9.24   One way around the problems of restrictive covenants is to draft a long notice clause for both parties – called a 'garden leave' clause. If the employee then gives shorter notice than that required by his contract, the employer may be able to enforce the notice period by refusing to release the employee from his requirement to give the required notice, to offer to pay the employee for the duration of the notice period and to obtain an injunction to prohibit that employee from working for anyone else during this period (*Evening Standard Co Ltd v Henderson [1987] IRLR 64*). These 'garden leave' clauses must be drafted carefully because the practice of long periods of 'garden leave' is obviously open to abuse.

In this case, Mr Henderson's contract required twelve months' notice on either side. When he gave only two months' notice in order to go to work for the rival London newspaper which was about to be launched, his employers were able to enforce the twelve months' notice clause by way of an injunction restraining Mr Henderson from working for any other employer during his paid notice period (he was not required to continue working for the Evening Standard during his notice period and his employer had undertaken to pay him his salary and other contractual benefits throughout that time). The balance of convenience was in favour of granting the injunction.

Obiter, Lawton LJ said that when the need for skilled personnel, particularly in industries using highly sophisticated technology is very great, there is a great temptation for employees to break their contracts and go to other employers, usually for far higher salaries: 'It is time that some court examined the matter fully'.

However such relief is discretionary and whether the court will grant an injunction to prohibit an employee from working for anyone else during the currency of the contract will depend on what detriment the employer will suffer if the clause is not enforced by injunction and the exact wording of the contract. If the employer wishes to restrict the employee from working for anyone else during the notice period, there must be an express clause to this effect prohibiting such conduct.

In *Provident Financial Group plc and Whitegates Estate Agency Ltd v Hayward* [*1989*] *IRLR 84*, Mr Hayward was employed by the Provident Financial Group as the financial director of their estate agency business. His contract contained a clause restricting him during his employment with the company from working for or having any financial interest in any other business. Although his contractual notice period was twelve months, when he tendered his resignation, in July 1988, it was agreed his employment would terminate at the end of 1988. From September 1988 he went on 'garden leave' but in October he informed the company that he was planning to start work for another chain of estate agents the following Monday.

In refusing an injunction enforcing the clause that he would not work for anyone else during the continuance of his contract, the Court of Appeal held that they would not enforce a 'garden leave' clause where the other business for which the employee wishes to work has nothing whatever to do with the business of the employer.

On the other hand, the courts may grant an injunction where there is an express clause restraining the employee from working during the notice period or where working for another employer would be in breach of the duty of good faith.

The Court of Appeal held that:

'. . . employers often have exaggerated views of what will or may affect their business. The court is entitled to find on the facts objectively considered and despite the fears of the employer that the proposed employment is nothing whatever to do with the employer and therefore it is not appropriate as a matter of discretion to grant an injunction . . . .

If the period during which the employee is not required to work out his notice is not excessive it may be said forcibly and correctly for the employer that the risk of his going to a rival and fostering the rival's business before the expiration of his notice, is one against which the employers are entitled to be protected because of the damage it would do to them. Equally it may be said that the amount of confidential information that he must have in his head which would be highly prejudicial to the employer if he was working for a rival is such that, on the mere principle of policing confidential information, it is right that the covenant should be enforced to prevent him from working for a rival until the expiration of a reasonable period of notice.'

In this case there was only ten weeks of Mr Hayward's notice to go, his job was an administrative one and there was no prospect of any serious or significant damage to the appellant's business. The confidential information which he had would not be relevant to the other employer.

The courts also take due regard to the nature of the occupation. In this case, Dillon LJ ruled that:

'. . . the concern of the employee to work and to exercise his skills . . . has been recognised in cases involving artists and singers who depend upon publicity and this applies equally to skilled workmen and even to chartered accountants. The practice of long "garden leave" clauses is clearly open to abuse. It is a weapon in the hands of the employer to ensure that an ambitious and able executive will not give notice if he is not going to be able to work for anyone at all for a long period of notice. Any executive who gives notice and leaves his employment is very likely to take fresh employment with someone in the same line of business not through any desire to act unfairly or to cheat the former employer but to get the best advantage of his own personal expertise.'

Other clauses

9.25   Other clauses concerning a prohibition on poaching staff for the benefit of another employer, contacting the press or media other than in their own personal capacity, misrepresenting themselves after their employment has ceased that they still work for or are an authorised agent for the employer and matters relating to security are other matters which can properly be dealt with by express terms in the contract. They can all be found in **Precedent 5**.

Key Points

- Ensure there is a clause covering outside business interests and working in spare time; a register of outside interests may be appropriate with a requirement for declaration of any such interests.

- Ensure that when drafting all clauses they are drafted as separate clauses and it is clearly stated that if any restriction which would be deemed valid but for some part which is deemed void, then that part should be severed and the remainder of the clause should stand.

- Consider drafting a confidentiality clause giving examples of trade secrets; ensure that all contractors and consultants sign confidentiality agreements if relevant.

- Ensure that all clauses are drafted solely to protect the legitimate business interests of the Company and are reasonable in scope, duration and geography.

- Ensure non-solicitation clauses restrict the employee to clients, suppliers, and customers with whom he has dealt.

- Draft non-dealing clauses for all staff (to apply for a period of time after they have left) for anyone who might be able to conduct business with your clients in their own right after they left and which could seriously harm your business.

- Draft a specific clause prohibiting any 'touting' for potential business before the employee leaves your employment.

- Draft warranties and indemnities for new staff who may be subject to restrictive covenants and the like from their former employment.

- Consider drafting long notice clauses in place of restrictive covenants.

- Consider drafting other clauses to protect your business such as restrictions on employees talking to the press or representing themselves as connected with your business after they have left your employment.

PRECEDENT 1

Clause 1 – Outside business interests

It is expected that you will devote your whole time and attention to this Company during your working time. During your employment, you are not expected to undertake any other paid employment outside working hours, nor are you permitted to have any interest in any business or undertaking or engage in any other activities which might interfere with the performance of your duties or cause a conflict of interest or otherwise.

If you should be engaged in any other employment or have any outside business interest whether financial or otherwise, you may first seek the written permission of the Chief Executive which will not be unreasonably withheld. You are required to declare any interests in the Company's register of interests (see Clause 3 below).

Clause 2 – Accepting or offering improper inducements

It is strictly forbidden to offer to any third party or accept any benefit whether financial or in kind from any other party (other than your proper remuneration from the Company).

It is strictly forbidden to accept gifts or hospitality other than by way of a token nature from any person or business with whom you are involved on Company business. You must always clear the position with your section head or Chief Executive before accepting any gift or hospitality whatever the nature.

Clause 3 – Declaration of interests

The Company will maintain a register of interests and all members of staff must declare any interests they have. This may include family relationships with consultants, contractors or suppliers to the Company, private work and membership of other voluntary organisations, statutory bodies etc. If in doubt, you must discuss the matter with your section head or Chief Executive.

You will also be required to sign a declaration that you have no interests as defined above. The register of interests is a document designed to protect both the Company and its employees. The contents of the register will not normally be open to inspection by members of the public or other external bodies.

Clause 4 – Using the Company's consultants, contractors and suppliers

*A. Wherever possible staff should avoid making use of the services or purchasing goods from any consultant, contractor or other suppliers of goods or services to the Company. Where you may wish to do so, you must inform the Chief Executive and obtain his written permission *prior* to any contact whatsoever being made on a personal basis. Where the value of any goods or services exceeds an amount to be set by the Chief Executive and reviewed from time to time, permission will not normally be granted. The register of interests referred to in Clause 1 above must be kept up to date in relation to these matters.

Should you breach this clause of your contract, the Company reserves the right to treat this as gross misconduct for which you may be summarily dismissed.

(Replace the above paragraph with the following in relation to:
Chief Executive, Section Heads, Technical Officers, Development Officers/ Assistants and any others as applicable.)

*B. You are not permitted to make use of any services or be supplied with goods on a personal basis from any consultant, contractor or other suppliers of goods and services to the Company because of the possible conflict of interest. Should any such conduct come to the attention of the Company, the Company reserves the right to treat this as gross misconduct for which you may be summarily dismissed.

PRECEDENT 2

Confidentiality Clauses

In the event that any restriction defined in the clauses below shall be found to be void would be valid if some part thereof were deleted, such restrictions shall apply with such modifications as may be necessary to make them valid or effective.

Clause 1* – Duty of Confidentiality

You must not, whether during your employment with the Company or after the end of it, whether you resign or are dismissed by the Company, unless expressly authorised in writing by your Head of Department, disclose to any unauthorised person or use any confidential information relating to the business affairs or trade secrets of the Company. This includes any details about the Company's products, technical data, any matter or product in the research or testing stage at the termination of your employment, clients and employees, actual, potential or past, and all details relating to information on the Company's database.

Clause 1* – Confidentiality Clause for Medical Staff/Research Staff and Personnel

During the course of your employment you may have access to, gain knowledge of or be entrusted with information of a confidential nature. This may include policy, organisation, research and development of new products, scientific or medical test results, future plans, staffing of the Company, customers, clients, suppliers, manufacturers, medical practitioners etc. (past, present or potential) and the terms upon which they do business, the nature, origin, composition of the Company's stocks and products (whether in production or in research stage) and the manufacturing processes which the Company or any associated company undertakes. You may also gain knowledge of or be entrusted with sensitive, personal or medical information concerning other members of staff or colleagues.

You agree, not at any time, during or after the end of your employment with the Company (or any associated Company), unless expressly authorised by the Company or as a necessary part of the performance of your duties, to disclose to any person or make use of such confidential information as described above.

If such disclosure or misuse of information occurs during the course of your employment, the Company will treat such conduct as gross misconduct and reserves the right to terminate your employment without notice or payment in lieu. Such misconduct is described in the Company's disciplinary procedure which forms part of your contract of employment.

242

Clause 2

Confidentiality Agreement for Third Parties

(*Covering letter*)

Name.................................. Date ....

Address....................................... Ref ....

Dear (name)

ABC Co Ltd is prepared to declare to you certain information in confidence. This information should under no circumstances be declared to any third party without prior written consent from the company. The only exceptions to confidentiality are when information:

(a) is in the public domain prior to the date thereof;

(b) was already known to be and can be shown to have been known;

(c) comes subsequently into the public domain other than by a breach of ABC Co Ltd confidence.

The information referred to herein as 'confidential information' is to enable you to develop......................for ABC Co Ltd for use in the.........process.

By signing this letter you agree to keep secret this confidential information to yourself and to other authorised persons who have signed or agree to sign a similar letter in favour of ABC Co Ltd.

Signed for ABC Co Ltd   Signed for X Ltd (Company name)

....

                                          (Name of representative of X Ltd)

Third Party Confidentiality Agreement

This Agreement is made on 1990

BETWEEN ABC CO LTD ('The Company')

AND

......................('The Contractor/Consultant')

A. The Company has entered into an agreement with 'The Contractor/ Consultant' to undertake work in respect of (specify the process etc.).

B. The Company is in possession of confidential information and Know How in relation to this process, which terms are defined as follows:

(a)   'Confidential Information' means that part of the Know How not in the public domain otherwise than by breach of this Agreement and specifically includes all manuals and other material including but not limited to all information bulletins, drawings and other documents relating to the......process marked as 'confidential'.

(b)   'Know How' means all technical information, ideas and techniques relating to......process owned by or licensed to the Company and includes confidential information.

C. In the course of undertaking work in respect of the......process, the Company may or will have to disclose to 'The Contractor/Consultant' Know How or confidential information belonging to the Company. 'The Contractor/Consultant' may make modifications or improvements in the Know How or confidential information in the course of performing the work.

D. It is the parties' intentions that the confidential information and Know How remain the sole and absolute property of the Company and that all improvements and modifications to the Know How or confidential information become the sole and absolute property of the Company.

E. 'The Contractor/Consultant' agrees that it will not communicate or divulge to any other person any of the information relating to the......process made available to it by the Company or its representatives and expressly acknowledges that such information is only made available to it for the purpose of undertaking the work in respect of the......process and no other purpose.

F. 'The Contractor/Consultant' agrees that if in the course of undertaking work in respect of the......process, it shall develop any improvements or modifications to the......process then all such information shall be disclosed immediately in writing to the Company and will become the sole and exclusive property of the Company which shall have the sole and exclusive rights to any patentable invention, copyright, design or other rights as might exist in the said improvements or modifications.

Signed on behalf of the parties

Signed by .... Date............ 19....
for and on behalf of the Company

Signed by .... Date............ 19....
for and on behalf of the Contractor/Consultant

PRECEDENT 3

Clause 1 – Non-solicitation/Non-competition/Non-dealing

A. You will not during your employment with the Company or any associated or subsidiary companies or for a period of (*one/two*) year(s) afterwards, attempt to solicit custom or accept work for private gain and/or for any third party from any private individual, firm or company who within the period of (*one/two*) year(s) before the termination of your employment had been a client or customer whom you had introduced to the Company or with whom you had any business dealings or knowledge.

After your employment has ceased (whether by your resignation or termination by the Company), you also agree that you will not, except in a purely social capacity, contact, deal with, attempt to solicit custom from, any customer or client with whom you had any business dealings in the (*one/two*) year(s) prior to the termination of your employment. Nor will you attempt to interfere with the existing business relations between any client or employee and the Company.

Clause 2 – Touting for business

You are strictly forbidden from making any contacts whether formal or informal, written or oral, to any of the Company's past, current or prospective suppliers, customers or clients for any purpose other than for the legitimate business interests of this Company. Such purpose might include but is not limited to an intention to set up a competing business or work for a rival after leaving this Company. Any breach of this clause may render you liable to serious disciplinary action which will result in summary dismissal if the circumstances warrant it.

Clause 3 – Non-dealing clause for purchase of business

A. You agree to use your best endeavours to enhance the value of the goodwill of the business (name of company) and in that connection you agree to act as consultant to the company for a minimum of (*two*) years and to be bound by certain restraints set out below.

B. You agree not to solicit any existing customer of the practice for the purpose of selling a product competing with (name of company).

C. You agree for a period of (*one/two*) year(s) following the termination of the Consultancy Agreement with the company that you will not be involved in any capacity in a business which competes either directly or indirectly (in any way) with that of the Company or any of its associated companies or subsidiaries.

Clause 4 – Non-competition/Restrictive covenant

In order to protect the legitimate business interests of the Company you agree that you will not during the period of (*one/two*) years following the termination of your employment, howsoever caused, within a radius of......miles of any premises at which you have, during the last (*one/two*) years preceding termination, been employed, either on your own account or for any other person, firm, corporation or company and in competition with the Company directly or indirectly engage in or be concerned with any trade or business carried on by this Company as at the date of termination of your employment.

Clause 5 – Non-enticement

You agree that at no time while you are in the Company's employment will you approach any other employee of the Company with a view to him or her ceasing to be employed with the Company.

PRECEDENT 4

The Executive hereby warrants and represents to the Company that he will not be in breach of his existing or his former terms of employment whether express or implied or of any other obligation binding on the Executive by reason of his entering into this Agreement.

PRECEDENT 5

Clause 1 – Copying/Making abstracts etc.

You are not permitted to make any copy, abstract, summary or precis of the whole or part of any document belonging to the Company except where expressly authorised so to do or in the proper performance of your duties.

Clause 2 – Security

You will be required to ensure that all documents, papers, correspondence etc. are kept secure at all times and are carefully locked away at night and that all the security procedures are properly maintained at all times. You are not expected to take any papers or documents belonging to the Company, home with you when you leave at the end of the day except where this is strictly necessary for the proper performance of your duties. Any unauthorised conduct in this respect which causes loss or damage to the Company or to any Client (past, present or future) will be regarded as serious misconduct for which you may be dismissed should the circumstances warrant it.

Clause 3 – Outside communications

You must not make contact with or communicate with any members of the press or media or anyone so connected on behalf of the Company unless you have obtained the prior written permission of the Head of Corporate Communications or Divisional Head.

You are not permitted to publish any letters, articles or otherwise purporting to represent the Company (other than in your personal capacity) unless you have obtained prior permission in writing from the Head of Corporate Communications or Divisional Head. Failure to comply with any of the Clauses (1-3) may if the circumstances warrant it be regarded as gross misconduct for which you may be liable to summary dismissal.

Clause 4 – Property to be returned on termination

You are required to deliver to the Company before the end of your employment or immediately after should your employment terminate without notice all papers, documents, keys, credit cards, cars and all property properly belonging to the Company. You will be required to sign an undertaking that all such property has been duly returned.

Clause 5 – Representing the Company

You are not permitted to represent yourself as an authorised agent for the Company except in the course of the proper performance of your duties or where authorised so to do. When your employment ceases, you must not hold

248

yourself out in any business context as being an employee of this Company. Should there be any misrepresentation or intention to deceive in this respect, or any attempt to interfere with the existing business relations between this Company and its existing or potential clients, suppliers or agents, then the Company may take proceedings against you to prevent any recurrence and to recover any losses incurred as a result.

The Company's policy is to comply fully with the requirements of the Data Protection Act 1984 and it is essential that you follow the Company's rules and instructions very carefully on all aspects of Data Protection. In particular your attention is drawn to the 'Data Processing Security Policies and Standards Manual' which is published and updated regularly.

PRECEDENT 6

Secrecy Agreement for Existing Staff

(Headed notepaper of employing company)

I, the undersigned, hereby agree that I will at all times, whether or not in the employ of this Company:

(a) Maintain the strictest secrecy with regard to the business affairs of the Company and its customers, products and product lists, except to the extent that I may be authorised to disclose them by the Board of Directors of this Company, a Court of Law or any authorised or enforcement agency such as the police, Regulatory Body given powers under the Financial Services Act, Customs and Excise, Inland Revenue etc.

(b) Refrain from revealing or using confidential information regarding systems and programme design and data for personal gain.

(c) Refrain from using computer equipment except when authorised to do so and for official Company business as unauthorised usage could result in damage to the equipment and loss of stored data.

I undertake to familiarise myself with the Data Protection procedures set down by this Company as a result of the Data Protection Act 1984 and I understand that the Company is obliged as a consequence to view any breach of these procedures as a serious matter of discipline.

I understand that any breach of this agreement could result in the Company's sensitive and confidential data being disclosed to competitive or other interested parties and any such conduct on my part may render me liable to summary dismissal under the disciplinary procedure.

Signed ....

Name in full ....

Position held ....

Date: ....

Chapter 10

Notice

What is notice?

10.1 Notice to terminate the contract may be given orally or in writing by either party. When it is given by the employer it is a dismissal in law. [*EPCA 1978, s 55(2)(a)*]. The American expression for such action is an MIT – a Management Initiated Termination! It is important to ensure that the words used are clear and unambiguous, otherwise the tribunal will consider whether any reasonable employee upon hearing those words would have taken them to be words of dismissal (*Tanner v DT Kean Ltd [1978] IRLR 110*). It is therefore prudent to communicate notice of termination in writing.

When notice is given by the employee it is a resignation and save in one particular case (constructive dismissal – see EPCA 1978, s 55(2)(c)), he will lose all rights to bring an action for wrongful dismissal, unfair dismissal and/or a redundancy payment. The resignation must be clear and unequivocal (*Sothern v Franks Charlesly & Co [1981] IRLR 278*) and if the words are unambiguous, employers are permitted to treat them as such. In some cases, however, an employee may utter words whilst under great emotional strain or in the heat of the moment. Employers are not entitled to treat these words as words of resignation in circumstances where the employee is mentally disabled or emotionally disturbed and could not have been expected to have understood the full impact of his words.

In *Barclay v City of Glasgow District Council [1983] IRLR 313*, the Employment Appeal Tribunal held that where the words were uttered 'in the heat of the moment' or by an 'immature employee' then those words should be taken to mean what a reasonable employer would have taken them to mean. In such cases where 'idle words' have been used under emotional stress which the employer knew or ought to have known were not meant to be taken seriously, the tribunal will find that the employee has not resigned.

In *Millars of Falkirk Ltd v Chapman, EAT 156/86*, an employee who was under severe emotional strain told his employers that he 'felt like packing in his job'. His employers refused to allow him to return to work despite his sending in medical certificates to cover his subsequent absence. The EAT concluded that he had no intention of resigning and those words used were not intended to create any such impression. They held that a reasonable employer would not have believed that he was giving his calm considered view.

In *Sovereign House Security v Savage [1989] IRLR 115*, a security guard who

10.1 *Notice*

told his firm that 'he was jacking in his job' after being accused of dishonesty, was held not to have resigned by the Court of Appeal. Here it was held that 'where there may be something in the context of the exchange between the employee and employer or in the circumstance of the employee himself, the Tribunal may conclude that notwithstanding appearances, there was no real resignation despite what might appear at first sight'.

If there is ambiguity or any element of doubt in the context of the exchange between the employee and the employer it is open to a tribunal to conclude that despite appearances there has not been a resignation but a dismissal (*Goodwill Incorporated (Glasgow) Ltd v Ferrier, 11 August 1989, EAT 157/89 IRLIB 391*).

There may however be 'special circumstances' which should make an employer delay accepting a resignation. In *Kwik-Fit (GB) Ltd v Lineham* *[1992] IRLR 156*, Mr Lineham, a manager, threw his depot keys at the reception counter and drove home following a heated exchange with his manager which took place after one of the fitters had seen a written warning that he had been given concerning a previous incident. These 'special circumstances' when an employer should not accept a resignation at face value were cases of resignations in anger, in the heat of the moment and under extreme pressure. In such circumstances 'a reasonable time period' should be allowed to elapse during which time the employer will be able to ascertain whether the resignation was really intended. A 'reasonable period of time' would be relatively short, say a day or two.

In view of the above, it is therefore prudent to request that all resignations should be in writing!

More recently, the EAT held that a supervisor's conduct in reprimanding an employee in front of other staff for making a dental appointment without first obtaining permission, was 'humiliating, intimidating and degrading to such an extent that there was a breach of trust and confidence which went to the root of the contract'. The reprimand being 'officious and insensitive' was deemed to be an act of the employer and conduct on the part of the employer amounting to constructive dismissal under EPCA 1978, 55(2)(c). This was the case even though the particular supervisor had no authority to dismiss (*Hilton International Hotels (UK) Ltd v Protopapa [1990] IRLR 316*).

However, an unreasonable demotion and pay cut (in April, while an appeal was pending) which led the employee's solicitor to write a letter stating that if he did not hear from the company by 26 June he would initiate constructive dismissal proceedings was held by the EAT to be a resignation when the company did not reply to the letter. In all the circumstances of the case, the letter was clear and explicit enough to establish resignation on 26 June (*McDonald v Lowndes Queensway Group Ltd, 2 April 1991, EAT 651/90*).

Once the resignation has been accepted, the employee may not unilaterally withdraw it (*Riordan v War Office [1950] 3 All ER 552*). It can only be withdrawn by mutual consent. If however he is not paid what is due to him by way of his wages up to his termination date he will have a claim for breach of contract or a claim under the Wages Act 1986 (*Alsop v Star Vehicle Contracts Ltd* [*1990*] *IRLR 83*; *Kournavous v JR Masterton & Sons (Demolition) Ltd* [*1990*] *IRLR 119*; and see Chapter 5 above).

It is more common to include a term providing for written notice. The terms of the notice must be clear and unambiguous – merely warning staff they are to be dismissed will not constitute notice of termination (*Morton Sundour Fabrics Ltd v Shaw* [*1966*] *2 ITR 84*). They must take care not to leave their employment before proper notice is given otherwise they will be deemed to have resigned and will not be entitled to any redundancy payments or compensation for unfair dismissal.

The letter set out in **Precedent 1** is a typical letter warning staff about impending redundancies. The letters in **Precedent 2** set out the terms of notice of termination by reason of redundancy.

Statutory notice provisions

10.2   There are statutory minimum periods of notice which provide that employers must give one week's notice where an employee has between one month and less than two years' continuous service. [*EPCA 1978, s 49 (1)(a)-(c) as amended*]. For each additional continuous year of service up to twelve years, an additional week's notice is due, providing for a maximum of twelve weeks' notice. Employees with at least one month's continuous service must give at least one week's notice to terminate their contract. [*EPCA 1978, s 49(2)*]. If either the employer or the employee terminates the contract without giving the requisite notice to the other party (whether statutory or common law – see 10.3 below), the other party will have a right of action for breach of contract. Where the employer is the party terminating the contract without due notice, this is generally referred to as 'wrongful dismissal'. (For remedies for no notice or short notice, see 10.4 below.)

Any term in a contract providing for less than the statutory minimum shall be deemed to provide for the minimum statutory notice; however, either party has a right to waive his right to notice. [*EPCA 1978, s 49(3)*].

Section 49 does not affect the common law right of either party to treat the contract as terminable without notice, because of the conduct of the other party. [*EPCA 1978, s 49(5)*]. Thus, if an employee is guilty of gross misconduct, the employer can dismiss the employee without notice and will be able to resist an action by the employee for wrongful dismissal. Similarly, if an employer is guilty of a fundamental breach of contract, the employee will be entitled to terminate the contract without notice and will have a right of action against the employer for wrongful dismissal, on the basis that he had been 'constructively dismissed'.

Note, however, that in the instances referred to above (and indeed, as is always the case), the issue of whether the dismissal is *unfair*, as opposed to *wrongful*, is a separate one. Whether or not a dismissal is unfair is a matter to be determined by the industrial tribunal, in accordance with the provisions of section 57 of EPCA 1978.

No notice provisions

10.3 Where there are no notice provisions, employees are entitled to rely on common law notice. This is defined as 'reasonable' notice. The county court or High Court has the power to determine what length of notice is reasonable, taking into account the status of the employee. In most cases this will be more generous than statutory notice. It will also not normally be in excess of what other staff with similar seniority enjoy under their contracts and will not be determined by the pay intervals, i.e. a month's notice for monthly paid staff and a week for weekly paid staff. In one case (*Hill v CA Parsons & Co Ltd [1971] 3 All ER 1345*), a skilled engineer was held to be entitled to at least six months' notice and possibly twelve months. Here Lord Denning held:

> 'For a professional man of the plaintiff's standing (chartered engineer) and . . . . his length of service (35 years), reasonable notice would be at least 6 months and may be 12 months.'

Remedy for no notice or short notice

10.4 Whilst the normal remedy for no notice or short notice will be damages, the courts have granted declarations and injunctions particularly where the purported notice of termination is a wrongful repudiation of the contract.

In the *Hill* case referred to above, the Court of Appeal held (as summarised in the headnote) that:

> 'Ordinarily where an employer insists on the employment ending on the date specified in the unlawful notice, the employment relationship comes to an end since it is inconsistent with the confidential nature of the relationship that it should continue contrary to the will of one of the parties. This rule is not however inflexible and *where special circumstances exist*, the court has power to grant a declaration that the relationship still subsists and an injunction to prevent the employer from treating it as at an end.
>
> In the present case there were special circumstances justifying the grant of an injunction. The plaintiff had suffered a wrong by receiving notice which was too short and damages were an inadequate remedy. If the proper notice had been given his employment would probably have continued until Part II of the Industrial Relations Act 1971 came into operation in which case his rights would be safeguarded and he would not be obliged to join the union. Furthermore personal confidence continued to exist between the parties and therefore one of the main grounds for refusing an injunction was not applicable.'

This point was discussed again in a later case (*Gunton v London Borough of Richmond-upon-Thames [1980] IRLR 321*), where the issue in question was whether or not an employee had to accept the repudiation of his contract by his employer or whether he had an option to waive the breach and permit his contract to continue.

The majority of the Court of Appeal held that:

> 'The general doctrine that a repudiation by one party does not terminate the contract applies to contracts of employment as it applies to the generality of contracts. There is no reason in principle why (this) doctrine . . . should operate differently in the case of contracts of personal service from the way in which it operates in respect of other contracts.'

Lord Justice Shaw (dissenting, although he agreed with the majority decision for other reasons) suggested that such a notion 'in the sphere of employment . . . could not be reconciled with the realities of life. The preservation of the contractual relationship is necessarily coterminous with the ability of the law to compel performance and it has long been recognised that an order for specific performance will not be made in relation to a contract of service'.

When does the contract terminate?

10.5   Determining the effective date of termination is a crucial matter since certain critical time limits for bringing claims will apply from the effective date of termination, e.g. three months for unfair dismissal claims, six months for claims for redundancy payments.

The normal rule is that where notice is given orally – unless otherwise agreed, notice may be oral – the period of notice is exclusive of the day on which it is given (*West v Kneels Ltd [1986] IRLR 340*). The contract does not terminate when notice is given, it terminates when the notice expires. This applies even where the employee is told that he need not work out his notice (*Brindle v HW Smith (Cabinets) Ltd [1972] IRLR 125*).

It is, however, open to the parties to agree to waive notice or to agree to short notice. The employer may decide to dismiss without due notice and elect to pay wages in lieu of notice as damages for breach of contract (*Dixon v Stenor Ltd [1973] IRLR 28*). Where no notice or insufficient notice has been given, statutory notice will be added in order to determine (*a*) the effective date of termination for the purpose of the three-month time limit for presenting a claim for unfair dismissal [*EPCA s 55(4)*], and (*b*) the relevant date for the purposes of entitlement to a redundancy payment [*EPCA s 90(3)*]. These notional additional weeks will count for the computation of a period of continuous employment for both unfair dismissal and redundancy purposes. [*EPCA Sch 13, para 11(1), (3)*]. Statutory notice will be tacked on even where the employee has waived his right to notice or accepted a payment in lieu (*Staffordshire County Council v Secretary of State for Employment [1989] IRLR 117*).

10.5 *Notice*

It is well settled law that in cases of summary dismissal, the dismissal will take immediate effect, i.e. the date when the employer tells the employee that he is dismissed 'with immediate effect' unless there is an express clause in the contract to the contrary (*West Midlands Co-operative Society v Tipton* [*1986*] *IRLR 112*). In *Savage v J Sainsbury Ltd* [*1980*] *IRLR 109*, the contract provided that 'pending any appeal against the decision to dismiss, the employee would be suspended without pay but if reinstated will receive full back pay'.

In *Savage's* case, the Court of Appeal ruled that:

'. . . the effective date of termination was the original date of his summary dismissal because upon a correct analysis of the terms of his contract suspension without pay meant that if the appeal was successful he would be reinstated with full back pay and if not successful the original decision to dismiss would be affirmed and the dismissal would take effect on the original date. Since the contract made it clear that if an appeal fails the employee is deprived of his right not only to pay but to work from the original date of the dismissal, the contract must terminate at the date of dismissal.'

This will be the case even though the dismissal may have been in breach of a contractual disciplinary procedure (*Batchelor v British Railways Board* [*1987*] *IRLR 136*). The Court of Appeal ruled that the wording of the employee's dismissal letter dated 5 February 1985 stating that she was dismissed 'with immediate effect' meant just that 'and left no room for doubt whatsoever'.

This is an interesting judgment since in the *Tipton* case referred to above, the court suggested that an express clause in the contract may provide for some other date of dismissal where a decision to dismiss has been taken but an appeal is pending. In this case, British Railways' own disciplinary procedure provided that only in 'cases of exceptionally grave misconduct' would dismissal take immediate effect. This was not a case of exceptionally grave misconduct and the employee had a right of appeal against any punishment 'to be inflicted' – arguably showing that a dismissal under this clause only took effect after the appeal. The Court of Appeal however concerned themselves only with the document handed to the employee on 5 February which made it clear that she was dismissed with immediate effect. They were arguably wrong to do so and employers should be careful not to act inconsistently with contractual procedures.

Two more recent cases have considered the difficulties of establishing the effective date of termination in cases of summary dismissal and the necessity for being careful, consistent and clear when dismissing employees. In some cases, where employees are nearing their two years' service, employers may wish to dismiss immediately and give a payment in lieu of notice in order to avoid the possibility that the employee will be covered by the majority of the employment protection legislation. This appears to be a most cynical approach and in some cases the employer may be too late even when it looks at first blush as though the employee is one week short of two years' service. Perhaps in these cases a telephone call to a lawyer may be sensible!

In the first case, *Naidu v West Lambeth Health Authority, EAT 17/92*, the EAT affirmed the fact that the common law rules of repudiation and acceptance have no relevance to the statutory date of dismissal established by section 55(4). In this case the applicant had refused to accept certain terms and conditions of employment (which the employer was entitled to expect her to abide by) and she was suspended from duty. A letter date 24 May was read out to her at a meeting held on 30 May. The letter stated that if she did not accept the terms and return to work immediately her employment would be terminated summarily. She refused to return to work and on 6 June a letter was sent to her confirming her date of termination as 30 May.

The EAT held that the wording of the letter of 24 May and what had taken place at the meeting on 30 May clearly pointed to her employment being terminated on 30 May. She did not have the requisite two years' service to bring a claim for unfair dismissal.

In the second case, *Sister Rose Ltd v Garratt, EAT 101/90*, a manageress of a consulting room was purportedly dismissed with immediate effect by a letter dated 19 May 1989 which was handed to her on that day and also posted to her. Included with the letter was the P45, two weeks' pay in lieu of notice and her outstanding salary to date. Her employment had commenced on 26 May 1987 so on the face of it, it looked as if she lacked the two years' service.

The employer believed that by offering pay in lieu of notice and the employee accepting the payment, the employee had effectively waived her right to notice, as set out in section 49(3) which excludes the operation of a minimum notice period (i.e. extending the service by the minimum one week's statutory notice) in cases where it can be shown that the employee has waived his or her right to notice or accepted a payment in lieu.

However the tribunal, supported by the EAT, held that the employee had not waived her right to notice or accepted – in the sense of agreed to – a payment in lieu. The terms of the letter of 19 May and the employer's action in changing the locks at the workplace left her no choice. As a result one week's statutory notice could be tacked on to her period of employment enabling her to bring a claim. Moreover the EAT held:

> 'The right under s 55(5) to extend the effective date of termination when notice should have been given by the employer expires was intended to prevent the employer excluding the employee from the remedies that he or she would otherwise have, by prematurely terminating the period of employment. A cheque, even when cashed, if tendered as payment of damages for fundamental breach by an employer cannot have retrospective effect on the employer's termination by that fundamental breach . . .'

Consequently the EAT upheld the tribunal's ruling as to the employee's qualifying service and allowed her to bring her claim of unfair dismissal.

Counter-notice by employee

10.6 Section 55(4)(a) of the EPCA 1978 provides that where a contract of employment is terminated by notice given by either party, the effective date of termination (EDT) is the date upon which that notice expires.

Section 55(3) provides for circumstances where an employer gives notice to an employee and before that original notice has expired, the employee gives a counter-notice to end the employment earlier than the date specified in the employer's notice.

Despite the counter-notice, the employee shall be taken to have been dismissed by the employer and the dismissal will be for the reasons given by the employer when giving notice.

However, since the effective date of termination is crucial for determining the start of the three-month time limit for applicants to present their claim before an industrial tribunal, the effective date of termination is critical in cases where the employee gives counter-notice and terminates the employment at an earlier date.

In such a case, the EAT has held that the effective date of termination was the date when the applicant had terminated her employment by her own counter-notice i.e. on 21 September 1990 and not 9 November 1990 when the employer's notice would have run out (*Thompson v GEC Avionics Ltd [1991] IRLR 488*).

Option of pay in lieu of notice

10.7 It is prudent to provide for an option in the contract itself to make a payment in lieu of notice and in such circumstances there is no breach of contract involved when the employer elects to pay in lieu of the employee working out the notice period. Here the payment must include compensation for the loss of all contractual benefits due during the notice period. This may include the use of or compensation for the loss of the company car, mortgage subsidy, pension contributions, private health insurance etc.

The employer may wish to elect to require the immediate return of the company car since in some cases ex-employees have failed to return their cars at the end of the notice period or have returned them in an unfit and dilapidated state. A special clause is shown in **Precedent 3**.

The importance of a provision in the contract for payment in lieu of notice can be seen in cases where restraint clauses will operate after the contract has ceased. Any employer who breaches the contract – for example, by dismissing summarily in circumstances where the employee has not committed gross misconduct, or dismissing without notice and offering a payment in lieu of notice where there is no provision for such payment in the contract – will not be entitled to enforce any of the restraint clauses against the ex-employee.

Under a well-established principle (*General Billposting Co Ltd v Atkinson* [*1909*] *AC 118*), any party who breaches the contract – e.g. an employer who wrongfully dismisses – will normally not be permitted to rely on thereafter or enforce thereafter any clauses of the contract. However where it is the employee who is in serious breach of contract, then the employer may elect to bring the employment to an end without bringing the contract and the restrictive covenant to an end (*Thomas Marshall (Exports) Ltd v Guinle* [*1978*] *IRLR 174*). The employee is not permitted to take advantage of his wrongdoing by committing a fundamental breach of contract and then claiming that the contract and the covenant is at an end. Indeed, the employer is not obliged to accept the repudiation of the contract by the employee and he is best advised not to when the employee is attempting to leave his employment so as to compete without giving proper notice and in doing so is in breach of contract (see 'Garden Leave' clauses in Chapter 9).

It may, however, be possible to get around the principle in the *General Billposting* case noted above by an express clause providing for the employee's agreement to continue to be bound despite any breach of contract by the employer – see Clause 2(4) of **Precedent 3**.

In *Rex Stewart Jeffries Parker Ginsberg Ltd v Parker* [*1988*] *IRLR 483*, the employer was saved from such a predicament and was permitted to enforce a non-solicitation clause when he gave only one week's notice and six months' salary in lieu. Here the contract provided that the employee's service could be determined 'by the giving in writing of six calendar months' notice on either side or the payment of six months' salary in lieu'.

The Court of Appeal ruled that the clause offered two alternative methods of lawful determination – by six months' notice or six months' wages. Even though payment in lieu of notice is properly regarded as damages for breach of contract (see *Dixon v Stenor* referred to above), the Court of Appeal ruled that:

'. . . that did not establish the principle that in any case where the contract provides for money in lieu of notice, it is doing no more than quantifying damages which will be payable for a breach of the requirement to give a proper period of notice. The critical difference between the present case and *Dixon v Stenor* and cases in a similar category is that they were not cases in which the contract itself provided for a payment in lieu of notice.'

A model clause on notice appears in **Precedent 3**. This includes a series of model clauses for directors and senior executives. These clauses include conditions for automatic termination of the contract, such as insanity or bankruptcy, and certain requirements upon the executive upon termination such as resignation from his directorships and release of any shares, return of all papers and correspondence. There is also a clause which provides that even where the employer has breached the contract, the employee agrees to continue to be bound by the restrictions on competition, confidentiality etc.

Tax position on payments in lieu

10.8   The tax position on payments in lieu have been discussed in Chapter 5 ('Pay'). Where the contract provides for payments in lieu of notice they fall to be taxed in the normal way. [*ICTA 1988, ss 148, 188*]. Since payments in lieu are regarded as damages, the courts would normally only award any such sums with tax deducted.

However, where there is no provision in the contract for the termination payments in issue, the courts may regard them as being 'tax-free' – up to the statutory limit of £30,000. In one recent case (*Gothard v Mirror Group Newspapers Ltd [1988] IRLR 396*), Mirror Group Newspapers offered early retirement to some of their staff and letters were sent offering 'generous and fair financial arrangements for early retirement'. This included a lump sum pension, twice the statutory amount of redundancy payments, notice of six months plus seven weeks and 'a payment in lieu for any unworked notice at the date of termination'.

When one of the employees sued for his notice pay on the basis that he had only been given six months' notice not six months and seven weeks, the employers argued that any payments in lieu of notice should be paid with tax deducted and not gross. The Court of Appeal held that:

'The payment in lieu of notice made as part of an early retirement package should have been calculated on the gross pay not the pay net of tax.... This case was not one concerning damages in a case where no notice has been given but one concerning an offer made by an employer to an employee to accept voluntary early retirement. The question to be determined was what was meant by the employer's offer. In the context of an offer made which was said to be "generous and fair" and against a matrix that those under the age of 50 would receive tax-free payments for the unexpired notice and redundancy payments, the court was entitled to conclude that the natural meaning of the offer was that the payment in lieu of notice would be calculated on a gross basis .... If the appellants had wanted to argue that such payments are usually made on a net-of-tax basis, they should have called evidence to that effect.'

Employees who leave without due notice or short notice

10.9   Employers must also take heed should they withhold any payment of wages due in the event of their employees leaving without giving due notice or during their notice period. Frustrating as it may be, any refusal to pay wages due (including accrued holiday pay) will be a breach of the Wages Act unless of course the employee has given his prior written consent to such non-payment or this is provided for in the contract. This was established in *Pename v Patterson [1989] IRLR 195*, despite the employer's argument that the employee had been told at his interview that he would forfeit a week's wages should he leave without giving notice.

Not even the offer letter confirming this would satisfy the tribunal (or the EAT) because there was no evidence as to the employee's written agreement or consent to that term 'in writing' as required by section 1(1)(b) (although see the criticism of this decision by the Editor of IRLR – [*1989*] *IRLR 194*). In cases where the employer wishes to reserve the right to withhold accrued holiday pay in the case of gross misconduct (where there is no notice or pay in lieu due), he must set this out clearly in the contract. But the tribunal has the right to determine whether in the circumstances the employee has in fact committed gross misconduct and if the finding is to the contrary, then any failure to pay such moneys will be a breach of the Wages Act (*Greg May (CF&C) Ltd v Dring* [*1990*] *IRLR 19*).

It will be important therefore to include a clause in the contract covering this point. A model clause can be found in **Precedent 4**.

Notice by the employee

10.10 In many cases where an employee resigns and gives the proper written notice, he may ask to be released early – often because either he wishes to look for alternative work or he wishes to start work for his new employer during the notice period. In some cases, this may be acceptable to the employer but a prudent employer will confirm such matters in writing. This confirmation will refer to the agreement to release the employee early from his notice period with a termination date of............agreed. Should the employee be able to argue that the employer merely agreed to release him from his obligation to serve out his proper notice, then the employer will be obliged to pay the employee for the remainder of his notice period (subject to the normal doctrine of mitigation of loss). A model clause appears in **Precedent 5**.

Termination letter

10.11 A standard termination letter for a senior member of staff can be found at **Precedent 6**. A fuller discussion concerning terms of settlement can be found in Chapter 11, 'Settlements'.

Key Points

- Notice clauses in contracts should always refer to written notice.

- There should always be a provision for the employer to make a payment in lieu.

- There should be a provision for the withholding of any accrued holiday pay in cases of gross misconduct.

- There should be a clause stating that upon reaching normal retirement age the employee's contract will automatically terminate without further notice.

- Where there are no notice provisions the employee is entitled to common law notice which is 'reasonable notice' – in the case of a skilled engineer this amounted to six months' notice.

- There are statutory minimum periods of notice laid down by section 49 of the EPCA to which every employee becomes entitled unless the employer provides for longer notice periods in the contract.

- Termination becomes effective on the date specified in the letter of dismissal but where it is given orally the day on which it is given is normally excluded.

- Where no notice has been given in circumstances where it should have been, statutory notice will be tacked on to determine length of continuous service.

- If an employee accepts a payment in lieu of notice, he waives his right to notice but nevertheless, statutory notice will be added to the calculation of his service.

- Employees who leave without giving their required notice or leave during their notice period without permission may have a day's pay withheld if this is provided for in the contract.

PRECEDENT 1

Model Letters giving Warning of Redundancy

(*Headed company notepaper*)

Dear.............   Date ....

(Insert opening paragraph either giving brief reasons for the redundancy or alternatively referring to discussions at which the reasons were given.)

Every effort will be made to find you alternative employment but if by...........we have been unsuccessful it will be necessary to give you notice of termination of your employment due to redundancy.

We must emphasise that if you leave before notice of termination is given, you will not be eligible to receive a redundancy payment.

(OR: We must emphasise that if you leave without our written permission before we have given you notice of termination, you will lose any entitlement to a redundancy payment.)

We regret that this situation has arisen and will continue to make every effort to find a suitable alternative post for you.

Yours sincerely,

Managing Director

PRECEDENT 2

Letter giving Notice of Termination on Grounds of Redundancy

(*Headed notepaper*)
(RECORDED DELIVERY)

Date..............

Dear....................

Further to our previous letter of..........and the discussions that have taken place between yourself and ....I very much regret that the decision has had to be made to close the..........office at..........and therefore to declare you redundant. Below I set out the following terms of the termination of your contract:

1. NOTICE

By this letter I now give you twelve weeks' notice to terminate your contract irrespective of your minimum entitlement in law. Your contract of employment with the Company will therefore terminate on ....1993.

During this time you will be expected to work normally and co-operate with us to ensure a smooth closure of the office.

2. TERMINATION PAYMENTS

Assuming you honour the given period of notice and continue to work for us satisfactorily throughout this period, the Company proposes to make you the following payments:

(a)   Statutory redundancy payment of: £

(b)   Ex gratia payment made up of one
       week's gross pay for every completed
       year of service: £

(c)   Any accrued holiday pay in respect of
       holiday not taken up to the date of
       termination: £

       Total: £

Please note that in accordance with your contract of employment, the Company reserves the right to deduct from your final termination payment any moneys in respect of any holiday entitlement taken in excess of that due by the date of termination.

3. COMPANY CAR AND PROPERTY

I would like to remind you that on your last day at work you will be required to return your company car and keys in a satisfactory condition, the terms of which are set out in the Company Car Policy, a copy of which you already have. In accordance with the terms of your contract, you must also return all Company property in your possession, including any keys, petrol cards, equipment, documents, papers and correspondence.

4. TIME OFF TO LOOK FOR ALTERNATIVE EMPLOYMENT

You will be permitted a reasonable amount of time off during working hours if you need it to look for alternative work and attend job interviews. Prior agreement with your head of department must be obtained and evidence of appointments etc. may be required before permission may be granted.

5. REFERENCES

If you are successful in obtaining other employment or if you require a character reference in the future, a reference will be sent in the strictest confidence to your prospective employer or other appropriate person. Any request for a reference by such parties should be made in writing to.................

You may be assured that between now and your termination date, all possible efforts will continue to find you suitable alternative employment in the area within this Group of Companies. I regret the necessity of having to send you this letter and would like to thank you personally for your loyal service and hard work during your time with the Company. I wish you every success with your future employment.

Please will you sign both copies of this letter and return ONE COPY ONLY that you agree to all the conditions stated herein. A stamped, addressed envelope is enclosed for this purpose.

Yours sincerely,

Managing Director

I have read, understood and agree to abide by the conditions herein stated in return for which I shall receive the moneys set out in paragraph 2. Termination Payments.

....
(Employee)   (For and on behalf of the Company)

....(Date)   ....(Date)

PRECEDENT 3

Notice Clauses

Clause 1 – Management contract

'You will be entitled to receive and required to give X months' notice to terminate your contract. In cases of gross misconduct, no notice or pay will be due.

The Company reserves the right to make a payment in lieu of notice should it so wish or to require you to remain away from work during your notice period whichever may be appropriate. Any payment in lieu of notice will have PAYE tax and Class 1 National Insurance Contributions deducted at source.

Where the Company requires you to remain away from work during your notice period (whether you or the Company gave notice), you will be required to comply with any conditions laid down by the Company and whilst on full pay during such time you will not be permitted to work for any other person, firm, client, corporation or on your own behalf without the Company's prior written permission.

Unless your employment has terminated at any earlier date, it will terminate without any further notice at the end of the month in which your (60th/62nd/65th) birthday falls.

Should your employment terminate for whatever reason, the Company reserves the right to make a cash allowance in lieu of the use of the car during the notice period. The car will have to be returned upon leaving the Company or on any date determined by the Company in a clean and proper condition. The Company reserves the right to alter or withdraw any cash allowance to reflect the condition of the car or the need for any repairs.'

Clause 2 – Executive Director's contract

1. If the Executive

1.1. is prevented by illness, accident or other incapacity from fully carrying out his duties under this Agreement for a period exceeding [   ] consecutive months or at different times for periods exceeding in aggregate [   ] days (whether working or not) in any one period of [   ] consecutive months; or

1.2. if the Executive without reasonable cause neglects or omits or refuses to perform any of his duties under this Agreement or to observe and perform the provisions of this Agreement to the reasonable satisfaction of the Board; or

1.3. misconducts himself, whether during or outside the course of his employment, in such a way that in the reasonable opinion of the Board the business of any company in the Group will be affected prejudicially; or

1.4. becomes bankrupt or applies for a Receiving Order or has a Receiving Order made against him or enters into any arrangement or otherwise with his creditors; or

1.5. becomes of unsound mind or a patient within the meaning of the Mental Health Act 1983; or

1.6. shall be or become prohibited by law from being a Director of a company; or

1.7. shall for any reason otherwise than at the request of the Company resign as a Director of the Company,

it will be lawful for the Company, without prejudice to any other rights it may have at law in respect of any matters mentioned above, by written notice to the Executive, to terminate his employment forthwith.

2. The rights of the Company under Clause 1 are without prejudice to any other rights it may have at law to terminate the Executive's employment.

3. Upon termination of the Executive's employment for whatever reason the Executive:

3.1. will at the request of the Company and without claim for compensation resign his office as a director of the Company and as a director of any company within the Group or any Associated Company of which he is then a director and shall transfer to such company without payment any qualifying or nominee shares which he holds in or on behalf of the Company;

3.2. will immediately deliver up to the Company all price lists, lists of customers, correspondence and other documents and papers and property belonging to the Company which may have been prepared by him or have come into his possession in the course of his employment and shall not retain any copies thereof;

3.3. will cease to represent himself as being in any way connected with the business of the Company, the Group or any Associated Company.

4. The termination of this Agreement shall be without prejudice to the rights of either party against the other in respect of any antecedent breach of this Agreement. Such termination shall not, even in a case where the termination involves a breach of contract on the part of the Company, operate to affect those provisions in this Agreement which are intended to have effect after such termination. Without limiting the application of the two preceding

sentences, such termination shall not, even in such a case as mentioned above, release the Executive from the continuing observance and performance by him of the obligations on his part contained in Clauses..........(restraint, confidentiality etc.).

PRECEDENT 4

'Deductions from Pay during Notice Period'

Should you leave without notice or during your notice period without the permission of the Company, the Company reserves the right to deduct a day's pay for each day not worked during the notice period. This may include deduction of wages, accrued holiday pay or other moneys due to you. In any case where the Company agrees (in writing) to waive the need for you to work out your notice the above clause will not apply.

PRECEDENT 5

Agreement to Waive Notice

(*Headed company notepaper*)

Dear (Name)   Date........................

This is to confirm our conversation of today when you asked me whether the Company would agree to release you from your obligation to work out your three months' notice. You requested a leaving date of............(date).

I am pleased to confirm that we can agree to your request and therefore your contract will terminate accordingly on.............(date).

You understand that you have released the Company from any further obligation to pay you after............(date).

You also understand that you are still expected to comply with Clauses............of your contract which prohibit you from using or disclosing any confidential information, working for a competitor or soliciting our customers, suppliers or clients.

We wish you every success in your new venture.

Please will you sign the duplicate of this letter confirming your agreement to the above points.

Yours sincerely,

(name and position)

I agree with all that has been written above and I agree that I am fully aware of and agree to comply with all the terms of my contract in respect of the above matters.

Signed (Employee) .... Date..............

PRECEDENT 6

[Draft Termination Letter]

(Headed company notepaper)

Dear X,   Date.......................

Following our discussions, I am pleased to record the terms agreed in relation to the termination of your employment which takes place (took place) on..........(insert date of termination of contract of employment) which was, as was explained to you, by reason of redundancy.

The terms of your severance payment in compensation for loss of office are set out below. You will be required to agree to several conditions in consideration for your severance payment, the details of which are set out below:

1. The Company will pay you upon termination of employment the sum of £................ in compensation for loss of office which is made up of the following sums:

(a)	Payment in lieu of notice:	£
(b)	Accrued holiday pay:	£
(c)	Compensation for loss of other contractual benefits *including cash allowance for withdrawal of car for the period of the notice* (if applicable):	£
(d)	Redundancy payment as set out in Clause XX of your Contract of Employment (to include any and all statutory redundancy payments):	£
(e)	An ex gratia payment:	£
TOTAL:		£ (Gross)
		£ (Nett)

As we discussed the first £30,000 will be paid to you tax free, the remainder will be taxed at the rate of ......% on the basis of the salary element of your normal remuneration. Thus two figures are shown – the gross and nett figures. You will receive the nett figure and your final payslip will show the tax that has been duly deducted.

2. You agree to sign a COT 3 settlement form in full and final settlement of any claims you may have under the Employment Protection (Consolidation) Act 1978 in relation to the termination of your employment.

SUBSTITUTE IF 2. IS NOT TO BE INCLUDED – PLEASE INCLUDE THE FOLLOWING:

You agree to accept payments set out in Clause 1(a)-(c) as soon as you and the Company sign this Agreement. However, the payments set out in 1(d) and (e) will be paid:

either in three monthly stages, but only in so far as you have not accepted any other employment whether this be employment or self-employment, acting as agent or otherwise:

(i) the first third to be paid on (one month from the date of this Agreement);

(ii) the second third to be paid on (two months from the date of this Agreement);

(iii) the final third to be paid on (three months from the date of this Agreement);

OR

the whole of the payment as set out in 1(d) and (e) above to be paid four months after your employment has terminated.

You also agree that you will repay any and all payments paid on an ex gratia basis (i.e. all payments as stated in Clause 1(e) above) should you submit a claim for unfair dismissal or any other claim before an industrial tribunal which relates in any way to this termination of employment.

3. You agree to accept this payment, referred to above, in full and final settlement for any legal claims that you may have arising out of or in connection with your Contract of Employment or the termination thereof. This includes all claims that you may have at common law and under Statute against the Company or any of its authorised officers.

4. The Company agrees to provide a reference, upon written request from any prospective employer, the terms of which will be agreed between you and the Company.

You will be required to sign both copies of this letter. Please retain one copy and return the other duly signed.

Yours sincerely,

(Director)

I agree to all the above terms in consideration for the aforementioned severance payment made to me by the Company which is in full and final settlement for any claims that I may have at common law arising out of my Contract of Employment or in connection with the termination of my employment.

....   Date............
(Employee's signature)

Chapter 11

Settlements

11.1   In cases where the services of an employee are to be terminated, employers may seek to make some form of payment 'in full and final settlement'. Any such settlement reached between the parties will be regarded as void, permitting the employee to proceed against the employer for unfair dismissal or to bring any other proceedings before an industrial tribunal (if he satisfies the applicable service qualifications and all the other eligibility requirements). [*EPCA 1978, s 140(1)*]. However, as an exception to this rule and subject to the new provisions inserted by TURERA 1993 (see 11.2 below), settlements reached under the auspices of a conciliation officer employed by ACAS will be effective. [*EPCA 1978, s 140(2)(d),(e)*].

New compromise agreements

11.2   By virtue of section 39 of and Schedule 6 to TURERA 1993, amending section 140(2) of the EPCA, it will now be possible for employers and employees to make legally binding agreements to settle claims other than by effecting a settlement under the auspices of ACAS, provided that the following conditions are satisfied:

(*a*)   the agreement must be in writing;

(*b*)   the agreement must relate to the particular complaint;

(*c*)   the employee must have received independent legal advice from a qualified lawyer as to the terms and effect of the proposed agreement and in particular its effect on his ability to pursue his rights before an industrial tribunal;

(*d*)   the qualified lawyer who gives the advice must have a policy of insurance covering the risk of a claim by the employee in respect of loss arising in consequence of the advice;

(*e*)   the agreement must identify the adviser; and

(*f*)   the agreement must state that the conditions regulating compromise agreements under the Act are satisfied.

On a strict interpretation of the words in the 'particular complaint', in subsection (3)(b), it is unclear whether an agreement under this section could cover all possible claims as is commonly the case under the COT 3 arrangements. However, in introducing the amendment in the House of Lords, Viscount Ullswater stated that:

'We are proposing that the procedures should only be available in the context of an agreement which settles a particular complaint that has already arisen between the parties to that complaint. They will not allow an individual to compromise his right to present, or to continue with, a claim to a tribunal in respect of any matter other than the particular complaint which is the subject of the agreement.'

(Hansard (HL) Vol.545 No.135 Col.904 6 May 1993).

In view of the decision of the House of Lords in *Pepper v Hart* [*1993*] *IRLR 33* (see 5.20 'Pay') whereby references to Parliamentary materials can be used as an aid to construction, the above statement may be referred to by a court or tribunal in a future case should it consider that the meaning of the provision is ambiguous.

With regard to (3)(c), subsection (4) provides that the 'qualified lawyer' must be a barrister (in practice or employed) or a solicitor holding a practising certificate in England and Wales or an advocate or solicitor holding a practising certificate in Scotland. 'Independent' legal advice means that it is given by a lawyer who is not acting in the matter for the employer or an associated employer. This could therefore include an employer's solicitor so long as he is not acting for the employer in relation to the matter in question.

Readers should note that Schedule 6 which makes corresponding amendments in relation to claims under the Sex Discrimination Act 1975, the Race Relations Act 1976, the Wages Act 1986 and claims under TULRCA 1992 refers to 'Compromise Contracts', whilst section 39(3), in relation to EPCA claims, refers to 'Compromise Agreements'. According to a spokesman at the Employment Department, it was not intended to distinguish these agreements in any way and the difference in name is apparently irrelevant!

The introduction of these amendments, enabling the ACAS route to be by-passed will be a relief to lawyers and employers as ACAS has taken the view (supported by legal advice) that it has no statutory role to become involved in cases where the parties have already reached an agreement between themselves (see 11.3 below). The practice of 'rubber stamping' such agreements had become a considerable drain on ACAS's resources.

The new procedure will provide a simple and speedy means of reaching binding settlements without recourse to the tribunal system. The most important element of any such procedure, however, will be to safeguard the employee so that he does not sign away his rights without being fully aware of the implications.

These provisions are expected to come into force on 30 August 1993.

Settlements through ACAS

11.3 In July 1990 ACAS published a practice directive providing some guidance on how it intended to act in cases before a formal complaint has been made to an industrial tribunal. Since that date conciliation officers will not take part in any settlements in such cases unless:

(1) a dismissal has actually occurred or notice has been served;

(2) statutory employment protection rights have been infringed;

(3) the requisite qualifying period of service has been served where appropriate;

(4) a firm agreement has not already been reached (i.e. where there is no room for conciliation).

The conciliation officer will no longer become involved in cases of mutual agreement to terminate or where, in redundancy dismissals, the employer has clearly acted fairly and followed an agreed selection procedure or customary arrangement.

It will not be good enough to have agreed the terms, the officer must be satisfied that the terms could be changed as a result of his taking action and he will ask the parties if this is the case.

This procedure is explained in the leaflet COT 5, a copy of which is reproduced in **Precedent 1**.

Ways of achieving a binding settlement

11.4 In order to effect a satisfactory settlement so that no tribunal claim may be brought, it will be necessary either to:

(1) negotiate the whole agreement through the conciliation officer;

(2) negotiate an element of the settlement through the conciliation officer; or

(3) agree to make any additional payments other than payment in lieu of notice and statutory redundancy pay (if relevant) after the three-month time period has elapsed for presenting an unfair dismissal claim. This sum may be put into an interest-bearing account and any interest accruing will also be paid at the appropriate time.

It will be important to check with the Central Office of Industrial Tribunals in Bury St Edmunds that no claim has been presented. This may be done one or two weeks following the end of the three-month period for bringing a claim.

Role of conciliation officer

11.5 A settlement reached through ACAS is normally recorded on a COT 3 form, although an oral agreement secured through a conciliation officer has been regarded as binding notwithstanding that it was not recorded in writing (*Gilbert v Kembridge Fibres Ltd [1984] IRLR 52*).

Furthermore, a settlement will be deemed to have been effected through ACAS, and will be a valid settlement precluding any claim before a tribunal, even where the parties have agreed the terms before the ACAS officer has been called in. In one case, *Moore v Duport Furniture Products Ltd [1982] IRLR 31*, agreement was reached on the basis of a £300 settlement and the employee would be allowed to resign. The ACAS officer went through the terms with both parties. Both parties signed the COT 3. The employee was subsequently not prosecuted by the police and he brought a claim for unfair dismissal on the basis that the conciliation officer had a duty to promote a settlement that was fair to both sides and that simply to record a settlement reached was not 'action by a conciliation officer' pursuant to section 140(2)(d). The House of Lords disagreed. They held that:

> 'The expression "endeavour to promote" a settlement . . . should (not) be construed as involving the taking of a positive initiative by the Conciliation Officer concerned. The expression "promote a settlement" . . . must be given a liberal construction capable of covering whatever action by way of such promotion is applicable in the circumstances of the particular case.'

The tribunals have also made it clear that conciliation officers are under no duty to advise the employee on any relevant legislation, but an agreement reached with their assistance may be set aside if an officer acts partially or adopts unfair methods.

In *Slack v Greenham (Plant Hire) Ltd [1983] IRLR 271*, the EAT held that: ' . . . his (conciliation officer's) action and any resultant agreement can only be impugned if he is guilty of bad faith or if he adopts unfair methods'.

Effect of COT 3

11.6   Where an employer or employee has appointed a representative in relation to a complaint or claim, ACAS has indicated that its conciliation officers 'will deal with the representative unless and until they are instructed to the contrary . . .' (ACAS Annual Report 1988).

The importance of this practice can be seen in the decision of *Freeman v Sovereign Chicken Ltd [1991] IRLR 408* where the Citizens' Advice Bureau agreed a COT 3 settlement for Mrs Freeman without her express oractual authority. Nevertheless the EAT held that in cases involving claims arising out of statutory employment rights, the ostensible or implied authority 'must be somewhat wider [than usual] and include all actual and potential issues between the parties arising out of the employment relationship and which are or should be known to the parties at the time'.

However, the EAT went on to state that it would be good practice for any representative to 'ensure that the client has seen and approved the wording of the proposed settlement'.

Wording of COT 3

11.7   Great care must be taken when drafting the wording of a COT 3 since it has been held that the general wording 'in full and final settlement of all claims which the employee might have arising from his employment or its termination' will not cover future claims for discrimination.

In its 1988 Annual Report, ACAS advised that:

'Where parties concerned in a complaint falling under the EPCA wish to include possible complaints under the discrimination jurisdictions in the terms of a wider settlement, we believe it is necessary to identify such complaints separately in the settlement wording . . .'

In *Livingstone v Hepworth Refractories plc [1992] IRLR 63* Mr Livingstone signed a COT 3 drawn up by a conciliation officer agreeing to accept £20,402 in 'full and final settlement'. However, following the decision of the ECJ in *Barber v Guardian Royal Exchange Assurance Group [1990] IRLR 240*, he presented a sex discrimination complaint arguing that he had been discriminated against under the company's pension scheme contrary to section 6 of the Sex Discrimination Act, Article 199 of the Treaty of Rome and various EC Directives. The EAT held that the COT 3 did not preclude his complaint since a COT 3 made under the EPCA did not apply to claims made under the Sex Discrimination Act.

Suggested wording for COT 3 is included as **Precedent 2**.

Jurisdictional limits

11.8   Conciliation officers have no statutory powers to conciliate over redundancy payments since their powers to promote a settlement are limited to unfair dismissal complaints, discrimination cases and Wages Act complaints.

Set-off

11.9   It is important for employers to understand the effect of any payments made other than under the auspices of ACAS. In particular, the rules on set-off are complex and any *ex gratia* payments made by an employer may not always be set off against any awards of compensation.

The general rule is that any *ex gratia* payments made by an employer are to be taken into account and deducted from any award of compensation (*Horizon Holidays v Grassi [1987] IRLR 371*). However, tribunals will determine the loss before deducting any payments already made. Briefly, tribunals will determine the loss suffered by any unfairly dismissed employee under various heads such as loss of present earnings, future earnings, loss of fringe benefits, pension rights etc. (*Norton Tool Co Ltd v Tewson [1972] IRLR 86*). The total loss will be calculated, subject to the duty on the part of the ex-employee to mitigate his loss. The tribunal will then deduct any payments in lieu of notice and will then determine the consequent loss. Should this figure exceed the statutory limits [*EPCA 1978, ss 74-76*], the tribunal will award the maximum permitted amount (£11,000 from 1 June 1993) subject to any reduction for contributory fault [*EPCA 1978, s 74(6)*]. An appellate tribunal can overturn an industrial tribunal's decision on the question of contribution only where there has been an error of law or the decision is perverse (*Hollier v Plysu Ltd [1983] IRLR 260*).

Mutual agreement to terminate

11.10   In some cases where an employer reaches an agreement with an employee and both parties agree that the contract will end, there will have been no dismissal and no resignation but a mutual agreement to terminate. The courts may take the view that a separate contract has been agreed, which terminates the contract of employment by mutual agreement. As stated in 11.3 above, ACAS will no longer conciliate where there is a mutual agreement to terminate (see **Precedent 1**, COT 5).

The tribunals have been reluctant to enforce such agreements, since the argument that there has been a mutual agreement to terminate will preclude any claim for unfair dismissal. The tribunals will only determine that a mutual agreement has been reached where they are satisfied that:

(*a*)   the employee has entered into the agreement freely and without duress;

(*b*)   he has benefited from a financial consideration; and

(*c*)   he has had the opportunity to take independent advice.

In *Logan Salton v Durham County Council [1989] IRLR 99*, a social worker was in the process of appealing against a decision to redeploy him when his employers decided to institute disciplinary proceedings for several matters, disclosed in a seven page document to him, which set out numerous complaints against him. He decided to resign rather than face the hearing and he asked his union official to negotiate terms with his employer. As a result of those negotiations a written agreement was drawn up and signed by both parties. The agreement stated that: 'The employee's contract of employment with the Council will terminate by mutual agreement on 31.3.87'. A financial settlement was agreed and a loan for his car of £2,750 was wiped off. Here the EAT held that:

> 'The agreement between the appellant and respondents was not a contract of employment or a variation of an existing contract. It was a separate contract which was entered into willingly, without duress and after proper advice and for good consideration. Termination of employment did not depend upon the happening of some future event which may have been envisaged, nor upon the possible happening of events which were not envisaged and which, had they been, might well have caused the employee not to agree with the proposed terms.'

Employers may be tempted to rely on a mutual agreement to terminate as it avoids any question of dismissal. However, in practice, a termination based on a mutual agreement will be rare. In most cases, the employer will dismiss the employee in question with an offer of damages for breach of contract and or an ex gratia payment.

Extended leave agreements

11.11 Some employers have attempted to obtain the agreement of an employee that upon a non-return to work on an agreed date, his contract will automatically terminate. The Court of Appeal in *Igbo v Johnson Matthey Chemicals Ltd [1986] IRLR 215* has ruled that such an agreement is void. There is a clear prohibition on any agreement which purports to exclude or limit any of the employment protection rights. [*EPCA 1978, s 140(1)*]. In *Igbo*, the Court of Appeal held that:

'The effect of a provision for automatic termination upon a failure to report for work on a specified future date, introduced by way of a variation of a subsisting contract of employment, is to "limit" the operation of ss 54 and 55 of the EPCA 1978 contrary to section 140(1)(a) in that it converts a right not to be unfairly dismissed into a conditional right not to be unfairly dismissed.'

Agreements on early retirement

11.12 Any invitation or offer made by an employer to employees to apply for early retirement may be valid in which case there may be no dismissal by the employer, simply an agreement to retire early. Here the Court of Appeal, in *Birch and Humber v University of Liverpool [1985] IRLR 165*, ruled that such an agreement may be valid where:

'. . . an employer envisaging that some time in the future, for example, because of new technology, he will have to slim down his workforce, makes an offer to those who are prepared to resign rather than wait to volunteer and supports that offer with a financial inducement which is far in excess of what is likely to be obtained under redundancy legislation, assuming no question of coercion of any kind, there can be no question of there having been a dismissal if that offer is accepted'.

The case above is to be distinguished from voluntary redundancies where the employees are still regarded as having been dismissed – all they have done is volunteer for dismissal! They will still be entitled (if they qualify) for redundancy payments.

Particular note should be taken of the latest Inland Revenue guidance on the taxation of early retirement payments which have been disguised as redundancy payments (Memorandum 104, March 1991, Joint Office of Inland Revenue Superannuation Funds Office and Occupational Pensions Board). The £30,000 tax-free payments on top of pension benefits is only allowable on genuine redundancy and not for voluntary early retirement.

11.13 *Settlements*

What amounts to pressure?

11.13 The question of coercion was discussed in a case where an employee was to be the subject of a disciplinary hearing (*Martin v MBS Fastenings (Glynwed) Distribution Ltd [1983] IRLR 198*). His regional director told him that it would be in his best interests to resign. Here the Court of Appeal held that tribunals might well address their minds to questions such as 'whether the employer intended that the employment should in any event be ended, whether the employer imposed some degree of pressure on the employee and whether that pressure in fact caused the resignation' in deciding whether the employee resigned or was dismissed. However, that question was a question of fact for the industrial tribunal and would only be reviewed on appeal if the decision reached was one which no reasonable tribunal could have reached on the evidence.

Thus, employers must take care that pressure does not 'force' the employee to resign or accept the agreement. If this is the case, the employer may be deemed to have been dismissed.

Financial advantages of settlement

11.14 Apart from the obvious advantages for the employer to settle a case (time, legal costs, stress etc.), one major financial advantage is often overlooked. Where an award of compensation is made by tribunals, any award is subject to the Employment Protection (Recoupment of Unemployment and Supplementary Benefit) Regulations 1977 (SI 1977 No 674, as amended by SI 1980 No 1608). Any unemployment benefit or income support paid by the Department of Employment or Department of Social Security to the applicant will be deducted from any award but those moneys (called the 'prescribed element') will have to be repaid by the employer, under an order attached to the copy of the tribunal's decision, within 21 days. Where a settlement has been reached with the tribunal, no such order is made.

Tax implications of settlements

11.15 Any payments made by an employer to an employee in consideration for his entering into a termination agreement containing obligations or restrictions is subject to tax. This is particularly so where the employee is required to enter into a restrictive covenant (whether or not it is valid and enforceable) or required to remain at work until the end of his contract (see section 313(1)(2) of the Income and Corporation Taxes Act 1988 and Tolley's 'Taxation of Employments' under Chapter 11 on Termination Payments and Signing-on Fees). The 1993 Inland Revenue Guide to PAYE at R1 states that:

'Restrictive covenants are undertakings which restrict the employees' freedom of activity in some way, and for tax purposes do not have to be legally enforceable. These undertakings can take many different forms but will commonly restrict the employees' freedom to compete with you after they stop working for you.'

280

R1 also makes it clear that payments made to employees in return for their entering into restrictive covenants, count as pay for tax purposes even if the payments take the form of payments in kind.

Settlement terms

11.16 It is suggested that the termination letter should be drafted in straightforward terms – see **Precedent 6**, Chapter 10 for an example. In addition employers may consider entering into a Declaration of Trust with the individual. A copy of a simply drafted version can be found at **Precedent 3** at the end of this chapter. Other undertakings pursuant to termination can be found at **Precedent 4**.

Key Points

- Any settlement should be determined under the auspices of ACAS and agreed on a COT 3.

- Conciliation officers will not negotiate the terms but will go through the terms with both parties to ensure that both are satisfied and both understand the legal effect of the settlement.

- Any ex gratia payments and payments in lieu of notice will be set off against any losses calculated by the tribunal.

- By reaching a settlement employers will avoid repaying unemployment benefit and income support under the recoupment provisions.

- Mutual agreements to terminate if accepted will disbar any ex-employee from complaining of unfair dismissal since he will not have been dismissed.

- Agreements to terminate should only be concluded if the employee has had an opportunity to take independent advice, has been put under no duress and is to receive a monetary settlement.

- Any pressure from the employer exerted on the employee to conclude such settlement will be deemed to be a dismissal in law.

- Agreements which purport to terminate the contract automatically if a future event happens or does not happen will be deemed to be void.

- Agreements for staff to retire early may be valid where there is a financial settlement and a clear option on the staff to stay in employment or retire on agreed terms.

- Asking for volunteers for redundancy will still be deemed to be a dismissal by the employer and any employee volunteering will still be entitled to sue for unfair dismissal (and a redundancy payment if this has not been paid) – the employee is volunteering to be dismissed in law.

PRECEDENT 1

Conciliation in Complaints by Employees to Industrial Tribunals

Information about ACAS assistance

INDIVIDUAL CONCILIATION WHERE COMPLAINTS ARE NOT MADE TO TRIBUNALS

COT 5 leaflet explains that it is not necessary for individuals who believe their employment rights have been infringed to make a formal complaint to an industrial tribunal before conciliation can be available. A claim that rights have been broken or withheld, which could become a formal complaint to a tribunal, can be made direct to ACAS. This 'insert' explains ACAS's approach in such cases in greater detail. If I am asked in such cases to try and promote a settlement, I will need to be sure that I have a duty in law to do so before I can begin to conciliate.

This means:

1. I will need information about the claim. In cases where there is a claim of unfair dismissal, I will need to be satisfied that dismissal has actually occurred; or that notice of dismissal has been given; or, in claims of constructive dismissal, that notice of resignation has been given. I will not be able to help where employment has ended voluntarily or by mutual consent, or where there was clearly a redundancy under customary arrangements or agreed procedures which had been fairly applied.

2. I will need to be sure that a claim is being made about the infringement of statutory employment rights which provide for conciliation officers to take action.

3. In cases where the employment rights only exist after a qualifying period of employment (e.g. 2 years is necessary for claims of unfair dismissal), I will ask for information about the length of the employment. If the qualifying period has been served I will then seek to promote an agreed settlement, in exactly the same way as if a formal complaint had been made to a tribunal.

4. If a firm agreement has been reached before I am asked to help, it will not be possible for me to do so because the dispute has already been settled, and there is thus no room for conciliation. If such an agreement is said to be conditional on a conciliation officer taking action, I will need to ask whether it is accepted that its terms might be changed as a result of that action. I will only be able to act if that possibility exists.

DATA PROTECTION ACT

Some information given to ACAS is placed on computer for ACAS's own record purposes. It is not made available to any other body or individual.

PRECEDENT 2

Suggested Wording for COT 3

'We the undersigned have agreed that the Company will pay to ....
(name of employee) the sum of £...................... on the terms as set out in the
attached Schedule [not included here]. .... agrees to accept this sum
in full and final settlement of all and any claims that he/she may have
regarding any and all rights for which a Conciliation Officer has a statutory
duty to conciliate. This includes but is not limited to claims for unfair
dismissal, sex or race discrimination, equal pay, any discrimination or equal
pay claims arising out of any EC Directive or Article of the Treaty of Rome,
statutory redundancy payments and any and all claims under the Wages Act
1986. .... also agrees not to pursue any claims that he/she may have
against the Company or any subsidiary or associated companies, arising out of
her contract of employment with the Company and in relation to the
termination of the contract of employment. This Settlement does not affect
any rights that .... may have in relation to industrial injury claims or
the Company Pension Scheme.'

PRECEDENT 3

Declaration of Trust (1)

(Company headed notepaper)

This Declaration of Trust is made The .... Day of 1993

BETWEEN:

The ABC Company Ltd

Hereinafter called 'the Company'

AND

(Name) ....
(Address) ....

Hereinafter called 'the Beneficiary'

In consideration of the payments to be made to the Beneficiary by the Company hereinafter contained, the Beneficiary agrees:

(a) To keep confidential all confidential information and trade secrets belonging to the Company, its staff, clients and customers, its business dealings, computer systems and all the information on the Company's databases etc.

This includes (but is not limited to) giving a written undertaking that the Beneficiary has not nor will not engage or be engaged nor has not nor will not set up any computer sabotage including but not limited to any computer or systems software 'bomb(s)' or any other device(s) which would interfere in any way with any of the Company's computer programs or systems etc.

(b) To make no untrue, derogatory or unflattering statements about any member of the Company (or any associated or subsidiary companies), Director (whether executive or non-executive, former or current), client or customer (former or current), agent, distributor, supplier or consultant nor make any statements whether oral or in writing which would tend to have the effect of lowering the reputation of the subject of the statement in the estimation of right-thinking members of society.

(c) Not to misuse for your own use or disclose to any third party any information of a personal or sensitive nature concerning any member of the Company's staff (present or past).

285

(d) To confirm that any and all keys, property, books, files, documents, correspondence, codes etc. belonging to the Company including the Security Pass, AMEX card and mobile telephone, have been duly returned to an Authorised Officer of the Company.

(e) To confirm that any and all files, papers etc. have been handed over to an Authorised Officer of the Company.

(f) To confirm in writing that all papers, disks, computer hardware and/or software have been handed to an Authorised Officer of the Company.

(g) To confirm that no contact has been or will be made during business hours with any member of staff other than .... (Name). This includes but is not limited to telephoning or contacting by any other means any other member of staff at the Company's premises, all outside specialists, contractors etc. with whom the Company has business dealings.

(h) To confirm no representation or misrepresentation as an authorised agent/employee or otherwise of the Company has been or will be made at any time after the termination of employment.

(i) To keep the terms of this Settlement and the circumstances giving rise to its making strictly confidential and agree not to disclose these terms to any other third party. You agree that you will not disclose any information regarding the terms of this Settlement nor give any interview or make any statement to any person, television company, radio station, newspaper, magazine or other media organisation save and except as required by law and save and except that you will be permitted to disclose this information only to your spouse.

(j) Not to represent yourself as an authorised agent/employee or otherwise for this Company or any other associated company once your employment has ended.

(k) Not to, for a period of twelve months after your employment ends, attempt to solicit custom for private gain and/or deal with any private individual, firm or company who within the period of one year before the termination of your employment had been a customer, client, supplier, broker, dealer or authorised agent, of the Company (or of an associated company) with whom you had any personal dealings in the last twelve months of your employment. This does not affect your rights to continue to deal with Clients whom you personally introduced to this Company.

You also agree that you will not attempt to interfere with the existing business relations between any customer, client, supplier or authorised agent or employee and the Company.

(l) That at no time after the end of your employment, will you approach any other employee of the Company with a view to him or her ceasing to be employed with the Company.

(m) To repay any outstanding loans by any means deemed acceptable to the Company and to release the Company as guarantor for any loans or agree to any other arrangement in relation to any Bank guarantees as may be acceptable to the Company.

(n) To represent and warrant to the Company that at the date of signing this agreement, you have not received or accepted an offer of employment or taken up any consultancy or agency arrangements either on your own behalf or with any other third party. You agree to repay any or all of the payments as set out above.

(o) To resign immediately from any Directorships which you may hold in this Company, a subsidiary or associated company within the Group.

The Company, through an Authorised Officer, HEREBY declares that it will pay to the Beneficiary the sum of £35,980 gross, £33,588 PAYE deducted at source, in two equal six-monthly instalments. The first instalment will be paid on the date hereof, following the execution of This Declaration, by cheque.

The second instalment will be paid by cheque six months from the date of this Declaration subject to the above conditions having been fully met and complied with to the satisfaction of the Company.

In addition, the Company agrees to provide to you for your private use your Company car for the period of six months from 4 January 1993, Private Medical Insurance cover for the period of six months from 4 January 1993 and your continued use (with no repayments) of your Season Ticket.

DECLARED BY ....
                            (Authorised Officer For and On Behalf of the Company)

IN THE PRESENCE OF
WITNESS

Signature ....
Name ....
Address ....
Occupation ....

Prec 3 *Settlements (11)*

Declaration of Trust (2)

(Company headed notepaper)

This Declaration of Trust is made The .... Day of 1993

BETWEEN:

The ABC Company Ltd

Hereinafter called 'the Company'

AND

(Name) ....
(Address) ....

Hereinafter called 'the Beneficiary'

In consideration of the payments to be made to the Beneficiary by the Company hereinafter contained, the Beneficiary agrees:

(a) To keep confidential all confidential information and trade secrets belonging to the Company, its staff, clients and customers, its business dealings, computer systems and all the information on the Company's databases etc.

This includes (but is not limited to) giving a written undertaking that the Beneficiary has not nor will not engage or be engaged nor has not nor will not set up any computer sabotage including but not limited to any computer or systems software 'bomb(s)' or any other device(s) which would interfere in any way with any of the Company's computer programs or systems etc.

(b) To make no untrue, derogatory or unflattering statements about any member of the Company (or any associated or subsidiary companies), Director (whether executive or non-executive, former or current), client or customer (former or current), agent, distributor, supplier or consultant nor make any statements whether oral or in writing which would tend to have the effect of lowering the reputation of the subject of the statement in the estimation of right-thinking members of society.

(c) Not to misuse for your own use or disclose to any third party any information of a personal or sensitive nature concerning any member of the Company's staff (present or past).

(d) To confirm that any and all keys, property, books, files, documents, correspondence, codes etc. belonging to the Company including the Security Pass, AMEX card and mobile telephone, have been duly returned to an Authorised Officer of the Company.

(e) To confirm that any and all files, papers etc. have been handed over to an Authorised Officer of the Company.

(f) To confirm in writing that all papers, disks, computer hardware and/or software have been handed to an Authorised Officer of the Company.

(g) To confirm that no contact has been or will be made during business hours with any member of staff other than .... (Name). This includes but is not limited to telephoning or contacting by any other means any other member of staff at the Company's premises, all outside specialists, contractors etc. with whom the Company has business dealings.

(h) To confirm no representation or misrepresentation as an authorised agent/employee or otherwise of the Company has been or will be made at any time after the termination of employment.

(i) To keep the terms of this Settlement and the circumstances giving rise to its making strictly confidential and agree not to disclose these terms to any other third party. You agree that you will not disclose any information regarding the terms of this Settlement nor give any interview or make any statement to any person, television company, radio station, newspaper, magazine or other media organisation save and except as required by law and save and except that you will be permitted to disclose this information only to your spouse.

(j) Not to represent yourself as an authorised agent/employee or otherwise for this Company or any other associated company once your employment has ended.

(k) Not to, for a period of twelve months after your employment ends, attempt to solicit custom for private gain and/or deal with any private individual, firm or company who within the period of one year before the termination of your employment had been a customer, client, supplier, broker, dealer or authorised agent, of the Company (or of an associated company) with whom you had any personal dealings in the last twelve months of your employment. This does not affect your rights to continue to deal with Clients whom you personally introduced to this Company.

You also agree that you will not attempt to interfere with the existing business relations between any customer, client, supplier or authorised agent or employee and the Company.

(l) That at no time after the end of your employment, will you approach any other employee of the Company with a view to him or her ceasing to be employed with the Company.

(m) To repay any outstanding loans by any means deemed acceptable to the Company and to release the Company as guarantor for any loans or agree to any other arrangement in relation to any Bank guarantees as may be acceptable to the Company.

(n) To represent and warrant to the Company that at the date of signing this agreement, you have not received or accepted an offer of employment or taken up any consultancy or agency arrangements either on your own behalf or with any other third party. You agree to repay any or all of the payments as set out above.

(o) To resign immediately from any Directorships which you may hold in this Company, a subsidiary or associated company within the Group.

The Company, through an Authorised Officer, HEREBY declares that it will pay to the Beneficiary the sum of £35,980 gross, £33,588 PAYE deducted at source, in two equal six-monthly instalments. The first instalment will be paid on the date hereof, following the execution of This Declaration, by cheque.

The second instalment will be paid by cheque six months from the date of this Declaration subject to the above conditions having been fully met and complied with to the satisfaction of the Company.

In addition, the Company agrees to provide to you for your private use your Company car for the period of six months from 4 January 1993, Private Medical Insurance cover for the period of six months from 4 January 1993 and your continued use (with no repayments) of your Season Ticket.

DECLARED BY ....
                 (The Beneficiary)

IN THE PRESENCE OF
WITNESS

Signature ....
Name ....
Address ....
Occupation ....

PRECEDENT 4

Undertakings upon Termination of Employment

I, ..., hereby undertake and confirm that I have duly returned all Company property properly belonging to the ABC Company Ltd. This includes but is not limited to all correspondence, documents, files, disks, manuals, papers, hard copies of any data from any of the Company's databases, keys, security pass(es), AMEX card, mobile telephone etc.

I further declare that to my knowledge there are no security devices, passwords or details of the computer hardware or software, databases etc. or any information relating thereto, known personally only to me.

I further declare that I have personally not engaged nor will I engage in the future nor will I cause, induce, incite or otherwise any other person(s), company, partnership, corporation or otherwise, to engage in any activity(ies) which may or might affect any of the Company's security systems, databases, software facilities or any computer facilities or any other processes by which the Company carries on its lawful business activities.

Signed .... Date 1993

Other Useful Clauses

12.1   Employers might wish to include additional clauses covering issues such as the requirement to report the misconduct or breaches of company rules of others and the duty to co-operate with outside agencies; the exclusion of new employees from the requirement to give warnings before dismissing; rules on smoking at work; dress and appearance and standards of conduct; rules concerning gambling on and off duty; insider trading rules; personal transactions rules; a requirement to inform of any changes of personal circumstances; drinking on and off duty; requirement to wear a uniform/ protective clothing and equipment etc.; staff purchase and discount rules; rules concerning personal liability; right of search.

Duty to report wrongdoings of others

12.2   The duty of confidence, i.e. to keep confidential information secure and not to misuse it or disclose it to any other unauthorised third party, does not by implication include the duty to disclose the misconduct or wrongdoings (or suspected wrongdoings) of others. The only persons who are under an implied duty to do so are directors, who are under a fiduciary duty which includes the duty to report the wrongdoing of others even if this implicates themselves. The courts have made this clear in several cases. They have also made it clear that should this be a requirement, then a very clear term must be included in the employees' contracts (see, for example, *Sybron Corporation v Rochem Ltd [1983] IRLR 253*).

In *The Distillers Company (Bottling Services) Ltd v Gardner [1982] IRLR 47*, Lord McDonald held that:

> 'It is asking a lot of an employee to require him to report the misdemeanours of his colleagues, but if this is to be the rule it should in our view be very clearly spelled out.'

In *Ladbroke Racing Ltd v King, EAT 202/88*, the EAT held that any rules regarding such a requirement 'must be crystal clear'. Any rules which leave it to the discretion of the employee would entitle any tribunal to find that the employee's conduct, in not reporting any breaches of rules by another member of staff, was not a sufficient reason for dismissal since it could not properly be regarded as an act of gross misconduct on the employee's part.

In this case the Company attempted to rely on a clause in the Staff Handbook which read:

'Please note that the Company does not give authority for any member of its management to waive compliance with or condone breaches of rules by others. Therefore should there be any instances wherein you have been told to breach a rule, or such a breach is condoned, it will be without the knowledge or consent of the Company and will not protect the employee to whom permission is given.'

The EAT ruled that such a clause did not imply or express any duty on an employee to report the misdemeanours of other employees. All the rule did was to warn that employees who were instructed to break, or condone a breach of, company rules would do so without the consent of the company and would not have its protection.

The EAT held that: '. . . the rule had to be written clearly – in capital letters if necessary – to impress that obligation upon all concerned'.

There was, however, no breach of a duty of confidence where an employee disclosed breaches of FIMBRA regulations and tax irregularities to FIMBRA and the Inland Revenue. In *Re a Company's Application (7 February 1989, High Court)*, a company providing financial advice and managing clients' investment portfolios, and hence subject to FIMBRA regulations under the Financial Services Act 1986, attempted to obtain an injunction against their former compliance officer (whose duty it was to ensure that the company fully complied with its legal duties). The company sought an injunction to restrain him from making any disclosures concerning tax irregularities and alleged breaches of FIMBRA regulations, arguing that such disclosures would be breaches of confidential information. The High Court held that these were matters within the province of those authorities to investigate, that the information would only be disclosed to those bodies and not to the world at large, and that it would be contrary to the public interest for employees who believed that they should disclose information to FIMBRA or the Inland Revenue to be inhibited from doing so by the thought that they may be injuncted.

Some staff may be warned that if they disclose the misconduct of others, they may themselves face retaliatory action. This may occur where there is an issue of product or environmental safety. Some organisations guarantee protection to so-called 'whistle blowers'.

A model clause on all these issues appears in **Precedent 1**.

Exclusions from the disciplinary procedure

12.3   Where a disciplinary procedure forms part of the contract (or is referred to in the contract and is contained in some other document) care must be taken by the employer to follow all the stages, allow for all the hearings and appeals etc., otherwise an employee may have a claim for breach of contract. Here quantum will be assessed on the basis of the length of time the employee would have been employed had the procedure been properly followed (*Gunton* *v London Borough of Richmond-upon-Thames* [*1980*] *IRLR 321*). If employers do not wish to face actions for breach of contract, they should reserve the right in the contract to reduce the number of official warnings or waive them for an initial period of time in relation to an individual's employment, if it is company policy not to follow all the warning stages of the disciplinary procedure during the first few months of employment.

There have been some very interesting developments in this area where employees have been dismissed in breach of the disciplinary procedure – in some cases they have been dismissed without reference to the warning stages, nor have they been given a disciplinary hearing and right of appeal as laid down in the procedure. In some cases the employee concerned has been successful in obtaining an injunction, restraining the employer from carrying out the dismissal decision until the proper procedure has been followed.

Developments in injunctive relief

12.4   In an early case in this area, *Dietman v London Borough of Brent* [*1988*] *IRLR 299*, the Court of Appeal held that the London Borough of Brent had broken Mrs Dietman's contract when they dismissed her without first following their disciplinary procedure. Here Mrs Dietman's contract referred to the disciplinary procedure which provided that: 'Any breach of disciplinary rules will render you liable to disciplinary action'.

In cases of less serious misconduct, there was a three-stage warning procedure with a disciplinary interview and appeals procedure. For acts of gross misconduct, examples of which were confined to acts involving intention on the part of the guilty party and all of which involved conduct which was dishonest or disruptive, the procedure provided for instant dismissal (without any further definition).

Some 17 months after the death of Jasmine Beckford, the inquiry report was published which stated of Mrs Dietman: 'By her non-intervention in flawed social work she was grossly negligent'. The Council immediately dismissed Mrs Dietman without notice or pay in lieu; neither did they give her a hearing.

The Court of Appeal held that her admitted gross negligence did not amount to gross misconduct because, as stated above, her contract defined gross misconduct in terms of an element of intention on the part of the guilty employee and all the examples of gross misconduct involved dishonesty or disruptive behaviour.

Hence if she had not committed gross misconduct, she should have been taken through the warning stages of the procedure and at the very least been given one formal warning before any decision to dismiss was taken. The Council were then under an obligation to provide her with a formal disciplinary interview as laid down in their procedure since this was part of her contract.

Several other cases illustrate the courts' attitude towards the granting of injunctions against public sector employers.

In one case, *Powell v London Borough of Brent* [*1987*] *IRLR 466*, Mrs Powell sought an injunction to stop the Council re-advertising the post to which she had been promoted some three months earlier. In another case, a team of hospital-based social workers obtained an injunction preventing the Council from unlawfully transferring them to area team work. In that case, *Hughes v London Borough of Southwark* [*1988*] *IRLR 55*, Mr Hughes and the other plaintiffs were social workers working in a multidisciplinary team at the Maudsley Hospital. They obtained an interlocutory injunction against the Council restraining it from enforcing its decision to order the plaintiffs to cease working at the Maudsley Hospital on certain days and carry out area team work for three days a week. Since this instruction was a breach of the plaintiffs' contracts and 'there was no question of the employers not having confidence in the plaintiffs . . . . It was clear that they had great confidence in them' an interlocutory injunction would be appropriate.

In that case the High Court laid great stress on the aspect of the continuing trust and confidence. Indeed they held that: 'The most important criterion for such an order is whether there is mutual trust and confidence'.

In contrast to that case, the High Court granted an injunction against the London Borough of Brent preventing the dismissal of one of their social workers taking place, even though it was accepted by the court that the mutual trust and confidence had broken down. In this case, the social worker agreed to give an undertaking that he would obey the lawful instructions of his new superior until his claim for breach of contract came to trial (*Wadcock v London Borough of Brent* [*1990*] *IRLR 223*).

In another case, *Robb v London Borough of Hammersmith and Fulham* [*1991*] *IRLR 72*, the High Court granted an injunction to restrain the local authority from dismissing Mr Robb until the full disciplinary procedure provided for in his contract of employment had been completed.

The authority was involved in the disastrous capital market transactions and interest rate swaps which were later declared unlawful by the courts. Mr Robb was the Director of Finance. In May he was told to drop all his duties and help in a preliminary investigation into his part in the swaps deals. There was already an independent enquiry going on into the capital market transactions.

In June he was told to take special leave until the preliminary investigation was completed. He was at that time attempting to negotiate a severance package. Unfortunately these negotiations broke down and on 5 July the Council abandoned the disciplinary procedure and dismissed him summarily on 26 July (on the instructions of the 'Urgency Committee') on the grounds that they no longer had any confidence in his ability to perform his duties as finance director.

His contract of employment incorporated the conditions of service for Chief

12.4   *Other Useful Clauses*

Officers. The procedures included one for 'Discipline' and one for 'Capability'. In the former case any disciplinary complaint had to be investigated on a preliminary basis and if the complaint warranted a full investigation it then had to be referred to the investigating committee and, if appropriate, the employee concerned suspended from duty and given the reasons for his suspension. Under the latter procedure, the officer was to be advised informally of the nature of the complaint, told of ways of improving and given a period in which to effect the improvements (unless there is a previous outstanding warning or there is evidence of a serious act of incompetence which is unlikely to be remedied within a reasonable time).

Mr Robb argued that the Council should be forced to conclude the proper procedures and that he would be content to remain suspended pending the outcome. This would mean that he was nominally employed by the Council and entitled to his pay.

An injunction was granted by the High Court. Although the established principle remained true that an injunction to preserve the contract would only be granted where the mutual trust and confidence in the employee's ability remained, that was the position where the employee sought to be reinstated so as to actually carry out the job. But on the principle of the 'balance of convenience' the court favoured Mr Robb for the granting of the injunction for the following reasons:

(1) the Council had on its own admission acted in breach of the contract by ending the disciplinary procedures and summarily dismissing Mr Robb;

(2) damages for that breach would not be an adequate remedy because these would only reflect the losses arising from his dismissal and would not compensate him for the manner of his dismissal and for depriving him of the proper disciplinary procedure;

(3) without an injunction Mr Robb would lose the opportunity to ventilate his case and justify his actions – and an industrial tribunal was not an adequate alternative forum for adjudicating upon his capabilities in such complex matters as interest swaps;

(4) the disciplinary procedure was a workable one now but could become unworkable if delayed until the conclusion of full trial of the matter;

(5) an injunction would restore Mr Robb to the position he was in until he was unlawfully deprived of entitlement to the disciplinary procedures and if it were not granted the Council would be 'snapping their fingers' at the legal rights of Mr Robb.

Here Mr Robb was attempting to obtain an injunction to preserve his employment (and his pay) until the outcome of the disciplinary hearing as opposed to attempting to return to his employment. This is the first case in which the courts have granted an injunction on this basis, i.e. they had to decide not whether the Order would make the employment relationship unworkable but merely whether the Order sought was workable.

As in the *Wadcock* case (above), the court here considered the 'workability' of the situation rather than the rigid reliance on the establishment of trust and confidence. In neither case was the employee seeking to return to his original job on exactly the same terms as before. However unlike Mr Wadcock, Mr Robb had given undertakings that he would not carry out any of his previous duties or functions and would not go to his place of work unless requested or instructed by his employers.

In *Jones v Gwent County Council [1992] IRLR 521*, the High Court granted a permanent injunction after it had heard evidence that two disciplinary hearings were invalid as they did not comply with Mrs Jones's contract of employment. Here the procedure provided for ten days' notice in writing if the Council wished to call a hearing which would consider dismissal and she had to be informed in writing of all the detailed charges. This was not done in her case. Her letter did not inform her that the hearing would consider her dismissal and the charges as formulated merely stated that her return to work would cause an irrevocable breakdown in relationships between management and staff based on her past behaviour.

In this case the injunction was granted under Order 14A preventing the authority from dismissing the plaintiff until it had followed the correct procedure. The new Order 14A provides that:

'The Court may determine any question of law or construction of any document arising in any matter at any stage of the proceedings where it appears to the Court that (a) such question is suitable for determination without a full trial of the action and (b) such determination will finally determine (subject only to any possible appeal) the entire cause or matter or any claim or issue therein.'

The High Court granted a permanent injunction (restraining the Council from dismissing Mrs Jones until full trial) and a declaration that her suspension was invalid since it would only be valid if the decision to dismiss Mrs Jones was justified.

The argument that the mutual trust and confidence had been destroyed could not be accepted as this was irrelevant to the issue of whether the letter of dismissal was a valid notice or not.

Main lesson

12.5   The implications of the decision in *Robb* (12.4 above) are far-reaching and solicitors who draft contracts of employment or service agreements ought to ensure that a reference to the disciplinary procedure is made in the agreement/contract. In the event of the Managing Director or Chief Executive whose contract provides for relatively short notice being summarily dismissed in breach of procedure, quantum may be far higher than a simple payment in lieu of notice.

12.6 *Other Useful Clauses*

It is important to include in the list of gross misconduct offences, 'gross negligence' or 'gross dereliction of duty' along with the other examples of gross misconduct. The Council in the *Dietman* case (12.4 above) lost their argument that Mrs Dietman had committed gross misconduct because there was no such reference to 'gross negligence' in the list of examples of gross misconduct.

Although Mrs Dietman had also applied for an injunction to prevent the dismissal decision going ahead, she was unsuccessful because the High Court and Court of Appeal found she had accepted her wrongful termination since she had already applied for other jobs.

In other cases, employees have been unsuccessful in obtaining injunctions either because the matter was not a proper matter for the disciplinary procedure and therefore the employer did not breach procedure by not following it or there was a significant breakdown in mutual trust and confidence and damages would be an appropriate remedy.

The remedy of injunctive relief becomes even more important following the *Jones* decision, since the new Order 14A enables a plaintiff to obtain an injunction on the basis of the true construction of his contract and not on the basis of the existence of mutual trust and confidence.

Solutions for employers

12.6 One obvious option for employers would be to take the disciplinary procedure out of the contract and make it discretionary. This may give difficulties to employers who defend unfair dismissal claims and wish to argue that the employee has broken contractual rules or whose work performance has fallen below the standard required by his contract. The tribunals may take the view that since the disciplinary procedure does not fall within the contract, the employee has not committed any offence or has not fallen below any standards which would be sufficient to dismiss him. Some tribunals take the view that if a standard or a rule is important, employers should make sure that they include it and the consequences of failure to conform to such standards, or breach of the rule, as part of the contract.

Another option would be to introduce an exclusion clause in relation to the procedural stages (whilst leaving the rules and standards within the terms of the contract) for employees with minimum service. A model exclusion clause appears in **Precedent 2**.

Undertaking to behave

12.7 There may be disciplinary incidents arising at work where the employer wishes to ensure that despite issuing a formal warning, the employee agrees to undertake that he will not repeat the conduct in issue. In some cases this involves a refusal to obey a lawful or reasonable instruction.

298

The tribunals have indicated that it is reasonable to require the employee to give an indication that a similar refusal will not occur on any further occasion – see *Devlin v Hamilton District Council (S), EAT 2/91*. In *Devlin's* case, Mr Devlin, a gardener/groundsman, refused to work because it was raining and he regarded it as being too wet to work. He was provided with appropriate protective clothing with which to work during wet weather. Despite three requests to work from his chargehand, foreman and area manager, he persisted in his refusal. Management told him that if he would agree to work in the rain in the future only mild disciplinary action would be taken against him. He made it clear that he would not accept management's authority to decide whether he should work in wet weather in the future.

The EAT held that the employer had acted within the band of reasonable responses in taking into account Mr Devlin's indication that he would not abide by his managers' authority in the future. The Council had spent considerable time in trying to convince him to change his mind, pointing out the terms of the national working agreement and stating that the penalty would be less severe if he agreed to obey orders in the future. His attitude that he would not abide by the terms of his contract was a major factor in making this decision fair.

Furthermore, in *Gosling v Ford Motor Company Ltd, EAT 221/90*, the fact that Mr Gosling, a Branch Chairman of a notoriously active union branch (he had no official status as a union official on the shopfloor), refused to sign an undertaking after being given a final written warning, that he would not call any further unconstitutional and unofficial industrial action, led the tribunal to reduce the unfair dismissal compensation awarded by 75%. The dismissal was held to be unfair because of the long time delay in taking the decision to dismiss Mr Gosling for inciting unconstitutional industrial action.

A model Undertaking to Behave appears in **Precedent 3**.

Relationships at work – 'Consensual relations'

12.8   Several employers have asked the author recently to draft some guidance on relationships at work. This is not for any moral reasons but more for concern that improper or undue influence is not exerted on one of the parties by the other. In one a Director became infatuated by his secretary – both parties were married. He promoted his secretary to a grade far higher than could be justified and sanctioned her first class travel round the world with him. This caused consternation on the part of senior management and prompted a claim for equal pay for work of equal value from higher graded male employees paid less than her!

In extreme cases, employers may have 'some other substantial reason' for dismissal where the employer can show that there is a real risk of a leak of confidential information as a result of the marriage or relationship of the two parties and there was no alternative employment within the organisation or associated employers. Employers have got into trouble when they have dismissed the female party in the relationship on the basis that 'the woman is not the breadwinner'. This has been held to be an act of sex discrimination (*Coleman v Skyrail Oceanic, trading as Goodmos Tours [1981] IRLR 398*).

Whilst it may be fair to dismiss for a workplace affair, particularly if the relationship continues at the office or where obvious favours have been awarded or confidences broken, it will be sex discrimination to dismiss the woman for allegedly having an affair with a male colleague. In *Brocks Explosives Ltd v Montgomery (14 November 1991, EAT 419/91)*, the only evidence of an affair that the employer had was that the employees in question were seen on holiday together. The EAT held that the employer did not have valid evidence upon which to base his belief. The comparison was two men going on holiday together without any evidence of any intimate relationship. The EAT concluded that the woman had been treated less favourably in being dismissed on such evidence than a man would have been. In addition she had not been given any opportunity to explain her actions before she was dismissed – her male colleague had!

However it is possible for employers to request or require that employees who do form relationships at work inform their head of department or personnel manager (if the head of department is involved in the relationship!) and action will be taken to move one or other of the parties. This action should be taken in the context of an adequate mobility and flexibility clause in the contract giving the employer the right to transfer the party and done after consultation and explanation and proper notice. Employers must in any event be able to justify why the one party was required to be transferred rather than the other, otherwise a claim for sex discrimination may be brought if the practice is to transfer the female employee.

See **Precedent 4** for a typical clause.

New Code for 'Consensual relations'

12.9   In 1993, a British University published a new Code of Conduct aimed at regulating sexual affairs or romantic encounters between lecturers and students. It is attached as a new **Precedent 5**. The main thrust of the Code aims to discourage such relationships which are seen to be incompatible with and likely to compromise the relationship of academic trust.

Staff so involved are advised to declare any such relationships in the first instance to their head of department or Registrar. Staff are warned that to leave undeclared any such relationship may lead to their being accused of misconduct and could open them to disciplinary action.

There is also mention of the possibility of complaints of sexual harassment if the relationship goes horribly wrong. The Code ends on the rather sombre and cautious note:

'Staff should note that it could prove exceedingly difficult to defend themselves against such complaints on grounds of mutual consent.'

Dress and appearance

12.10　Rules relating to dress and appearance, and to the wearing of uniforms and protective clothing, are dealt with in Chapter 4 above; see 4.18 and **Precedent 7** at the end of that chapter.

Gambling, financial impropriety etc.

12.11　It may be necessary in financial institutions to state the rules concerning gambling or taking bets whilst at work and other such activities outside work. In addition there may be a restriction on employment for anyone in debt, with an overdraft or in arrears with any repayments such as mortgage payments. A model clause in **Precedent 6** sets out some guidelines.

Entertaining clients

12.12　If entertainment plays a part in anyone's employment it is sensible to set out the limits and the rules. For example, a member of staff may have authority to take clients out to lunch but may not have authority to take them to nightclubs or on expensive trips on 'Concorde'. A clause in **Precedent 6** sets out one company's rules.

Insider dealing

12.13　There are very strict rules for anyone working in financial institutions concerning insider dealing. Reference must be made to them in the contract with the consequences of any breach. **Precedent 7** contains some of these rules.

Personal transactions

12.14　Those working in financial institutions must take great care should they wish to speculate or invest. It is essential to lay down clear guidance for them so that the employer or clients are not compromised. Some rules appear in **Precedent 8**.

Change of personal circumstances

12.15　It is essential that staff keep the employer informed about any change of name, address, dependants, loss of driving licence, gain of any qualification, criminal convictions etc. so that the employer's files may be kept up to date. A reminder that the employee is required to do so may be included in the contract and a typical clause appears in **Precedent 9**.

Smoking policy

12.16   Those organisations with 'No Smoking' rules may consider it prudent to include the rules as part of the terms and conditions of employment, breach of which may result in disciplinary action. It is important to remember that any new rules must be introduced after consultation with staff, proper notice and consideration of alternative measures for any existing smokers (*Watson v Cooke, Webb and Holton (Case No 13852/84)*). Employers who comply with such guidelines should have no worries about claims for constructive dismissal or breach of contract (*Rogers v Wicks and Wilson Ltd (Case No 22890/87)*).

One organisation known to the author excludes from the occupational sick pay scheme any smoking-related illnesses or injuries as part of its policy. It does however offer paid time off for 'Quit Smoking' classes. Another organisation offers additional days' leave to non-smokers.

A model set of rules appears in **Precedent 10**.

Rules on alcohol and drugs

12.17   Those employers with special rules concerning alcohol will need to specify what those rules are, to whom they apply and the consequences of any breach. Model rules appear in **Precedent 11**.

Rules relating to prescribed drugs and controlled substances are also outlined in **Precedent 11**. It is becoming increasingly more common for employers to cover such matters in light of the problems of side effects of prescribed drugs and the effects on work and the rise in drug abuse in this country.

Personal search

12.18   Since there is no common law or implied right for employers to carry out searches, it is essential that this is spelt out in the contract. It is wise to ensure that two members of management are always present and a representative on behalf of the employee to act as an impartial observer to ensure fair play. A typical clause appears in **Precedent 12**.

Personal liability

12.19   Some employers have clarified the position as to personal liability under the anti-discrimination legislation and the Health and Safety at Work etc. Act 1974 which impose civil liability in the former case and criminal liability in the latter. Certain guarded assurances on the question of payment of costs may be appropriate. A typical clause appears in **Precedent 13**.

Patents and inventions

12.20   A model clause concerning the rights and duties of employees who research or are involved in any invention or patentable item is set out in **Precedent 14**.

Lecturing and writing

12.21   Some organisations specify when staff may carry on writing and lecturing activities which are closely allied to their position and status. For example, art historians, museum curators and the like who are specialists in their field are often called upon to write articles and contribute lectures.

It would be reasonable for employers in such cases to include in the contract of employment terms to govern the situation under which an employee may write or lecture on a subject which is directly or indirectly connected with his employment.

A typical clause appears in **Precedent 15**.

Requirement to work efficiently and with speed

12.22   Some occupations require speed and accuracy and attention at all times to the job in hand. For example some computer staff are required to work with great speed and their work involves the rapid transfer of information. Instructions often come from the electronic display unit and not from a manager. In this regard, a term in the contract is required which reads:

> 'Employees will promptly carry out all instructions given by the unit's management or an electronic display.'

Behaviour at offices

12.23   It is still commonplace for employers to invite their staff and partners and sometimes clients and suppliers to office parties around Christmas time. Unfortunately a few such parties have been marred by the drunken behaviour of a small minority of employees. Several employers have considered operating a Model set of rules for such occasions and this is printed at **Precedent 17**.

Precedent 16 contains a letter sent to one such errant member of staff!

PRECEDENT 1

Duty to Report Misconduct

Due to the nature of our business it is expected that you will act with due diligence and utmost honesty at all times. Should any matters of concern come to your attention, you must report them immediately to your immediate manager or Head of Department or a member of Personnel. The Company sees it as your duty to report any acts of misconduct, dishonesty, breach of company rules or breach of any of the rules of the relevant regulatory bodies committed, contemplated or discussed by any other member of staff or other third party.

The Company will treat whatever you have reported with confidentiality as far as this is practicable.

Should you fail to act in accordance with the above provisions the Company reserves the right to treat this as a disciplinary matter which could if the circumstances warrant it lead to summary dismissal.

(ALTERNATIVE CLAUSE FOR FINANCIAL SECTOR)

1. The Company is a member of IMRO and you are therefore required as a condition of your employment to observe and comply carefully and diligently with all the Rules as laid down by IMRO from time to time. Since you act in an authorised capacity on behalf of the Company, you must ensure that at all times you are fully complying with all the IMRO Rules. Failure to do so may result in legal action being taken against the Company and disqualification from trading.

Any employee committing any serious breaches of IMRO or other Rules may be summarily dismissed in accordance with the Company's Disciplinary Procedure.

2. You are required to co-operate fully with all directions and requests properly made or imposed by or on behalf of IMRO. This may include, but is not limited to, a requirement that you make yourself readily available for and truthfully answer all questions put to you in the course of any inspection investigation, Summary Process or Proceeding of any Appeal Tribunal.

Any breach of these undertakings will be a matter of serious misconduct which may entitle the Company in any case it deems fit to dismiss without notice or payment in lieu.

'The Whistle-blowing Clause'

(A) The Company will guarantee that whatever you report will be treated with the utmost confidentiality as far as this is practicable. You are also assured that no discriminatory or retaliatory action short of dismissal or dismissal action will be taken against you in any case where you make such reports to management neither shall any adverse action of any kind be taken against you now or in the future. On your part you agree that you will not disclose any matter of a sensitive nature, e.g. relating to product safety or health and safety or any environmental matter to the enforcing authorities or to any member of the press or media unless you have taken all such reasonable steps to draw the matter to the attention of management.

(B) The Company is a member of .... and you are therefore required as a condition of your employment to observe and comply carefully and diligently with all the Rules as laid down by [........] from time to time. Since you act in an authorised capacity on behalf of the Company you must ensure that at all times you are fully complying with all the relevant Regulatory Body Rules. Failure to do so may result in legal action being taken against either the Company or you personally [and disqualification from trading].

Breach of the above undertakings will be a matter of serious misconduct which may entitle the Company in any case it deems fit to dismiss with or without notice or payment in lieu.

PRECEDENT 2

Disciplinary Procedure

This procedure will apply only to employees who have..........(insert) continuous service at the date of the commission of any offence. Where any offence is committed or work performance falls below the standard required in relation to employees with less service, management will at its discretion determine whether disciplinary action short of dismissal will be taken bearing in mind the gravity of the offence and the record of work and conduct which the employee has. Management reserves the right to terminate the contract with proper notice where appropriate or pay in lieu in cases of poor work performance or unacceptable conduct without reference to the following procedure of warnings (or may reduce the number of official warnings) where the employee concerned has less than..........service.

All employees are subject to all the Company's rules and procedures from the commencement of their employment.

PRECEDENT 3

Undertaking to Behave

(Headed company notepaper)

To: Mr XYZ, Managing Director, ABC Ltd

Date ....

Following the disciplinary hearing held on 28 August 1992, I hereby warrant and undertake the following matters:

1. I accept that I have blatantly and consistently refused to co-operate with Mr XYZ and others when asked to undertake routine, reasonable and legitimate requests. That, on several occasions I have refused to speak to Mr XYZ or attend meetings when requested to do so and more seriously I have refused to carry out tasks when asked to do so which has seriously affected Mr XYZ and the running of the business.

2. I have apologised for all these matters and hereby give an undertaking to Mr XYZ, being a duly authorised officer of the Company, that I will desist in this negative and obstructive behaviour immediately and that I will from now on co-operate fully both in spirit as well as to the letter with Mr XYZ and any other third parties conducting business with the Company. I further give an undertaking that I will respond to any reasonable and legitimate requests in a friendly and cheerful manner and that I will work in a constructive way in the future.

3. I understand that, in return for the undertakings given in 1. and 2. above, my employment has not been terminated. I accept that a Final Written Warning will be placed on my record recording the facts raised in my disciplinary hearing and I understand that this Warning will not lapse until a minimum of three years from that date of issue. If during that time there is any repetition of incidents that led to the disciplinary hearing, or any matters concerning my conduct or competence, I understand that the Company will terminate my employment.

Signed ....   Date ....
(Position in the Company)

PRECEDENT 4

Relationships at work – 'Consensual relations'

'Because of the nature of our business and the position you hold, you have access to confidential information and have authority to make decisions and sanction budgets. For this reason, the Company regards it as undesirable that employees who form close personal relationships should work in the same department or division of the organisation. As a result, the Company operates a rule that no member of staff who has formed a close personal relationship with another member of staff may work together in the same department or division. Such a relationship must be reported in confidence to the Head of Department or Personnel Director (as appropriate) and the parties will be counselled with a view to transferring one or both to another department or division where this is possible.

Where no re-deployment is found to be possible and after all efforts have been made to try to resolve the situation or find alternative employment, the Company reserves the right to terminate with notice or payment in lieu of notice, the contract of either of the parties involved. The Company will give an assurance that as long as no impropriety such as the leak of confidential information has occurred, the employee to be dismissed will be given a reference for future employment and every help possible to try to find alternative employment outside the Company.

It is regarded as gross misconduct and a serious breach of contract for any member of staff not to report any relationship at work immediately they believe that it is appropriate to do so . . . .'

PRECEDENT 5

Guidelines on Professional Relations between Student and Academic Staff

To be proposed formally to the University authorities

The relationship between student and lecturer (or supervisor) is an integral part of the educational development of the student. In order that enquiry and learning can be facilitated, this relationship must be a supportive one characterised by good communication, trust and confidence. Unprofessional behaviour on the part of staff can lead to abuse of such a relationship, made more serious by the unequal power of the two parties. The University therefore expects good professional relationships between academic staff and students within the classroom and laboratory, in one-to-one tutorials and in social gatherings.

Lecturing and supervisory staff are strongly advised not to enter into any sexual/romantic or other potentially incompatible relationships with students which compromises the relationship of academic trust, or could reasonably appear to do so in the eyes of other students.

If such a relationship does occur, it is the duty of the member of staff to declare it so that alternative arrangements can be made for the tutoring, supervision and assessment of the student concerned. The declaration can be made in the first instance either to his/her Head of Department, and, where appropriate, to the student's Head of Department, or to representative(s) of the Registrar's Department (such person(s) to be nominated with the Association of University Teachers' (AUTs') agreement). In the case of a Head of Department, the declaration can be made in the first instance either to the Vice-Chancellor or the Registrar. A member of staff in doubt about his position is encouraged to discuss this with member(s) of the AUT Committee nominated for this purpose.

To leave undeclared a sexual/romantic or other potentially incompatible association where a lecturer or supervisor is also in professional contact with the student may be regarded as misconduct and could leave the member of staff open to disciplinary action.

Members of staff should be aware that such an abuse of professional relationships may also lead to complaints of sexual harassment. Staff should note that it could prove exceedingly difficult to defend themselves against such complaints on grounds of mutual consent.

PRECEDENT 6

Gaming and Standards of Financial Propriety

In particular you are expected to ensure that your own personal financial transactions always reflect the highest standards of financial propriety. The Company has specific rules about the prohibition of margin accounts and you must acquaint yourself with them.

The Company also has a specific rule prohibiting gambling in any form or book-making whilst on any of the Company's premises. The making or arranging of bets between brokers and principals (dealers) is expressly forbidden.

Similar rules prohibit the use for any purpose of the City Index, IG Index or similar devices. Please note that these rules form part of the Company's Disciplinary Procedure and breach of any of them amounts to gross misconduct which may render you liable to summary dismissal.

Debts or Arrears of Payments

It is a condition of your employment that you are not nor have been in debt or in arrears with any repayments e.g. mortgage payments. This rule is self-evident since you are expected to manage your own finances with the same degree of propriety, sense and honesty as that required of you in relation to the Bank or any of its customers.

You will be required to notify your immediate manager immediately should you be in debt or in arrears with any payments. ('Debt' for this purpose includes debts against credit cards or credit agencies, and gambling debts.) All the circumstances will be taken into account but it may prove necessary to move you from your position in the Bank to another position where there is less risk to the business. In certain cases, failure to comply with the above requirements may render you liable to summary dismissal.

Offering or Accepting Entertainment

1. All entertainment must be recorded in one of the Treasury diaries either available on the..........desk or..........desk or from the Group Manager's secretary.

2. Principals and brokers are responsible for ensuring that entertainment offered in the course of business does not exceed reasonable limits. The same applies if you are offered such items.

'Reasonable' here means:

  (a) a few drinks;
  (b) lunch or dinner;
  (c) a 'show';
  (d) lunch or dinner at the weekend to include spouses.

3. Nightclubs of the explicitly sexual kind and casinos are expressly forbidden.

4. Any other entertainment will be looked at on a 'case by case' basis such as:

  (a) a day at the races or other such 'hospitality tent' type events;
  (b) extra special dinners/lunches of the 'Concorde', 'Orient Express', 'Paris' type;
  (c) any other event that is clearly not covered by 2.

These categories of entertainment *must* have the prior written approval of the Group Manager. This will be requested in writing by a Director or the broking house concerned.

Settlement of Differences

Small differences of a few points, say up to five points on a deal, may be accepted so long as they occur in the natural course of business as it is unreasonable to expect a broker to always justify his prices 100%.

However, any small differences must be resolved that day without any balance being carried over. Any other differences must be settled through the 'Association' (Foreign Exchange and Currency Deposit Brokers Association) in the prescribed manner.

In addition to the above Bank of England Regulations, all staff are reminded of the strict code of secrecy and of the totally confidential nature of our business, inside and outside the Bank.

Any breach of the above guidelines will result in disciplinary action, the nature of which will depend upon the particular offence but may include suspension or termination of employment if the offence is serious enough.

PRECEDENT 7

Insider Trading Rules

In addition there are very important rules concerning Insider Trading and these can be found in the 'Insider Trading Rules' a copy of which has been given to you on joining. All UK Bank staff will be required to sign an undertaking which forms part of the Contract of Employment that they will comply with the rules set out below on Insider Dealing and Personal Transactions and any others which may be published from time to time. Failure to do so may result in your summary dismissal since breach of these rules is regarded as gross misconduct.

Insider dealing is a criminal offence under the Company Securities (Insider Dealing) Act 1985 which makes it an offence to use unpublished price sensitive information in order to make a profit or avoid a loss when dealing in securities.

'Unpublished price sensitive information' is defined as any information in relation to specific matters concerning the company which is not generally available and will be likely to have a material effect on the market price of those securities if it was generally known.

Insider dealing includes:

(a) dealing by directors, senior staff and professional advisers of a company in that company's securities;

(b) dealing in the securities of another company with which one's own company is connected;

(c) secondary insider dealing where an individual deals in securities of a company on the basis of information obtained from a person who is closely connected with that company;

(d) take-over dealing: dealing in shares by an individual in a proposed target as the potential bidder or on information received from the potential bidder;

(e) tipping: passing price sensitive information to someone else who will use it for insider dealing;

(f) counselling and procuring insider dealing.

The Financial Services Act 1986 makes certain consequential amendments to the Company Securities (Insider Dealing) Act 1985 and widens the scope of the 1985 Act and provides for the appointment of inspectors to investigate insider dealing offences with the use of wide-ranging powers.

PRECEDENT 8

Personal Account Transactions

Individuals who wish to deal on their own account in the securities market may do so subject to the following rules:

(1) all transactions are reported in writing to the Bank's Compliance Officer, unless an arrangement is in place for the Compliance Department to receive a copy of the contract note issued to you in respect of such a transaction;

(2) prior approval must be obtained from a senior member of executive management and the Chief Operating Officer before dealing in bullion, precious metals and foreign exchange options, futures or other margined transactions;

(3) whenever you instruct a firm to execute a transaction for you, you should identify yourself as an employee of this Bank and inform them that the Bank has permitted the transaction;

(4) if you know that the Bank intends to publish on that day or within the following five business days a research recommendation which you know or should know is likely to cause an immediate and substantial price change in the investment concerned, you should not deal the same way as that recommendation until the recommendation has been published and the customers for whom the recommendation was principally intended have had a reasonable opportunity to react to it;

(5) if you know that the Bank has accepted a customer's order or made a decision to deal for a discretionary customer, you should not deal the same way for your own account until the relevant order or decision has been executed or cancelled;

(6) you should not deal in an investment at a time or in a manner which you know is likely to have a direct adverse effect on the particular interests of a customer of the Bank;

(7) you should not arrange for the Bank to enter into a transaction, if you know or have any reason to believe that it involves an employee of another company (which is an authorised person) who is contravening or attempting to evade the Company Securities (Insider Dealing) Act 1985 or any similar rule made by The Securities Association, the Bank of England, the Securities and Investments Board or any other Self-Regulatory Organisation or Recognised Professional Body;

(8) if as part of your duties you give investment advice to others or enter into investment transactions for the Bank, you should not accept from any other person any benefit which cannot be properly regarded as justifiable in all the circumstances;

(9) in all dealings, employees are directed to the Bank's Standards of Conduct which provides guidance as to your responsibilities in the management of your personal finances.

PRECEDENT 9

Change of Personal Circumstances

It is very important that you inform your Personnel Officer of any changes to your personal circumstances such as change of address and or telephone number, next of kin, bank or building society details, dependants, marriage, gain of qualifications, criminal convictions, loss of driving or other relevant licences etc.

It is expected that you have given all the correct details concerning age, dependants, qualifications, grades of examinations passed etc. Should the company discover that you have provided any false information in this or any other material respect, the Company reserves the right to terminate your contract with or without notice or payment in lieu.

PRECEDENT 10

Smoking Rules

It is a rule of this Company that you are not permitted to smoke* in..........(state where) at any time whether during normal business hours or during any overtime hours. This was explained to you both at your interview and on induction. Please note that smoking is only permitted in..........(state where) at..........(state times if appropriate). Should you wish to take a smoking break you must obtain the permission of your superior in advance. This will not be unreasonably refused but you should note that if the needs of the business or your department dictate, permission may on any occasion be refused. You are expected to conform to sensible practices in this regard and should any abuse be suspected, permission to smoke, other than in meal breaks (or other designated times), may be withdrawn from you or from the department as a whole.

Please note that breach of the Company's smoking rules is defined in the Disciplinary Procedure (a copy of which you have received) as an act of misconduct. The Company will make every endeavour to persuade you to adhere to the rules but after initial informal counselling, you may receive formal warnings should you persist in breaking the rules. This could ultimately lead to your dismissal.

Please note also that any absences, illnesses or injuries, which in the opinion of our Company doctor or any independent specialist, are smoking-related may be excluded from the Company's sick pay scheme. In such a case only Statutory Sick Pay will be paid. This exclusion from sick pay also covers any illnesses or pre-existing medical conditions which are exacerbated by or aggravated by the employee's smoking habits. Due regard will be had to any employee who tries to give up smoking and paid time off may be granted for 'Quit Smoking' classes or any other recognised medical treatment pursued in order to stop smoking.

*The terms 'smoke' and 'smoking' relate to tobacco products only. Controlled substances are not covered here.

(All non-smokers are entitled to take . . . days' paid leave in any holiday year in addition to normal holiday entitlement.)

PRECEDENT 11

Rules on Alcohol and Drugs

Alcohol

From June 1990 the Company has introduced an Alcohol Policy after due consultation with the unions/workforce/staff. The following rules apply to all staff and should anyone break any of the rules they will be subject to the Company's disciplinary procedure which may eventually lead to dismissal.

Please note that anyone who admits to alcohol dependency and seeks help will be treated sympathetically by the Company. However they will still be expected to comply with the following rules at all times:

1. No alcohol is permitted to be drunk during working hours whether on or off company premises. It is also forbidden for staff to drink any alcoholic drinks during any meal breaks or rest breaks or whilst waiting to come on duty/ waiting for a flight etc.

2. It is strictly forbidden for any member of staff to bring any alcohol onto Company premises at any time or to carry any alcohol in any company vehicle or on their person whilst on Company business or during working hours.

3. It is regarded as gross misconduct to be drunk on duty.

4. It is strictly forbidden to come to work under the influence of alcohol.

5. Any entertaining on or off Company premises must be conducted sensibly and whilst you may offer alcohol to your guest, you will be required to drink non-alcoholic drinks only. There may be alcoholic drinks at Company social functions which are held after business hours but anyone who is driving a car, whether a company car or private car, is expected to drink non-alcoholic drinks and must certainly keep well within the legal limits (80 milligrammes of alcohol per 100 millilitres of blood).

6. Any act of random, excessive drunkenness may be regarded as gross misconduct for which summary dismissal may be the penalty.

7. Anyone who is considered by their superior to be unfit for work due to alcohol will be required to return home either driven by a colleague or in a taxi. A full report will be made at the time and a counselling interview will be conducted by personnel, normally the following day, where the individual will be asked to give his own account. Everything said in this interview will be treated in confidence and should any referral to the Occupational Health Department be deemed necessary an appointment will be made with the employee's agreement. The employee will be referred to the Employee Assistance Programme.

The Company's Employee Assistance Programme is set out elsewhere.

8. It is now Company Policy to screen for alcohol and drugs at pre-employment and job applicants will be told about these tests and required to give their permission for such tests to be done before any job will be offered.

We are now introducing a similar rule for existing staff in any cases where there is reasonable cause. This would include any accident at work where alcohol or drugs are suspected or any other case where alcohol or drug abuse is suspected of being implicated. You will be expected to comply with all reasonable requests to undergo any blood or urine tests as deemed necessary. The proper protocol for testing will be carried out including the retesting of any positive specimens.

Confidentiality is assured and no-one other than the Occupational Health Physician will have access to the results apart from yourself and a named member of management. Your written consent to such disclosure will be obtained prior to any tests being carried out.

Drugs

1. Anyone taking any prescribed drugs will be required to report to Occupational Health with the drugs so that a note can be made of the items, dosage etc. and the identity of the person who prescribed the drugs can be checked.

Any side effects will be discussed with the individual and should there be any concerns for health and safety, Occupational Health will make any recommendations it deems necessary for redeployment.

Employees are required to continue to take any medication prescribed by their doctor and should it come to the attention of Occupational Health or any other member of staff that this is not the case, management reserves the right to require that the employee refrain from work on (pay/no pay).

2. It is a criminal offence to use, possess or deal in any controlled substances and anyone caught on company premises involved in any of those activities will normally be dismissed for gross misconduct. The Company reserves the right to call in the police in any case it deems necessary.

3. Anyone convicted outside work of any offence in connection with controlled substances will not automatically be dismissed. Matters such as the nature of the conviction and the sentence, whether the conviction affects the employee's ability to do the job, the effect on the Company's image and reputation will be taken into account.

However anyone who admits to a problem in relation to controlled substances and who seeks help will be treated sympathetically but will be required to agree to refrain from any involvement or use of any controlled substances whilst at work.

4. Screening for drugs will be carried out as per paragraph 8 of the Alcohol section above.

PRECEDENT 12

Right of Search

It is a requirement of this Company that you submit to a personal search and search of all baggage, personal items, lockers, car etc. when requested to do so. A body search will only be carried out in a private room by a security officer in the presence of another member of management and an employee representative.

Anyone caught in unauthorised possession of company property, property belonging to any other employee or other third party will be suspended on pay and will be the subject of further investigation which may lead to serious disciplinary action.

PRECEDENT 13

Personal Liability

Three employment Statutes impose personal liability as well as corporate – the Health and Safety at Work etc. Act 1974; the Race Relations Act 1976 and the Sex Discrimination Act 1975. Under the Health and Safety at Work Act there is criminal liability, breach of which may render the company or an individual liable to a fine and/or imprisonment. The other two Statutes impose civil liability.

Whilst the Company has primary responsibility for ensuring compliance with these Statutes, individual employees may also be held liable where they have consented, connived or been neglectful or have deliberately ignored or disobeyed correct instructions.

It would be contrary to public policy for any Insurance Company to offer any indemnity for any penalty imposed under these Statutes although limited insurance cover is available for legal expenses incurred under certain prosecutions under the Health and Safety at Work Act subject to certain conditions laid down in the Insurance Policy.

The Company would look carefully at any case where an individual employee is held liable and a senior Executive will determine whether it would be appropriate to grant any financial (in which case, the level of any financial assistance) or any other assistance.

PRECEDENT 14

Patents and Inventions

Your duties include a review of the Company's products with a view to improving them by new and original inventions and implementing improvements by means of such inventions and of applying established techniques, designs, processes, and methods not previously used or used in that particular application by the Company.

The following shall apply to your employment:

1.1. Any invention (relevant to or capable of use in the business of the Company) made by you in the course of your employment by the Company whether or not in the course of your duties, is, unless it is otherwise the exclusive property of the Company, hereby assigned by you to the Company, and you undertake at the expense of the Company to execute any formal and additional assignment required by the Company to vest or to confirm the vesting in it of such invention.

1.2. The Company has no liability to account to you for any revenue or profit derived or resulting from any invention belonging to the Company but this does not prejudice any rights you may have under section 40 of the Patents Act 1977.

PRECEDENT 15

Lecturing and Writing

Because of the nature of your position in the Company/profession/ professional status/reputation in our industry, you may be invited to or upon your own initiative you may write articles, manuals, publications etc. on a subject closely connected with or similar to the work for which you are employed by this Organisation.

The copyright in any company manuals, publications, handbooks, documents, guidance etc. remains the exclusive property of the Company and cannot be used for any other purpose other than the legitimate business of the Company.

It is therefore strictly forbidden to use any material whatsoever whether in hard copy or computerised data for your own personal use or for the use of any other unauthorised third party.

Should you be asked or wish to write or publish or lecture on a subject which is directly or indirectly connected with your employment with this Company, then you must obtain the prior written permission of ....
It will then be decided whether you may do so in Company time or your own time and the copyright of and royalties and fees for all materials, articles, media appearances etc. written or made by you will be clarified.

It is a requirement of your employment that you obtain the express, prior written permission of .... before undertaking any private work from which personal financial gain may accrue, such as publication, authorship, lecturing, consultancy and contributions to the media.

Even where consent has been given, such activities should not interfere with the proper performance of your duties.

Detailed rules about the preparation of such work will be discussed with you at any material time and this will include:

1. Number of hours to be spent on the work i.e. a realistic schedule of the time to research and write.

2. Whether extra time is envisaged in order to meet a copy deadline; overtime to be claimed etc.

3. Whether any written publication relating to the employer's field of activity has been first offered for publication to the employer; any fee or royalty in the event that the employer wishes to publish the work.

4. Undertaking to spend own time on work not to be published by employer.

5. Approval of text by employer in any event.

6. Lectures and interviews to take place in work time and agreement over fees; if outside work time, agreement in advance from employer.

7. Consultancy to any other organisation – permission must first be sought.

PRECEDENT 16

Letter Confirming Behaviour at Christmas Party

To:
From:
Date:

This is to confirm the conversation that I had with you this morning. You were informed last week by memo that the office party is to take place on Friday 22 December at 5.00 pm. As you know, last year you had to be escorted off the premises and we investigated a complaint following the party that you sexually harassed the Chairman's wife and daughter and were generally verbally abusive to fellow employees and other guests. You were given an informal warning about this and a note still remains on your file to that effect.

In order to avoid any recurrence of these events this year, I would remind you that it would be sensible in your case if you restricted your consumption of alcohol to the minimum – probably one pint of beer or one short or two glasses of wine at the most.

There will be ample supply of soft drinks and many of your colleagues will be restricting their intake of alcohol particularly in light of driving home afterwards.

You have confirmed to me that you are prepared to comply with this request. I repeat my offer to you that you are welcome to seek help and assistance from Occupational Health if you have any personal problems. Anything you say will be treated in the strictest confidence.

It leaves me to thank you for your co-operation in this matter and I hope that we all have a good time at the party this year.

Yours

Signed

PRECEDENT 17

Model Rules for Drinking of Alcohol and Office Parties

To: All Staff
From: The Managing Director

Date:

The festive season is upon us and I would like to remind all staff about our rules concerning the consumption of alcohol:

1. No alcohol can be consumed on Company premises during working hours *save in the staff restaurant at meal times or on the occasion of entertaining business clients where so authorised to do subject to the rules set out below.*

2. Drinks cabinets in senior management offices must be kept securely locked at all times and only used for specific business entertaining.

3. Where you are authorised to entertain business clients, we would expect you to drink sensibly and moderately. Normally one alcoholic drink would be regarded as sufficient; soft drinks are always available. We do not expect you to drink spirits at such times but you may offer spirits if appropriate.

4. OPTION A: *If you should drink any alcohol during your lunch hour off the Company premises, you must limit yourself to a small amount, say one pint of beer, one glass of wine, one single spirit. The Company does not encourage you to drink alcohol during your breaks.*

OPTION B: *It is against Company Policy and Rules to drink any alcohol during any meal breaks whether these are paid or unpaid. You may drink soft drinks only.*

It is particularly important that you observe these sensible/no drink rules since those of you who drive a Company car must be in a fit and competent state to drive. In this regard the Company does not accept the limit set for the purpose of the Road Traffic Act of 80 milligrammes of alcohol per 100 millilitres of blood.

5. Anyone who is deemed by his supervisor as unfit for work because he is under the influence of alcohol will be suspended from work immediately and sent home (normally driven by a colleague or sent home in a taxi). Once the employee is fit for work, he will be counselled about his behaviour and if appropriate reminded of the disciplinary action which may follow if there is any repetition. Anyone who admits to alcohol dependency problems will be referred to Occupational Health for advice, counselling and referral for treatment (where appropriate).

6. At the office Christmas party, where guests are invited, you are expected to conduct yourself sensibly. A wide variety of non-alcoholic drinks will be available all evening.

You will be representing the Company and whilst we want everyone to enjoy themselves and have a good time, you should consider limiting the amount of alcohol you drink, particularly if you know a small amount has an adverse effect on you or if you are driving home afterwards.

It is expected that you will either make arrangements to be driven home, in which case your driver should abstain from alcohol (or limit the amount of alcohol to one or at the most two units).

The Company will lay on transport for all those who put their names down – minicabs will be ordered and paid for by the Company (optional).

The bar staff will be instructed to limit the amount of alcohol that they serve to any one individual and will refuse to serve alcohol to anyone who in their opinion (or senior management's) has had too much.

7. A senior member of Personnel is organising this party and he will be supervising all evening. Any person who becomes violent or breaches the code of normal, social conduct will be refused entry or required to leave. Disciplinary action may be taken against anyone whom management believes has committed an offence.

We trust that with these guidelines, everyone will be able to enjoy themselves and we will be able to show our normal hospitality to all our invited guests.

Appendix 1

MANAGEMENT CONTRACT

Contract of Employment

OTHELLO INVESTMENTS LTD

This document sets out your principal terms and conditions of employment which incorporates the written particulars required by the Employment Protection (Consolidation) Act 1978 as amended and together with your Offer Letter and the Staff Handbook and any Rules and Procedures published by the Company constitutes the Contract of Employment between:

.... (Employee)

and

....(Employer, hereinafter referred to as 'The Company')

Your employment as ....

commences on the.........day of .... 19....

*No previous employment counts as continuous employment for any statutory purposes

*Previous employment which counts as continuous employment commenced on the.........day of .... 19....

*(*Delete whichever is not applicable.*)

1. Job responsibilities

Your job title is..........Your duties will be fully explained to you when you commence employment with the Company. *Your job description is attached as Schedule A to this Contract.* It is the Company's intention that any oral instructions or written descriptions of your job duties and responsibilities should serve as a guide to the major areas for which you will be accountable. Because of the changing nature of the business the obligations upon you will inevitably vary and develop. The Company reserves the right at any time during your employment, upon reasonable notice, to require you to undertake any duties which fall within your capabilities.

2. Salary

2.1. Your basic salary is £..........per annum payable monthly by direct credit transfer to your personal bank or building society account. This will normally be paid on..........day of each month. It will be your responsibility to ensure that your Personnel Officer has a note of your Bank or Building Society Account Name and Number and Sort Code Number.

2.2. You are/are not entitled to the payment of any overtime for hours worked in excess of the normal business hours of this Company.

2.3. The Company operates a profit sharing scheme in respect of your employment. The Board of the Holding Company meets each year to determine the percentage award to be made, based on the Company's profits for the preceding year. Any payments are distributed in the January of each year to employees on the payroll on the previous 31 December and the amount payable (if any) is announced in January of each year.

Please note that this profit-sharing scheme and any payments paid are discretionary and this scheme does not constitute a contractual term.

The Company reserves the right at any time to vary or withdraw the scheme with your prior agreement and you will be given four weeks' written notice of any such changes.

2.4. You are entitled to a 'living out' allowance if you do not live in Company accommodation. It will be clearly spelt out in your Offer Letter whether you qualify for this 'living out' allowance.

2.5. Your basic salary will be reviewed annually. There is no contractual entitlement to any increase in your basic salary but you will be notified in writing in any case where there is any change to your salary. An itemised pay statement of your earnings and deductions will be sent to you in the middle of each month.

The Tax Office which deals with this Company is:

HM Inspector of Taxes

    Ref:

3. Hours of work

Your normal working hours are..........per week, Monday to Friday inclusive from..........am to..........pm. You are entitled to take one hour for lunch. The times at which lunch may be taken may vary from department to department depending on the needs of the business.

Due to the particular needs of our business, you may be required to work additional hours from time to time. This may include weekends or Bank,

Public or Statutory Holidays. If this is the case, your name will be included in the Duty Rosta and you will be paid at the rate of..........................for such days. You will be entitled to time off in lieu.

4. Staff Handbook, Rules and Procedures

The details of many of your terms and conditions are set out in the Staff Handbook and in other documents published by the Company in the form of Rules and Procedures.

Your attention is drawn in particular to the Compliance Manuals, Rules and Procedures published by the TSA/LAUTRO/FIMBRA and any other appropriate Regulatory Body, the Company's Personal Transaction Rules and the Rules on Data Security.

You have been given a copy of the Staff Handbook and all the above-mentioned Rules and Procedures as well as those referred to in Clause 5 below and other relevant Rules and Procedures, on joining. You should note that all these Rules and Procedures and the Staff Handbook (as amended from time to time) form part of your Contract. If there is anything that you do not understand, please make sure that you discuss it as a matter of urgency with your Supervising Officer/Head of Department or your Personnel Officer.

The Company reserves the right to add, delete, vary or modify any such Rules and Procedures and you will be given due notice of any such changes as well as copies of any additions or changes.

5. Conduct, dress and appearance

Because of the nature of our business, you are expected to conduct yourself at all times as would be expected of anyone working in the Finance Sector. *(SPECIFY if there are any dress rules or whether uniforms must be worn. If so state that these rules form part of the contract and that staff are required to wear this uniform at all times when on duty and have a duty to keep the uniform in a clean and tidy condition. SPECIFY whether the Company will pay cleaning costs etc.)*

The Company has published a booklet entitled 'Rules Book – General Standard of Conduct' and you are encouraged to read this carefully so that you are fully acquainted with all these rules.

In particular you are expected to ensure that your own personal financial transactions always reflect the highest standards of financial propriety. The Company has specific rules about *the prohibition of margin accounts and you must acquaint yourself with them. SPECIFY whether any other rules apply to your Company.*

The Company also has a specific rule prohibiting gambling in any form or book-making whilst on any of the Company's premises. Similar rules prohibit the use for any purpose of the City Index, IG Index or similar devices. Please note that these rules form part of the Company's Disciplinary Procedure and breach of any of them amounts to gross misconduct which may render you liable to summary dismissal.

In addition there are very important rules concerning Insider Trading and these can be found in the 'Insider Trading Rules' a copy of which has been given to you on joining.

6. Change of personal circumstances

It is very important that you inform your Personnel Officer of any changes to your personal circumstances such as change of address and/or telephone number, next of kin, bank or building society details, dependants, marriage, gain of qualifications, criminal convictions, loss of driving or other relevant licences etc.

It is expected that you have given all the correct details concerning age, dependants, qualifications, grades of examinations passed etc. Should the Company discover that you have provided any false information in this or any other material respect, the Company reserves the right to terminate your contract with or without notice or payment in lieu.

7. Place of employment

Your place of employment is at our location in London.

During the course of your employment you may be required to work in the same or any similar capacity in any of the Company's Departments, Branch offices, subsidiary or associate companies or locations within the UK. You may be required to travel in the UK or Overseas as Management may from time to time require should the need arise. Reasonable expenses will be paid for such travel as laid down in the Staff Handbook or any other document concerning expenses.

LIVING-IN ACCOMMODATION

SPECIFY whether required to live in and any other rules about using company accommodation.

8. Expenses

You will be reimbursed all reasonable expenses relating to travel, accommodation, entertainment and other out-of-pocket expenses incurred on authorised Company business upon production of all reasonable receipts in accordance with the Company's Travel and Entertainments Policy.

9. Holidays and time off

9.1. General

The rules for holidays and time off can be found in the Staff Handbook. It is important that you read them carefully in order that you do not lose any of your entitlement. A summary of the more important rules are set out below:

9.2. The 'Holiday Year'

The 'Holiday Year' runs from 1 January each year.

9.3. Entitlement

In addition to Bank and Public Holidays your entitlement in each complete year of service will be according to the following scale:

Grade and Service	*Entitlement*
Grades 1 – 11	20 working days
Grade 12 and above	22 working days
Employees with 25 years' service or more	25 working days

9.4. Rules

You are entitled to your full salary when on holiday. You may take your holiday at any time in the year subject to the agreement of your Head of Department/Supervising Officer. It is expected that you will give at least one month's prior notice of any leave to be taken. You must take at least ten working days at any one time. Should you wish to take leave in excess of this, you must get the agreement of your Head of Department/Supervising Officer. Permission will be granted only if adequate cover in the office can be maintained.

The Company requires that you reserve *two* days' annual leave in any holiday year in order that you take such days during the Christmas/New Year period when the office is shut. You will be given due notice every year, before the Christmas break, exactly which days these will be.

9.5. Year of commencement

In your first year of employment, your holiday entitlement will depend upon the month in which your employment started. The scale used to determine entitlement is shown in the Staff Handbook. You will normally only be permitted to take the holiday actually accrued.

9.6. Holiday pay upon termination

If you leave the Company's employment you will receive pay for any accrued holiday outstanding and untaken at the effective date of termination of your contract. Please note that you may be required to take any outstanding holiday entitlement reckoned by the Company during any period of notice and should you fail to do so you will then lose any entitlement to holiday pay in lieu.

The Company may at its entire discretion require you not to take any holiday during any period of notice and may require you to work out your notice period in full or in part in order to effect a smooth handover or finish any outstanding work. Any holiday pay due to you upon termination will be calculated by deducting holidays already taken from the amount of holiday accrued in that holiday year to the date of leaving.

Should holiday already taken exceed entitlement, the Company shall require you to repay an amount equivalent to the number of days by which you have exceeded your entitlement. The Company reserves the right to deduct this sum from any moneys, whether final salary, bonus or commission outstanding, expenses etc., from your final salary payment.

The Company reserves the right to withhold any accrued holiday pay to which you may have been entitled should you be summarily dismissed for gross misconduct.

Holiday pay may also be withheld in whole or in part should you fail to give proper notice of termination of your contract or should you leave before the said notice has expired. In such a case your holiday pay will be reduced by the number of days' notice not worked. In any case where the Company agrees to waive the need for you to work out your notice, the above paragraph will not apply.

10. Absence and sick pay procedure

10.1. Statutory Sick Pay (SSP)

The Company pays Statutory Sick Pay (SSP) as long as you have complied with all the statutory rules. These are clearly laid out in the Staff Handbook.

10.2. Additional sick pay

The Company may pay sick pay in addition to SSP at its entire discretion. In any case, the rules set down in the Company's Sick Pay Policy must be followed.

It is essential that you follow the absence reporting procedure otherwise your absence may be deemed to be unauthorised for which you may not be paid and for which disciplinary action may be taken.

10.3. Medical examinations

You may be required at any time to undergo a medical examination by a doctor of the Company's choice the cost of which will be borne by the Company.

11. Accidents at work

Any accident at work however minor must be reported to the Health and Safety Officer immediately and recorded in the Accident Book.

12. Car

If you are entitled to receive a car you will be notified of this in your Offer Letter. The car is provided in accordance with the Company's Car Policy which may be amended from time to time. The car is provided to you on condition that you have and retain a valid full UK driving licence.

The Company will meet the costs of repair, tax and the insurance premium of the car together with any petrol.

The Company reserves the right to institute any rules which are reasonable relating to cars and may change the rules at any time. The Company may also withdraw the car at any time or amend the value of the car permitted at any time. Due written notice will be given to you of any such changes.

Should you leave the Company's employment for whatever reason, the Company reserves the right to make a cash allowance in lieu of the use of the car during the notice period. The car will have to be returned upon leaving the Company or on any date determined by the Company in a clean and proper condition. The Company reserves the right to alter or withdraw any cash allowance to reflect the condition of the car or the need for any repairs.

13. Pension, Life Insurance, Long Term Disability and Medical Insurance Plans

The Company operates a voluntary, non-contributory/contributory Pension and Life Insurance Scheme for all employees over the age of .... There is a Contracting-Out Certificate in force in respect of all employees covered in this Scheme. An explanatory booklet entitled 'Pensions and Long Term Disability Plans' is given to you on engagement. It is assumed that all employees over the age of .... wish to participate in the Scheme unless Personnel is notified to the contrary. You will also be covered by a Long Term Disability Plan.

The rules on eligibility and benefit etc. for the Pension, Life Insurance and Long Term Disability Plans are governed exclusively by formal documents which are available for inspection in the Personnel Division.

The Company reserves the right to withdraw or amend any of the rules or benefits of the Schemes at any time and reserves the right to terminate any employee's participation in the Schemes at any time.

The Company also has a Medical Insurance Scheme which is paid for by the Company. The Scheme operates on the terms and conditions which are in force from time to time. The Company reserves the right at any time to amend or withdraw these Schemes or vary the scale or level of benefit currently in force and may at its entire discretion terminate any employee's participation in the Scheme.

Please note that all employees working eight (8) hours a week or more and who satisfy the conditions of the Scheme are eligible to join the Pension Scheme.

14. Lunch

A subsidised lunch is provided for all employees other than those who, by reason of their hours of work or office location, cannot make use of the Company's dining facilities. Such employees will be eligible to receive a meal allowance (which is taxable) in lieu.

15. Notice

In all cases other than gross misconduct, should the Company decide to terminate your contract for any other reason, you will be entitled to the following written notice or payment in lieu:

GRADES 1-11

Continuous Service	Notice
Less than six months	One week
Less than one year but more than six months	Two weeks
Less than five years but more than one year	Four weeks
Each additional year of continuous service up to twelve years	One week's notice for each complete year of service
Twelve years' continuous service or more	Twelve weeks' notice

SENIOR STAFF GRADES 12 AND OVER

You will be entitled to receive and required to give 3/6/12/24 months' notice to terminate your contract. In cases of gross misconduct, no notice or pay will be due.

The Company reserves the right to make a payment in lieu of notice should it so wish or to require you to remain away from work during your notice period whichever may be appropriate. Any payment in lieu of notice will have PAYE tax and Class 1 National Insurance deducted at source.

Where the Company requires you to remain away from work during your notice period (whether you or the Company gave notice), you will be required to comply with any conditions laid down by the Company and whilst on full pay during such time you will not be permitted to work for any other person, firm, client, corporation or on your own behalf without the Company's prior written permission.

Please note that during any such notice period or should the Company decide to pay you in lieu of giving you notice, the special rules about your car set out in Clause 12 above may apply.

Unless your employment has terminated at any earlier date, it will terminate without any further notice at the end of the month in which your (60th/62nd/65th) birthday falls.

16. References

Your employment is subject to satisfactory references and the Company's decision is final as to whether the references meet with our requirements. Your references will be taken up before we confirm our offer of employment to you but your current employer will not be approached for a reference until you confirm your acceptance of the position unless you allow us to do so earlier. If any delay is incurred in our taking up this or any other reference and should you commence employment whilst we are waiting for a reply, it is understood that your employment is terminable forthwith (with no notice) in the event of such references falling short of our requirements. Every effort will be made to obtain references as quickly as possible.

17. Qualifications/Experience/Licence under appropriate Regulatory Body

Your employment (and continued employment) is conditional upon you having and retaining all the educational, vocational, professional and any other appropriate qualifications that you stated you had when you completed your application form. It is also expected that the grades of all examinations taken conform with what you have stated on your application form.

The Company also expects that you have had the work experience that you have stated on your application form or at your interview. The Company reserves the right to terminate your employment with or without notice or payment in lieu in any case where it is discovered you do not have the said qualification or experience or where for whatever reason you fail to acquire any appropriate examination or licence or become disbarred from the appropriate Regulatory Body or Authority.

You will be required to bring the originals of all examination, undergraduate and post-graduate certificates and the certificates of any professional qualifications with you on your first day at work.

18. Outside business interests

It is expected that you will devote your whole time and attention to the Company during your working time. During your employment with the Company you are not permitted to undertake any other employment outside working hours, whether paid or unpaid, nor are you permitted to have any interest in any business or undertaking which directly or indirectly competes with the same or similar field of activity of this Company or any associated or subsidiary companies. If you should be engaged in any other employment or have any outside business interest, you must first seek the written permission of your Head of Department or Supervising Officer and Personnel Officer which will not be unreasonably withheld.

19. Duty of confidentiality

The restrictions contained in Clause 19 below are considered reasonable by the parties, but in the event that any restriction shall be found to be void, would be valid if some part thereof were deleted or the period of application reduced, such restrictions shall apply with such modifications as may be necessary to make them valid and effective.

19.1. Copying/Making abstracts etc.

You are not permitted to make any copy, abstract, summary or precis of the whole or part of any document belonging to the Company except where expressly authorised so to do or in the proper performance of your duties.

19.2. Disclosing or using confidential information

You must not, whether during your employment with the Company or after the end of it, whether you resign or are dismissed by the Company, unless expressly authorised in writing by a Supervising Officer or Head of Department, disclose to any unauthorised person or use any confidential information relating to the business affairs or trade secrets of the Company. This includes any details about the Company's clients and employees, actual, potential or past and all details relating to information on any of the Company's databases.

19.3. Outside communications

You must not make contact with or communicate with any member of the press or media or anyone so connected on behalf of the Company unless you have obtained the prior written permission of the Head of Corporate Communications or Divisional Head.

You are not permitted to publish any letters, articles or otherwise purporting to represent the Company (other than in your personal capacity) unless you have obtained prior permission in writing from the Head of Corporate Communications or Divisional Head. Failure to comply with any of the provisions (19.1-3) above may if the circumstances warrant it be regarded as gross misconduct for which you may be liable to summary dismissal.

19.4. Property to be returned on termination

You are required to deliver to the Company before the end of your employment or immediately after should your employment terminate without notice all papers, documents, keys, credit cards, cars and all property properly belonging to the company. You will be required to sign an undertaking that all such property has been duly returned.

19.5. Representing the Company

You are not permitted to represent yourself as an authorised agent for the Company except in the course of the proper performance of your duties or where authorised so to do. When your employment ceases, you must not hold yourself out in any business context as being an employee of this Company. Should there be any misrepresentation or intention to deceive in this respect, or any attempt to interfere with the existing business relations between this Company and its existing or potential clients, suppliers or agents, the Company may take proceedings against you to prevent any recurrence and to recover any losses incurred as a result.

20. Non-solicitation/non-competition

The parties agree that the following clauses are wholly necessary and are reasonable to protect the legitimate business interests of the Company. The restrictions contained in Clause 20 below are considered reasonable by the parties but in the event that any restriction defined below shall be found to be void would be valid if some part thereof were deleted or the period of application reduced, such restrictions shall apply with such modifications as may be necessary to make them valid or effective.

20.1. You will not, during your employment with the Company or any associated or subsidiary companies, or for a period of *six (6)* months afterwards, attempt to solicit custom, for private gain and/or for any third party, or deal with or accept orders from any private individual, firm or company who, within the period of one year before the termination of your employment, had been a client or customer of this or any associated company with whom you directly or indirectly dealt during this period. This clause does not apply to such individuals, firms, clients etc. whom you had personally introduced to the Company or with whom you had no business dealings.

Nor will you attempt to interfere with the existing business relations between any client or employee and the Company.

20.2. In order to protect the legitimate business interests of the Company you agree that you will not, at any time during the *six (6)* months immediately following the termination of your employment, howsoever caused, either on your own account or on behalf of any other person, firm, corporation which is involved in the same or similar activity as this Company within [a radius of..........miles of any of the Company's licensed offices OR the UK], engage or undertake the trade or business carried on by this Company as at the date of termination of your employment howsoever this is caused.

21. Non-enticement

You agree that at no time while you are in the Company's employment or after your employment has ceased, howsoever this is caused, will you approach any other employee of the Company with a view to him or her ceasing to be employed with the Company.

22. Additional duties

Due to the nature of our business it is expected that you will act with due diligence and utmost honesty at all times. Should any matters of concern come to your attention, you must report them immediately to your supervising officer or Head of Department or a member of Personnel. The Company sees it as your duty to report any acts of misconduct, dishonesty, breach of company rules or breach of any of the rules of the relevant regulatory bodies committed, contemplated or discussed by any other member of staff or any other third party. Please note that any failure to do so on your part may be regarded as serious or gross misconduct depending on the circumstances.

The Company will guarantee that whatever you report will be treated with the utmost confidentiality as far as this is practicable. You are also assured that no discriminatory or retaliatory action will be taken against you in any case where you make such reports to management, neither shall any adverse action of any kind be taken against you now or in the future.

The Company is a member of IMRO/LAUTRO/TSA/FIMBRA and you are therefore required as a condition of your employment to observe and comply carefully and diligently with all the Rules as laid down by [.....] from time to time. Since you act in an authorised capacity on behalf of the Company, you must ensure that at all times you are fully complying with all the relevant Regulatory Body's Rules. Failure to do so may result in legal action being taken against either the Company or you personally [and disqualification from trading].

You are required to co-operate fully with all directions and reasonable requests properly made by or on behalf of the Company or [........]. This may include, but is not limited to, a requirement that you make yourself readily available for and truthfully answer all questions put to you in the course of any

Appendix 1

Inspection, Investigation, Summary Process or Proceeding of any Appeal Tribunal.

Breach of the above undertakings will be a matter of serious misconduct which may entitle the Company in any case it deems fit to dismiss with or without notice or payment in lieu.

23. Cash handling and till procedures

Because of the particular nature of your job, the Company has very strict rules and procedures concerning the handling of stock and cash and accounting and till procedures. You are required to follow strictly the Company's laid down procedures. Any failure to do so may render you liable to dismissal should the circumstances warrant it. It is strictly forbidden to grant any credit, take IOUs or borrow any sums of money from any tills. Anyone suspected or caught committing such acts will be subject to serious disciplinary action which could lead to summary dismissal.

24. Security

You will be required to ensure that all documents, papers, correspondence etc. are kept secure at all times and are carefully locked away at night and that all the security procedures are properly maintained at all times. You are not expected to take any papers or documents belonging to the Company, home with you when you leave at the end of the day except where this is strictly necessary for the proper performance of your duties. Any unauthorised conduct in this respect which causes loss or damage to the Company or to any Client (past, present or future) will be regarded as serious misconduct for which you may be dismissed should the circumstances warrant it.

The Company's policy is to comply fully with the requirements of the Data Protection Act 1984 and it is essential that you follow the Company's rules and instructions very carefully on all aspects of Data Protection. In particular your attention is drawn to the 'Data Processing Security Policies and Standards Manual' which is published and updated regularly.

25. Inventions and patents

Your duties include a review of the Company's products with a view to improving them by new and original inventions and implementing improvements by means of such inventions and of applying established techniques, designs, processes, and methods not previously used or used in that particular application by the Company.

The following shall apply to your employment:

25.1. Any invention (relevant to or capable of use in the business of the Company) made by you in the course of your employment by the Company

340

whether or not in the course of duties, is, unless it is otherwise the exclusive property of the Company, hereby assigned by you to the Company, and you undertake at the expense of the Company to execute any formal and additional assignment required by the Company to vest or to confirm the vesting in it of such invention.

25.2. The Company has no liability to account to you for any revenue or profit derived or resulting from any invention belonging to the Company but this does not prejudice any rights you may have under any statutory provisions including section 40 of the Patents Act 1977.

26. Company indemnity/deductions and overpayments

Where any losses are sustained in relation to the property or moneys of the Company, client, customer, visitor or other employee, during the course of your employment caused through your carelessness, negligence, recklessness or through breach of the Company's rules or any dishonesty on your part, the Company reserves the right to require you to repay any of the said losses, either by deduction from salary or any other method acceptable to the Company. The Company may also require you to repay any damages, expenses or any other moneys paid or payable by the Company to any third party for any act or omission for which the Company may be deemed vicariously liable on your behalf.

This clause will also apply in cases of overpayment of any remuneration or any other payments (statutory, discretionary etc.) made by mistake or through any misrepresentation or otherwise.

The Company also reserves the right to withhold payment or deduct from salary a day's pay for each day of unauthorised absence. Any decision concerning this matter will be made by your immediate superior who will notify Personnel and Payroll.

27. Conflict of interests

Because of the nature of our business and your senior position, it is essential that your business dealings are above reproach. For this reason, the Company has set the following rules:

27.1. Offering or accepting gifts

It is not permitted to offer to any third party or accept any benefit whether financial or in kind from any other party (other than your proper remuneration from the Company).

It is not normally permitted to accept gifts or hospitality other than by way of a token nature (i.e. under £20 in value) from any person or business with whom you are involved on Company business or who may place business in the future. You must always clear the position with a Director before accepting any gift or hospitality whatever the nature.

27.2. Declaration of interests

You will be asked to inform your Director of any business interests that you or any close family member may have. This may include but is not limited to family relationships with consultants, contractors or suppliers to the Company, private work and membership of voluntary organisations, statutory bodies etc.

27.3. Use of Company contractors, consultants, suppliers etc.

Wherever possible staff should avoid making use of the services or purchasing the goods from any consultant, contractor or other suppliers of goods or services to the Company. Where you may wish to do so you must inform your Director and obtain his/her written permission *prior* to any contact whatsoever being made on a personal basis. Should you breach this clause of your contract, the Company reserves the right to treat this as gross misconduct for which you may be summarily dismissed.

28. Grievances

If you have an individual problem or complaint about your work or relating to the Company as a whole, you must bring this to the attention of your immediate manager within five working days of any such grievance arising. Everything possible will be done to resolve the problem. If an acceptable solution cannot be found, then the matter may be referred to an appropriate senior manager/Director, in writing if you so prefer. His/her decision will be final. At any stage of this grievance procedure you may be represented by a fellow member of staff should you so request this. In most cases the Personnel Officer will also be involved.

29. Disciplinary procedure

The Company has detailed Disciplinary Rules and a Procedure for dealing with misconduct and poor performance issues. It operates so that employees are treated fairly and consistently and everyone is given a chance to improve their conduct and their performance. These are set out in the Staff Handbook in the section dealing with Disciplinary Rules and Procedures. Please make sure that you have read and fully understand them since you are expected to comply with all the rules set out in the Procedure.

During (*the first twelve months of your employment/your probationary period*) the Company reserves the right in all cases other than gross misconduct to waive any or all of the official warnings and terminate your contract by giving you the required written notice or payment in lieu. This may mean that no official warnings will be given during this period. Please note that you are subject to the Rules and Policies from the start of your employment.

30. Maternity

Any female member of staff who becomes eligible either for Statutory Maternity Pay, and/or the statutory or any other maternity rights must comply with all the rules which are set out in the Company's Maternity procedure. The .... should be informed when a member of staff becomes pregnant so that all the maternity rights, rules and procedures can be fully explained.

31. Changes

Any major changes to your terms and conditions will be agreed and in any event all changes will be notified to you within four weeks of any change.

Signed on behalf of .... Date...............19....
(Employer)

I have read, understood and accepted the Terms and Conditions of Employment as stated and referred to in this Document relevant to my employment with Othello Investments Ltd.

Signed .... Date.............19....
(Employee)

Schedule A

Job Description

Appendix 2

Written Statement of Terms and Conditions of Employment

NUTS AND BOLTS & PARTNERS

This document sets out some of your terms and conditions of employment and incorporates the written particulars required by the Employment Protection (Consolidation) Act 1978 as amended. This Statement, your Offer Letter, job description and Staff Handbook form your Contract of Employment and all these documents are now contained in the Staff Handbook which has been given to you.

This Statement dated .... sets out certain particulars of the Terms and Conditions on which .... (Employer's name) (known hereafter as 'The Firm')

At .... (Address)

Employs .... (Employee's name)

Your employment with us began on ....

*Previous employment which counts as continuous employment commenced on:
....

OR

*No previous employment counts as continuous employment with this or any associated employer.

*(*delete as appropriate*)

1. Place of work

Your normal place of work is ....
but you will be required to travel within reasonable commuting distance of Greater London/your local office as part of normal job duties as you may be directed by management from time to time. You will also be required to relocate to any office of the Firm in the United Kingdom whether current or future. As much notice as possible will be given should we ask you to travel to another office or relocate to another office and reasonable relocation expenses will be paid.

344

2. Job title

Your job title is..............................and you will be required to undertake all the duties that are within your capabilities within the context of this job title.

3. Salary

Your salary is £..............per annum. You are paid monthly on the last calendar day of each month by credit transfer. In addition, you may receive, at the entire discretion of the Partnership, an annual bonus which is normally paid in December of each year.

4. Job duties and job description

Your job description is attached to this Written Statement (Schedule A) and forms part of your Terms and Conditions of Employment. Because of the evolving nature and changing demands of our business, you must understand that your job description is to be seen as a guide only as examples of the kinds of job duties you are expected to undertake. Your duties may vary from time to time and you will be given due notice of any such changes.

You will also be required to work in any department in the Firm as you may be directed from time to time in order to meet the needs of the business.

5. Staff Handbook

The Staff Handbook contains the details of your terms and conditions together with our policies and procedures. This Handbook forms part of your Contract of Employment. It is therefore very important that you read and fully understand everything in the Handbook and should you have any queries you should ask your Manager or the Staff Partner.

6. Hours of work

Your normal hours of work are..........am to..........pm, Monday to Friday, with one hour for lunch. However you will be required to work whatever additional hours the needs of the business may from time to time demand. Any overtime is paid at time and two-thirds of basic pay. The Firm operates flexible working hours and the terms which apply can be found in the relevant section of the Staff Handbook.

7. Holidays

You will be entitled to 20 working days' holiday in each calendar year, calculated at one and one-third days per completed calendar month. In your first year of employment you may only take the amount of holiday actually accrued in the year. You are also entitled to 8 statutory Bank Holidays. You will be subject to all the rules of the holiday policy which is set out in the Staff Handbook. In particular your attention is drawn to the special rules relating to holidays during your first year of employment. Details of the calculation of holiday pay etc. are also set out in the Handbook.

8. Sick pay

The Firm operates a sick pay scheme the details of which can be found in the Staff Handbook. Sick pay will only be paid according to the rules and conditions laid out in the Handbook. During your first year of employment any payment over and above any statutory sick pay (SSP) for which you may qualify will be subject to the entire discretion of the Partners. You may also be eligible to join the Private Medical Insurance Scheme which at the present time is provided by BUPA. Details of this are available from the Staff Partner.

9. Pension

The Firm operates a contributory staff Pension Scheme. You are eligible to join the Pension Scheme in accordance with the rules that are laid down in the relevant section of the Staff Handbook. A Contracting-Out Certificate is in force in respect of your employment. Upon joining the scheme, you will be required to complete an Expression of Wish Form for the purposes of the Pension Scheme.

You will retire on your 65th birthday and this Statement constitutes notice that your contract of employment will expire on that date (unless it has terminated at any earlier date) without any further notice being issued.

10. Notice

You will receive one calendar month's written notice to terminate your employment during the first four years' completed service. Thereafter you will receive one additional week for each completed year of service up to a maximum of twelve weeks' notice for twelve or more years' completed service. You are required to give the Firm one calendar month's written notice. The Firm reserves the right to make a payment in lieu of notice except in cases of gross misconduct where no notice or pay in lieu will be given.

11. Disciplinary Rules and Grievance Procedure

You are subject to the Disciplinary Rules and Procedures set out in the Staff Handbook. In cases of gross misconduct the Firm reserves the right to dismiss you without notice or pay in lieu. Your rights of appeal against any decision to dismiss are set out in the Disciplinary Procedure referred to in this paragraph.

In all other cases, should you be dissatisfied with any other decision affecting your employment you have the right to raise the matter with your immediate Manager/Partner. If no satisfactory solution has been found, you should then set out your grievance in writing to the Partner in charge of your office within five working days of the initial decision being made. Your final appeal lies with the Chairman to whom you should address your grievance in writing within five working days of receiving the Partner or Staff Partner's decision. Should you fail to pursue any grievance within these time limits, you will be deemed to have accepted any decision made.

12. Office Rules and Procedures

You are expected to acquaint yourself with all the Office Rules and Procedures set out in the Staff Handbook. The Firm reserves the right to modify, withdraw or initiate any rules or procedures as it deems fit. Due notice of any such changes will be given to you in writing.

In addition, you will receive a copy of the Office Manual where this is relevant to your job and you will be expected to acquaint yourself with its contents and follow all the rules set down in this Manual.

13. (optional) Temporary contract

This employment will continue until the final audit of our major clients, ABC plc and XYZ plc, have been completed. It is expected that this will be in approximately six months from the start date of this contract.

14. (optional) Overseas work

You will be working in Saudi Arabia as discussed for approximately eighteen months starting on 1 January 1994 to oversee the commissioning of the new hospital built by our associated company.

You will be paid in US dollars into your bank account in Switzerland. You will be eligible to receive the overseas allowances payable to staff working abroad and to four flights (first class air fares) during that time.

Upon your return you will receive the disturbance allowance as set out in the Policy and to four extra weeks' holiday in the year of your return.

Signed on behalf of Nuts and Bolts & Partners ....

Date................19....

I have read, understood and accept the Terms and Conditions of Employment as stated and referred to above and those contained in my Offer Letter and set out in the Staff Handbook which are relevant to my employment with Nuts and Bolts & Partners.

Signed....................(Employee)

Date................19....

Schedule A

Job Description

Appendix 3

Executive Service Agreement

THE ABC COMPANY LIMITED

Agreement between

.... (The Executive)

and

....(Employer, hereinafter referred to as 'The Company')

1.   Preamble

1.1. Any reference to any statutory provision shall be deemed to include a reference to all and every statutory amendment, modification, re-enactment and extension in force on or after the date of this Agreement.

1.2. Any reference to a clause shall be deemed to be a reference to a clause of this Agreement.

1.3. Words denoting the singular number shall include the plural number and vice versa and words denoting the masculine gender shall include the feminine gender.

2.   Appointment

2.1. With effect on and from....................(insert date), the Company will employ the Executive and the Executive shall serve the Company as............ (or such other title or titles as the Company may from time to time assign) upon the terms set out in this Agreement provided that the Company or a duly authorised nominee may from time to time require the Executive to serve the Company in some other capacity or capacities involving duties carrying a comparable or higher degree of responsibility in addition to and/ or in substitution for the capacity referred to above.

2.2. The Company shall be entitled to employ any other person or persons jointly with the Executive in the capacity referred to in Clause 2.1. or in any other capacity or capacities which the Executive may be required to assume in accordance with that Clause.

2.3. If the Executive is at any time unable through illness, accident or other incapacity to carry out his duties under this Agreement for any consecutive period of fourteen (14) days the Company may (without prejudice to the provisions of Clause 15) temporarily employ any person or persons to perform those duties in the Executive's place until such time as the Executive is able to resume fully the performance of his duties.

2.4. The Executive hereby warrants and represents to the Company that he will not be in breach of his/her existing or his former terms of employment whether express or implied or of any other obligation binding on the Executive by reason of his entering into this Agreement.

3.   Duration

3.1. The Executive's employment will commence on the Commencement Date of this Agreement and will continue unless terminated by either party giving to the other not less than [90] days' notice in writing provided that during the first three months of this Agreement the Company shall be entitled to terminate this Agreement by [30] days' notice in writing.

OR FOR A FIXED TERM CONTRACT

3.1. The Executive's employment will (unless lawfully terminated earlier under the provisions of Clause 15) be for a minimum term of ....(   )* years (calculated from the Commencement Date) and will terminate automatically without any further notice at the end of this Term

OR, and will continue thereafter unless and until terminated by either Party giving to the other not less than three (3) months' notice in writing in advance to that effect (unless the Party receiving the notice is willing to accept less notice or waive any or all notice).

*[Companies Act 1985, s 319 provides for a maximum term of five (5) years for a fixed term in a Director's Service Agreement. If the term is to exceed five years, then this has to be approved by the Company in a General Meeting. The Cadbury Report 1992 has recommended that this be reduced to a maximum term of three (3) years.]

3.2. In all cases, other than in the case of Gross Misconduct, the Company reserves the right to make a payment in lieu of notice or to require the Executive to remain away from work during the notice period whichever may be appropriate.

Any payment in lieu of notice will have tax and Class 1 National Insurance deducted at source.

Where the Company makes a payment in lieu of notice, the special rules about the car set out in Clause 13. 4 will apply.

3.3. Where the Company requires the Executive to remain away from work during the notice period (whether the Executive or the Company gave notice), the Executive will be required to comply with any conditions laid down by the Company and whilst on full pay during such time the Executive will not be permitted to work for any other person, firm, client, corporation or on behalf of the Executive himself without the Company's prior written permission.

3.4. Notwithstanding the provisions of Clause 1, the Executive's employment will automatically terminate without notice when he attains the Company's normal retiring age (years of age).

3.5. The Executive's period of continuous employment with the Company shall be deemed to have commenced on.....................[his employment with ....being counted as part of such continuous period of employment with the Company] OR [No previous employment will count for the purposes of continuous service with this employment].

4.   Powers and duties

4.1. The Executive shall exercise such powers, carry out such duties (if any) and observe such directions and restrictions in connection with the business of the Company as in each case the Board or any other authorised nominee of the Board from time to time may lawfully and reasonably confer and impose upon him.

4.2. In addition the Executive shall carry out such duties and responsibilities as are included in Schedule 1 attached [not included here].

5.   Other obligations

The Executive:

5.1. shall use his best endeavours to maintain and improve and extend the business of the Company and will observe all proper and lawful directions given to him from time to time;

5.2. will devote his whole time and attention to the performance of his duties (if any) under this Agreement (except when on holiday as hereinafter provided) and [unless otherwise agreed between the Executive and the Company there will be no specific terms and conditions relating to the Executive's hours of work under this Agreement] OR [the Executive's normal hours of work are from........am to ....pm Monday to Friday inclusive of one hour for lunch daily but the Executive shall conform to such hours of work as may be reasonably required of him for the proper performance of his duties and shall not be entitled to receive any additional remuneration for work outside his normal hours];

5.3. will if required by the Company serve the Company in accordance with this Agreement at any location used, owned, managed, leased or operated by the Company whether such place is now used, owned, managed, leased or operated by the Company or is acquired hereafter.

Appendix 3

6. Remuneration

6.1. By way of remuneration for his services the Executive will as from the Commencement Date be paid by the Company during the continuance of his employment a basic salary at the rate of £........................per annum or at such higher rate as may from time to time be approved by the Board.

6.2. The Company shall not less frequently than once a year review the basic salary in the light of increases in the Cost of Living, rates of remuneration then being paid to Executives holding similar positions in the UK and the general economic climate prevailing.

There is no contractual entitlement to any increase in basic salary and any increase will be notified in writing in any case where there is any change to basic salary.

6.3. The Executive's salary shall be deemed to accrue from day to day and (unless otherwise agreed) will be payable in monthly instalments on the last day of each month.

7. Other rules and procedures

The Company has produced a Staff Handbook which, with other documents provide more detail about the terms and conditions of employment, rules and procedures for the proper performance of the Executive's duties. In particular the rules concerning Conflict of Interest, the Code of Conduct and Common Responsibilities and all the rules on Data Security as they may change from time to time apply to the Executive's employment.

A copy of the Staff Handbook is given to every member of staff upon joining the Company's employment. All these Rules and Procedures and the Staff Handbook (as amended from time to time) form part of this Agreement.

The Company reserves the right to add, delete, vary or modify any such rules and procedures and due notice will be given of any such changes as well as copies of any additions or changes.

8. Codes of conduct

It is expected that the Executive will perform his duties to the highest level of competence and integrity in accordance with the requirements of the Company and that the reputation of the Company is safeguarded at all times. All Executives act as the Company's representatives whether on or off duty and it is essential that the good name and high standing of the Company is maintained at all times. A Code of Common Responsibilities and Good Conduct has been published and is printed in the Staff Handbook. This contains important information for all staff and forms part of the Contract of Employment. Breach of any of the rules of this Code as amended from time to time, if sufficiently serious, may constitute gross misconduct which would warrant summary dismissal.

9.   Change of personal circumstances

It is very important that the Company is informed immediately of any changes to personal circumstances such as change of address and or telephone number, next of kin, bank or building society details, dependants, marriage, gain of qualifications, criminal convictions, loss of driving or other relevant licences etc.

It is expected that the Executive has given all the correct details concerning age, dependants, qualifications, grades of examinations passed etc. Should the Company discover that any false information in this or any other material respect has been given, the Company reserves the right to terminate this employment with or without notice or payment in lieu.

10.   Expenses

All reasonable expenses relating to travel, accommodation, entertainment and other out-of-pocket expenses incurred on authorised business will be reimbursed upon production of all reasonable receipts in accordance with the Company's Travel and Expenses Rules.

11.   Holidays and holiday pay

11.1. In each Holiday Year, the Executive will be entitled to take (in addition to Bank and other statutory holidays)........................working days' paid holiday (of which not more than............................working days may be taken consecutively) at such time or times as the Board may from time to time approve.

The 'Holiday Year' runs from 1 April each year.

11.2. In the first year of employment, the Executive's holiday entitlement will depend upon the month in which the Executive's employment started. The scale used to determine entitlement is shown in the Staff Handbook. This is worked out on a pro rata basis.

11.3. Untaken holiday entitlement at the end of any Holiday Year may [may not] be carried forward to the next Holiday Year [but the Executive will be entitled to receive holiday pay in respect of that entitlement calculated and paid in accordance with Clause 11.4 below as if the Executive's employment had terminated at the expiration of the Holiday Year].

11.4. If the Executive's employment terminates (otherwise than by reason of any default on the Executive's behalf or by reason of gross misconduct) during or on the expiration of any such twelve-month period and at that time he has not taken his holiday entitlement for that period in full he will (subject to the following provisions) be entitled upon leaving the Company's employment to holiday pay in direct proportion to salary and length of service from the commencement of the Holiday Year. If the Executive has already taken part of his holiday entitlement for that period at the time of such termination of his employment, his entitlement to holiday pay will be the amount resulting from calculating his entitlement on the basis stated above and then deducting the salary the Executive has received in respect of the number of days' holiday already taken prior to the termination save that in no circumstances will the Executive be required to repay any holiday pay already received.

The Company may at its entire discretion require the Executive not to take any holiday during any period of notice and may require the Executive to work out the notice period in full or in part in order to effect a smooth handover or finish any outstanding work.

12. Illness

12.1. If the Executive is at any time prevented by illness, accident or other incapacity from fully carrying out his duties under this Agreement, then medical evidence must be furnished to the Director in charge of the Board or any lawful nominee of the Board which satisfies the said party(ies). Subject to the following clauses, the Executive will be paid by way of sick pay in lieu of any remuneration to which he otherwise would be entitled under this Agreement, his basic salary for the first [   ] consecutive months of each such incapacity less any tax and National Insurance Contributions and inclusive of any Statutory Sick Pay to which he may be entitled OR [less any State benefits claimed and received by way of State Sickness Benefit or Invalidity Benefit], less all other authorised deductions applied to his remuneration.

12.2. If the Executive's incapacity continues for a longer period than [   ] consecutive months or if he is incapacitated at different times for periods exceeding in aggregate [   ] (whether working days or not) in any twelve months, then any further payment to the Executive of any nature whatsoever during the continuance of such incapacity will be at the sole discretion of the Board or any lawful nominee of the Board.

12.3. If the Executive is absent from duty as a result of an accident in the United Kingdom, then no remuneration during this period will be paid by the Company if there is a claim for damages against a third party in respect of the accident, but sums amounting to not more than the sums which would have been paid had the absence been due to ordinary sickness shall be advanced to such a person after abatement to take account of any entitlement to statutory sick pay. He will be required to undertake to refund, from any damages received, the full amount of the sums advanced, less such part of that amount as is proportionate to any contributory negligence or fault on the part of that person, or, if the claim is settled by a lump sum in which no specific amount is identifiable as loss of earnings, to refund the advance to the same extent as the total claim is successful, or such other amount as is, in the opinion of the Company, fair and reasonable.

Any period of absence in such a case shall, if a refund of the sums advanced is made in full, be ignored for the purposes of reckoning sickness absence or, if a refund is made in part only and covering therefore part only of the period of absence, there shall be reckoned as sickness absence only that part of the total period of absence for which no refund is made.

'Accident' includes any event which causes personal injury.

12.4. The Executive agrees that at any time during the continuance of this Agreement he shall undergo a medical examination by a doctor of the Company's choice, the cost of which will be borne by the Company. The Executive may also be required to give his consent to certain details contained in any medical report prepared being disclosed to a senior member of management of the Company in the strictest of confidence.

13.   Motor car

13.1. To enable the Executive to perform his duties under this Agreement the Company will provide him or cause him to be provided with a motor car and will replace the same with a new motor car of an equivalent type and engine size not later than [   ] and thereafter at [   ] yearly intervals.

OR

To enable the Executive to perform his duties under this Agreement, the Company will provide him or cause him to be provided with a motor car of an age and type appropriate in the opinion of the Company to his responsibilities and position in the Company.

13.2. The Company will meet the costs of repair, tax and the insurance premium of the car together with any petrol. The Company reserves the right to institute any rules which are reasonable relating to cars and may change the rules at any time. The Company may also withdraw the car at any time or amend the value of the car permitted at any time. Due written notice will be given to you of any such changes.

13.3. Whilst on Company business and driving a car provided by the Company it is an absolute rule that EITHER [the Executive agrees not to drink alcohol] OR [the Executive agrees to restrict the amount of alcohol consumed]. Should the Executive be charged with a drink/driving offence or be convicted of such an offence he may be liable to have his car withdrawn without compensation.

13.4. Should the Executive's employment terminate for whatever reason, the Company reserves the right to make a cash allowance in lieu of the use of the car during the notice period. The car will have to be returned upon leaving the Company or on any date determined by the Company in a clean and proper condition. The Company reserves the right to alter or withdraw any cash allowance or to deduct any sums from final salary or moneys due to the Executive to reflect the condition of the car or the need for any repairs.

14. Pension

14.1. In addition to the benefits provided above the Company will maintain (*at its own expense*) a pension policy with [   ] to provide the following benefits to the Executive and his dependants:

Widow's and Widower's Pension;
Death in Service;
Established Maturity Value;
Established Pension.

14.2. Normal retirement age of the Executives employed by the Company is [   ] years of age.

14.3. The Executive shall, at the Company's expense, cause to effect or have effected a 'Keyman' Insurance Policy and the Executive agrees to ensure that this Policy is maintained during the currency of this Agreement. The Executive agrees to comply with any lawful or reasonable instructions of the relevant Insurance Company or any authorised nominee of the relevant Insurance Company in relation to maintaining proper and effective cover at all material times. The Beneficiary of this Policy will be at all material times 'the Company'.

15. Notice

15.1. If the Executive:

15.1.1. is prevented by illness, accident or other incapacity from fully carrying out his duties under this Agreement for a period exceeding [   ] consecutive months or at different times for periods exceeding in aggregate [   ] days (whether working or not) in any one period of [   ] consecutive months; or

15.1.2. without reasonable cause neglects or omits or refuses to perform any of his duties under this Agreement or to observe and perform the provisions of this Agreement to the reasonable satisfaction of the Company; or

15.1.3. misconducts himself, whether during or outside the course of his employment in such a way that in the reasonable opinion of the Company, the operation of the Company will be affected prejudicially; or

15.1.4. becomes bankrupt or applies for a Receiving Order or has a Receiving Order made against him or enters into any arrangement or otherwise with his creditors; or

15.1.5. becomes of unsound mind or a patient within the meaning of the Mental Health Act 1983; or

15.1.6. becomes ineligible for cover, renewal or benefit or the Policy is declared void or otherwise unenforceable;

It will be lawful for the Company, without prejudice to any other rights it may have at law, in respect of any matters mentioned above, by written notice to the Executive to terminate his employment forthwith.

15.2. The rights of the Company under Clause 14.1 are without prejudice to any other rights it may have at law to terminate the Executive's employment.

15.3. Upon termination of the Executive's employment for whatever reason the Executive:

15.3.1. will immediately deliver up to the Company all lists belonging to the Company or any suppliers, contractors etc. correspondence and other documents and papers and property belonging to the Company which may have been prepared by him or have come into his possession in the course of his employment and shall not retain any copies thereof;

15.3.2. will cease to represent himself as being in any way connected with the business of the Company or being its lawful or appointed agent.

15.4. The termination of this Agreement shall be without prejudice to the rights of either party against the other in respect of any antecedent breach of this Agreement. Such termination shall not, even in a case where the termination involves a breach of contract on the part of the Company, operate to affect those provisions in this Agreement which are intended to have effect after such termination. Without limiting the application of the two preceding sentences, such termination shall not, even in such a case as mentioned above, release the Executive from the continuing observance and performance by him of the obligations on his part contained in Clauses 17-21 (Outside Business Interests, Restraint clause, confidentiality etc.).

16. References

All employment with the Company is subject to satisfactory references and the Company's decision is final as to whether the references meet with its requirements. References will be taken up before any offer of employment is confirmed in writing but any current employer will not be approached for a reference until the Executive's written acceptance of the position has been received by the Company. If any delay is incurred in taking up this or any other reference and should employment have commenced whilst waiting for a reply, it is understood that the Executive's employment is terminable forthwith (with no notice) in the event of such references falling short of the Company's requirements. Every effort will be made to obtain references as quickly as possible.

17. Qualifications and experience

The Executive's employment and continued employment is conditional upon his having and retaining all the educational, vocational, professional and any other appropriate qualifications that the Executive stated he had when applying for the position. It is also expected that the grades of all examinations taken conform with what has been stated on any relevant application form.

The Company also expects that all the employment experience stated at the time of applying for the position is correct in every detail. The Company reserves the right to terminate the Executive's employment with or without notice or payment in lieu in any case where it is discovered the said qualification(s) or experience are not as stated.

The Company requires that all originals of examination, undergraduate and post-graduate certificates and the certificates of any professional qualifications are produced either at any interview or upon commencement of employment or at any time during the employment.

18. Outside business interests

It is expected that the Executive will devote his whole time and attention to the Company. During the Executive's employment with the Company, the Executive is not permitted to undertake any other employment outside working hours, whether paid or unpaid, nor have any interest in any business or undertaking which directly or indirectly competes with the same or similar field of activity of the Company or any associated or subsidiary businesses. If the Executive should wish to be engaged in any other employment or have any outside business interest, the prior written permission of the Board or any lawful nominee of the Board must be obtained. This will not be unreasonably withheld.

19. Conflict of interests

Because of the nature of the Company's business and the seniority of the Executive's position, it is essential that all business dealings are above reproach. For this reason, the Company has set the following rules:

19.1. Offering or accepting gifts

It is strictly forbidden to offer to any third party or accept any benefit whether financial or in kind from any other party (other than any proper remuneration from the Company).

It is strictly forbidden to accept gifts or hospitality other than by way of a token nature from any person or business with whom the Executive has any business dealings involved on Company business. The Board or any lawful nominee of the Board must give their prior approval before any Executive is authorised to accept any gift or hospitality whatever the nature.

19.2. Declaration of interests

The Company will maintain a register of interests and the Executive will be required to declare any business interests that he or any close member of his family may have. This may include but is not limited to family relationships with consultants, contractors or suppliers to the Company, private work and membership of other voluntary organisations, statutory bodies etc. If in doubt, the Executive is expected to discuss the matter with the Board or any lawful nominee of the Board.

The Executive will be required to sign a declaration that he has no interests as defined above. The register of interests is a document designed to protect both the Company and its employees. The contents of the register will not normally be open to inspection by members of the public or other external bodies.

19.3. Use of Company contractors, consultants, suppliers etc.

OPTION A

Wherever possible the Executive should avoid making use of the services or purchasing the goods from any consultant, contractor or other suppliers of goods or services to the Company. Where an Executive may wish todo so, the Board or any lawful nominee of the Board must be informed inadvance and his permission granted *prior* to any contact whatsoever being made on a personal basis. A register of interests referred to in Clause 19.2 above must be kept up to date in relation to these matters.

Should there be any breach of this clause of this Agreement, the Company reserves the right to treat this as gross misconduct for which the Executive's employment may be terminated without notice or payment in lieu.

OPTION B

The Executive shall not be permitted to make use of any services or be supplied with goods on a personal basis from any consultant, contractor or other suppliers of goods and services to the Company because of the possible conflict of interest. Should any such conduct come to the attention of the Company, the Company reserves the right to treat this as gross misconduct for which the Executive's employment may be terminated without notice or payment in lieu.

20. Confidentiality

The restrictions contained in Clause 20 below are considered reasonable by the parties, but in the event that any restriction shall be found to be void, would be valid if some part thereof were deleted or the period of application reduced, such restrictions shall apply with such modifications as may be necessary to make them valid or effective.

The parties agree that the clauses as set out below are reasonable and strictly necessary for the protection of the Company's legitimate business interests.

All the following subclauses are to be read as separate and severable clauses. In the event that any of the subclauses are in the event found by a Court of Law to be unenforceable or void, then the parties agree that the other clauses may be enforced.

20.1. Copying/making abstracts etc.

The Executive is not permitted to make any copy, abstract, summary or precis of the whole or part of any document belonging to the Company except where expressly authorised so to do or in the proper performance of his duties.

20.2. Disclosing or using confidential information

The Executive will not, whether during his employment with the Company or for a period of...............(months) after the end of it howsoever caused, unless expressly authorised in writing by the Board, disclose to any unauthorised person or use any confidential information properly belonging to the Company and relating to the business affairs of the Company. Confidential information in this context includes but is not limited to details about the Company's clients and employees, contractors, suppliers actual, potential or past, financial status, future plans and all details concerning the Company properties and their contents and all details relating to information on any of the Company's databases.

20.2.1. Trade secrets

The Executive shall not at any time before or after the termination of his employment (howsoever caused) use, disclose or communicate to any person whatsoever any trade secret(s) of which he has or may have become possessed during the continuance of his employment with the Company except in the proper course of his duties or as authorised in writing by the Board or as ordered by a court of competent jurisdiction. Trade secrets in this context include but are not limited to [GIVE EXAMPLES].

20.3. Outside communications

It is strictly forbidden for the Executive to make contact with or communicate with any member of the press or media or anyone so connected on behalf of the Company unless the Executive has obtained the prior written permission of the Board or any lawful nominee of the Board.

It is strictly forbidden for the Executive to publish any letters, articles or otherwise purporting to represent the Company (other than in any personal capacity) unless prior permission in writing has been obtained from the Board or any lawful nominee of the Board. Failure to comply with any of the provisions (20.1-3) above may if the circumstances warrant it be regarded as gross misconduct for which the Executive's employment may be terminated without notice or payment in lieu.

20.4. Property to be returned on termination

All papers, documents, keys, credit cards, cars and all property properly belonging to the Company must be delivered to the Company before the end of the Executive's employment howsoever caused or immediately after should the employment terminate without notice. The Executive will be required to sign an undertaking that all such property has been duly returned.

20.5. Representing the Company

The Executive agrees that he will not represent himself as an authorised agent for the Company except in the course of the proper performance of his duties or where authorised so to do. When the Executive's employment ceases howsoever it is caused, the Executive agrees that he will not hold himself out in any business context as being an employee of the Company.

Should there be any misrepresentation or intention to deceive in this respect, or any attempt to interfere with the existing business relations between the Company and its existing or potential clients, suppliers or agents, then the Company may take proceedings against the Executive to prevent any recurrence and to recover any losses incurred as a result.

21. Other restrictions

The restrictions contained in Clause 21 below are considered reasonable by the parties, but in the event that any restriction shall be found to be void, would be valid if some part thereof were deleted or the period of application reduced, such restrictions shall apply with such modifications as may be necessary to make them valid or effective.

The parties agree that the clauses as set out below are reasonable and strictly necessary for the protection of the Company's legitimate business interests.

All the following subclauses are to be read as separate and severable clauses. In the event that any of the subclauses are in the event found by a Court of Law to be unenforceable or void, then the parties agree that the other clauses may be enforced.

21.1. The Executive will not during his employment or for a period of twelve months (12) afterwards, attempt to solicit custom for private gain and/or for any third party from any private individual, firm or company who, within the period of one year before the termination of the Executive's employment, had had business dealings or proposed business dealings with the Company and with whom the Executive had any personal business dealings or knowledge of. The Executive agrees that he will not attempt to interfere with the existing business relations between any client, customer, supplier, contractor, firm or corporation or employee and the Company.

OR

For a period of twelve months (12) from the termination of his employment howsoever caused, the Executive shall not either solicit or seek to obtain orders by way of trade in respect of goods with which he shall have dealt on behalf of the Company or goods of a substantially similar nature from any person, firm or company with whom during the period of twelve months (12) the Executive shall have had such dealings on behalf of the Company.

OR

The Executive shall not for a period of twelve months (12) from the date of termination of employment howsoever caused, canvass, solicit or deal with, in connection with products made, sold or fixed by the Company or such persons' products similar to such products, any person, company or firm carrying on business within any such area as aforesaid who was during the twelve months (12) before the termination of the Executive's employment, a customer of the Company or accustomed to deal with the Company.

21.2. In order to protect the legitimate business interests of the Company the Executive agrees that he will not, during the period of one year following the termination of his employment, howsoever caused, within a radius of...............miles of any of the Company's premises at which he had, during the last twelve (12) months preceding the termination of the employment, taken employment of any kind either on his own account or for any other person, firm, corporation or company and in competition with the Company directly or indirectly engage in or be concerned with any trade or business carried on by the Company or any of its subsidiaries as at the date of termination of the Executive's employment.

21.3. The Executive also agrees that he will not whilst he is still in the employment of the Company, except in a purely social capacity, contact, deal with, or attempt to solicit custom from, any customer or client with whom he had any business dealings in the twelve months (12) prior to the termination of his employment. Nor will the Executive attempt to interfere with the existing business relations between any client, contractor, supplier or employee and the Company. This Clause is without prejudice to Clause 20.1 above.

22. Non-enticement/Non-poaching

The Executive covenants that he shall not without the consent in writing of the Board during the continuance of his employment or during the period of twelve months (12) after the termination of his employment howsoever caused, either on his own account or in conjunction with or on behalf of any other person solicit or entice away or endeavour to solicit or to entice away from the Company or any of its associated or subsidiary companies, any individual who was:

(a) an employee, Director, or Consultant of the Company or any of its associated or subsidiary companies; or

(b) contracted to render services to any such company during the period specified in paragraph 21 above; and

(c) during which period (whether in whole or in part) the Executive had dealings; whether or not such person would commit a breach of contract by reason of his leaving.

23. Touting for business

The Executive covenants that he will not make any contacts whether formal or informal, written or oral, with any of the Company's past, current or prospective suppliers, customers or clients for any purpose other than for the legitimate business interests of this Company. Such unlawful purpose might include but is not limited to an intention to set up a competing business or work for a rival after leaving this Company. Any breach of this Clause may render the Executive liable to serious disciplinary action which may result in summary dismissal if the circumstances warrant it.

24. Reporting misconduct

Due to the nature of our business it is expected that the Executive will act with due diligence and utmost honesty at all times. Should any matters of concern come to the Executive's attention, he must report them immediately to the Board or any lawful nominee of the Board. The Company sees it as the duty of all Executives to report any acts of misconduct, dishonesty, breach of Company rules or breach of any other relevant rules or codes of conduct, committed, contemplated or discussed by any other member of staff or any other third party. Please note that any failure to do so may be regarded as serious or gross misconduct depending on the circumstances.

The Company agrees that whatever is reported will be treated with the utmost confidentiality as far as this is practicable.

25. Security

It is a strict rule that all documents, papers, correspondence etc. are kept secure at all times and are carefully locked away at night and that all the security procedures are properly maintained at all times. It is not expected that any papers or documents belonging to the Company will be taken home at the end of the day except where this is strictly necessary for the proper performance of the Executive's duties. Any unauthorised conduct in this respect which causes loss or damage to the Company or to any third party will be regarded as serious or gross misconduct.

The Company's policy is to comply fully with the requirements of the Data Protection Act 1984 and Computer Misuse Act 1990. It is essential that all the rules and instructions are followed very carefully on all aspects of data protection. Any misuse of any data on any of the Company's databases or unauthorised access to any databases or computerised data or any breach of the Company's rules on security may be regarded as gross misconduct for which summary dismissal may be warranted.

26. Inventions and patents

The Executive's duties may include a review of the company's products with a view to improving them by new and original inventions and implementing improvements by means of such inventions and of applying established techniques, designs, processes, and methods not previously used or used in that particular application by the Company. The following shall apply to the Executive's employment:

26.1. Any invention (relevant to or capable of use in the business of the Company) made by the Executive in the course of his employment by the Company whether or not in the course of his duties, is, unless it is otherwise stated, the exclusive property of the Company, hereby assigned by the Executive to the Company, and the Executive undertakes at the expense of the Company to execute any formal and additional assignment required by the Company to vest or to confirm the vesting in it of such invention.

26.2. The Company has no liability to account to the Executive for any revenue or profit derived or resulting from any invention belonging to the Company but this does not prejudice any of the Executive's rights under section 40 of the Patents Act 1977.

27. Indemnity etc.

Where any losses are sustained in relation to the property or moneys of the Company, client, customer, visitor or other employee, during the course of the Executive's employment caused through his carelessness, negligence, recklessness or through breach of the Company's rules or any dishonesty, the Company reserves the right to require the Executive to repay any of the said losses, either by deduction from salary or any other method acceptable to the Company. The Company may also require the Executive to repay any damages, expenses or any other moneys paid or payable to the Company to any third party for any act or omission for which the Company may be deemed vicariously liable on the Executive's behalf. This will apply to any excess in relation to the Company's Car Insurance Policy for any claim relating to damage to a motor vehicle for which the Executive is deemed to be responsible.

This Clause will also apply in cases of over-payment of any remuneration or any other payments (statutory, discretionary etc.) made by mistake or through any misrepresentation or otherwise.

28. Grievances

If the Executive has an individual problem or complaint relating to his employment or the Company as a whole, he should bring this to the attention of the Board or any lawful nominee of the Board within five working days of any such grievance arising. Everything possible will be done to resolve the problem. If an acceptable solution cannot be found, then the matter may be referred to [   ]. Their decision will be final. At any stage of this grievance procedure the Executive may be represented by a fellow member of staff.

29. Disciplinary Rules and Procedures

The Company has detailed Disciplinary Rules and a Procedure for dealing with misconduct and poor or unsatisfactory performance. These are set out in the Staff Handbook in the Section dealing with Disciplinary Rules and Procedures. These rules apply to the Executive's employment.

During [   ] months' of the Executive's employment, the Company reserves the right in all cases other than gross misconduct to waive any or all of the official warnings and terminate the Executive's employment by giving him the required written notice or payment in lieu, as stated in Clause 3 of this Agreement. Please note that the Executive is subject to the Rules and Policies from the commencement of this Agreement.

OR

There is no disciplinary procedure applicable to the Executive's employment.

30. Cancellation and amendments

30.1. This Agreement will operate as from the Commencement Date in substitution for and to the exclusion of any terms of employment in force between the Company and the Executive without prejudice to the rights, liabilities and obligations (if any) of either party accrued or accruing prior to that date.

30.2. No Agreement made between the Company and the Executive nor any amendment to this Agreement will be legally binding on the Company unless and until such agreement or amendment is confirmed in writing by the Company.

31. Governing law

This Agreement shall be interpreted and operate in accordance with the law of England.

Signed .... Date..............19...
(The Board or any lawful nominee of the Board on behalf of the Company)

I have read, understood and accepted the Terms and Conditions of Employment as stated and referred to in this Agreement relevant to my employment with the Company.

Signed .... Date.....................19...
(Executive)

Contract of Employment – Firm of Accountants

THE ABC COMPANY LIMITED

Contract of Employment

This document sets out your principal terms and conditions of employment which incorporates the written particulars required by the Employment Protection (Consolidation) Act 1978 as amended and together with your Offer Letter and any Rules and Procedures issued by the Firm constitutes the Contract of Employment between:

....

and
.... (Employer, hereinafter referred to as 'the Firm').

Your employment as...
commences on the....................day of ....19....

No previous employment counts as continuous employment for any statutory purposes.

1. Career progression

1.1. Trial period

Your initial employment with the Firm will be on the basis of a trial period of up to six months. During this time either party shall give one month's prior written notice to terminate the contract (other than in the case of gross misconduct or gross incompetence or negligence when the Firm reserves the right to dismiss without notice or payment in lieu). In any case deemed appropriate by the Firm, this trial period may be extended and in any such case you will be notified in writing.

1.2. Future partnership(s)

Provided that the Firm is satisfied with your performance, it is expected that you would be offered a salaried partnership to take effect six months after the start of your employment i.e. after the satisfactory completion of the trial period. Please note that this depends upon your performance and conduct during your initial employment with us and the Firm reserves the right to suspend any decision concerning the offer of a partnership if there is any doubt in the minds of your superiors about your suitability.

It is the Firm's policy that a salaried partnership is a normal preliminary to full equity partnership. The normal progression to equity partnership would be two to two and a half years of appointment to salaried partner. It would be our expectation that you would, in the normal case, be offered an equity partnership on or after 1 May 1995. Any such offers either to salaried or equity partnership are made at the entire discretion of the Firm and do not form part of any contractual entitlement on your part or obligation on the part of the Firm.

It is a condition of your engagement that if you are offered an equity partnership, you will accept such offers subject to the terms being agreed. Because of the investment the Firm will have made in you, should you unreasonably decline any such offer of equity partnership, the Firm will deem this to be a breach of these terms and conditions and will terminate your contract of employment with immediate effect.

2. Job responsibilities

2.1. Job title

You are employed as a Senior Manager.

2.2. Duties

Your duties will be fully explained to you when you commence employment with the Firm. It is the Firm's intention that any oral instructions or written descriptions of your job duties and responsibilities should serve as a guide to the major areas for which you will be accountable. Because of the changing nature of the business the obligations upon you will inevitably vary and develop. The Firm reserves the right at any time during your employment, upon reasonable notice, to require you to undertake any duties which fall within your capabilities.

3. Hours

The normal office hours are Monday to Friday, ...am to ....pm. Because of the nature of your position in the Firm you will be required to work whatever hours are necessary for the proper performance of your duties and this may on occasion mean that you will work in excess of normal business hours and in some cases on weekends or Bank or Public Holidays.

4. Remuneration package

4.1. Basic salary

Your basic salary is £.....................per annum payable monthly by direct credit transfer to your personal bank or building society account. This will normally be paid on ....day of each month. It will be your responsibility to ensure that .... has a note of your Bank or Building Society Account Name and Number and Sort Code Number.

You are not entitled to the payment of any overtime for hours worked in excess of the normal business hours of this Firm.

4.2. Bonus Scheme

The Firm operates an annual bonus scheme in respect of your employment.

(INSERT DETAILS OF BONUS SCHEME as per para .... of the Offer Letter)

Please note that this bonus scheme and any payments paid are discretionary and this scheme does not constitute a contractual term.

The Firm reserves the right at any time to vary or withdraw the scheme and will give you four weeks' notice of any such changes.

4.3. Annual review of salary

Your basic salary will be reviewed no later than 1 November 1993 and annually thereafter. There is no contractual entitlement to any increase in your basic salary but you will be notified in writing in any case where there is any change to your salary.

An itemised pay statement of your earnings and deductions will be sent to you on ....

The Tax Office which deals with this Firm is:

HM Inspector of Taxes

Ref:

4.4. Payment of subscriptions

The Firm will pay your annual subscriptions to the Institute of Chartered Accountants in England and Wales and to the Institute of Taxation.

4.5. Payment of telephone expenses

The Firm will reimburse you all the costs of the business telephone line that you maintain in your home. All calls must be recharged to Clients where appropriate as identified for write-off as practice development costs.

5.   Place of employment

Your place of employment is at our office in ....London.

During the course of your employment you may be required to work in the same or any similar capacity in any of the Firm's Departments, Branch offices, subsidiary or associate companies or locations within the UK. Due to the nature of our business, you may be required to travel to our Clients' locations in the UK (or Overseas) as any of the Partners may from time to time require should the need arise. This was discussed with you at your interview. You will be given as much notice as possible if you are required to travel or relocate and reasonable travel and relocation expenses will be paid to you as laid down in the Firm's Policy on Expenses, Travel and Relocation.

6.   Rules and procedures

There are certain internal office rules concerning your work and conduct and these will be spelt out to you in writing when you start with us. You are also expected to observe all reasonable rules which have been laid down by any of our Clients where you may be working.

We and you are governed by the Financial Services Act 1986 and the body which regulates such conduct – The Institute of Chartered Accountants in England and Wales (ICAEW). You are required to comply with all the professional rules and codes of conduct which apply to your employment and to co-operate in any way with any internal or external enquiry, investigation, meeting etc. initiated either by the relevant regulatory body or any Partner of this Firm.

7.   Rules concerning conduct

Because of the nature of our business, you are expected to conduct yourself at all times as would be expected of anyone working in the Finance Sector.

In particular you are expected to ensure that your own personal financial transactions always reflect the highest standards of financial propriety. The Firm has specific rules about the use of insider information and confidential information relating to Clients or the Firm's business or proposed business. Any breach of such information constitutes gross misconduct for which you may be summarily dismissed.

(PLEASE INSERT A REFERENCE TO YOUR SPECIFIC RULES)

8.   Change of personal circumstances

It is very important that you inform .... of any changes to your personal circumstances such as change of address and/or telephone number, next of kin, bank or building society details, dependants, marriage, gain of qualifications, criminal convictions, loss of driving or other licences, loss of membership of ICAEW etc.

It is expected that you have given all the correct details concerning age, dependants, qualifications, grades of examinations passed etc. Should the Firm discover that you have provided any false information in this or any other material respect, the Firm reserves the right to terminate your contract with or without notice or payment in lieu.

We also require you to notify a Partner immediately should any complaint about your professional conduct be made to the ICAEW or any other body, party or organisation or where you are subject to any disciplinary charge by the ICAEW.

9. Expenses

You will be reimbursed all reasonable expenses relating to travel, accommodation, entertainment and other out-of-pocket expenses incurred on authorised Firm's business upon production of all reasonable receipts in accordance with the Firm's Policy.

10. Annual holidays

10.1. Entitlement

In addition to the eight Bank and Public Holidays you are entitled to 25 days' annual leave in any year. The 'Holiday Year' in this Firm runs from 1 January to 31 December.

Annual entitlement rises to 30 days' annual leave when you become a salaried partner.

You are entitled to your full salary when on holiday. You may take your holiday at any time in the year subject to the agreement of the Senior Partner. It is expected that you will give at least one month's prior notice of any leave to be taken. Permission will be granted unless in exceptional cases there is an urgent matter which requires your attention or there are not sufficient staff in the office at that time.

10.2. Year of commencement

In your first year of employment, your holiday entitlement will depend upon the month in which your employment started. You will normally only be permitted to take the holiday actually accrued.

10.3. Holiday upon termination

If you leave the Firm's employment you will receive pay for any accrued holiday outstanding and untaken at the effective date of termination of your contract. Please note that you may be required to take any outstanding holiday entitlement reckoned by the Firm during any period of notice and should you fail to do so you will then lose any entitlement to holiday pay in lieu.

The Firm may at its entire discretion require you not to take any holiday during any period of notice and may require you to work out your notice period in full or in part in order to effect a smooth handover or finish any outstanding work. Any holiday pay due to you upon termination will be calculated by deducting holidays already taken from the amount of holiday accrued in that holiday year to the date of leaving.

Should holiday already taken exceed entitlement, the Firm shall require you to repay an amount equivalent to the number of days by which you have exceeded your entitlement. The Firm reserves the right to deduct this sum from any moneys, whether final salary, bonus or commission outstanding, expenses etc., from your final salary payment.

The Firm reserves the right to withhold any accrued holiday pay to which you may have been entitled should you be summarily dismissed for gross misconduct.

Holiday pay may also be withheld in whole or in part should you fail to give proper notice of termination of your contract or should you leave before the said notice has expired. In such a case your holiday pay will be reduced by the number of days' notice not worked. In any case where the Firm agrees to waive the need for you to work out your notice, the above paragraph will not apply.

11. Absence and sick pay procedure

11.1. Statutory Sick Pay (SSP)

The Firm pays Statutory Sick Pay (SSP) as long as you have complied with all the statutory rules. These are clearly laid out in the Staff Handbook.

11.2. Additional sick pay

The Firm may pay sick pay in addition to SSP at its entire discretion. In any case, the rules set down in the Firm's Sick Pay Policy must be followed.

It is essential that you ring in and speak to your immediate superior as early as possible on the first morning of your absence.

11.3. Medical examinations

You may be required at any time to undergo a medical examination by a doctor of the Firm's choice, the cost of which will be borne by the Firm.

12.   Car

The Firm will provide you with a car of a cost equivalent to a Citroen BX19 1.6 subject to the paragraph below.

It has been agreed that we would take over the lease on your existing car which has some 18 months to run, providing that your former employer, XYZ, agrees to assign the lease to us. If they do not agree then we will provide you with a new car on a three-year lease. We will be responsible for all tax, reasonable insurance and maintenance costs assuming that you have a 'No Claims' bonus and are not loaded.

The car is provided to you on condition that you have and retain a valid full UK driving licence.

The Firm reserves the right to institute any rules which are reasonable relating to cars and may change the rules at any time. The Firm may also withdraw the car at any time or amend the value of the car permitted at any time. Due written notice will be given to you of any such changes.

Should your employment terminate for whatever reason, the Firm reserves the right to make a cash allowance in lieu of the use of the car during the notice period. The car will have to be returned upon leaving the Firm or on any date determined by the Firm in a clean and proper condition. The Firm reserves the right to alter or withdraw any cash allowance to reflect the condition of the car or the need for any repairs.

13.   Pension, Life Insurance, Long Term Disability and Medical Insurance Plans.

The Firm does not operate a Group Pension Scheme and we will therefore match your contributions to a personal pension up to a maximum of 5% of your basic salary.

We will provide you with life cover for death in service of three times your basic salary.

You are also entitled to join the Private Medical Insurance Scheme which is paid for by the Firm for you, your wife and children. The Scheme operates on the terms and conditions which are in force from time to time. Currently the Scheme in operation is run by Private Patients' Plan (PPP).

The Firm reserves the right at any time to amend or withdraw these Schemes or vary the scale or level of benefit currently in force and may at its entire discretion terminate any member of staff's participation in the Scheme.

14.   Notice

In all cases other than gross misconduct, should the Firm decide to terminate

your contract for any other reason, you will be entitled to ....weeks/
months' written notice or payment in lieu. This paragraph will only apply after
the satisfactory completion of the trial period referred to in Clause 1 of this
Contract.

The Firm reserves the right to make a payment in lieu of notice should it so
wish or to require you to remain away from work during your notice period
whichever may be appropriate. Any payment in lieu of notice will have PAYE
tax and Class 1 National Insurance deducted at source.

Where the Firm requires you to remain away from work during your notice
period (whether you or the Firm gave notice), you will be required to comply
with any conditions laid down by the Firm and whilst on full pay during such
time you will not be permitted to work for any other person, firm, client,
corporation or on your own behalf without the Firm's prior written
permission.

Please note that during any such notice period or should the Firm decide to
pay you in lieu of giving you notice, the special rules about your car set out in
Clause 12 above may apply.

Unless your employment has terminated at any earlier date, it will terminate
without any further notice at the end of the month in which your 60th birthday
falls.

Should you leave without notice or during your notice period without the
permission of the Firm, the Firm reserves the right to deduct a day's pay for
each day not worked during the notice period. This may include deduction
from your salary, any bonus due, accrued holiday pay or other moneys due to
you. In any case where the Firm agrees (in writing) to waive the need for you
to work out your notice the above clause will not apply.

15.   References

Your employment is subject to satisfactory references and the Firm's decision
is final as to whether the references meet with our requirements. Your
references will be taken up before we confirm our offer of employment to you
but your current employer will not be approached for a reference until you
confirm your acceptance of the position unless you allow us to do so earlier. If
any delay is incurred in our taking up this or any other reference and should
you commence employment whilst we are waiting for a reply, it is understood
that your employment is terminable forthwith (with no notice) in the event of
such references falling short of our requirements. Every effort will be made to
obtain references as quickly as possible.

16.   Qualifications and experience

Your employment and continued employment is conditional upon having and
retaining all the educational, vocational, professional and any other

appropriate qualifications that you stated you had when you completed your application form and as stated at your interview. It is also expected that the grades of all examinations taken conform with what you have stated on your application form.

In particular you are required to be and remain a member of the Institute of Chartered Accountants in England and Wales (ICAEW). Should you lose your membership or be 'struck off' or where any serious disciplinary action has been taken against you by the ICAEW, the Firm reserves the right to terminate your contract forthwith as being gross misconduct on your part.

The Firm also expects that you have had the work experience that you have stated on your application form or at your interview. You will also be asked at any time during your employment to show to a Partner the originals of all examination, undergraduate and post-graduate certificates and the certificates of any professional qualifications.

17. Outside business interests

It is expected that you will devote your whole time and attention to the Firm during your working time. During your employment with the Firm you are not permitted to undertake any other employment outside working hours, whether paid or unpaid, nor are you permitted to have any interest in any business or undertaking which directly or indirectly competes with the same or similar field of activity of this Firm. If you should be engaged in any other employment or have any outside business interest, you must first seek the written permission of a Senior Partner, which will not be unreasonably withheld.

18. Duty of confidentiality

The parties agree that the restrictions set out below are reasonable and wholly necessary to protect the legitimate business interests of the Firm.

In the event that any such restriction shall be found to be void, would be valid if some part thereof were deleted or the period of application reduced or in the event that either no time limit has been specified or a time limit specified, such restrictions shall apply with such modifications as may be necessary to make them valid or effective.

18.1. Copying/Making abstracts etc.

You are not permitted to make any copy, abstract, summary or precis of the whole or part of any document belonging to the Firm except where expressly authorised so to do or in the proper performance of your duties.

18.2. Disclosing or using confidential information

You must not, whether during your employment with the Firm or after the end of it, whether you resign or are dismissed by the Firm, unless expressly authorised in writing by a Senior Partner disclose to any unauthorised person or use any confidential information relating to the business affairs or trade secrets of the Firm. This includes any details about the Firm's clients and employees, actual, potential or past and all details relating to information on any of the Firm's databases.

18.3. Outside communications

You must not make contact with or communicate with any member of the press or media or anyone so connected on behalf of the Firm unless you have obtained the prior written permission of a Senior Partner.

You are not permitted to publish any letters, articles or otherwise purporting to represent the Firm (other than in your personal capacity) unless you have obtained prior permission in writing from a Senior Partner.

Failure to comply with any of the provisions (18.1-3) above may if the circumstances warrant it be regarded as gross misconduct for which you may be liable to summary dismissal.

18.4. Property to be returned on termination

You are required to deliver to the Firm before the end of your employment or immediately after should your employment terminate without notice all papers, documents, keys, credit cards, cars and all property properly belonging to the Firm. You may be required to sign an undertaking that all such property has been duly returned.

18.5. Representing the Firm

You are not permitted to represent yourself as an authorised agent for the Firm except in the course of the proper performance of your duties or where authorised so to do. When your employment ceases, you must not hold yourself out in any business context as being an employee or partner or agent of this Firm. Should there be any misrepresentation or intention to deceive in this respect, or any attempt to interfere with the existing business relations between this Firm and its existing or potential clients, suppliers or agents, then the Firm may take proceedings against you to prevent any recurrence and to recover any losses incurred as a result. Such representation shall include but is not limited to advertising your services using the name of this Firm in some connection.

19. Non-solicitation/non-dealing

19.1. You will not during your employment with the Firm or any associated or subsidiary companies or for a period of twelve months afterwards, attempt to solicit custom from for private gain and/or for any third party or deal with any private individual or Firm, Corporation,

Organisation etc. who within the period of one year before the termination of your employment (howsoever caused) had been a Client or Customer with whom you had any business dealings or knowledge of other than any Client whom you had personally introduced to the Firm. Nor will you attempt to interfere with the existing business relations between any Client or employee and the Firm.

19.2. Non-enticement

You agree that at no time while you are in the Firm's employment will you approach any other employee of the Firm with a view to him or her ceasing to be employed with the Firm if this causes him/her to breach any term whether express or implied of his/her contract of employment.

20. Duty of fidelity

Due to the nature of our business it is expected that you will act with due diligence and utmost honesty at all times. Should any matters of concern come to your attention, you must report them immediately to a Senior Partner. The Firm sees it as your duty to report any acts of misconduct, dishonesty, breach of Firm rules or breach of any of the rules of the relevant regulatory bodies committed, contemplated or discussed by any other member of staff or any other third party. Please note that any failure to do so on your part may be regarded as serious or gross misconduct depending on the circumstances.

The Firm will guarantee that whatever you report will be treated with the utmost confidentiality as far as this is practicable.

21. Security and Clear Desk Policy

You will be required to ensure that all documents, papers, correspondence etc. are kept secure at all times and are carefully locked away at night and that all the security procedures are properly maintained at all times. You are not expected to take any papers or documents belonging to the Firm home with you when you leave at the end of the day except where this is strictly necessary for the proper performance of your duties. Any unauthorised conduct in this respect which causes loss or damage to the Firm or to any Client (past, present or future) will be regarded as serious misconduct for which you may be dismissed should the circumstances warrant it.

22. Grievances

If you have an individual problem or complaint about your work or relating to the Firm as a whole, you must bring this to the attention of a Partner within five working days of any such grievance arising. Everything possible will be done to resolve the problem. If an acceptable solution cannot be found, then the matter may be referred to an appropriate Senior Partner, in writing if you so prefer. His decision will be final. At any stage of this grievance procedure you may be represented by a fellow member of staff should you so request this.

Appendix 4

23. Disciplinary Procedure

The Firm has detailed Disciplinary Rules and a Procedure for dealing with misconduct and poor performance issues. Copies of the Rules and Procedures are kept......................(insert where) and open to you to read upon giving reasonable notice.

During your trial period referred to in Clause 1 of this Contract, the Firm reserves the right (in all cases other than gross misconduct) to waive any or all of the official warnings without proceeding to any disciplinary hearing or appeal to terminate your contract by giving you the required written notice or payment in lieu. Please note that you are subject to the Rules and Policies from the start of your employment.

24. Changes

Any changes to your terms and conditions will be notified to you within four weeks of any change and in some cases you will be given due notice before any changes are implemented.

Signed on behalf of.. Date.................19...
(ABC Ltd)

I have read, understood and accepted the Terms and Conditions of Employment as stated and referred to in this Document relevant to my employment with ABC Ltd.

Signed.. Date....................19...
(Senior Manager)

378

Appendix 5

Contract of Employment – Hairdressing Salon

Contract of Employment

between

Employers: .... (name and address)

....

....

(known in this Agreement as 'Salon' or 'Management')

Employee: .... (name and address)

....

....

Tel. No: ....

Date of commencement of employment: ....199....

1.   Job title

Your job title is ....

2.   Salary

Your salary will be £.................. per week after deduction of income tax and Class 1 National Insurance Contributions (NIC), payable in arrears weekly. Your employers will be responsible for paying the tax and NIC which becomes due and proper records will be maintained of all such payments. Your salary will be reviewed .... (*annually*). Any tips paid or payable to you will be in addition to your salary. Please note that you will be taxed on such gratuities in line with the Inland Revenue rules.

3.   Hours of work and days off

Your working week will be *five/six* calendar days with *two* days off, those days being notified to you when you commence employment. These may vary depending on circumstances and you will be notified in advance if your normal days off are to be changed. The normal working hours are ....am to ....pm but these may vary according to the needs and requirements of the business. You are required to work any such additional hours as the needs of the business demand, for which *no* additional payment will be made.

4. Holidays

You will be entitled to .... weeks' paid annual holiday for a complete year's service and a pro-rata amount should you leave at any earlier date. In addition you may be entitled to all or some of the eight Bank and Public Holidays in addition to your annual leave. *Should you be required to work on any such Bank or Public Holidays, extra time off in lieu will be granted.*

Any accrued and untaken holiday when you leave will either be paid on a daily basis of £......... per day or be taken at a mutually agreed time. Any holiday taken in excess of any entitlement will have to be repaid on any basis acceptable to your employers, normally by deducting the amount from your final wages.

Your paid leave may be taken during the course of the year commencing on your start date of employment, subject to the provisions below, the dates of which are to be notified and agreed with management in advance.

No holiday (i.e. annual leave) may be taken until the first *three* calendar months' service have elapsed and have been satisfactory but if you have made any prior arrangements, these will be honoured but may have to be taken as unpaid leave. If you should leave during this period and any holidays have been taken, management reserves the right to deduct a day's pay for each day taken, from your final salary.

5. Sickness

Should you fall sick during your employment we will pay Statutory Sick Pay (SSP) in accordance with the relevant Regulations as from time to time published. Any failure to follow the requirements to produce satisfactory evidence of sickness or injury or any other omission on your part may lead to non-payment of SSP. Any additional sick pay will be made at management's discretion.

6. Notice to terminate employment

Both parties agree to give *at least* four weeks' notice to terminate this contract. Longer notice will normally be given in order for both parties to make alternative arrangements. Shorter notice may only be given with the mutual agreement of both parties.

7. Pension

There is no pension scheme associated with this position.

8. Outside employment

Whilst you are working in this employment, you may not work for any other person, firm, or company nor undertake any hairdressing duties on your own account or in partnership or association with any other person, except with management's written consent. You will devote your whole time, attention and energies to this employment.

9. Working for a competitor/Setting up a rival business after employment

9.1. You agree that you will not, for six months after you leave this employment, within three-eighths of a mile of this salon, work in any other hairdressing salon in the same or similar capacity as you have worked in this employment.

9.2. You agree that you will not, whether solely or jointly or on behalf of any other person, firm or company, directly or indirectly, for six months after your employment with us has ceased, carry on or assist in carrying on or establish in any way or be in any way concerned with the business of a hairdresser or any business providing services the same or similar to those provided by this salon.

10. Non-solicitation of clients

You agree that you will not during your employment or for six months after your employment has ceased for whatever reason, whether through advertising or by any other means whatsoever:

10.1. canvas, solicit, approach or entice away any other employee or agent of this salon employed or engaged at this salon for the three months prior to the termination of your employment;

10.2. canvass, solicit, approach or entice away any person who shall have been during the period of twelve months prior to the termination of your employment, a regular customer of this salon.

11. Advertising your services

You shall not for six months after your employment has ceased (howsoever caused) directly or indirectly assist any company, firm, partnership or person by whom you may be employed or for whom you work, to advertise that you are employed by or work for that company, firm, partnership or person with a view to canvassing, soliciting or enticing away any person who shall have been during the period of twelve months prior to the termination of your employment a regular customer of this salon.

12. Meaning of Clauses 11, 12 and 13

In this Contract the following words bear these meanings:

1. 'Advertising' means advertising by use of your photograph and/or use of your name (first name and/or surname and/or any other name by which you are known) and/or by reference to place or places at which you worked for this salon. The word 'advertise' bears the same meaning.

2. 'Regular customer' means a customer of this salon to whom hairdressing and/or beauty services have been given at least eight times during the twelve months prior to the termination of your employment.

13.   Confidential information

You are not permitted to disclose or misuse any confidential information of this employer or relating to this salon, whilst you are in employment or for twelve months after this employment has ceased, howsoever caused (save with the written consent of management).

Signed by the Employers   Date

....

Signed by the Employee   Date

....

ABSENCE FROM WORK DUE TO SICKNESS OR INJURY

Rules, Procedures and Benefits

1. Preamble

The following sections set out information about the Company's Scheme for sick pay and absence from work due to injury or sickness. It is a condition of your employment that you abide by the terms of this Scheme.

Any benefits, whether sick pay or permission to be absent, will only apply where you have complied fully with the letter and spirit of the following points. Please make sure that you read very carefully the rules of the Scheme and that you understand exactly what you must do in the event of any sickness or injury which prevents you from working.

Any sick pay paid by the Company is paid at its entire discretion and none of the benefits described below form part of any contractual entitlement.

The Company reserves the right to withdraw or modify any or all of the terms of this Policy at its discretion. Any change will be notified to all employees and will affect both existing or any new staff.

Payments made under this Policy are made as full or part payment for any wages during any period of absence due to sickness or injury, subject to all the rules and conditions laid down in this Policy. Any such payments shall include any Statutory Sick Pay (SSP) payments where they fall due.

During the first six months of employment, members of staff are normally only eligible for SSP when this becomes due.

2. Purpose of the Sick Pay Scheme

The Company will provide generous sick pay at its discretion where the circumstances and/or the member of staff merits it. Sick pay is designed to alleviate hardship and anxiety in cases where an employee is unable to carry out his/her duties because of illness or injury.

The Sick Pay Scheme operates on trust and the Company leaves it to the integrity and honesty of individual employees to comply with the spirit of the Scheme as well as the detailed rules set out below.

It should be understood that anyone who is suspected or caught abusing the Scheme will be dealt with under the disciplinary procedure which may result in a formal warning or in serious cases, dismissal with or without notice or pay in lieu depending on the seriousness of the case.

Appendix 6

Please note that in any case an employee may be requested to attend the Company's premises if he/she is fit enough to do so either at the start or during any sickness absence. In the alternative management reserves the right to ask any member of management to visit a sick employee at home or in hospital – such visits will not normally be unannounced. Appointments that are mutually convenient will be made. Only in the event of any failure to contact the employee or where serious abuse of the Scheme or Company rules is suspected will management reserve the right to make a visit to the employee's home without an appointment.

The Company reserves the right, upon proper medical advice, to determine whether an employee is fit or unfit for any duties which it would be reasonable to expect that employee to perform. Employees will be given every opportunity to put forward their own medical evidence before any final decision is taken.

3.   Your sick pay

If you are absent from work and your illness or injury prevents you from working, you may be entitled to four weeks' full pay inclusive of SSP in any 'rolling twelve months' provided that you have complied with all the rules of the Scheme set out in this booklet and provided that the Company is satisfied with the reasons given for the absence. Additional sick pay may be provided with the consent of your manager. The 'twelve-month' period will start on the first day of absence from work. Periods of absence occurring at intervals will be treated as cumulative within the rolling twelve months. Once you have returned to work for a period of ....complete weeks of work, sick pay 'entitlement' is resumed. Please note that any employee who has a record of persistent or excessive sickness absence may be refused Company sick pay for any future period of absence.

Absences due to accidents arising outside work or at work and are the subject of legal action are treated separately and may be subject to the rules contained under the heading 'Loans during periods of absence'.

How your sick pay is made up

The pay you receive when you are off sick is made up of the following:

• Sick Pay – paid directly to you by the Company; and

either

• Statutory Sick Pay – paid directly to you by the Company on behalf of the DSS

or if you are not entitled to receive Statutory Sick Pay

• State Sickness Benefit – you must claim this direct from your local DSS office. We will send you form SSP1 in order for you to claim State Benefit.

384

The total amount of your sick pay which is made up of either full pay paid by the Company inclusive of SSP or Sick Pay and State Sickness Benefit will not exceed your normal net pay.

All sick pay whether SSP or normal pay is subject to deduction of PAYE income tax and National Insurance. State Sickness Benefit is not subject to PAYE income tax or National Insurance.

4. Definition of authorised absence

Any absence from work will only be authorised, for which payment may be made, where one of the three following conditions is satisfied:

(a)   your absence from work is due to genuine personal sickness or injury and you have complied with the notification and evidence rules which entirely satisfy your Manager; or

(b)   you have had written prior permission from your Manager; or

(c)   your absence is due to a genuine reason(s) outside your control which is (are) acceptable to your Manager.

Please note that should the Company have any reason to doubt the validity of the illness or injury or the reason given for the absence, the Company reserves the right to withold pay for all or part of the absence and may issue a formal warning (which could eventually lead to dismissal) or even dismiss if such conduct was deemed to be gross misconduct under the disciplinary procedure, should the circumstances warrant it.

Any member of staff whose past absence record causes concern or whose absence record is higher than the average of those working in the same location/department may receive an extended written warning which may last longer than normal written warnings. If this should happen, the warning letter will make clear how long the warning will last and the reasons for the extended warning.

5. Notification of absence

If you are absent from work due to any illness or injury which incapacitates you from doing any work that you are employed to do, the following rules must be observed in order to qualify for payment and for authorised leave:

Notify your Manager

It is your responsibility to notify your Manager by telephone as soon as you fall sick and you know that you will be unable to attend work.

You must give sufficient details on the telephone about the nature of your illness or injury and you should give some indication as to when you will be able to return to work. Should your absence be caused by any illness or injury of a highly personal nature, then as long as the relevant Manager is satisfied with your explanation, he/she will authorise your absence but may want the absence verified by a doctor that there is some medical condition. You are expected to regularly update your Manager throughout your absence either by telephone or by post.

6.   Evidence of illness or injury

Self-certification (for seven calendar days or less)

Should your absence last less than seven calendar days (counting Saturday and Sunday) you will be required to report to your Manager immediately you return to duty and complete a self-certification Form. The reasons given by you for your absence must satisfy your Manager before he will authorise your absence and counter-sign the self-certificate. Should your Manager have any doubts about the reasons given by you or for any other reason, he may not counter-sign the self-certificate. This may result in either non-payment of sick pay or a delay in payment until a Manager has reviewed your case. Until your self-certificate is counter-signed by a Manager no sick pay can be authorised.

In such a case, the position will be discussed with you, first in the context of an informal counselling interview. Depending on the outcome of that meeting, you may be formally warned should the circumstances warrant it.

When your self-certificate has been counter-signed by your Manager, it will then be forwarded to the Wages Department.

Medical certificates (for more than seven calendar days)

If you are absent for more than seven calendar days (including Saturdays and Sundays) or as soon as you know that you will be away from work for more than seven calendar days, you must get a medical statement from your own doctor. This must be sent immediately to your Manager who will forward a copy to Wages. You will be required to let your Manager know when you will be fit to return to work.

Your Manager will send a copy of any self-certificates to the relevant Manager if necessary.

All medical statements obtained from your doctor covering the total absence save for the first seven days must be sent straight to your Manager.

You should ensure that your absence is covered by a current medical statement at all times. Please note that all medical statements submitted must satisfy your Manager and whilst medical statements normally provide adequate evidence of unfitness for work, they may not be conclusive evidence depending upon other factors and the circumstances surrounding your particular case.

For example, a man with a medical statement from his doctor certifying 'sciatica' may be suspended from the sick pay scheme and disciplined if he is seen marching on a rally or conducting himself in any way which is inconsistent with such a diagnosis.

Should there be any query or problem regarding any medical statements submitted, this will be discussed with you and the matter may be referred to senior management for investigation and further action may be taken if necessary.

7.   Conduct during sickness absence

To help you understand what might raise doubts or queries in the mind of your Manager concerning any medical statements (or self-certificates), the Company has drawn up some guidelines for employees concerning their conduct and activities during any periods of absence due to sickness or injury.

In all cases of sickness or injury which necessitates taking time off work, it is expected that the employee will do his utmost to facilitate a speedy return to fitness and to work. In this regard, employees are expected to act sensibly and honestly.

The Company would not in the normal case expect any employee who is absent from work due to sickness or injury to:

- participate in any sports, hobbies or social or any other activities, meetings etc. which are in any way inconsistent with his alleged illness or injuries or which could aggravate the illness or injury or which could delay recovery;

- undertake any other employment whether paid or unpaid. If you declare yourself incapacitated from work in relation to your employment with us, it will be deemed gross or serious misconduct to undertake any other duties whilst off sick – clearly the Company would expect you to do everything to aid a speedy recovery;

- engage in any work around the home in terms of home improvements or the like;

- engage in any activity which is inconsistent with the nature of the alleged illness or injuries (e.g. be seen walking round town with bags of shopping with an alleged injury).

Holidays/Days of leave during periods of sickness absence

If you are off work due to illness or injury, whether this period is covered by a medical statement from your doctor, self-certification or otherwise, you are not expected to take any day(s) of leave whether pre-booked or not during your sick leave. If you should wish to honour any leave pre-booked or take a day(s) leave, you may do so only once this is approved by your Manager prior to the leave being taken. Please note that your Manager may at his discretion deem this day/these days as ordinary leave and as such sick pay will be suspended and days of normal leave taken (at the rate of pay paid for holiday leave).

Any employee who takes any such days, whether this be holiday or attending conferences, meetings, sports or leisure activities and the like, without prior authorisation, will be deemed to have breached the rules of this Company and as such will become liable to disciplinary action. This may include but not be limited to suspension of sick pay for all or part of the sickness absence, suspension without pay as a disciplinary measure and a formal written warning. In any serious case, the Company may deem this to be an offence of gross misconduct which may result in summary dismissal.

Normally any holidays or attendance at any outside activity or location during sick leave will only be authorised as still counting as sick leave if it is convalescent leave specifically authorised in writing by your own doctor.

8. Medical examinations

You may be required to submit to a medical examination during or after any absence from work due to sickness or injury or at any time deemed necessary by the Company during your employment. You will be required to give your consent to a report being sent to management concerning your fitness or otherwise to work or on any other relevant matter.

Should the doctor appointed by the Company require details of your medical history, you will be required to give your written consent giving him permission to contact your doctor (your GP or your Consultant) for your medical records or for a medical report – subject to your rights under the Access to Medical Reports Act 1988 and Access to Health Records Act 1990.

You may also or in the alternative be required to submit to a medical examination by an independent consultant (whether medical or otherwise) at the Company's expense. You will be required to give your written consent to a report being sent in confidence to the Company doctor who in turn will disclose to management any relevant details regarding your fitness to work. No confidential medical details will be disclosed to management neither will any diagnosis be given except in cases where any doctor regards this as paramount for your or other people's health and or safety. In any event your consent will be sought first before any such disclosure is made.

The doctor appointed by the Company will be responsible for liaising with your own GP who will be kept fully informed about your case. It is expected that you will co-operate in this procedure and you will be required to give such consent as necessary in order to progress your claim for sick pay.

All medical information will be kept confidential but you may be required to give your consent to any medical reports or records kept by your GP being sent to the doctor appointed by the Company for him/her to base a report on your fitness or otherwise. That report may then be sent to a senior Manager.

Until the Company is satisfied with the outcome of those enquiries, the Company reserves the right to withhold all or part of Company sick pay and if the circumstances warrant it, Statutory Sick Pay (SSP).

You should also report any contact with anyone suffering from an infectious or contagious disease and it will be up to the Manager in charge of your office to determine whether you should come to work or stay home on full pay. Such leave would not count against any sick pay.

9.   Second opinions/Light work

The Company reserves the right to ask for a second opinion (normally from a qualified medical practitioner or nurse) on whether any particular illness or injury would necessarily incapacitate an employee from doing such work for the Company.

In addition, the Company reserves the right to require an employee to undertake any reasonable duties having due regard to the nature of the illness or injury and this may mean that the employee will be able (after being signed off as fit for work by his doctor) to attend for work and undertake alternative or light duties or work on shorter hours for a period of time. In such a case the Company may, at its discretion, 'red circle' (maintain) the employee's normal earnings or may offer the rate of pay applicable to those alternative duties/ shorter hours. This will in any event be fully discussed with you first.

10.   Return to work

Upon your return to work you may in certain circumstances be required to present a certificate from your doctor confirming that you are fit for work. In any such case you will be contacted and asked to obtain such a certificate. You may also be required to submit to a medical examination by a doctor appointed by the Company before being allowed back to work. The decision of management will be final, following consultation with the doctor, as to whether you are fit to return to work. Management, at its entire discretion, reserves the right to refuse to permit any member of staff to return to work should the circumstances warrant it.

11.   Exclusions

There is no entitlement to any sick pay (this may include the withdrawal or non-payment of SSP in some cases) where in the opinion of the Company:

- you have knowingly entered false information on any form (including a self-certification or application form); this is regarded as serious misconduct which could result in serious disciplinary action being taken;

- you have failed to follow the policy and rules explained in this part of the Handbook;

- there are any serious doubts about the circumstances surrounding your claim for sick pay;

- your absence record in previous years is in the opinion of management excessive;

- your absence is caused by negligence, recklessness or carelessness by you in observing standard safety practices or by wilful misconduct at work – in addition to withholding sick pay management reserves the right to take any appropriate action it deems fit including disciplinary action where necessary;

- your absence is caused by any self-inflicted illness or injury as defined by management from time to time; this may include any illness or injury which was in the opinion of management primarily caused by your failure to heed medical advice;

- your absence is caused through injury in any dangerous sport as defined by the Company – in this respect you are advised to take out your own personal accident insurance cover;

- your absence is caused through illness or injury occasioned at any outside employment (whether paid or unpaid) or activities such as a charity parachute jump or run;

- your absence is caused through any smoking-related illness or disability, in the written opinion of a medical practitioner;

- your absence is caused by elective surgery or medical treatment unless undertaken upon the advice of a registered medical practitioner and confirmed as necessary by any doctor appointed by the Company – this may cover cosmetic surgery or dental treatment; treatment for infertility; sterilisation operations etc.

12. Loans during periods of absence

If you are absent through injuries caused by the actionable negligence, nuisance or breach of statutory duty of a third party in respect of which damages are recoverable, you must inform your Manager immediately. Any payment that may be made for all or part of any such absence (other than SSP) shall be by way of a loan which must be repaid in full. If damages are settled on a proportionate basis, the Company will require full details. The amount of any repayment required in those circumstances will be determined by the Company but will not exceed the actual damages recovered or the part thereof identified as loss of earnings.

In circumstances where no claim is made or where no claim can be made, you may, at management's discretion, be paid sick pay.

You will be required to sign a Loan Form in respect of this loan.

13. Private Health Insurance

If you are eligible to join the Group Private Health Insurance Scheme (currently administered through BUPA), it will state this in your Terms and Conditions of Employment document. The appropriate forms are available from ....

This will cover you and your dependants. Please note that this benefit is discretionary and management reserves the right at any time to modify or withdraw the Scheme at any time and will give four weeks' due notice of any changes being made.

14. Sickness before or during a holiday

Subject to the Rules as set out in the section on 'Conduct during sickness absence' if you should fall ill before you are due to start your annual holiday and you inform your Supervisor or Manager immediately, the Company may at its entire discretion treat that absence as sick leave and further annual leave may be granted at a time to be agreed with senior management.

However should you fall sick once your holiday has commenced, then the Company reserves the right to treat that as holiday and not as sick leave. In such cases, holiday pay will be paid and the absence will not be regarded as counting towards your sickness entitlement.

In genuine cases, however, where you are actually prevented from taking your holiday through sickness or injury, if you notify your Manager immediately and submit medical evidence which satisfies the Company, the Company at its entire discretion may grant you further leave either paid or unpaid. You will have to return to work for an uninterrupted period of .... weeks before you may take any further holiday entitlement and the normal rules will prevail.

15. Accrual of holiday during sick leave

OPTION 1

Holiday entitlement will accrue during any period of sick leave where the employee is in receipt of full pay or SSP only. If the employment is terminated as a result of sickness or injury then all holidays which have accrued during that holiday year will be paid with the final salary.

OPTION 2

Holidays will only accrue during any period of sick leave at the discretion of a senior Manager. The Company reserves the right to withhold all or part of any holiday pay which may have accrued during any period of sick leave.

If the employment is terminated as a result of sickness or injury the Company reserves the right to withhold all or part of any holiday pay which may have accrued during this period.

Appendix 6

Supervisor's Guide

(1)   If an employee is absent from work due to sickness or injury, the Supervisor will be notified initially. He/she will complete the Notification of Absence form in triplicate and will send the Yellow copy to the Personnel Department, the White copy to Wages and the Pink copy to the Head of Department.

(2)   The Supervisor must interview the employee when he/she returns to work and notify Wages of the return to work as follows:

If the employee is sick for seven days or less (counting Saturday and Sunday):

— as early as possible on the day of the employee's return to work, give the employee a self-certification form to be completed in the presence of the Supervisor;

— the form should be counter-signed by the Supervisor only if he/she is satisfied with the reason given and all the circumstances;

— the Supervisor must send the Yellow copy to the Personnel Department, the White copy to Wages and the Pink copy to the Head of Department.

If the employee is sick for more than seven days (counting Saturdays and Sundays) then:

— the Supervisor will receive a medical statement from the employee to cover the absence. Wages will be sent a copy;

— as early as possible on the day of the employee's return to work the Supervisor should give the employee a self-certificate to complete in his/her presence;

— the self-certificate should be counter-signed only if he/she is satisfied with the reason given and all the circumstances.

Important Notes

1.   If a new employee hands his/her Supervisor a 'Linking Letter' or a Leaver's Statement (form SSP 1(L)) from a previous employer, it must be sent by the Supervisor to Wages as soon as possible.

2.   The Supervisor/Wages must check whether the employee falls into any of the categories excluded from receiving Statutory Sick Pay. If he/she does, the Supervisor must advise Wages, or vice versa, and the employee will be notified. The appropriate Exclusion Form will be sent by Wages to the employee.

3.   If the employee is not receiving Statutory Sick Pay and is claiming State Sickness Benefit, Wages should take copies of the medical certificates sent by the employee and forward the originals to the employee's local DSS office.

4.   If an employee has received State Sickness Benefit he/she must send Wages the DSS form BS 12 stating how much benefit has been paid. Wages will then be able to make the appropriate deductions from the employee's pay.

5.   If an employee has received State Sickness Benefit, he/she must give his/her Supervisor a 'Linking Letter' from the DSS. This should be sent to Wages as soon as possible.

6.   If there is any reason to doubt an employee's claim for sick pay, this should be discussed with the Supervisor or the Personnel Department before Wages is notified to continue to pay any salary.

Appendix 7

HOLIDAY POLICY

1.1. General

The Holiday Entitlement Year runs from 1 April to 31 March. You are required to take your holiday between those dates (i.e. between 1 April to 31 March the following year).

You may not carry forward any holiday untaken by 31 March in any year nor will any pay in lieu be made.

All holidays MUST be taken at times approved by your Manager or a Director. Two weeks is the maximum that can be taken at any one time.

1.2. Holiday pay

Holiday pay is calculated on the basis of your current basic rate of pay (i.e. basic excluding any overtime, bonuses etc.).

There will be no payment in lieu of any holidays not taken.

1.3. Public and Bank Holidays

All Public and Bank Holidays are permitted as paid holidays in addition to holiday entitlement specified in 1.4 below. You will not be paid for any Bank or Public Holiday however should you be absent (other than on Company business or unless expressly authorised) immediately before or after a holiday occurs. If the absence was caused by genuine sickness, you may be paid at the entire discretion of the Company should your Manager so agree, whether or not you provide a Medical Certificate to cover the said absence.

1.4. Holiday entitlement

Your holiday entitlement is four weeks in any holiday year calculated at one and one-third days per completed calendar month. For the purpose of calculating the amount of accrued holiday entitlement only complete calendar months will count.

Holiday entitlement will be rounded up or down to the nearest half day.

1.5. Holidays in year of commencement

During your first year of service unless otherwise agreed by your immediate superior, you will not normally be allowed to:

(i) take any holiday before you have completed three months' service;

(ii) take more holiday than you have actually accrued.

1.6. Holiday pay on termination of employment

If you leave the Company's employment you will receive pay for any accrued holiday outstanding. This pay will be calculated by deducting holidays already taken from the amount of holiday accrued in that holiday year to the date of leaving.

Should holiday already taken exceed entitlement, the Company shall require you to repay an amount equivalent to the number of days by which you have exceeded your entitlement. The Company reserves the right to deduct this sum from any moneys, whether final salary, bonus or commission outstanding, expenses etc., from your final salary payment.

The Company reserves the right to withhold any accrued holiday pay to which you may have been entitled should you be summarily dismissed for gross misconduct.

Holiday pay may also be withheld in whole or in part should you fail to give proper notice of termination of your contract or should you leave before the said notice has expired. In such a case your holiday pay will be reduced by the number of days' notice not worked.

In any case where the Company agrees to waive the need for you to work out your notice, the above paragraph will not apply.

1.7. Sickness during holidays

As a general rule once annual leave has started, no claims for sickness will be permitted. However, if you are prevented from going on your holiday or are ill or sustain a serious injury during your holiday, the Company may at its entire discretion be prepared to treat that leave (or part thereof) as sick leave PROVIDED THAT you are able to provide satisfactory medical evidence (i.e. to the satisfaction of the Company). In such a case you may be permitted further paid or unpaid leave later on in the holiday year.

No claim for sickness is permitted on any Public or Bank Holiday and no further time off in lieu of pay will be given.

1.8. Accrual of holidays during sick leave

Holidays will accrue during any paid or unpaid sick leave at the entire discretion of the Company. If your employment is terminated whilst on sick leave, it will be up to the Company to determine whether or not any accrued holiday pay will be paid.

Appendix 7

1.9. Holiday entitlement and maternity leave

Holiday entitlement will/will not continue to accrue during maternity leave. Should you have any outstanding holiday before you start your maternity leave you may be required to take it prior to your maternity leave commencing or you may be paid accrued holiday pay or you may be permitted to 'bank' it and take it after your maternity leave. This will be discussed with you before the start of your maternity leave.

Index

References are to the paragraph numbers and chapters of this book.

Index

checking criminal records, 1.10
photographs, requests for, 1.12
Rehabilitation of Offenders Act 1974, effect of, 1.9
Job share contract, 3.11

L
Lecturing and writing, 12.21
Loans
during absence, 6.18
fringe benefit, as, 8.6
Long service awards, 8.13

M
Malingerers, 6.24
Management Contract, App 1
Medical examinations
during employment, 6.15
offer of employment, as condition of, 2.4
questionnaire, 2.4
return to work, as condition of, 6.16
Misconduct, duty to report, 12.2
Misrepresentation, 1.7, 2.5
Mobility clause
employer's duty arising from, 4.7
express, 4.9
implied, 4.7
sex discrimination and, 4.11

N
Notice
common law, 10.3
effective date of termination (EDT), 10.5
employee, by, 10.1, 10.6, 10.10
holidays and, 7.16
meaning, 10.1
no notice or short notice
– effect of, 7.18
– pay, withholding of, 10.9
– remedy, 10.4
pay in lieu of, 10.7, 10.8
relocation, reasonable notice of, 4.8
statutory provisions, 10.2
termination, effective date of, 10.5

O
Occupational sick pay
benefits, 6.10
conduct during absence, 6.14
contractual or discretionary, 6.5
eligibility, 6.9
evidence of sickness, 6.13
exclusions, 6.17
holiday, accrual during sick leave, 6.20
legal position, 6.3
loans during absence, 6.18
malingerer, 6.24
medical examinations, 6.15
– return to work, as condition for, 6.16
notification rules, 6.12
permanent health insurance, 6.22
private medical insurance, 6.21
purpose, 6.7
scope, 6.6-6.21
'sick year', 6.11
sickness during holidays, 6.19
unauthorised absence, definition, 6.8
Offer of employment
conditions, 2.2-2.6
confirmation, 2.8
documentary evidence, 2.3
engagement, expenses on, 4.12
medicals, 2.4
probationary periods, 2.9
qualifications, 2.7
references, 2.2
reneging on, 2.9
trade union membership, 2.5

P
Patents and inventions, 12.20
Pay
bonus or commission payments, 5.5
date of, 5.18
deductions from (see *Deductions from pay*)
definition of, 5.1
holiday, 7.8
– termination of employment, effect of, 7.17
itemised pay statement, obligation to provide, 5.1
no notice or short notice, 7.18, 10.9
notice, payment in lieu of, 5.11, 10.7, 10.8
– damages or unpaid wages, 5.11
– industrial tribunals, extension of jurisdiction, 5.12
– tax and national insurance, deduction from, 5.17, 5.18
overtime allowance, 5.4
profit-sharing scheme, 5.5
reductions in, damages for, 5.22
review of, 5.3

Index

scale or rate of, obligation
to state in writing, 5.1
school fees, 5.19
– payment of, 8.14
– tax implications of payment
of, 5.19, 5.20
shift allowance, 5.4
variations in, 5.2
Payment in lieu of notice
tax and NI treatment of, 5.18, 10.8
termination of contract, 10.8, 10.9
Wages Act, 5.11
Pensions, 8.4
Permanent contract, 3.6, 3.7
Permanent Health Insurance
(PHI), 6.22, 6.23
Personal circumstances, change of, 12.15
Personal liability, 12.19
Personal search, 12.18
Personal transactions, 12.14
Private medical insurance, 6.21, 8.4
Private sector employees, contract
applicable to, 3.6
Probationary period, 3.9
Promises at interviews, 1.6
Public servants, contract
applicable to, 3.7

Q
Qualifications
misrepresentation of, 2.5
requirement to gain, 2.6
requirement to hold, 4.15

R
References, 2.2
Rehabilitation of offenders, 1.9
Relationships at work, 12.8, 12.9
Relocation
payment of expenses on, 4.8, 4.12
reasonable notice of, 4.8
Restrictive covenants (see also
*Competition, confidentiality and
restrictive covenants*)
area, 9.12, 9.16
drafting, 9.4
non-dealing clauses, 9.15, 9.17
non-solicitation clauses, 9.15, 9.16
scope, 9.13
severance, 9.19
time limit, 9.14
Retirement, agreement for early, 11.12

S
Seasonal workers, 3.5

Settlement
ACAS, role in promoting, 11.1-11.7
early retirement agreement, 11.12
extended leave agreements, 11.11
financial advantages, 11.14
mutual agreement to terminate, 11.10
pressure to settle, 11.13
set-off, 11.9
tax implications of, 11.15
Share option schemes, 8.10
exclusion clauses relating to, 8.11
Sick pay (see *Occupational sick
pay* and *Statutory sick pay*)
Smoking policy, 12.16
Statutory sick pay
damages, deduction from, 6.18
evidence of sickness, 6.13
exclusions, 6.17
introduction, 6.4
period of incapacity for
work, 6.11
purpose, 6.7

T
Telephone charges, payment of, 8.9
Temporary employment, 3.1, 3.5
Tenured employment, 3.7
Termination of employment, effective
date of, 10.5
holiday pay, on, 7.17
Trade secrets, 9.5, 9.6
Trade union membership, 2.6, 4.6
Travel, requirement to, 4.10

U
Undertaking to behave, 12.7
Uniform, requirement to wear, 4.18,
12.10
Unions, de-recognition of, 3.13

V
Vicarious liability
criminal acts, 1.8

W
Warranties and indemnities, 9.22
Wedding gifts, 8.12
Work, efficiency of, 12.22
Work, hours of, 4.17
fringe benefit, as, 8.6
long service awards, 8.13
Work permits, 4.16
Writing, lecturing, 12.21
Written statement, employment
particulars, 1.1, 4.1-4.6

400

TAX REFERENCE SERVICES

'...excellent value for money.'

TOLLEY'S TAX REFERENCE ANNUALS 1993-94

Including legislative developments and changes, together with detailed coverage of official documents, and notes of practice and concessions from all available sources, these invaluable guides have become firmly established as the most accurate and easy to use. Written by technical experts to provide authoritative advice, each title follows the same practical and highly readable style, presented in a handy, portable format and includes:

◆ Chapters arranged alphabetically for ease of reference
◆ Clear, concise yet comprehensive explanations
◆ Worked examples to clarify points of detail
◆ References to statutes, case law, Inland Revenue Statements of Practice, Extra-Statutory Concessions and Press Releases in Income Tax, Corporation Tax, Capital Gains Tax and Inheritance Tax annuals
◆ References to Customs & Excise Notices in VAT annual
◆ References to DSS Leaflets in National Insurance Contributions annual
◆ Full coverage of the law and practice for at least the past six years
◆ Tables of cases, statutes and statutory instruments where appropriate
◆ Full cross-references throughout the text
◆ Comprehensive contents lists and indexes

Tolley's Income Tax 1993-94

Glyn Saunders MA and David Smailes FCA
Order Code IT93   £29.95
720 pages approx
0 85459 770-0 September 1993

Tolley's Corporation Tax 1993-94

Glyn Saunders MA and Alan Dolton MA(Oxon)
Order Code CT93   £25.95
400 pages approx
0 85459 771-9 September 1993

Tolley's Capital Gains Tax 1993-94

Patrick Noakes MA FCA ATII and Stephen Savory PhD
Order Code CGT93   £26.95
470 pages approx
0 85459 772-7 September 1993

Tolley's Inheritance Tax 1993-94

Patrick Noakes MA FCA ATII and Stephen Savory PhD
Order Code IHT93   £23.95
260 pages approx
0 85459 773-5 September 1993

Tolley's Value Added Tax 1993-94

Robert Wareham BSc (Econ) FCA and Nicholas Bowen, Barrister
Order Code VAT93   £26.95
700 pages approx
0 85459 774-3 September 1993

Tolley's National Insurance Contributions 1993-94

Neil Booth FCA FTII
Order Code NIC93   £31.95
500 pages approx
0 85459 775-1 September 1993

Tolley

SPECIALIST TAX GUIDES

Tolley's Interest and Penalty Provisions

John T Newth FCA FTII AITP

Covers the provisions of all the main UK direct taxes, providing practical advice on everyday problems regarding mitigation and negotiations with the Revenue.

◆ Examines both criminal and civil penalty proceedings

◆Chapters devoted to specific topics, such as the implementation of the Keith Report, time limits, and regulations governing pay and file

Order Code IAP £34.95

350 pages approx

0 85459 580-5 May 1993

'...practical information in an easily accessible form...'

THE LORD CHANCELLOR

Tolley's Tax Appeals to the Commissioners

Eric Harvey FCA with Foreword by the Lord Chancellor

This highly practical work on the law and procedure of tax appeals ensures a full understanding of what happens before, during and after the hearing.

◆ Written from the perspective of a tax consultant who is himself a General Commissioner

◆ Uses a step-by-step approach to guide you through every stage of the proceedings

Order Code TAC1 £15.95

136 pages 0 85459 370-5 July 1990

Tolley's Tax Compliance and Investigations (Third Edition)

David Jeffery MA MSc, Brian Sturgeon, Terry Donaldson and
Michael O'Brien FTII PhD
(Williams Jeffery Barber)

A detailed guide to the various investigation techniques and strategies of the Inland Revenue, with practical advice on everything from a simple district office enquiry to a full-scale Special Office investigation.

◆ Numerous illustrative examples

◆ Appendices include Inland Revenue Press Releases, Statements of Practice and CCAB notes

◆ Concludes with an account of a hearing before the Commissioners

Order Code TI3 £34.95

424 pages 0 85459 681-X December 1992

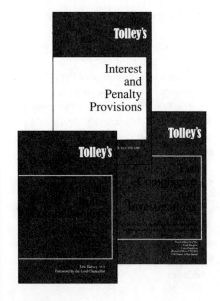

SPECIALIST TAX GUIDES

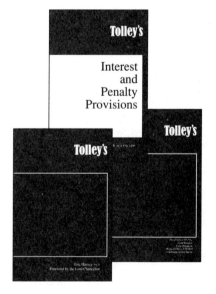

FOR TAX READ TOLLEY

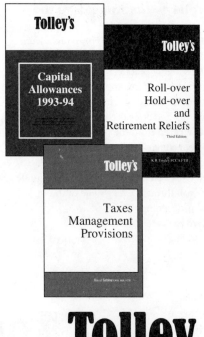